For Appearance' Sake
The Historical Encyclopedia of Good Looks, Beauty, and Grooming

Victoria Sherrow

Oryx Press
2001

The rare Arabian Oryx is believed to have inspired the myth of the unicorn. This desert antelope became virtually extinct in the early 1960s. At that time, several groups of international conservationists arranged to have nine animals sent to the Phoenix Zoo to be the nucleus of a captive breeding herd. Today, the Oryx population is over 1,000, and over 500 have been returned to the Middle East.

© 2001 by The Oryx Press
A division of Greenwood Publishing Group, Inc.
88 Post Road West
Westport, CT 06881
(203) 226-3571, (800) 225-5800
www.oryxpress.com

Published simultaneously in Canada
Printed and bound in the United States of America

∞ The paper used in this publication meets the minimum requirements of American National Standard for Information Science—Permanence of Paper for Printed Library Materials, ANSI Z39.48, 1984.

Library of Congress Cataloging-in-Publication Data

Sherrow, Victoria.
  For appearance' sake: the historical encyclopedia of good looks, beauty, and grooming/by Victoria Sherrow.
    p. cm.
Includes bibliographical references and index.
  ISBN 1-57356-204-1 (alk. paper)
  1. Beauty, Personal—Encyclopedias. 2. Beauty, Personal—Social aspects. I. Title.
GT499.S49 2001
646.7'042--dc21

00-010107
CIP

CONTENTS

GUIDE TO SELECTED TOPICS

The Body
Body Hair, Men's and Women's
Breasts
Ears
Eyes
Face
Facial Hair, Men's
Feet
Hands
Head
Legs
Lips
Neck
Nose
Skin
Teeth

Companies
Alberto Culver Company
Avon Products, Inc.
Body Shop, The
Colgate-Palmolive Company
Coty Company
Creed, House of
Guerlain
Houbigant
International Flavors
    and Fragrances (IFF)
Johnson Products
L'Oreal
Max Factor & Company
Michaeljohn
Pola
Procter & Gamble Company

Revlon Company
Shiseido Corporation
Yardley of London

Ethnic Groups/Cultures *See also*
    PLACES, SOCIAL ISSUES
African Americans
Hispanic Americans
Wodaabe

Grooming Techniques/Practices
Baths
Beauty Regimens
Body Decoration
Body Hair, Men's and Women's
Body Odor
Body Ornamentation
Breasts
Breath, Bad
Cellulite
Chemical Peels
Ears
Eyes
Face
Facial Hair, Men's
Facial Patches
Feet
Fragrance
Grooming Products, Children's
Hair Care
Hair Color
Hair Loss
Hair, Styling of
Hair Straightening
Hair Transplants

PREFACE

For Appearance' Sake: The Historical Encyclopedia of Beauty, Good Looks, and Grooming discusses the universal human interest in physical appearance. Throughout history, people around the world have devoted time, energy, money, and other resources to changing and/or enhancing their appearance. How and why they have done so illuminates the social history, attitudes, and values of many different cultures. The subject also encompasses sociological, psychological, political, and economic matters.

Attitudes about beauty and good looks differ, often dramatically, among different cultures. Each group has its own view of what makes for physical attractiveness and how the features of the body should be groomed or adorned. People living in different cultures may compare their own looks and the looks of others to the beauty standards of their culture. Ideas about what constitutes a "desirable" appearance for men or women affect the lives of individuals and social groups.

In modern times, the pursuit of personal attractiveness has also had major economic implications, and mass media has both defined and spread "standards" that define attractiveness and good grooming. The advertising and sale of beauty and grooming products are multibillion dollar industries. In response to concerns about safety and effectiveness, more laws have been passed to regulate grooming products, and government agencies oversee some aspects of these industries. Cosmetics and consumer advocates have become more numerous, as have critics of the beauty industry.

For Appearance' Sake brings together information on appearance and grooming from ancient times to the present and around the world. The book does not offer advice for selecting and using beauty and hair products or give tips on personal grooming but rather covers the history of these products and techniques. The book focuses primarily on the care and appearance of the face, hair, hands, skin, and nails and on the social/historical, health-related, regulatory, and other general aspects of these topics. The book also discusses methods of cleansing and scenting the body, ornamentation, such as scarification, tattooing, piercings, body painting, and other body decoration, as well as clothing, fashion, dieting, health, nutrition, and fitness as they relate to major aspects of beauty/appearance. People who have developed large businesses in the cosmetics, fragrance, or hair products industries are profiled, along with some of the people throughout history who have been widely regarded as attractive or trendsetters. Entries on every fad, fashion, person, diet, and medication are not included. Entries on consumer advocates, critics, and feminism address some controversial aspects of the beauty industry, mass advertising, and beauty standards. There are entries on only those models who have set trends, epitomized the "look" of their era, and/or had a significant influence on the fashion and/or beauty industries.

Information for this book was gathered over a period of several years from a variety of primary and secondary sources. Material about ancient times comes from descriptions of cave-paintings and archaeological finds, which illuminate the customs and grooming and beauty materials used long ago. Translations of works by ancient writers—for example, Ovid (ancient Rome) and Al-Kindl (ancient Arabia)—contain fascinating details about beauty standards and cosmetic use in these societies, as do other written works, including literature, diaries, and letters. Firsthand accounts written by those who have visited indigenous peoples around the world offer information about the grooming practices of those groups. Authoritative biographies, autobiographies, and published interviews provided information for entries about well-known people in the beauty industry, including cosmetics entrepreneurs Mary Kay Ash and Esteé Lauder, makeup artist George Masters, consumer advocate Paula Begoun, and hairstylist Vidal Sassoon. Much of the information about the history and activities of specific organizations and companies came from the organizations themselves.

More than 300 entries, listed alphabetically, make up the book, and cover grooming (e.g., baths, body hair, men's facial hair; hair care); parts of the body (e.g., ears, eyes, nose, breasts, hands, feet); products and materials (e.g., cosmetics, henna, perfume, soap); practices and procedures (e.g., plastic surgery, hair transplants; permanent makeup); changing ideals of attractiveness (e.g., beauty standards, "looks"); health/safety/ environmental issues (e.g., animal testing, laws and regulations, safety); "firsts," (e.g., first manufactured fragrances, first products of their type, first African American woman to own a large cosmetic company, first laws passed to "police" various products); award-winning fragrances; people (barbers, product developers, trend-setters, famous beauties, founders of companies, beauty industry critics and supporters, models); advertising and endorsements; events (e.g., beauty pageants, various cosmetic and fragrance awards); associations and organizations (e.g., American Beauty Association, Fragrance Foundation, Society of Cosmetic Chemists).

The book will be useful for people who want to learn more about the social history and customs of different societies, as well as the changing social attitudes about beauty and the way those attitudes affect individuals. The *Encyclopedia* includes information useful for students, librarians, teachers and professors, researchers, and general readers who want to learn more about how people from different cultures approach grooming and beauty and about the people, products, services, and social issues related to beauty and personal products businesses.

Although it is impossible to cover all aspects of every topic in a work of this length, readers will find basic information and many lesser-known facts, along with suggestions for further readings. Most entries contain cross-references, directing the reader to additional information on the subject, and an extensive bibliography directs readers to books, articles, and Web sites for more in-depth information. A subject index completes the book.

A

Abdominoplasty *See* PLASTIC SURGERY.

Acne *See* SKIN.

Adair, Eleanor (1867–?)

Eleanor Adair, who was born in Ireland, became one of the first modern beauty culturists at the turn of the nineteenth century. She founded successful beauty salon businesses based in New York, London, and Paris.

During the 1890s and early 1900s, Adair produced several skin care products for women, including creams, oils, and tonics, that were used and sold in her salons. Her staff of specially trained "treatment girls" gave expensive facials using what Adair called the "Ganesh muscle-strapping method." The treatment involved strapping the client's lower jaw tightly shut so the jaw would not move during the treatment. ("Ganesh" may have come from a French word, ganache, which means "lower jaw")

Adair influenced social attitudes about the use of beauty products and beauty salons. She gave her salons and products snob appeal by charging high prices and advertising that her products and services were for "Ladies only." She claimed that "beauty culture must be taken up by gentlewomen of social standing." (Lewis and Woodworth, 1972) Advertisements for Adair's salons appeared in the top women's magazines of that era, including *Vogue.* Her clients included socialites and titled European women. One of Adair's former receptionists and treatment girls, Elizabeth Arden (1884–1966), went on to found successful beauty salons of her own, as well as a world-famous cosmetics company. By 1915, Adair, Arden, and actress Lillian Russell were considered America's top beauty experts. *See also* ARDEN, ELIZABETH; RUSSELL, LILLIAN.

Further reading: Alfred Allan Lewis and Constance Woodworth, *Miss Elizabeth Arden* (1972); Kathy Peiss, *Hope in a Jar* (1998).

Advertising (U.S.)

United States companies use advertising widely to promote beauty and grooming products and services and thus encourage consumers to use these products. Over the years, methods of advertising have changed dramatically as new forms of communication developed, and new products became available.

The 1880s brought the first serious advertising of commercial cosmetics and personal grooming products. Makers and sellers of these products have used posters, signs, banners, placards, business cards, display wagons, and billboards, as well as newspapers and other periodicals, for promotion. During the twentieth century, the mass media, direct mail, and the Internet offered new and more far-reaching means of advertising products. Today, television ads are common for cosmetics, soaps, hair care products, deodorants, shaving products, and other personal care items. Most of the advertisements in beauty and fashion magazines are for cosmetics and grooming products.

Early Advertisements

Advertising cards, also called trade cards, were among the earliest techniques used to sell cosmetics in America. During the 1840s, perfume manufacturers in New York City distributed cards soaked in the scents that they were marketing. Along with the manufacturer's name and the name of the product, the cards contained drawings designed to appeal to customers. A card intended to attract more conservative women to use certain scents, for example, might feature delicate pictures of angels, sweet-faced children, and flowers. These were often colorful and detailed prints.

The first American magazines did not contain advertising, but ads began appearing during the late 1870s, in newspapers as well. These print advertisements touted skin care products, soaps, and such products as shaving soaps and tooth cleaners. The ads lured women into buying them by suggesting that use of the products would lead to

1863 advertisement showing woman with container of liquid pearl skin conditioner. *Library of Congress.*

delightful results. An early beauty-related ad appeared in 1884 that promoted a book that described various cosmetics. The caption read, "For Homely Women Only," and the text said that the book was for "the plainer sisterhood who look in the glass and are not satisfied with what they see." (Ayer, 1897).

Soap ads were among the first to appear in print, and some of them claimed that a person could use the product to clean just about anything. In 1882, an ad for Slidall's Soap called it "The Soap for All Uses," saying it could be used for "the toilet, laundry, kitchen, housecleaning, babies, dogs, for brushing teeth, washing old running sores, harness, and carriages." In addition, the ad claimed, "Artificial teeth will retain their old brilliance."

Some newspaper advertisements in 1882 for a new brand called Ivory Soap were effective and creative enough to remain in use, with some variations, for decades. The ad said simply "Ivory Soap–99 44/100th percent pure." The makers went on to claim the soap was superior to other brands then available because Ivory was purer and more pleasant and effective. To underscore the claim of "purity," the ads pointed out that Ivory soap would "float."

Ads for Pear's soap, made by an English company, appeared in 1897. The Pear's campaign to sell soap is considered groundbreaking in the history of advertising because it attempted to attract a particular consumer—upper class—by associating the product with a more elite image. This the company did, somewhat circuitously, by adapting a painting by one of the premier artists of the time, John E. Millais, and using it in a soap advertisement. (Twitchell, 2000) Pear's wanted to promote the soap as a product that would lighten the skin and hence separate the upper class from those who "toiled out in the sun." (Twitchell, 2000) It was not socially acceptable to make that distinction openly, but by using the image of a light-skinned, innocent child in a painting, the company got its message across.

Manufacturers tried to enhance the credibility of their claims with endorsements from well-known people. Celebrity endorsements were increasingly used after the late 1800s.

Companies sought testimonials from society women, beauty experts, and actresses. As a beauty expert of the 1890s, cosmetics company founder Harriet Hubbard Ayer was often sought for endorsements, and she was among those who promoted Pond's Extract Cream for the face, emphasizing its healing properties. Pear's hired the actress Lillie Langtry to endorse its complexion soap. Athletes, models, and celebrated beauties also lent their names to some products' advertisements. The women's suffrage leader Elizabeth Cady Stanton endorsed "Fairbanks' Fairy Soap" in a series of ads that appeared in 1899. She was quoted as saying, "I . . . find it delightful. It leaves the skin soft and velvety and I particularly like it because it is as free from odor as the air and sunshine." Parts of the ad seemed clearly aimed at the competing Ivory Soap, because they stressed that Fairy Soap was "different from any other floating white soap— purer, more scientific and delicate, made of better materials and by the latest perfected methods . . ." Ads like these, for soaps and shampoos, appeared in magazines like *Pictorial Review*, *Ladies Home Journal*, and *Good Housekeeping*. (Watkins, 1959)

Before the 1900s, women in America were discouraged from using color cosmetics (or "painting" themselves), which was condemned as unnatural, deceptive, and something a respectable woman would never do. With time, however, cosmetic ads attempted to counter this belief by conveying the idea that beauty products were both acceptable and respectable. Even conservative women used face creams, and manufactured creams were among the first products to be widely advertised. In 1912, ads for Pompeian Massage Cream declared that this product would beautify the complexion. The ad copy assumed that a respectable young lady would want to appeal to both her beau and his parents, and the illustration showed a proud young man introducing his girlfriend to his mother above a caption that read, "Look, Mother, here she is." An ad for Pond's Cream said, "She's lovely. She's engaged. She uses Ponds."

Talcum powder, household salve, face creams, hair pomade, and face powder manufactured by the C.L. Hamilton Co. of Washington, DC. *Library of Congress.*

Celebrity testimonials became increasingly popular. Some ads featured the images of prominent people and their comments on the product, while other ads merely informed readers that certain people they admired used the product in question. Ads for Pond's Cold Cream pointed out that the Queen of Romania was a satisfied customer. A 1918 ad for Watkins Mulsified Cocoanut Oil for Shampooing featured photographs of the most famous American actresses of that era, including Norma Talmadge, May Allison, and Ethel Clayton.

During the early 1900s, cultural attitudes about race and beauty were reflected in the text and pictures for many ads. They promoted a standard of beauty based on the appearance of white Europeans. Ads for skin bleaches and hair straighteners, along with products to remove unwanted facial hair, targeted women of color or women whose ancestors came from places outside Northern Europe. Before and after photographs emphasized a light-skinned, hair-free face with small boned features as the "ideal."

New Media and Methods

By the 1920s, ads were being presented on radio as well as in print. The first grooming products advertised on radio were soaps, including Gold Dust Soap Powder and Palmolive in 1922. Listeners began to call certain radio programs "soap operas," because soap companies sponsored most serials—a name still used today for both the programs and any melodramatic and convoluted situation.

Lever Brothers used endorsements to boost sales of its new Lux toilet soap in 1925. To show that their soap was better than high-priced imported ones, the company launched an effective ad campaign in 1925 featuring screen stars who praised the product. The ad claimed "9 out of 10 screens stars care for their skin with Lux toilet soap," and the leading film studios in Hollywood had made this their official soap. The ad pictured sixteen female stars—among them Clara Bow, Joan Crawford, Janet Gaynor, and Billie Dove—and included a longer list of the

soap's users. The photo captions included testimonials from the stars, saying that the soap kept their skin "exquisitely smooth" and "in perfect condition." A similar sales campaign continued for about twenty years, and sales of the soap remained high. These techniques encouraged people to identify with their products and aspire to become like the people in the ads

They also warned about the social dangers of poor grooming, and body odor in particular. In 1928, the makers of Lifebuoy soap hired an agency that launched an effective campaign depicting their soap as just right for men, especially those who wanted to prevent body odor. Illustrations in the print ads for this soap showed robust-looking men.

Listerine, the antiseptic and mouthwash, is another example of a grooming "need" created by astute marketing. Gerard Lambert, in the early 1920s, used advertising to convince the public that unpleasant mouth odor, common in those days, was in fact a social problem called halitosis (the medical term for bad breath) and that his product could cure it. People had not considered mouth odor abnormal or problematic before; they have since then. (Twitchell, 2000)

In the 1930s, ads for Listerine played even further on social anxiety. One showed a solitary woman playing with her two dogs. The text said, "What she really wanted was children" and that the woman "yearned for love, marriage, motherhood." However, the men who were initially attracted by her charm and beauty did not stay. The reason was that she had "halitosis (unpleasant breath) . . . the unforgivable social fault." (Watkins, 1959)

During the 1920s, sex in advertising became more obvious. Fashionable women wore lighter, shorter clothing , and silk stockings were more widely available, so women's legs were on view for the first time. Artists prepared ads that drew attention to the legs, even when the product had nothing to do with stockings.

Ads continued to promote the idea that certain products would aid romantic relationships. The 1927 ad for Palmolive soap featured a lovely young bride with the caption, "and . . . I promise to keep that schoolgirl complexion." The image of a beautiful bride was used often to sell not only soap, but also various cosmetics and household products. (Goodrum and Dalrymple, 1990) In the years since, ads for numerous other products have claimed they will freshen breath, eliminate underarm smells, and get rid of other body odors that have been defined as worrisome and socially unacceptable.

Taking this notion a step further, ads for cosmetics and grooming products often focused on how people who used certain products would become more popular and sexually desirable. The J. Walter Thompson Agency, a large advertising firm in New York City, used this tactic when it created the slogan "The Skin You Love to Touch" for Woodbury Soap. Woodbury gave this same title to a booklet about skin care that the company produced. Ads showed an affectionate-looking man embracing an attractive woman. Customers were told how to cleanse their skin to give it the "Woodbury treatment." The ad was first used in May 1911 in *The Ladies' Home Journal* and continued to appear into the 1920s. Carl Naether, author of a 1928 book called *Advertising to Women*, called the ad "a lure to make women believe that, by using the soap in question, she will be able to cultivate a skin sufficiently beautiful to constitute an infallible safeguard against the waning of male affection." (Naether, 1928).

The "skin you love to touch" campaign was so successful that the company used it into the 1940s. Ads described the "radiant complexion and soft velvety skin" that would come from using Woodbury. (Goodrum and Dalrymple, 1990)

Endorsements and expert testimonials continued to be popular in ad campaigns. Palmolive soap featured the famous Dionne Quintuplets in a 1937 ad, showing pictures of the five little girls and text saying their doctor had recommended Palmolive for their sensitive, tender skin.

A more daring note also began to creep into some ads. In 1936, Woodbury was one of the first companies in America to use a nude woman in its advertisements. A photograph taken by the photographer Edward Steichen and called "The Sun Bath," showed a rear/side view of a reclining woman wearing sandals. The ad claimed that the Woodbury formula had been enriched with "filtered sunshine" and that this new product was an "amazing scientific soap!" (Foster, 1967)

The Age of Television

Television, which first entered households in the late 1930s, offered opportunities to promote products in new and more dramatic ways. Few people owned televisions in the 1930s and early 1940s, but by the early 1950s, millions of American homes had televisions, and the number continued to grow steadily. Ads, developed especially for this medium, touted the virtues of various cosmetics, perfumes, and hair products and often featured attractive models or celebrities. Revlon gained a reputation for its striking graphics and captivating ad copy. Sales of Revlon cosmetics rose dramatically after the company began advertising on a popular television quiz show.

Hair care products were a particular focus in the 1950s in all advertising media. Competing companies vied to capture a larger share of the growing hairspray market. Hair dyes produced a more natural look, and companies used that in their advertisements. In its 1956 campaign, the Clairol company used the slogan "Does she or doesn't she? Only her hairdresser knows for sure." That same company also came up with "If I have only one life, let me live it as a blond."In 1953, actress Marilyn Monroe, celebrated for her glamour, endorsed Lustre-Crème Shampoo, in an ad that claimed the shampoo was favored by "4 out of 5 top Hollywood stars . . ." During the 1940s and 1950s, Elizabeth Taylor, Betty Hutton, Jane Russell, June Allyson, and other prominent female film stars were also featured in Lustre Crème ads, which appeared in *Vogue, Ladies Home Journal, Good Housekeeping,* and other periodicals with many female readers. (Goodrum and Dalrymple, 1990)

More full-color ads began appearing during the 1950s, and ad campaigns became increasingly slick and sophisticated, and continued with celebrity endorsements. During the 1970s, an ad campaign for Clairol hair care products featured Olympic gold-medal figure skating champion Dorothy Hamill, whose performance had been seen on television worldwide. Many women and girls who admired her looks asked for a "Dorothy Hamill haircut." The likable athlete became a popular spokesperson and signed a contract to endorse a new line of hair products by Clairol called "Short and Sassy." Ads for the products featured Hamill's image on television and in the print media.

Celebrities endorsed other best-selling hair care products. One of the best known was actress Farrah Fawcett, who appeared in ads for Wella Balsam shampoo and conditioner. Fawcett was known for her thick, layered blonde hair, a style that became very fashionable during the 1970s.

Ads for hair coloring products also featured celebrities. Among the actresses who endorsed L'Oreal's Preference were Meredith Baxter, Cybill Shepherd, and Andie MacDowell. The memorable tag-line for these television and print ads was "I'm worth it," a reference to the fact that this brand was slightly more expensive than a number of other brands.

A Vast Industry

By the late twentieth century, the cosmetics industry was spending billions of dollars a year on advertising and was the largest client for the American advertising business. The top 10 television advertisers during the 1990s included several companies that made grooming and beauty items: Procter & Gamble (which spent about $1.3 billion each year on ads), Lever Brothers, Colgate-Palmolive, Bristol Meyers, and American Home Products. (*Advertising Age*, February 1999; Tucker, 23 March 1999). Common in all forms of media were ads for cosmetics, hair care products, and fragrances and for soaps, toothpaste, mouthwash, deodorants, and other personal care products.

Celebrity endorsements continue to be popular and powerful advertising tools. Companies offer top models or celebrities multi-

million dollar contracts to represent their products. Top models have signed exclusive contracts to represent products for particular cosmetics companies. They included Christy Turlington, who appeared in ads for Maybelline cosmetics, and Cindy Crawford, a Revlon spokesperson. In recent years, more female singers have contracted to represent various cosmetics. They include country/pop stars Shania Twain (Revlon) and Faith Hill (Cover Girl).

To sell their products as effectively as possible, members of the beauty industry have developed increasingly sophisticated methods of analyzing consumers and specific groups of consumers. They gather statistics about different sectors of the population to find out who bought what and why. Ads have also become more visually sophisticated and colorful. Magazine fragrance ads for both men and women may contain samples in the form of papers that can be rubbed on the skin. Discount coupons promote new and old products both.

For many years, most women's fashion magazines used top models on the covers—*Vogue, Elle, Harper's Bazaar*, and *Cosmopolitan*. These models often became well known and received a great deal of publicity about both their professional and personal lives. By the late 1990s, however, the owners and editors of beauty and fashion magazines also noted that more copies sold of issues featuring celebrities on the cover. In 1997, the best-selling covers for *Mirabella, Harper's Bazaar*, and *Cosmopolitan* had movie actresses on them.

Further analysis supported this notion. In 1998, when comparing news-stand sales figures, the editors of *Vogue* magazine found that an August issue, with a cover featuring a top model, sold 520,000 newsstand copies, while the October issue, with a cover photo of popular talk-show host/actress Oprah Winfrey, sold a record 810,000 newsstand copies. (Kuszynski, 1998) During 1998, *Vogue* used photos of celebrities on 8 of its 12 covers. Magazines with other celebrities on the cover, such as Oscar-winning actress Gwyneth Paltrow, were also big sellers.

The advertising industry concluded that consumers were more likely to buy products associated with celebrities they admired than they were to buy products advertised by models. Some analysts went so far as to predict that the era of the supermodel might be over in America and that this trend seemed to be extending into Europe as well. (Kuszynski, 1998)

People have tried to explain why consumers might relate more to celebrities than to models. Cultural historian and author Neil Gabler concluded: "In the eyes of the public, models are unidimensional. They are purely visual, whereas celebrities have these lives we can attach to and they seem more fully dimensional to us."(Kuszynski, 1998) Other analysts have said that people prefer to see ads and magazine covers featuring people with less than perfect bodies and features. People can identify more with celebrities whose looks seem more attainable and whom they associate with a certain personality. Many of the celebrities are also older than the typical model, which again makes them more like the average consumer.

In response to this trend, some top modeling agencies developed links to record companies and agencies that represented singers, actors, and other performers. Some of these groups handled contracts in which celebrities became spokespersons for lines of hair-care products or cosmetics.

Some of these celebrities appeared on television in a genre known as "infomercials." These special advertising programs of varying lengths appear on regular television channels and on special "shopping networks." They first emerged in recent decades as a way to sell various consumer goods, including cosmetics, hair and skin care products, exercise equipment, and grooming aids. Lori Davis hair products, Victoria Jackson Cosmetics, and Jose Eber hair extensions are among the products that began their sales campaigns through infomercials featuring celebrities.

Critics of infomercials contend that the promoters may make unsubstantiated, exaggerated, or false claims about the products. People who appear on the programs may not have used the products they are promoting, or their clear skin, thick glossy hair, or lovely coloring may be unrelated to use of the product. *See also* AGING AND APPEARANCE; BEAUTY INDUSTRY (U.S.); HAIR COLOR; MODELING AND MODELS.

Further reading: Margaret Allen, *Selling Dreams* (1981); *Advertising Age,* February 1999; Allen G. Foster, *Advertising: Ancient Market Place to Television* (1967); Stephen Fox, *The Mirror Makers: A History of American Advertising and Its Creators* (1984); Charles Goodrum and Helen Dalrymple, *Advertising in America: The First 200 Years* (1990); Michael Gross, *Model: The Ugly Business of Beautiful Women* (1995); Dorothy Hamill, *Dorothy Hamill On and Off the Ice* (1983); Alex Kuszynski, "Trading on Hollywood Magic," *The New York Times,* 30 January 1998, C1, C4; Vance Packard, *The Hidden Persuaders* (1957); Richard S. Tedlow, *New and Improved: The Story of Mass Marketing in America* (1990); Randy Tucker, "P & G Puts $1.72 Billion into Ads," *Cincinnati Enquirer,* 23 March 1999, http://www.Enquirer.com.editions/1999/03/23; James B. Twitchell, *Twenty Ads that Shook the World* (2000); Julian Lewis Watkins, *The 100 Greatest Advertisements, Who Did Them and What They Did* (1959).

African Americans

Grooming practices and modes of hairdressing and cosmetics usage among African Americans have reflected both a distinctive heritage and the prevailing styles in the larger society. Beauty trends that began with, or were popularized by, African Americans have also influenced people throughout the United States and other countries.

For centuries, African Americans endured discrimination on every front, including attitudes about their looks, because the notion of "attractiveness" was based on European standards. Such attitudes led some African Americans (and people of color from other regions of the world) to try and lighten their skin to look more "Caucasian." They did this not only to make their looks match the mainstream ideas but also to avoid the mistreatment and legal and social discrimination that came with being nonwhite. During the 1800s and early 1900s, some women of color and a smaller number of men used household bleaches, among other substances, for this purpose. As time went on, companies began selling more commercial skin-bleaching products, especially for the face. Products designed to lighten the skin were vigorously marketed to African Americans during the early part of the twentieth century. Many of these creams, treatments, and lotions were made from damaging chemicals, including laundry bleach. Ads for these products openly denigrated dark skin and made assumptions that white or light-colored skin was "better" and "more attractive."

These same promoters urged African Americans to change their natural hair texture to achieve a straighter and smoother look typical of the white majority. They used topical products (pommade, etc.) and hot irons to achieve this look, including some products invented and sold by other African Americans. At the turn of the nineteenth century, Madam C.J. Walker and Annie Turnbo Malone created successful hair care products businesses for African American women and men.

African Americans got negative messages about their physical features from many fronts, including advertisements and images in the mass media. Beauty contests in the United States were segregated by race (as were many other things). In response, African American newspapers sponsored contests for black women. For example, in 1914, the *New York Age* newspaper sponsored a beauty contest for African American women in that area. When the first Miss America pageant was held in 1921, African Americans began organizing a national "Miss Bronze" for women of color; the first "Miss Bronze" title was awarded in 1927, and the pageant continues to the present. A "Miss Black America" pageant was also organized and is held annually. (The first African American to participate in the Miss America contest was not until 1970.) Black women used such pageants and contests as one way of combating their exclusion from other contests or from contests biased in favor of white women. New pageants, such as the "Miss Black Swimwear" contest, expanded opportunities to showcase African American beauty.

During the 1920s, during what was known as the "Harlem Renaissance, African Americans celebrated their own beauty and distinctive physical traits and rejected the limiting view of white European ideals. Black writers praised women's charms, comparing their skin colors to cinnamon, honey, ginger, and other appealing representations. They also wrote of African Americans' own attitudes toward how they looked and called on them to recognize their own standards of beauty. People of all races admired Josephine Baker and other African American celebrities who appeared on the stage and in nightclubs, such as Harlem's Cotton Club, for their beauty, style, and glamour.

Later, other performers also overcame obstacles to build successful careers and reach broad audiences, although often at considerable personal cost. Singers Billie Holliday and Lena Horne and actress Dorothy Dandridge are among the black women who won acclaim for their talent and beauty; singers Nat King Cole, Johnny Mathis, and Harry Belafonte are among the men who were admired for their good looks and talent by Americans of all colors and ethnic backgrounds.

During the 1960s, the African American community experienced a new and widespread movement to change negative attitudes and discriminatory practices. The slogan "Black Is Beautiful" is associated with the civil rights and Black Pride movements of this era. People discussed how stereotyped ideas about appearance were used to prop up the power of the dominant white society and to oppress people of color and members of other minority groups. They contended that these standards of appearance were also used as a way to deny the validity of black culture and to promote feelings of inferiority, according to authors Lakoff and Scherr (1984).

During this time, African Americans declared their pride in their heritage and physical appearance, rejecting the idea that white standards were superior or should apply to everyone. Many women and men wore their hair in a "natural" or "Afro" style and did not artificially straighten it. They adopted styles that reflected African heritage, such as cornrows, braiding, hair wrapping and, later, dreadlocks, and various curled, and twisted styles. Traditional styles of clothing in both vivid and earth colors were popular, worn with African jewelry and accessories, including beads and cloth wrappings for the hair.

The cosmetics industry, never far behind a trend, began marketing new products for these new hairstyles, including a line called Afro Sheen developed by the Johnson Company. A 1972 ad for these products showed a well-dressed father and son wearing natural Afro hairstyles admiring an African sculpture. The text, which included some words in an African language, described the grooming and conditioning properties of the shampoo, conditioner, dressing cream, and hairspray in the product line.

The Black Pride movement had an empowering effect not only on African Americans but on other ethnic groups, such as Native Americans, who expressed renewed pride in their own heritage and appearance. It brought more attention to the racist and stereotyped attitudes about appearance that had become part of American culture. Fashion and cosmetics advertisements became more diverse and featured far more women and men of color from different parts of the world.

Magazines played an important role in promoting black models and products made especially for people of color. In 1945, John H. Johnson, the founder of Johnson Publishing Company, launched *Ebony Magazine,* which became the world's best-selling magazine for blacks. It featured articles on beauty, fashion, health, and fitness, as well as articles on people, current events, history, sports, entertainment, and other subjects. Johnson's company expanded to include a new magazine called *Jet* (a weekly magazine that includes a feature called "Beauty of the Week"), and also produced Fashion Fair Cosmetics and Supreme Beauty Products, as well as sponsoring the still-popular Ebony Fashion Fair.

The Ebony Fashion Fair began in 1958 when four African American models displayed American fashions in ten cities. Later

tours have included cities throughout the world and both male and female models, including twin brothers in 1983 and a large-sized female model in 1982. The Fashion Fair has raised millions of dollars for charities and scholarships.

Fashion Fair Cosmetics debuted in 1973 and are now marketed in the United States, Canada, Africa, the Caribbean, Europe, and other places. They are especially designed to complement African American skin tones and hair and eye color. Other companies developed lines especially for African Americans during and after the 1970s.

The first issue of *Essence* magazine debuted in 1970 and was another groundbreaking publication created by African Americans. Geared to the interests of black women, the magazine showcases black models and celebrities in its fashion and beauty features. In doing so, it has provided a new forum for these models and for black designers, makeup artists, photographers, stylists, and writers. Lavish color photos and advertisements present black women and men in exciting fashions, hairstyles, and accessories, and feature articles about important issues and events.

This expanded standard of what constitutes "beauty" touched other areas of the culture. More black performers appeared in prominent roles on television and in feature films, as well as in ballet, opera, and the theatre. In the 1950s, singer/actress Dorothy Dandridge won leading roles as a film star and was nominated for an Academy Award as best actress in *Carmen Jones*. Actress and singer Diahann Carroll broke ground as a leading lady on Broadway, then as the star of her own television series, *Julia*. Dandridge, Carroll, and other glamorous black women greatly increased audiences' exposure to images of African Americans, since, in the past, they had mostly seen black women in small, supporting roles. Carroll later appeared in the hit television series *Dynasty*.

During the 1960s and 1970s, more African American women wore a traditional hairstyle called cornrows, which consisted of numerous small braids woven all over the head. African American celebrities, including Cicely Tyson, popularized the hairdo by wearing it at performances and public events. The hairstyle was well suited to the texture of black women's hair and required no chemical hair straighteners and relaxers.

Some white women also adopted this style. In 1979, a 19-year-old California actress, Bo Derek, wore a hairstyle featuring cornrows for her starring role in the film *10*. (Her male co-star, comedian Dudley Moore, described Derek's film character as a "Perfect 10," giving rise to the use of numerical rankings of 1–10 to describe a woman's appearance.) Derek's long blonde cornrows, decorated with beads, received much attention and prompted more white women to try this look. Tourists also enjoyed trying the hairstyle while on vacation on islands in the Caribbean where beaded cornrow hairdos are popular.

During the 1990s and into the twenty-first century, the two young tennis champions, sisters Venus and Serena Williams, have worn

Serena and Venus Williams. © *Kelly Jordan/Globe Photos, Inc.* 2000.

cornrows adorned with colorful beads on and off the courts, making the style one of their trademarks. These tall, attractive, athletic young women have been featured in fashion and beauty magazines.

Natural hairstyles worn to reveal the texture of unprocessed hair have become a source of pride and affirmation. According to *Essence* magazine, the last quarter of the twentieth century brought "the liberating freedom to wear hair kinky or straight, to wear cornrows or dreadlocks (called 'locks'), weaves or wigs, to be braided or clean shaven. Indeed, what we've come to understand and appreciate is that the real beauty of black hair lies in its enormous versatility." (Edwards, 1995)

Since the 1960s, more African American models of both genders have been pictured in beauty and fashion ads, as well as in high-fashion runway shows. Beverly Johnson was one of the first African American models to reach national and international prominence. Many more African American models and supermodels have followed, including Naomi Campbell, Iman, Naomi Sims, Veronica Webb, and Tyra Banks. The first black Miss America was crowned in 1983 (Vanessa Williams, now a well-known singer and actress), and another black woman was the first runner-up that same year.

Many black performers are well known for their looks as well as their talents or athletic abilities. African American performers who are often cited on "Most Beautiful" and "Best-Looking" lists include Billy Dee Williams, Denzel Washington, Will Smith, Michael Jordan, Taye Diggs, Whitney Houston, Janet Jackson, Halle Berry, and Vanessa Williams.

African American designers and hairstylists continue to influence popular trends in fashion and beauty. The black pop music world has also contributed various trends. Shaved heads on men became more common and popular after superstar basketball player Michael Jordan and other well-known African American athletes, musicians, and actors opted to go hairless. Although conservative looks for men of all colors have been the norm in the workplace, some men of color are breaking that mold. Men with shaved heads and dreadlocks can now be seen in executive offices, hospitals, and other work settings. *See also* BAKER, JOSEPHINE; DANDRIDGE, DOROTHY; DREADLOCKS; FRAGRANCE; HAIR COLOR; HAIR STRAIGHTENING; HAIR, STYLING OF; IMAN; JOHNSON, BEVERLY; JOHNSON PRODUCTS; MALONE, ANNIE TURNBO; MODELING AND MODELS; SKIN; SKIN COLORING AGENTS; WALKER, MADAME C.J.

Further reading: Audrey Edwards, ed. *Essence: 25 Years Celebrating Black Women* (1995); Robin Tomach Lakoff and Raquel L. Scherr, *Face Value: The Politics of Beauty* (1984); Melba Miller, *The Black Is Beautiful Beauty Book* (1974); Kathy Peiss, *Hope in a Jar* (1998). Noliwe M. Rooks, *Hair Raising: Beauty, Culture, and African American Women* (1996).

Aging and Appearance

The quest for perpetually youthful looks has been underway, at least in some cultures, for millennia. Although many societies traditionally venerated their elders, the desire to look forever young is nevertheless powerful and pervasive.

Around the world, people have looked for magic potions or formulas for eternal youth. They tried to find special health- and youth-giving waters and made pilgrimages to sites where they believed these powerful waters were. Sixteenth-century explorers searched for a place in North America that was known as the "fountain of youth." In more recent decades, people have turned their attention to hormones, foods, and nutritional supplements that might promote youth and vitality and stop the clock at an age when they thought they looked good.

Social scientists contend that a desire to turn back the clock, in terms of appearance, is often linked to a fear of death and age-related problems—for example, health problems, losing friends and loved ones, increasing loneliness, loss of sexual potency and attractiveness, and diminishing mental and physical abilities.

At the same time, the media bombard us with images of youth and beauty, and a large number of advertisements are for products to maintain that appearance. The term "ageism" refers to discrimination against older people, and some have contended that a more mature appearance has cost them a job or promotion. Looking young is associated with success in professional and personal life. During the late twentieth century, for example, some women filed lawsuits against their employers when they lost their jobs as television newscasters, contending this occurred because they were looking older.

Effects of Aging

Scientists study the physical and mental effects of aging and seek to understand how and why the body ages. In recent years, experts have claimed that skin looks old mostly because of exposure to the sun and other elements, although heredity probably plays a role as well.

As they age, most people's bodies change in characteristic ways. They get lines and wrinkles on the face, neck, and elsewhere, as well as loose and sagging skin. The contour of the face and jaw may change due to the loss of muscle tone, and skin may fade or yellow. These changes occur because tissue degenerates, skin loses elasticity, some cellular processes slow down, and the skin cannot retain moisture as efficiently. During the aging process, collagen and elastin fibers tend to break down, in large part because of exposure to sunlight; changes occur mainly on body parts that are exposed to sunlight. Dropping levels of once-abundant hormones and enzymes and the weakening of the immune system contribute to the visible signs of aging as well.

The Quest for Youth

People have used different substances to look younger and try to reverse the effects of aging, often applying colored cosmetics and other grooming products. Cheek and lip rouge are both used for this purpose and have been for millennia in Europe, Asia, and the Middle East; rosy cheeks and lips are associated with youth and vitality. Likewise, various moisturizing agents have been used since antiquity to give skin a more youthful appearance, as well as to protect it from the elements. People wore wigs to cover thinning hair or bald heads. They applied liquid tonics and masques containing plant materials, mud, or honey to their faces to reduce the signs of aging. A visitor to China wrote about the great attention women paid to their bodies, saying, "Nowhere are they better skilled or more practiced in the art of arresting or repairing the ravages of time." (Genders, 1972)

More recently, people have turned to increasingly sophisticated preparations, technology, and surgical techniques in their quest. In youth-oriented cultures such as the United States, people may spend a great deal of time and money pursuing a more youthful appearance; skin treatments, cosmetics, hair dyes, hair transplants, wigs, hairpieces, nutritional supplements, diets, and cosmetic surgery are all weapons in the battle. Just as a "beauty culture" gave rise to a huge and profitable industry, so the "youth culture" has its own industry.

Products and Treatments

The early years of the twentieth century saw the beauty and toiletries industries respond to the quest for a youthful appearance with what have now become thousands of different products and treatments. The face has been and remains the focus of many of these products—women's faces in particular. The treatments were quite complicated. For example, an article in a 1908 issue of the American magazine *Woman Beautiful* described a way to combat facial wrinkles with a process that involved cleansing, creams, an astringent, lotion, wrinkle paste, and massage using an electric vibrator. An analogous treatment, however, could readily be found today.

As more beauty salons sprang up their operators offered facial treatments that promised to create a younger appearance or help to prevent signs of aging. Today, salons continue to offer anti-aging facials and massages, as well as hair dyeing to cover gray hair, and other treatments.

Consumers could also buy devices to use at home. During the 1940s, facial sauna machines were first sold throughout Europe, and the manufacturers claimed these machines could aid aging skin. The devices were popular in Austria, Germany, France, and later in the United States, and are still around today, although never scientifically proved effective. Now, advertisements and infomercials encourage people to order special moisturizers, cosmetics, muscle-stimulating devices, facial exercise kits, hair restoratives, and other products to help them look younger. Special mail-order catalogues cater to the aging population, particularly women—one example is "As We Change"— their pages are filled not only with cosmetic treatments but also devices that are put in the mouth and used to exercise the facial muscles, thus supposedly countering any appearance of sagging. Anti-aging products are also promoted on-line, and their sales have increased with the growth of on-line shopping.

Cosmetics are also given names that in and of themselves make implicit claims (e.g. "visible difference" "anti-aging cream" "age-erase," "age-defying" "line eraser"). These words are not necessarily used again in the text of the advertisement or voiced in the television ads. Words like "rejuvenating" influence people to buy products that may have little or no effect or that are far more costly than other products with similar ingredients.

Consumer Issues

Controversy surrounds many topical skin care products that claim to be "anti-aging" or to "rejuvenate skin," "reverse the effects of aging," "get rid of wrinkles," or "prevent wrinkling." In 1987, the U.S. Food and Drug Administration took action on certain "anti-aging" claims. The FDA asked 23 prominent cosmetics manufacturers to verify the statements they were making in the media claiming their products contained ". . . anti-aging and cellular replacement ingredients." The presence of such ingredients would tend to classify a substance as a drug rather than a cosmetic, and drugs are subject to much stricter safety laws than cosmetics. The FDA said that if a company failed to withdraw such claims, it must immediately submit the products to be tested as drugs to determine safety and effectiveness. Daniel L. Michaels, the director of the FDA at that time, said, "We are unaware of any substantial evidence that demonstrates the safety and effectiveness of these articles. Nor are we aware that these drugs are generally recognized as safe and effective for their intended uses." (Michaels, 1987)

Scientists and critics of the cosmetics industry claim that such claims are unfounded and that, as of 1999, no cream or lotion can live up to such claims. Nor, say scientists, can any topical products live up to their claims to "feed the skin."

Critics of the beauty industry point out that ads for anti-aging products often refer to the results of "clinical studies," but the company that sells the product may commission the study and then design it in such a way that they prove the claims made in the ads. Critics also question the "before and after" pictures of people who are supposed to have used the product.

Also controversial are various devices or techniques, such as special massagers and "exercisers," that purport to make aging skin look young. Through the years, the FDA has removed some of these products from the market or forced their makers to change false and misleading ads. Critics state that some treatments and masks increase circulation or produce a refreshing feeling or temporary tightening of the skin, but these effects do not last.

Social Attitudes

Social scientists have studied and compared attitudes about aging and appearance in various cultures. Many cultures stress inner beauty or consider some features of aging to be visually attractive. In Africa, older women who are heavy, according to Western standards, walk with grace and pride and are called stately by many observers. Gray hair

is considered attractive in India and some other countries. Some Eastern cultures that stress physical and mental harmony state that a person's inner life is most important and will show in his or her movements, gestures, and facial expressions.

Beauty book author Michelle Dominique Leigh, who has lived in countries in Europe, Asia, Africa, and South and Central America, observed how some women in these regions deal with the effects of aging. She writes, "Using pure and natural ingredients and simple, empowering rituals, the women in traditional cultures whom I have known cultivate their beauty as they cultivate other aspects of their overall well-being—out of self-love and acceptance, not out of despair at the first signs of aging." (Leigh, 1996) (At the same time, it should be noted, Avon cosmetics salespeople also do business in remote parts of Latin American rainforests.)

Leigh repeats a Japanese saying: "Do not envy the fresh blossoms of youth. Accept yourself as you are. Jealousy, worry, and negative feelings will destroy your beauty far more than the natural wrinkles of age." (Leigh, 1996)

This is not a message common in American culture. Fashion and beauty magazines geared for women contain images of young, physically "perfect" models and celebrities, setting this youthful look as the standard. Numerous articles, books, and television features describe ways to care for the face and body and show ways to use cosmetics and hair care products to appear younger, get rid of gray hair, disguise lines and wrinkles, and lose weight (many people gain weight as they get older).

Critics of the American emphasis on youth and youthful looks claim there is also a double standard of aging, one for men and another for women. Women who show signs of aging are more likely to be dismissed, ignored, or considered less attractive, while men with facial lines or gray hair may be called distinguished or said to have more character in their faces. Female film actresses have complained about the lack of good roles for women over 40. They note that, in many films, older men are romantically paired with younger, sometimes much younger, women, while the reverse is seldom true.

Scientists say that one reason that the beauty ideal for women emphasizes youthful features for instance, glowing, soft skin, shining hair, a firm body, and rosy lips—is that these traits signify a fertile woman, and men are biologically programmed to seek a fertile mate. In contrast, men are able to father children at much later ages than women can conceive, and an older man may be perceived as having more economic means to provide for a family. In the past, men who were good providers might attract a younger mate considered more physically attractive than themselves, and men who marry for a second time frequently chose mates younger than they are. Images of older men with younger women were traditionally more common than the reverse, although it has become socially more acceptable for older women to affiliate themselves with younger men, as women's economic roles change in many societies.

Changing Views

As the Baby Boom generation ages, however, the cosmetics industry has recognized that their market is changing. During recent decades, more ads for cosmetics and hair care products have featured women over 40, including Lauren Hutton, Dayle Haddon, Andie MacDowell, and Melanie Griffith. Ads featuring images of more mature models were more likely to appeal to aging consumers, many of whom bought numerous beauty products each year.

Celebrities over 40, including Marilu Henner, Renee Russo, Tina Turner, Patti LaBelle, and Cheryl Tiegs, have expressed confidence and acceptance of their looks and said that women of all ages can be fit, attractive, and sexy. These women, as they pass 40, 50, and more, became role models for their noncelebrity counterparts, who welcomed the sight of glamorous, attractive, older women. French actress Catherine Deneuve, who had endorsed Chanel products during the 1970s, appeared in advertisements for a skin moisturizer. In the ad,

she acknowledged being over 40, then told TV viewers, "Come closer, I have nothing to hide." During the 1980s, actress Isabella Rosselini, born in 1952, was chosen to represent Lancome cosmetics (but later dropped). Actress Joan Collins (born in 1933), a star of the popular television series *Dynasty*, became the spokeswoman for a Revlon perfume named "Scoundrel." Collins portrayed alluring characters on film in her 40s, and, at age 50 she posed for *Playboy* magazine. Actress Linda Evans also symbolized that women over 40 can be beautiful. Evans endorsed Clairol hair color products and a perfume called "Crystal," among other things.

Targeting Older Consumers

The publishing industry has also taken note of the aging population. New fashion, beauty, and lifestyle magazines, including *More* and *Mirabella*, publish articles and features to attract these readers. Other new magazines, such as *Longevity*, address health, fitness, and appearance issues that concern women in their 40s or older. In speaking of the commercial impact of the maturing baby-boomers, makeup artist and author Victoria Jackson said, "Establishing 20-year-olds as the standard of beauty today is even more absurd than it has been in the past." (Jackson, 1993)

Author Nancy Friday pointed out that middle-aged Americans were "the fastest-growing major market, a culture of moneyed, educated men and women who expect to work, play, and have sex as long as possible. . . . Such a population has never existed before. Synthetic estrogen, testosterone, amazing beauty creams, revolutionary bodybuilding machinery, cosmetic surgery, none is going to disappear. In fact, they will flourish and multiply." According to Friday, the use of various means to stay healthy and look good is "not so much about eternal youth as about extended life." (Friday, 1975)

See also BEAUTY STANDARDS; BODY IMAGE; COSMETICS; FOUNTAIN OF YOUTH; HAIR COLOR.

Further reading: Lois W. Banner, *In Full Flower: Aging Women, Power, and Sexuality* (1993); Lynn

Darling, "Age, Beauty, and Truth," *New York Times*, 23 January 1994, sec. 9, p. 5; Nancy Friday, *The Power of Beauty* (1975); Roy Genders, *A History of Scent* (1972); Victoria Jackson, *Redefining Beauty* (1993); Norma Kinzer, *Put Down and Ripped Off: The American Woman and the Beauty Cult* (1977); Michelle Dominique Leigh, "Ageless Beauty," *Natural Health*, July–August 1996, 80–82, 145; Leigh, *The New Beauty: East-West Teachings in the Beauty of Body and Soul* (1995); Elissa Melamed, *Mirror, Mirror: The Terror of Not Being Young* (1983); Michaels, *FDA Consumer* (1987); Nicholas Perricone, M.D., *The Wrinkle Cure* (2000); Susan Sontag, "The Double Standard of Aging," *Saturday Review*, 23 September 1972, 29–38.

Alberto Culver Company

The Alberto Culver Company, a multinational firm with an annual income of $1.6 billion in 1999 (from "About Us"), manufactures and sells personal care products, as well as household products. The company's personal care brands include Alberto VO5 hair care products, St. Ives products for skin and hair, Consort men's hairspray, TRESemme hair products, and FDS feminine products.

The company was built on successful hairdressing products that were developed at a beauty supply company on the West Coast. The conditioning hairdressing product became popular with both Hollywood stylists and retail customers.

Chicago entrepreneur Leonard Lavin bought the company in 1955 and moved its headquarters to Chicago, where Alberto Culver focused on the VO5 hairdressing cream, which became the best-selling product of its kind in 1958. Advertising, especially on successful television programs, boosted sales. The company changed the TV advertising business in 1972 when it won the right to use 30-second spots instead of the traditional 60-second commercials. In 1983, Alberto Culver pioneered the 15-second commercial. The company introduced Alberto European Styling Mousse for hair to the United States.

In addition to its packaged products, the company makes and markets Sally Beauty Company products, which it bought in 1969, and is the world's largest seller of beauty supplies to the professional salon and barber markets. After purchasing this company, the Alberto Culver developed a chain of 2,000 stores in the United States, Great Britain, Canada, Japan, and Germany. Through its Beauty Systems Group, the company distributes Alberto Culver and other brands, including Clairol, Wella, Shiseido, and Redken to the professional beauty markets.

Alberto Culver has a large market-share of the hair care styling products sold in Great Britain and Canada. Its Indola label hair color is the leading brand for salons in Europe, Israel, and Southeast Asia, and Alberto Culver toothpastes are popular in Scandinavian countries. The company markets a VO5 deodorant brand in Latin America, where its hair care and skin care lines also sell well.

The company supports numerous charities, programs, and organizations that emphasize health care, education, childcare, and women in the workplace.

Further reading: "About Us," http://www.alberto.com/aboutus.html

Allergic Reactions

Consumers have experienced allergic reactions—often in the form of a skin condition called contact dermatitis—to grooming products and cosmetics, both homemade and commercially prepared. Some users also have nonallergic reactions to irritants in a product, as when soap gets in their eyes.

Allergens and Irritants

Substances used in cosmetics that may cause an allergic reaction include cornstarch, gum arabic, oil of spearmint, certain fragrances, preservatives, and coal tar hair dyes. Eye makeup is most likely to cause reactions because eye tissues are very sensitive.

Some people are also allergic to ingredients in hair care products, such as permanent waves, dyes, or bleaches. Classic reactions include redness, rashes, weeping skin, swelling, and papules (small, solid raised areas) on the skin. Bubble baths have also been known to cause rashes and skin irritation. In addition, bubble bath use can provoke Stevens-Johnson Syndrome, which is characterized by rashes, fever, joint pain, and eye disorders.

Determining the specific cosmetic ingredient that causes an allergy may be difficult, because the average consumer wears about 12 different products at a time. Also, some ingredients are not listed clearly on the label, but may fall under a larger heading, such as "fragrances."

A 1972 report issued by the President's National Commission on Product Safety estimated that about 60,000 Americans each year suffer from various allergic reactions, including itching, rashes, hair loss, burns, sneezing, and watery eyes. The report pointed out that most people do not report these reactions to a doctor unless they are severe. It noted too that many people did not initially realize that a cosmetic product had caused the allergic reaction, often because they had used the product many times in the past without any problems.

Most reactions to cosmetics are not life-threatening but may be severe or uncomfortable enough that people seek medical treatment. A survey conducted between 1977 to 1983 by the North American Contact Dermatitis Group (a task force organized by the American Academy of Dermatology) found about 210 reactions requiring medical care occurred per million cosmetic items purchased. Skin care products caused the most allergic reactions in this study, followed by hair products, including dyes. Facial makeup was third. The face ranked first among body parts likely to be affected, with 37 percent of the cases, followed by eyes, forearms, armpits, ears, entire body, neck, scalp, mouth, upper arms, fingers, and fingernails or toenails. Six percent of the cases affected "other" body parts, while in 7 percent of the cases, the body part affected was not known.

The group also listed the cosmetic ingredients most likely to cause reactions. They included fragrance ingredients, preservatives, p-phenylenediamine, lanolin and its derivatives, glyceryl monothioglycolate, propylene glycol, toluenesulfonamide/formaldehyde resin, sunscreens and other ultraviolet light absorbers, and acrylate or methacrylate.

The Food and Drug Administration (FDA) Division of Colors and Cosmetics is the agency set up to deal with reports from physicians and consumers about adverse effects of cosmetics. The FDA has the authority to remove a given product from the market if it appears to cause reactions in a significant number of people.

The FDA received 200 reports of adverse reactions to cosmetics in 1994. About 65 involved skin care products and makeup, and, of those, 22 involved products containing alpha hydroxy acid. Other complaints concerned hair products, soaps, toothpastes, and mouthwashes. (Stehlin, 1986)

Controlling Allergens

Manufacturers, agencies, and medical groups have used various approaches to the problem of allergens in products.

Removing potential allergens—or trying to—has been manufacturers' most common response. In the 1930s, an American company, Marcelle Cosmetics, claimed they had removed certain known irritants from their products, and they were permitted to advertise their products in the *Journal of the American Medical Association.*

The industry has also attempted to identify potential allergens. During the early 1980s, the cosmetics industry appointed a Cosmetic Ingredient Review Panel made up of scientists and other experts to evaluate the effects of thousands of ingredients that are used to make cosmetics and hair-care products.

Cosmetics companies may also test products or substances to see if they are likely to cause an allergic reaction. The patch tests is the most common method of doing this: placing a small amount of the product on the skin and watching for reactions over a period of time. A few cosmetics companies perform clinical tests of their products, but they have discretion in the way they conduct the testing.

Based on such tests and evaluations of ingredients, companies also applied the words "hypoallergenic," "allergy tested," and "fragrance free" to their products. ("Hypo" means less than normal, although consumers often interpret as meaning that the product will not cause allergic reactions at all.) Some manufacturers of hypoallergenic products have eliminated certain fragrance ingredients and preservatives that are often associated with allergic reactions. The International Fragrance Association has also listed chemicals they suggest should either be avoided or used in limited amounts in products because of their tendency to cause allergic reactions.

Using hypoallergenic products may reduce the possibility of many common reactions but does not mean the product is completely free of allergens. Critics, including the American Medical Association's Committee on Cutaneous Health, said that the term "hypoallergenic," when applied to cosmetics, is misleading.

Regulatory Efforts

Through the years, the FDA has proposed regulations that would require manufacturers to back up claims that a product is hypoallergenic. One such regulation was struck down in a federal court in 1978. In its official publication, *FDA Consumer,* the FDA has advised consumers that "there is no such thing as a 'nonallergenic' cosmetic—that is, one that can be guaranteed never to produce an allergic reaction." (Morrison, 1978) The FDA proposed ways to give consumers more accurate information and suggested that companies eliminate terms such as "medically proven" or "clinically proven" from their labels. The FDA also ruled that companies would not be permitted to make claims that imply that adverse reactions cannot occur. As of 2000, however, no legal standards existed regarding the use of the word "hypoallergenic." *See also* LAWS AND REGULATIONS (U.S.); SAFETY.

Further reading: Margaret Morrison, "Hypoallergenic Cosmetics," *FDA Consumer,* June 1974; Doris Stehlin, "Cosmetic Allergies," *FDA Consumer,* November 1986, http://vm.cfsan.fda.gov/~dms/cos-224.html; Stehlin, "Cosmetic Safety: More Complex Than at First Blush," FDA publication # (FDA) 95-5012, www.fda.gov/opacom/catalog/blush. html; David Steinman and Samuel

S. Epstein, M.D., *The Safe Shopper's Bible* (1995); U.S. Food and Drug Administration, Center for Food Safety and Applied Nutrition, Office of Cosmetics: 19 December 1994.

American Beauty Association (ABA)

The American Beauty Association, which has more than 250 member firms, was founded in 1985 when The National Beauty and Barber Manufacturers Association merged with The United Beauty Association. The ABA, based in Chicago, Illinois, states that its mission is to expand, serve, and protect the interests of the professional beauty industry by being a unified voice for the professional salon industry. Members of the association include manufacturers, manufacturer's representatives, and associated firms, including hair, skin, and nail care companies. The ABA also has subgroups to meet the needs of different industry segments, including the Nail Manufacturers Council and Esthetics Manufacturers and Distributors Alliance.

The ABA holds educational conferences and other industry events and advocates on behalf of members in regard to laws and political issues that affect the salon industry. It also sponsors the ABBIES Awards Program, which was created in 1996 to honor creative marketing in product development, advertising, packaging, salon education and public relations. The ABA also raises funds for charitable causes, including the Pediatric AIDS foundation and Breast Cancer Research Foundation.

Further reading: The American Beauty Association, *To Expand, Serve and Protect* (1999).

Animal Testing

Manufacturers have used animals to test cosmetics, personal care products, and other items throughout the twentieth century. Laboratories have used rabbits, rats, monkeys, and other animals for these tests, which animal-rights activists continue to protest.

Examples of Animal Testing

The most extreme type of animal testing is called acute toxicity testing. One early but still widely used acute toxicity test, called LD 50, was developed in 1927. The test is run until it least half of the animals die, which usually takes two to four weeks. In some tests, all of the test animals die. During the LD 50 tests, lab workers use tubes to force a substance into the animals' stomachs or through holes cut in their throats. At other times, substances are injected under the animal's skin or into their blood vessels or abdominal lining. The animals are observed to see what kinds of adverse reactions they have before they die, including convulsions, difficulty breathing, and bleeding.

Manufacturers use various other tests to gauge the safety of cosmetics or other personal care products. Workers may rub substances onto the animals' shaved skin or force the animals to inhale or swallow higher-than-normal amounts of test compounds.

Substances are tested to see whether they cause irritation, too, not only to gauge their toxicity when ingested. The Draize eye irritancy test, one common test, is conducted using albino rabbits. Laboratory workers insert liquid, granules, flakes, or powdered material into the eyes of the rabbits.

Over a period of time, ranging from an average of 72 hours up to 7 to 18 days, workers note the reaction to these substances. Damage to the eye tissue can include swelling, inflammation, ulcers, bleeding, and ultimately blindness, or the effects may be mild and transient.

The Debate over Animal Testing

As of 1999, United States' law did not require companies to test cosmetics on animals before they were marketed. The Food and Drug Administration (FDA), however, does require companies to substantiate the safety of their products or attach a warning label alerting consumers to potential hazards. Companies may continue animal testing because it provides one way to show consumers that products have been tested, and the company could use test results in its defense in case of lawsuits.

Critics of animal testing are many and vocal, at times more than vocal, as when they raid laboratories to free the animals. One of their major objections is that the tests are neither necessary nor valid. Federal laws do

Cosmetic testing on rabbits. *Courtesy of PETA.*

not require cosmetics manufacturers to test products on animals, and the test results cannot be applied to humans. Scientists have pointed out that the rabbit eye differs so from the human eye that the results of a Draize cannot be transferred to humans. In 1986, the Johns Hopkins Center for Alternatives to Animal Testing said, "The Draize test does not adequately reflect the degree of irritancy in human."

Critics also point out that although testing may be painful, animals are seldom given anesthetics or painkillers. They are sometimes placed in restraints during the tests, which may lead to injury and death. Animals have also been seriously injured trying to break free from restraints. For example, they argue that the Draize test causes animals unnecessary pain for which they rarely receive anesthetics or pain relievers. During most tests, the eyes of the rabbit are kept open with clips that are fastened to the eyelids.

Another major objection is that animal testing of cosmetics often involves luxury items and do not contribute to the relief of human suffering, cure diseases, or extend life, as is the case with laboratory animals used in medical research.

People for the Ethical Treatment of Animals (PETA), the National Anti-Vivisection Society (NAVS) and other organizations have lobbied Congress, demonstrated, and organized boycotts to show their disapproval of companies that use animal testing. They also urge consumers to boycott the products of these companies and have provided lists to consumers who wish to do so. During the late 1990s, PETA complained that one of the largest companies still testing on animals was Proctor & Gamble. PETA claimed that thousands of monkeys and other animals were killed in this company's laboratories each year.

A survey undertaken by the American Medical Association (AMA) determined that about 75 percent of Americans opposed the use of animals to test cosmetics. A 1996 poll of adult consumers conducted by Opinion Research Associates of Princeton, New Jersey, found that more than 52 percent of the respondents between ages 18 and 44 said it was extremely important or very important for them to know which companies did or did not test on animals.

In Europe, the controversy over animal testing is also intense. An organization called the European Center for the Validation of Alternative Methods has studied animal testing methods. Scientists involved with this organization claim that the scientific basis for using acute toxicity tests is "weak." The European Union (EU) proposed a ban on cosmetics tests using animals that would take effect by 1998, but delayed the ban after numerous companies complained about it. Some countries decided not to support the ban and their governments also planned to prevent companies that did not use animal testing from placing "Against Animal Testing" labels on their products.

Alternatives: Response by the Industry

Animal-rights advocates have long urged companies to seek alternative methods to animal testing to prove product safety. In 1959, animal protection activists in London published "The Principles of Humane Experimental Technique," which defined animal testing alternatives as the "Three Rs"—refinement, reduction, and replacement. Animal rights activists maintain that replacement of animal tests with alternative tests is the only acceptable outcome.

Between 1981 and 1998, the Cosmetic, Toiletry and Fragrance Association devoted $5 million for research into alternatives to the Draize test. Some critics note that alternatives already exist, including the use of human and animal corneas from eye banks, corneal tissue cultures, cell cultures, and frozen corneas that can be obtained from hospitals. In 1989, Avon became the first company in the United States to announce that it would no longer test products on animals.

By 1997 PETA listed 500 firms that do not test on animals. Others did fewer animal tests, and began to ensure humane treatment of animals. Companies that stopped testing on animals sometimes described themselves to consumers as "cruelty-free." In some cases, companies also stopped using animal products in their cosmetics or personal care items. Instead, they used plant products considered completely safe for human use, including herbs, flowers, and plant oils.

By 1999, cosmetics and personal grooming products companies were using alternative tests that included in-vitro tests, computer software, databases of tests that were already done in order to prevent duplication, cell or tissue cultures, and careful human clinical trials. Testing companies have devised innovative ways to test ingredients, for example using pumpkin rind to test skin reactions and growing skin tissue in sterile plastic bags for use in testing. One alternative test, the Chorioallantonic Membrane Vascular Assay (CAMVA), combines the use of screening materials and computers to predict toxicity. Some companies have themselves devised new methods to test products. For instance, Colgate developed artificial mouth systems to test oral health care products, using them to simulate actual conditions of the human mouth.

According to the FDA, nearly every ingredient that is used in cosmetics has at some point been tested on animals. Companies that say they do not test their products on animals are most likely referring to the finished product or mean that they have no plans to do any new animal testing on their products or ingredients in the future.

Some experts state that the alternative methods to animal testing have not been yet proven completely reliable, but that they might be substantiated in the near future.

Nevertheless, the Center for Alternatives to Animal Testing (CAAT), which was formed in 1992, commented that great progress had been made. Spokesperson Alan Goldberg said, "When we started the word alternatives and the 3Rs (reduce, refine, and replace) weren't known by 0.1 percent of the scientific community. It's quite remarkable. The whole scientific community has changed." (Canning, 1997) *See also* BODY SHOP, THE; CORPORATE STANDARD OF COMPASSION FOR ANIMALS; LAWS AND REGULATIONS (U.S.); SAFETY.

Further reading: Frank Ahrens, "Why Is This Rat Smiling?" *The Washington Post*, 17 August 1995; Christine Canning, "Animal Testing Alternatives: The Quest Continues," *Happi*, February 1997, http://www.happi.com/special/febmain2.html; Center for the Study of Responsive Law, *Being Beautiful: Deciding for Yourself* (1986); PETA Web site, http://www.peta-online.org; A.N. Rowan, *Of Mice, Models, and Men: A Critical Evaluation of Animal Research* (1984); U.S. Food and Drug Administration (FDA): Position Paper, October 1992.

Arabia (Ancient Times through Middle Ages)

Ancient Arabian societies were known for their highly developed bathing and grooming rituals and perfume industry, which was especially active in Aden. Both women and men used numerous preparations to care for their hair and skin and to beautify their faces. They also painted designs on their hands and other body parts using henna, a plant dye. Women developed special preparations to enhance their appeal. They pressed a fragrant almond unguent into their navels and used this same unguent as a cleansing cream.

Muslim tradition and the Qu'ran decree that both men and women cover their heads. Men used a turban, fez, or headcloth, and women were veiled in public. Men sometimes shaved their whole heads except for a long topknot. Women enhanced the color and shine of their hair with henna, a plant substance that yielded either a bluish or reddish tone. The genders had separate public baths.

The Arabs also created tooth powder from the bark of the walnut tree to clean their teeth, a substance still used today in parts of North Africa and the Middle East, where it is available in the form of chew sticks and powder. They invented a paste for removing unwanted body hair that contained turpentine, honey, and lemon.

Perfume, however, was the cosmetic of greatest importance, and its production became a major industry in Arabia. The land contained flowers, fruits, and plants that could be used to make fragrances, as well as animals that secreted substances also used in perfume making. The Qu'ran celebrated the scent of musk, and the seventh-century prophet Mohammed said that wonderful perfumes could be found in the Garden of Paradise.

Trade with other lands brought other raw materials for making scents. Traders brought oil from apricots that grew on trees in central and southwest Asia and the Mediterranean. Perfume ingredients were also exported. As early as 1500 B.C.E., the Egyptians gathered myrrh and frankincense from lands in south Arabia. Caravans of camels carried all the way to Rome frankincense, myrrh, cassia, and other materials used in perfumery. During the Roman Empire (27 B.C.E. to C.E. 476), the Romans used balsam of Makkah, costus, and calamus from Arabia to make incense.

By the fall of the Roman Empire, Arab ships were trading with India, China, and the East Indies, bringing back cinnamon from India, among other things, and new methods of producing perfume. Some of the earliest perfume recipes were recorded by Yaqub al-Kindl (c. C.E. 850), a historian, scientist, and philosopher. Powerful leaders of other lands who dominated the Middle East taxed the Arab peoples by demanding tons of fragrant materials. During the Middle Ages (mid-eighth through the mid-fourteenth centuries), Arab perfume makers greatly refined perfume-making techniques. A physician, Ibn Sina (980–1037), known in the west as Avicenna, developed techniques for extracting the oil (attar) from roses, a scent that the region's peoples valued highly. This was probably the first use of the distillation process to extract essential oils. Arab perfumers isolated the most strongly scented part of the rose and produced rosewater, or attar of roses. As they improved their distillation methods, they were able to make large quantities of attar of rose and other scents.

Baghdad became a world perfume center under the caliphs (762–1258), who also collected thousands of bottles of rosewater each year as a tribute from Persia. In addition to flowers and plant materials, Arab perfumers used animal ingredients, such as musk (secreted beneath the abdomen of the male musk deer), civet (secreted by the civet), and ambergris (believed to originate in the intestines of the sperm whale), as well as fruits, herbs, and spices. Some of these materials, such as ambergris, acted as fixatives. The liquids were dyed to achieve golden and red colors.

From the seventh to the sixteenth century, Arabia produced the finest perfumes in the world. The seventh-century ruler Muhammad ibn al-Haanifyah (637–710) was a particular promoter of perfume industry and surrounded himself with fragrances. During the eleventh, twelfth, and thirteenth centuries, European crusaders admired the perfumes and spices they found in the Middle East.. They brought them back to Europe and described the ways Arabians used them in their daily lives, such as to scent clothing and men's beards, for example. Many of these essences, including damask roses, red sandalwood, cloves, musk, aloes, ambergris, civet, and red cyprus, remained popular for centuries and have been used to make modern perfumes. *See also* BATHS; BODY DECORATION; FRAGRANCE; HENNA; PERFUME; TURKISH BATH.

Further reading: James Henry Breasted, *Ancient Times: A History of the Early World* (1944); Patricia Crone, *Meccan Trade and the Rise of Islam* (1987); Nigel Groom, *Frankincense and Myrrh: A Study of the Arabian Incense Trade* (1981); A. Verrill Hyatt, *Perfumes and Spices* (1940).

Arden, Elizabeth (1884–1966)

Elizabeth Arden founded one of the most famous and profitable cosmetics companies in the world. She was born Florence Nightingale Graham in Woodbridge, Canada, near Toronto, to a poor truck driver and his English-born wife, who died when Florence was six years old. Unable to afford a college education, Graham entered nurses' training but was unsuited for that profession. She later said, "I found I didn't really like looking at sick people. I want to keep people well, and young, and beautiful." (Lewis and Woodworth, 1972)

During her training, she met a biochemist working in the hospital laboratory to develop creams that would cure skin blemishes. Flo, as she was then called, tried to create face creams at home.

At age 30, after moving to Toronto, she held several clerical and sales jobs, then moved to New York City. There, she worked as a bookkeeper at E.R. Squibb, a pharmaceutical company, where she enjoyed visiting the labs. Soon, she changed jobs to work as a beauty culturist—known as "treatment girls"—in a salon run by Eleanor Adair, where she learned to give face treatments and manicures. As her income rose, she moved into a more comfortable apartment and sent money home to her family.

In 1909, she joined a beauty culturist named Elizabeth Hubbard, who had created some creams that Arden found superior to Adair's. The two women opened a Fifth Avenue beauty salon in an elegant neighborhood. Their advertisement in *Vogue* magazine described their new Elizabeth Hubbard Salon as "beautifully appointed" and reserved for "women socially prominent in the Metropolis and suburbs." They offered "Grecian Daphne" skin preparations, muscle creams, and oils, along with new treatment methods.

The two women soon dissolved their partnership over various disagreements. After Hubbard left, Florence Graham remained in the old salon, which she renamed "Mrs. Elizabeth Arden," the name by which she became famous. She improved the fragrances of the skin care products she offered at the salon and named her line "Venetian." With a $6,000 loan from her brother William, she furnished and decorated her luxurious salon, with its trademark red-painted door at the entrance. Arden invited two sisters to move their hairdressing business into a section of her salon so customers could conveniently receive more services in the same facility.

During these years, women's use of makeup was becoming more socially acceptable. Arden added rouges and tinted powders to her product line, and taught her staff to apply them expertly. Profits increased as more women came to the salon and bought her products. In 1914, she opened a second salon, in Washington, D.C., and then expanded the manufacturing end of her business, with the help of husband Thomas Lewis, whom she wed in 1915.

Within a few years, Arden added eye makeup and fragrances to her product line and began selling her products in Europe. Her sister Gladys de Maublanc managed the business in Paris. By this time, Arden was considered one of the top experts in the beauty business.

During the early 1920s, she developed hair care products and a new line of bath preparations. She also introduced the idea of exercise rooms as part of a beauty salon and made the first recordings giving instructions on specific exercises. They were based on Arden's personal experiences using yoga to relieve chronic hip pain. By 1925, the company had a gross income of more than $2 million a year just from its wholesale division in the United States.

Arden was known as a hard-working, perfectionistic, and sometimes temperamental executive. Her products were beautifully packaged and priced higher than average to appeal to a select clientele, primarily women in the upper 3 percent income bracket. Among her favorite Arden ads was a trademark photograph featuring French model Cecille Bayliss in a serene, elegant pose.

The company continued to expand, opening a new and more luxurious office building in New York City in 1929. In addition, Arden founded Maine Chance, the first American beauty spa/retreat, at her Maine country home and marketed Arden products in South America, Asia, Australia, and Africa. In 1929, Arden turned down an offer of $15 million (Lewis and Woodworth, 1972) to buy her business, to which she devoted most of her time and energy. She continued to introduce new ideas, such as kits containing different shades of lipstick and greater variety in shades of powder, rouge, and eye makeup.

In 1936, Arden introduced her first fragrance, "Blue Grass," a classic perfume created by George Fuchs of Fragonard, a French company. The scent, which contains floral and spice notes and a touch of Virginia cedar, was named for the landscape around Arden's Virginia estate, where she raised prize-winning racehorses.

Not only was Arden extraordinarily successful in the cosmetics field, at the time she died, she had earned more money than any other businesswoman in history. Her company, which was not sold until after her death in 1966, was grossing an estimated $600 million per year. (Lewis and Woodworth, 1972)

Today, in addition to the famous Elizabeth Arden Red Door salon in New York City, six other Red Door salons and spas operate in around the United States, including Arizona and Virginia. Arden cosmetics remain an upscale line that includes skin care products, color cosmetics, sunscreens, and fragrances. Elizabeth Arden fragrances are now part of the Unilever corporation, which distributes numerous home care products, food products, and personal care items, as well as several prestigious fragrance lines. In recent years, Arden has successfully launched new perfumes, including True Love, Fifth Avenue, and Splendor. *See also* ADAIR, ELEANOR; LIPS.

Further reading: Alfred Allan Lewis and Constance Woodworth, *Miss Elizabeth Arden* (1972).

Ash, Mary Kay (b. 1918)

Mary Kay Ash founded Mary Kay Cosmetics, which employs direct sales methods and offers customers personal consultations with trained representatives.

Ash was born Mary Kay Wagner in Houston, Texas. Her father was permanently disabled by tuberculosis, and her mother worked long hours to support the household, so Mary Kay was forced to assume adult responsibilities at a young age. Mary Kay cooked meals and ran the household in her mother's absence while maintaining excellent grades throughout her school years.

After she graduated from high school, Mary Kay Wagner married Ben Rogers, a local radio star. They had three children, and to help support the family, she began working in sales. She subsequently worked as a highly successful sales representative for Stanley Home Products, and was promoted to manager. Her husband returned from military service, and they divorced. She next worked for the World Gift Company, but decided to retire early when a man she had trained was promoted and became her supervisor.

In 1963, Ash retired and began writing a book about her professional experiences that she hoped would help other women succeed in the workplace. This made her decide to build a a company based on her values—Christian and family oriented—that would offer new opportunities for employees. She planned to sell skin care products made from formulas she had purchased. In addition, buyers would be able to try out these products before they bought them and salespeople would demonstrate the best ways to use them.

Just before the business was set to open, her second husband and her partner in this new venture, died of a heart attack. Nonetheless, she decided she would continue with her plans. With $5,000 (her life savings), she and her 20-year-old son established the first Mary Kay offices in a 500-square-foot storefront in Dallas, Texas. Initially, the company employed nine beauty consultants.

The company worked with independent salespeople who were paid commissions, depending on their sales. Their methods and products attracted loyal customers while offering employees high earning opportunities and opportunities for career advancement.

In 1964, Mary Kay became one of the first cosmetics companies to offer a full line of men's skin care products, with the trademark name "Skin Management," under the label "Mr. K." The men's products included moisture balm and cleanser and were packed in brown and silver containers.

The company continued to grow during the late 1960s. Ash, who adopted a company motto of "God first, Family Second, Career Third" and a signature color of pink for packaging her products, made headlines when she rewarded her top independent Sales Directors with pink Cadillacs. She went forward with the construction of a manufacturing plant about the size of three football fields, making it one of the largest manufacturing facilities in its region. She married Mel Ash and became Mary Kay Ash.

Beginning in the 1970s, Mary Kay Inc. expanded into international markets, such as Australia and Canada, as well as more than twenty other countries in Europe, Asia, and Latin America. When the company went public in 1976, Ash became a millionaire. By 1992, the company had sales of $487 million a year, and its worldwide sales for 1997 reached $2 billion. During 1998, wholesale sales were more than $1 billion and retails sales topped $2 billion. From 1993 to 1999, Mary Kay was the best-selling skin care and color cosmetic line in the United States. ("Frequently Asked Questions," http://www. marykay.com/marykay/About/faq/faq.html) During the 1990s, new factories opened in Switzerland and the People's Republic of China.

The company is known for its many female managers and successful female sales force, whose incomes are often substantial. Ash expressed pride that more women in her company are earning incomes upwards of $50,000 per year than in any other American company. (Ash, 1981)

Ash is also an author and philanthropist. In addition to her 1981 autobiography, she wrote *Mary Kay on People Management* (1993) and *You Can Have It All* (1995), which reached the best-seller list in one week. In 1996, she established the Mary Kay Ash Charitable Foundation, which has been especially active in raising money for cancer research, screening, and treatment.

Further reading: Mary Kay Ash, *Mary Kay* (1981); Ash, *You Can Have It All* (1995); Mary Kay "About Us," http://www.marykay.com/marykay/ About; "Mary Kay Ash," http://www. hergeneration.com.

Asian Markets (Modern)

During the last half of the twentieth century, Asian markets for cosmetics, personal care, and grooming products grew tremendously, although the countries are in different stages of development. This growth was fueled by a large population whose average income rose,

as did disposable income. At the same time, standards of living improved, as did distribution of goods, which gave people more access to consumer goods in stores. As the people in these countries learned more about styles around the world, the demand for cosmetics and toiletries also rose. In addition, more Asian women pursued higher education and careers, and they became more interested in beauty and health care.

During the early 1990s, Hong Kong, Singapore, and Japan were the most lucrative markets, and the demand within People's Republic of China was growing rapidly. East-West cultural differences are substantial, however, and western companies did not always understand Asian consumers. At times they introduced products that were successful in western nations but did not appeal to Asian consumers.

At a conference held in Singapore in 1997 called "Successfully Competing in the Cosmetics, Skin Care and Toiletries markets in Asia," research director Priya Tandan said, "In an image-laden industry such as cosmetics or fragrances, this is especially pertinent because the products reflect society's values and the fads of the day. The Asian consumer is fast becoming acutely conscious of these trends by choosing the right brands. There's a noticeable pursuit of material wealth and the symbols and status these confer." ("The Sleeping Giant Awakes," 1997)

Tandan noted, however, that Asians were looking more toward their own continent than the west as a source of fashion ideas and trends. Asian celebrities and designers were becoming increasingly influential and Asian entrepreneurs, such as Yue-Sai Kan of China, were developing lines of cosmetics, hair care products, and personal products that especially suited the styles and preferences of people in their own countries.

Experts who studied buying habits in Asia noted that Chinese women preferred cosmetics that were neutral in color, which were more acceptable in their culture, while women in India and Malaysia chose brighter tints, which also seemed more natural in their hot climates. Cosmetics companies were devoting more attention to the specific skin care needs and complexions of Asians. Experts noted that Asian skin was less likely to show age-related changes and that skin cancer rates were lower than in western countries.

Maybelline, a well-known multinational manufacturer of eye makeup and other cosmetics and now a division of L'Oreal, featured its first Eurasian model in 1998. Maybelline executives searched for a face that would appeal to consumers in different Asian markets and promote the young, fashionable look of its new Manhattan Mauves line of lipsticks and nail colors. They chose a model named Rosemary Vandenbrouke. The ads featuring Vandenbrouke were run in Hong Kong, China, Thailand, and Taiwan.

Shiseido Cosmetics, a top firm based in Japan, was also developing products for women in other Asian countries. The company, founded in 1872 in Tokyo, had previously focused on western markets and products for Japanese women. *See also* JA-PAN; KAN, YUE-SAI; SHISEIDO CORPORATION.

Further reading: Normandy Madden, "Maybelline Turns to Eurasian Model," *Advertising Age*, 21 September 1998, p. 12ff; "The Sleeping Giant Awakes," *Soap, Perfumery & Cosmetics*, 70(5) May 1997, p. 23ff.

Avon Products, Inc.

The international cosmetics firm Avon Products, Inc. was founded in the 1880s by American David McConnell, a traveling book salesman. It eventually became the world's largest direct seller of beauty products, and its advertising slogan "Avon calling" (preceded by the sound of a doorbell ringing) has been one of the best known in the cosmetics business.

McConnell came up with the idea of giving his potential customers a free bottle of inexpensive perfume to make them more willing to listen to his sales presentation or as a bonus for purchasing his books. Customers, however, became more interested in McConnell's perfume, which he had developed with the help of a chemist.

In 1886, McConnell went into the perfume business and called his new enterprise The California Perfume Company although it was based in New York City. From its earliest years, the business used direct sales methods.

Beginning in 1886, the company sold cosmetic products door-to-door when Mrs. P.F.E. Albee of Winchester, New Hampshire, became the first "Avon Lady." The company officially became Avon Products, Inc. in 1939. (McConnell changed the name, choosing "Avon" after the English town Stratford-on-Avon where William Shakespeare was born.) Avon products were sold with a reassuring 100-percent money-back guarantee. Selling Avon products also offered women an opportunity to earn money independently while working part-time. Customers could buy cosmetics in their homes, which was both more convenient and more private.

In 1959, another division of Avon opened in Britain, with a factory in Northampton to manufacture products for the European markets. During the mid-1900s, Avon was the largest cosmetics company in the world. More beauty products carried the Avon name than any other. Avon representatives continued to sell cosmetics in customers' homes, bringing small samples of new products or lipsticks, foundation, fragrances, and other items a customer wanted to try.

During the 1990s, the company expanded its international operations. Thousands of salespeople sold Avon products in Brazil, where the cosmetics were popular in both urban and rural areas, including the rain forests. Salespeople made their way to rugged areas by way of burros and boats. In South Africa, Avon built a sales force with thousands of people and sold more than 300 products. In 1996, Avon bought another direct sales cosmetics company named Justine. Justine Avon president Derek Loud said, "We have products for people of every colour. These are value-for-money products priced for all South Africans." (Koenderman, 1997) In 1987, Avon acquired the high-end perfume company, Giorgio Beverly Hills.

During the late twentieth century, Avon diversified and began selling clothing, jewelry, fashion accessories, and gift items. Cosmetics, toiletries, and fragrances continued to provide more than half of the company's revenues, which in 2000 totaled over $5.3 billion worldwide. A strong seller was Avon's "Anew" skin care product, which was introduced in 1992 as the world's first mass market alpha hydroxy acid (AHA) skin care product. Avon products are sold in 137 countries, including China, Poland, and the Czech Republic. The global sales force equals nearly 3 million, and the company also sells products online.

The company responded to consumer concerns in 1989 when it became the first major U.S. cosmetics company to announce that it would no longer use animals to test products. Avon has also actively promoted women's sports and breast cancer awareness and research.

By 1999, Avon was printing more than 600 million brochures annually in more than 12 languages. Fourteen million American women received Avon sales brochures every two weeks. In late 2000, however, Avon announced a major shift in its sales plans by planning to sell a new line of products at retail outlets such as Sears and J.C. Penney by mid 2001. *See also* ANIMAL TESTING.

Further reading: Avon Web site, http://www.avon.com; Fact Sheets: Avon Products, Inc.

(1998); Tony Koenderman, "The Avon lady comes calling in SA [South America] too," *Advertising/Marketing*, 11 July 1997, http://www.fm.co.za/97/0711/admark/avon.htm; Kathy Peiss, *Hope in a Jar* (1998).

Ayer, Harriet Hubbard (1849–1903)

Harriet Hubbard Ayer was one of the first Americans to start a large cosmetics business and to write a best-selling book on beauty. Ayer's astute business methods made her a fortune during a time when few women owned and ran businesses. She influenced the growth and development of the beauty industry in America.

Born in Chicago, Illinois, to an affluent family, Hubbard attended the Convent of the Sacred Heart and was graduated at age 15. Two years later, she married wealthy businessman and fellow Chicagoan, Herbert Copeland Ayer, with whom she had three daughters. The marriage ended in divorce in 1886, and Ayer experienced financial difficulties after her ex-husband lost his fortune, leaving her and her two surviving children with no means of support. She opened a decorating and antiques business, importing furniture and objects of art from Europe.

Avon products. *Courtesy of Avon Products, Inc.*

During a business trip to Paris in 1866, Ayer asked a French chemist to make her some face cream. Delighted with the results, she bought the recipe from the chemist. Her second husband provided financial help so she could produce and market the cream under the label "Recamier Preparations." Ayer devised an enticing story for her advertisements, which claimed that Madame Juliette Recamier, a famous French beauty of the Napoleonic era (1804–1814), had used the cream on her skin. At that time, U.S. laws banned advertising a product as a "beauty" cream as such, but Ayer's implicit message was clear to readers. At the same time,, she paid well-known beauties in America to endorse her face cream and used her social connections to place the cream in department stores. The business thrived and made Ayer a wealthy woman.

In 1896, Ayer lost control of her face cream company after a bitter battle with one of the primary stockholders. Her husband and one of her daughters claimed that she was mentally incapacitated, and they had her committed for treatment in a private psychiatric asylum, where she was confined for 14 months. After her attorneys secured her release, Ayer began lecturing around the country about the plight of the mentally ill and the problems of involuntary commitment.

In 1896, Ayer began writing a column in the *New York World* newspaper, offering advice about beauty. She emphasized good health habits, including nutrition, sleep, cleanliness, exercise, and fresh air. In 1899, she published her best-selling book, *Harriet Hubbard Ayer's Book: A Complete and Authentic Treatise on the Laws of Health and Beauty*. She produced new cosmetics, including La Belle Cocotte, which she described as an anti-wrinkle face cream, and promoted for the Cheseborough Ponds Company the use of Vaseline for the complexion.

Further reading: Margaret Hubbard Ayer and Isabella Taves, *The Three Lives of Harriet Hubbard Ayer* (1957); Lina Mainiero, ed., *Guide to American Women Writers* (1979).

B

Babylonia

Archaeological excavations from the ancient civilization of Babylonia (2105 B.C.E.–1240 B.C.E.), located in Mesopotamia and what is now Iraq, have yielded information about ancient bathing and grooming practices in this region.

Women were buried with their cosmetics and mirrors, as well as certain other possessions, suggesting the importance of cosmetics. The tomb of Queen Shubad contained elaborate gold and jeweled headdresses and a hair comb made of gold and lapis lazuli. The graves of some wealthy male Babylonians contain helmets made of beaten gold in the form of wigs that have locks of hair and individual hairs etched into the metal.

The Babylonians were among the first people to build indoor rooms for bathing. Royalty and wealthy Babylonians had bathrooms inside their palaces and homes, while poorer people bathed in canals or in cisterns located in courtyards.

People of every socioeconomic class used oils on their hair and skin to relieve the effects of their dry climate. They also used certain oils to kill parasites that attached themselves to the hair.

The typical Babylonian hairstyle was carefully arranged, sometimes with a metal or cloth band around the forehead to keep the hair in place. Babylonian men favored thick hair and a full beard—sometimes cut square—Men grew their hair long and curled it with heated curling irons, adding ringlets and, sometimes, false hair and wigs. Dying the hair black was also fashionable. High-ranking Babylonian men could be identified by the long, square cut of their beards, while commoners kept their beards trimmed short.

Babylonians developed perfume centers in the seventh century BCE and became a perfume trading center during the fifth century BC. They traded for the Arabian gums, Chinese camphor, and spices from India that they used to create scents. These were combined with cedar of Lebanon, cypress, pine, myrtle, and juniper.

Further reading: Georges Contenu, *Everyday Life in Babylon and Assyria* (1954); Richard Corson, *Fashions in Hair* (1865); Grant Frame, *Rulers of Babylonia* (1995).

Baker, Josephine (1906–1975)

Josephine Baker, an African American singer and dancer, became famous as an entertainer and woman of great individual style during the Jazz Age (post-World War I through the 1920s). She inspired trends in the world of beauty and fashion.

Baker was born in St. Louis, Missouri, where she left school at age eight to help support her family. She began performing before she reached her teens and was praised for her role as a chorus girl in the musical "Shuffle Along." After moving to New York

City, she performed at the famous Cotton Club in Harlem before moving to Paris in 1925 to perform in "La Revue Negre." She never returned to live in the United States.

At that time, Parisians were fascinated by African American culture and music, and they were captivated by this spirited American performer. Baker created a sensation during her appearances with the Folies Bergere and at the Casino de Paris. In one act, she appeared topless wearing a skirt made from a string of bananas. She also appeared in films, and the famous Russian-born ballet choreographer George Balanchine created a special dance for her in a Ziegfeld Follies review. Between 1925 and 1940, Baker was the highest-paid performer in Europe.

Baker was renowned for her exotic beauty and unique style. Many women copied her Marcel-waved hair (a short style featuring sculpted waves around the head), with "spit curls" on each cheek. Her use of cosmetics and the way she painted and adorned her toenails with jewels influenced other women, as did her glamorous costumes, with plumes and long ropes of pearls. Baker used kohl on her eyes and tried henna on her hands, a tradition in African cultures, but she stopped using it when the henna smeared some of her

Josephine Baker, Paris, 1949. *Library of Congress.*

costumes. One fashion and beauty magazine reported that Baker used the white of an egg on her face to give it a glossy appearance and that she highlighted her eyelids with white pencil. Off the stage, Baker made a dramatic picture as she strolled along the elegant Champs-Elysees Boulevard with leashed leopards and a pair of swans in tow.

During World War II, Baker worked undercover with the Free French Resistance against the Nazi occupation. After the war, she received the Legion of Honor award from the French government. Baker also spoke out against racism in America. She retired from performing in 1956 and established an orphanage in Bordeaux for children of different races and nationalities, which she supported with earnings from her career in show business. At the time of her death in 1975, a show celebrating her 50 years in Paris was being presented in the French capital.

Further reading: "Josephine Baker," Special Report: Remarkable American Women, *Life,* 1976, p. 91; Lynn Haney, *Naked at the Feast* (1996); Phyllis Rose, *Jazz Cleopatra: Josephine Baker in Her Time* (1991).

Barbers

Barbers (from the Latin "barba, meaning beard) provide hair-grooming services for men, including haircutting and styling, shaving, and beard and mustache care. Some barber shops may shine shoes and give manicures.

The profession has changed a great deal since ancient times, when barbers were medicine men and priests who held prominent positions in their tribes. Ancient superstitions held that spirits, both good and evil, entered the body through the hair, so hair-cutting took on a spiritual significance. Early barbers in Asia and other places played a key role in marriages and other rituals. At certain ceremonies, people wore their hair loosely so that evil spirits could leave the head, and good ones could enter. When these ceremonies ended, barbers cut and styled the hair against the head to keep good spirits inside and evil ones away.

In ancient Mesopotamian societies, religious leaders wore their beards in a special style, and community laws authorized barbers to shave the hair of priests and other religious figures. They were also brought in to shave slaves so that a brand or mark could be applied to their skin.

Ancient Egyptian barbers who served the upper classes were prominent members of the community and were well paid. Personal barbers visited the homes of the wealthier Egyptians to perform their services, while poorer citizens might visit itinerant barbers who worked outdoors. Among other things, they shaved off all body hair, which some Egyptians had done as often as every three days. This practice also helped people to stay clean because dirt was less likely to accumulate on hairless surfaces. Their tools included razors with curved handles made in the shape of small hatchets.

By about 500 B.C.E., barbers were important members of Greek society, where men prized a well-trimmed beard. Beards were often curled and scented with costly essences, so barbers polished their skills in this area, as well as in hair-cutting. In ancient Greece, barbers worked in shops where men gathered to socialize and exchange ideas as well as for grooming purposes. Wealthy people had personal barbers in their homes to attend to male members of the household or their guests.

A Sicilian, Ticinius Mena, brought barbers, called tonsors, to Rome in 296 B.C.E., and the Romans began shaving regularly. Roman barbers worked in shops and in the public baths. As in Greece, Roman barbershops served a social function, and barbers became prominent members of society. Some men, the dandies of Roman society, spent hours in barber shops, having their hair cut and styled, getting shaved and massaged, manicured, made up with cosmetics and anointed with lotions. A statue erected in memory of the ancient Roman barbers shows the esteem that the people gave these professionals.

Barbers also served royalty and chiefs in ancient Ireland and groomed their hair, beards, and mustaches. They were found in other parts of the British Isles and in Saxon and Frankish countries.

During the Middle Ages (mid-eighth through mid-fourteenth centuries), European barbers worked in monasteries, where monks were expected to be clean-shaven at all times, as specified in a papal decree dating back to 1092. Monks had been performing minor surgery and a medical procedure called blood-letting, based on the idea that illness resulted from an excess of blood in the body. In 1163, the Pope forbade clergymen to engage in any activities involving the shedding of blood, so the monks assigned this task to barbers, along with caring for wounds and certain other medical conditions.

Medieval barbers in different countries formed tradesmen's guilds, and new barbers were trained through apprenticeships. A group of barbers organized into a trade group in 1096 in France after the Archbishop of Rouen banned the wearing of beards. In the mid-1200s, a group of Parisian barbers called the Brotherhoods of St. Cosmos and St. Domain formed a school to train barbers in surgical procedures. In 1383, the King of France decreed that his personal barber and valet would be in charge of the barbers and surgeons throughout that country.

Similarly, English barbers organized trade guilds. The Worshipful Company of Barbers, which still exists (see their Web site at http://www.barbers.org.uk/), was formed in London in 1308; a Master of Barbers was empowered to inspect barbershops and discipline anyone who was not practicing in an appropriate manner. In 1462 King Edward IV granted the barbers' guild a charter. In 1540, however, King Henry VIII granted a royal charter to the United Company of Barber-Surgeons. This marked the first step toward separating the two professions; surgeons did not have to be barbers, and barbers could perform only dental surgery.

Barber-surgeons continued to practice until the eighteenth century.

By this time, barbers in some countries were also extracting teeth and performing other dental work in addition to providing tonsorial and surgical services. At this time, however, new medical discoveries were occurring regularly, and most barbers could not keep up with them. Many patients complained about the treatment they received, and physicians and dentists pushed for new laws that would limit barbers' activities.

In colonial America, the practice of combining the work of the surgeon, dentist, and barber continued. Signs reading "Barber and Chirurgeon" were displayed in towns, with the red-and-white striped pole that represented blood and bandages. These poles had once stood inside barber shops, where they held long white bandages used during the blood-letting process.

In 1745, a new law in England made barbering and surgery separate fields and banned barbers from practicing medicine. Similar laws were passed in France and other countries. Barbers then focused on hair cutting and styling, which included wig-making during times when false hair was popular. However, some continued to pull teeth and provide other services, such as baths.

Barber's schools were set up in the 1890s, replacing the apprenticeship system. In 1893, A.B. Moler set up the first such school in Chicago. The schools taught hair-cutting and shaving techniques, face and scalp treatments, and proper care of tools. A typical barber school training program lasted about 1,200 hours during the early and mid-1900s.

For men who insisted on being clean-shaven and well groomed, visits to the barber were a necessity. Ships provided barbers kept for sea travelers so they could maintain their appearance during voyages. Like other luxury liners of the early 1900s, the ill-fated RMS *Titanic* included barber shops for first-class male passengers, as well as a separate facility for second-class passengers so they could have professional shaves and haircuts during the trip, which was expected to last two weeks.

After the early 1900s, barbershops thrived as men began wearing short, clipped hairstyles, and beards went out of fashion. Some barbers in the United States were immigrants who trained in Italy and other countries, who

were apprenticed to established barbers before opening their own businesses. In America, states regulated the barbering profession and issued licenses to qualified operators. The National Association of Barber Boards was the official organization of barbers in the United States. In 1924, Hair International was formed as a professional organization for barbers and hair-stylists.

American barbershops were social as well as grooming facilities. Some stayed open six days a week from morning till late evening and midnight on Saturdays. During the 1930s, a haircut and shave typically cost 35 cents; by 1962, the price had risen to about $2 (Garver, 1997) and now it is from $10 on up.

Barbering changed in the 1960s. Men began wearing longer hairstyles, popularized by the Beatles, the British rock group, and other pop singers. The longer styles required far less frequent haircuts. At the same time, many men started going to hairstyling salons or "unisex" salons rather than traditional barbershops. Between 1975 and 1985, the number of licensed barbers fell dramatically. New Jersey, for instance, which had 12,000 barbers in the mid-1970s, had only about 7,000 in 1985, according to the state Board of Cosmetology and Hairstyling. The decline in numbers slowed but did not stop during the1980s and 1990s. (Garver, 1997)

This, however, may change. By the 1990s, American barbers saw a rising number of customers as shorter hairstyles, including flattops, fades, and buzzcuts, became popular. New versions of these old styles brought some young people to barbershops for the first time as they sought professionals who could cut hair using traditional razor or shaving techniques. In some locations, the demand for barbers exceeds the supply as older barbers retire and the number of new barbers declines.

Modern barbers continue to provide hair-cutting and some grooming services, although few do shaves any more, citing a concern about blood-transmitted AIDS from facial nicks and cuts. Some also say that giving a good shave is too time-consuming.

Barbers and cosmetologists both are represented by Hair International. The group also promotes ethical standards and works to strengthen relationships between hair professionals and the public and the government. It also works to advance scientific, technical, and economic research that affects these and related professions and industries. Members include owners, managers, and employees of hair-related businesses. Hair International sponsors seminars and conventions and informs members about legislation that could affect them and their businesses.

Although some men now go to stylists who serve both genders, other men prefer a traditional male-only barbershop. Barbershops have changed with the times and updated their facilities to attract more business, but many continue to display the traditional red-and-white striped pole. *See also* FACIAL HAIR, MEN'S; HAIR, STYLING OF; PERSONAL CARE PRODUCTS, MEN'S.

Further reading: Lois W. Banner, *American Beauty* (1983); Geoffrey Bibbey, *Four Thousand Years Ago: A World Panorama of Life in the Second Millennium* (1963); Rob Garver, "Bye-Bye Barbershops," *New Jersey Monthly,* October 1997, http://www.hairinternational.com/bar_conv.htm; Hair International "Purpose" and "Objectives," http://www.hairinternational.com/bar_conv.htm; Ian Jenkins, *Greek and Roman Life* (1986); William Chauncey Langdon, *Everyday Things in American Life, 1607–1776* (1937); Jack Lindsay, *The Ancient World: Manners and Morals* (1968); Richard A. Plumb and Milton V. Lee, *Ancient and Honorable Barber Profession* (1974); John Walton, *The Oxford Medical Companion* (1994).

Barbie Dolls

In 1959, the Mattel Toy Company introduced Barbie, a new "teenage fashion model" doll that was destined to become the best-selling doll of all time. Barbie became a symbol of the teenage culture that emerged in the United States during the 1950s. Playing with Barbie, girls could envision a future life as an attractive—even glamorous—well-dressed teen or young adult. Millions of children throughout the world, mostly girls, owned and played with one or more Barbie dolls, while some older people collected them

(and some still do). The dolls were widely sold in Europe and Asia and were even smuggled into Muslim countries, where they were not sold.

Ruth and Elliot Handler, who founded Mattel, named the doll after their daughter Barbara. Ruth Handler said that girls could use their imaginations when playing with the doll and that Barbie was "created to project every little girl's dream of the future."

Barbie was derived from a German doll called "Lilli," first sold in 1955. Lilli, who was based on a cartoon character created by Reinhard Beuthien, wore a black and white swimsuit, similar to Mattel's Barbie, and had a fashionable wardrobe, although her hairstyle was different. The first version of Barbie, which some Americans disliked, had slanted eyes, white irises, and thin, defined painted brows. Barbie's other physical attributes included long, slim legs, a tiny waist, huge breasts, and permanently arched feet to accommodate her high-heeled shoes.

Her worldly appearance struck many observers as inappropriate for a child's toy. They noted, too, that Barbie's long slim legs were not in proportion to the doll's large breasts. Actual women who had Barbie's proportions were very rare indeed. The Sears Company did not carry the doll in its stores or offer it in its mail-order catalogue, claiming it was "too sexy."

Girls and presumably their parents did not agree. Sales of Barbie increased dramatically after the doll was advertised on a popular television show, *The Mickey Mouse Club.* Children enjoyed playing with Barbie and her assorted outfits, inspired by clothing produced by top fashion designers, and detailed accessories.

Barbie was a reflection and product of the teen culture that developed after World War II. Children born after the war were the first generation to play with such dolls. Teen culture was a new phenomenon that arose during a time of unprecedented peace and prosperity. Teens had certain styles in clothing, jewelry, and makeup, as well as music, dancing, foods, and other activities, reflecting their special tastes and attitudes.

Through the years, Barbie's facial features, hairdos, fashions, and accessories changed with fashions and women's evolving roles. The first dolls had pale skin, arched eyebrows, molded eyelashes, dark lips, and red-painted fingernails and toenails. Blue eyeshadow was painted on the lids above the eyes, with blond or brunette hair styled in a ponytail. The 1960 version had rounder, blue eyes and smoother brows, although she still had red lips and painted fingernails. Skin tones were a more natural flesh tone. In 1961, the dolls were made with ponytails and "bubble cuts," influenced by the popular bouffant hairstyle. Mattel also introduced a red-haired Barbie called "Titian."

More than six million Barbie dolls were produced each year during the early sixties. Given the success of their first teen doll, Mattel began producing Ken, a male teen doll who was Barbie's boyfriend, in 1961. The first Ken, named for the Handlers' son, had a molded hairstyle that resembled the popular crew cut. The following year, Ken had the newer "Butch" hairstyle, which came with a stick of wax for grooming. During the 1970s, "New Look Ken" dolls featured stylishly long hair.

The first Barbie was sold as a "teen model," but the activities and professions changed greatly over the years. In the mid-1960s, "Fashion Queen Barbie" was sold with three wigs: a redheaded "flip," a platinum bubble cut, and a brunette pageboy. Other dolls, including Midge and Francie, were created as friends for Barbie.

In 1967, Mattel added an African American "Francie" doll to its collection of white "Francies." The following year, the company discontinued that doll and introduced Christie, a new black doll with her own identity. Some observers said this beautiful doll, which was produced until 1985, resembled a well-known African American model Naomi Sims. A male African American male doll, Curtis, was sold as Christie's boyfriend. Black Ken dolls were also available. Japanese Barbie and Ken dolls originated in the 1960s, with more childlike faces than those sold in America.

By 1985, Barbie came in white, Hispanic, and African American versions. International, fairy-tale, and historical Barbies were manufactured, and she had appeared as a teacher, majorette, prom queen, nurse, ballerina, equestrienne, flight attendant, physician, figure-skater, archeologist, astronaut, and basketball player, among other things. Girls could persuade their parents that they also needed Barbie makeup, clothing, accessories, houses, cars, pools, boats, camping equipment, sleeping bags, and many other products.

Critics have said that Barbie is an unrealistic depiction of the female body. Barbie, they note, represents unattainable images of "ideal" features and proportions that may leave girls feeling inadequate. They also criticized the dolls for perpetuating a limited white Anglo-Saxon ideal of beauty in a diverse

A recent Barbie Doll, called Jewel Girl. © *Reuters/Ho/ Archive Photos, Inc.*

world and for encouraging young girls to focus too much on appearance.

During the 1990s, Mattel introduced Barbies with greater variations in skin and eye colors, as well as a doll that used a wheelchair. A new, fuller-figured Barbie had a smaller bust and larger waist and hips, as well as a smaller difference between the bust and waist measurements.

Further reading: Billy Boy, *Barbie: Her Life and Times* (1987); Lois Firestone, "Barbie Arrived 40 Years Ago, Never Left," *The Salem (Ohio) News*, 23 March 1999, pp.1, 4; A. Glenn Mandeville, *Doll Fashion Anthology and Doll Fashion Anthology and Price Guide* (1987); Paris Manos and Susan Manos, *The World of Barbie Dolls* (1983).

Baths

Baths—the process of soaking and cleaning the body in water, steam, or another substance, such as mud or milk—have been part of grooming rituals for thousands of years. Bathing has been part of some cultures' rituals; people bathe to cleanse and purify the body; they bathe for pleasure and improved appearance.

Ancient Practices

People first bathed in lakes, rivers, oceans, or waterfalls. Facilities specifically for bathing, however, have been around for a long time. Writings and artifacts indicate that baths were common among the Babylonians, Romans, Greeks, Indians, and Turks. However, some ancient peoples, such as the Persians, believed that bathing was unsuitable for humans.

In earlier times and different cultures, baths were often part of a ritual. The ancient Hebrews greatly valued washing, bathing, and other forms of cleanliness, and used them in their religious observances, as well as to promote health. Bathing was integral to Egyptian spiritual practices. Egyptian priests had to take four baths per day, usually in cold water. Other Egyptians bathed twice daily, combining this activity with religious rituals. A bath that archeologists unearthed in present-day Pakistan, at Mohenjo-Daro, seems to date back to 4000 B.C.E. Scientists believe that the Egyptians devised showers as early as 3000 B.C.E.

The first indoor bathroom with a crude latrine, drain, and underground sewer system was apparently built in an area off the north coast of present-day Scotland called the Orkney Islands. Archeologists excavated this site, which is built using slabs of stone that date back to about 3000 B.C.E.

Ceramic pipes and special rooms for bathing were found in the ruins of Minoan Crete, a civilization that reached its peak around 1600 B.C.E. Archeologists found an ornate bathtub dating back to about 2000 B.C.E. at the site of the Palace of Minos. Terra cotta pipes brought water into the palace. This tub was apparently filled and emptied by hand, but other ancient Greek tubs had drains. Among the ancient Greeks, it was customary to offer guests a bath when they arrived for a visit. Ancient paintings found on Greek ceramics also indicate that the Greeks took outdoor showers while standing under a stream of water that ran out of spouts they placed on the sides of large fountains in their cities.

While wealthier Greeks had baths in their homes, the government built public bathhouses near gymnasiums where people could exercise. The Greeks and Romans both carried small flasks attached to their wrists to hold perfume unguents they took to the baths.

Early Greek physicians advocated exercise and cold baths as health measures. However, the public bathhouses had warm water, as well as soap produced from clay and wood ash. Bathers provided their own oil and perfumed soaps, along with a skin scraper (strigil) made of bronze. When water was unavailable for bathing, people cleaned themselves with oil and scrapers.

Archeologists have also found bathing facilities with working plumbing at sites once occupied by ancient civilizations of India and Syria.

Archeological finds also indicate that between 800 and 562 BC, wealthy Babylonians had separate rooms set aside for bathing. Slaves poured water over them while they washed themselves with a mixture of fats and plant ash.

More affluent ancient Mesopotamians also bathed indoors. The well-to-do people in this civilization lived in fairly large houses and set aside one room for bathing. Bathers used soap made of ashes and animal fat or special oils; here, too, slaves poured water on their bodies. Drains were put in the middle of the brick sloped floors. People who were too poor to have a bathroom inside their home bathed in the canals that brought water into the city from the river.

To the north, people in present-day Russia and Finland developed steam baths modeled on the bathing practices of the ancient nomads who had roamed the steppes of Eurasia. The Finnish saunas—small steam rooms with benches on which people could sit and perspire—are still popular, there and elsewhere. These hot steam baths are sometimes followed by a dousing of cold water or cold swim.

The people of ancient India developed steam rooms and combined bathing with massage. They also believed that scented baths attracted lovers and good spirits.

Bathing "Extras"

People have long augmented the simple water bath with additions and substitutions. The Arabs added scents to their baths in the form of rose water, orange flower water, willow water, and violet water. Greeks also added substances to make their baths smell or feel good—perfume essences, flower petals, goat's milk, and other types of milk. The Egyptian queen Cleopatra was said to bathe in milk, and Emperor Nero's wife, Queen Poppaea, supposedly took asses along on journeys so they could be milked for her baths. The Egyptians believed that minerals in the water of the Dead Sea had therapeutic and beautifying properties. Cleopatra asked her lover Marc Antony to give her this region as a gift so she could enjoy the benefits of the mineral-rich waters.

Large Public Baths

The first public Roman baths may have been built at Pompeii, Italy. Ancient Romans devised methods to bring large quantities of water into their cities, using rivers, springs, cisterns, and wells.

In parts of the empire that were especially dry, large numbers of slaves brought water to the royal palaces, with long lines of slaves passing jars of water from one to the other from the cisterns below the palace to the king's bathing chambers. Around 312 B.C.E., Romans began building complex aqueducts with channels made of stone and lead; earthenware or stone pipes carried the water along for miles. By the fourth century, the city of Rome had 11 public baths and about 856 private baths.

The Romans built fancy public baths in large buildings, one large enough to accommodate as many as 3,000 bathers at the same time. Baths were adorned with mirrors, paintings, and sculpture, and often featured intricate mosaics. Faucets were often silver, while other fixtures might be made from gold, marble, or bronze. Bronze tubs were common.

During the early days of the Roman Empire (27 B.C.E. to C.E. 476), people were likely to bathe about once a week, but as time went on, many Romans took at least one bath daily. During Nero's reign (C.E. 37–68), the Romans believed that taking a bath before eating would promote good digestion. They also believed in bathing after they exercised.

For the most part, women and men bathed at different times, with hours for women bathers usually scheduled from dawn until about 1 P.M. However there were times during the history of the empire when men and women could bathe together.

Upon entering the bath, a person paid a small fee and then undressed. Women could then proceed to the warm-air room, called a tepidarium, followed by a stay in the hot-air room (calidarium), in order to promote perspiration. This was said to help the body rid itself of impurities. There were facilities for men to exercise, run on a track, wrestle, play ball games, or throw a discus or spear.

Patrons could choose to bathe in water of different temperatures, because some pools in the Roman baths had warm water, while others (called caldaria) contained cool, even cold, water. Furnaces supplied heated air that warmed rows of hollow bricks that lay beneath the floor.

Before bathing, people rubbed their skin with sand and fragrant oils. These worked as detergents because when the sand and oils were scraped off, dirt was removed, too. Bath attendants were also available to rub oil or sand on peoples' bodies, scrape these substances off, and dry their bodies with towels. For an extra fee, bathers could also receive a massage.

The most famous and elegant public bath facility in the Roman Empire was probably the baths of Caracalla, a complex located in the center of Rome and measuring about 28 acres (11 hectares) in size, with more than 1,600 marble seats. The construction of the Caracalla baths was begun in C.E. 216 by the emperor Septemius Severus and completed during the reign of his son, Emperor Caracalla. The complex remained in use for about 300 years. The complex contained works of art and recreational facilities as well as baths. Inside were theaters, shops, restaurants, reading areas, exercise rooms, and

Thirteenth Century bath in Spain. *Art Resource.*

lounges where people could meet and talk. Besides indoor and open-air swimming pools, there were three major bath chambers with a cold room, hot room, and lukewarm room. A spacious garden area was used for exercise and games. Throughout the complex were sculptures, mosaics, frescoes, and abundant marble-work. In modern times, the excavated and restored site of the Baths of Caracalla has been used as a setting for outdoor musical and operatic performances.

Bathing in Asia

Public bathhouses could be found in Asia during ancient times. Cold baths were considered good for one's health at one time in parts of China. In China during the T'ang Empire (C.E. 600–900), wealthy people had bathrooms inside their homes and slaves prepared their baths. Their baths were scented with fine oils and aromatics. Certain scents were popular for promoting certain moods.

In Japan, baths were also popular and bathing was incorporated into religious rituals. The Japanese built large public baths in places that contained natural hot springs. People could also travel to special bathing places built near springs where the water contained special minerals or other substances with healing properties.

Most homes had baths either indoors or in the garden, and families sometimes bathed together in heated water. A Japanese saying that dates back to the tenth century lauds the pleasures of being clean and well-groomed: "To wash one's hair, make one's toilet, and put on scented robes . . . Even if not a soul sees one, these preparations still produce an inner pleasure."(Leigh, 145)

Hot water was regarded as the best way to wash and to relax the body. The Japanese found it acceptable for men and women to bathe together, whether in public bathhouses or private homes. The Japanese continued to bathe together until 1870, when a law banned the practice. The ban occurred after U.S. naval officer Commodore Perry arrived in 1853, and the Americans insisted that it was improper for men and women to bathe together.

The Americas

Ancient civilizations in Central and South America also built public baths, and bathing was often a part of their religious rituals. The Aztecs, who lived in present-day Mexico, had numerous bathing facilities, and bathed daily.

Steam baths, taken to purify, were part of many Native American cultures, including tribal groups that lived in the western Plains and the northwest Plateau of North America and those living in the what is now the southwestern United States. They built special buildings or huts made of mud and grasses for steam bathing. To prepare for the bath, rocks were made extremely hot over a fire, then put inside the building. As water was thrown against the hot walls, steam formed, and the bather went inside. Afterwards, they sometimes plunged themselves into the cooler water of a nearby stream. In the Apache version of the steam bath, a spiritual leader sprinkled water on the hot rocks. The men recited certain chants before they entered the bath and again afterwards before bathing in a cold stream. The tradition, with its spiritual significance, continues with some Native American groups to the present day. In modern times, non-Indians also use sweat lodges, as these facilities are called.

Changing Attitudes

Bathing practices changed in Europe between the 1200s and 1600s. People seldom bathed. Some public baths existed, but they were much less luxurious than the bathing complexes of ancient times. Medieval baths were used only for basic cleanliness or curative purposes. One reason was that physicians of that era still held to the theory put forth by the ancient Greek physician Galen, who believed that the body was made up or four "humours" that must be kept in balance. The medieval belief was that exposure to too much water upset the balance.

Just as some religions viewed bathing as integral to their practice, others viewed it as antithetical. Leaders of some religions advised people not to bathe because it was sinful. The early Christians rejected baths along with other Roman customs they considered vain or immodest. However, wealthy families were known to take occasional baths, and people kept basins and pitchers of water in their bedrooms to wash their faces, hands, and teeth.

The onset of plague in Europe further reduced bathing. During the 1300s and 1400s, when outbreaks of plague occurred, public baths closed down as fears of disease spread, and some people believed bathing was unhealthy. To hide body odors, people wore perfumes and scented powders.

In Europe, the public bath died out around the sixteenth century. In 1500, Henry VIII closed all public baths in England because they had become dirty places infested with insects and frogs and were often used as brothels. In 1538, public baths were banned in France. Some Europeans bathed their whole bodies only once or twice a month, usually in a wooden tub that had to be filled with water carried in from outdoors. Other people bathed even more infrequently, perhaps only a few times in their lifetime. Diseases flourished in this unclean environment, but people did not realize the connection.

During that same era, the fourteenth and fifteenth centuries, people who lived in Moslem countries and territories continued to take baths and build beautiful, comfortable rooms for bathing. Islamic bathhouses, often ornately decorated with mosaics, contained warm, hot, and steam rooms similar to those found in ancient Roman baths. Frequently, they also contained a cold room, or basins of cold water were placed in the warm room. Dressing rooms and rest areas were available, along with decorative pools and fountains. Men and women used separate facilities. Elaborate baths containing steam rooms and warm and hot steam rooms could also be found in the Ottoman Empire (late thirteenth century to 1918).

In England and Europe, bathing became slightly more acceptable during Elizabethan times (1558–1603). Elizabeth I is said to have bathed monthly; her cousin, Mary, Queen of Scots, bathed in wine. Because wine contains alcohol, washing with it served to kill some germs and parasites.

During the Renaissance in Europe (the fourteenth through the sixteenth century), people bathed every few weeks and sponged off their bodies in between baths. They used large wooden tubs filled by hand with water heated over a fire. Pitchers and basins were kept in bedrooms for this purpose and for cleaning teeth.

Late in that era, during the 1600s, people bathed at spas, built where the waters supposedly had curative powers. Examples included Bath and Tunbridge in England and Baden-Baden in Germany.

Early America

The Europeans who colonized North America brought European attitudes about bathing to their new homeland. Colonists seldom drank water, which contained germs and infected people with illnesses. For the same reason, they feared bathing, believing that it would give them pneumonia, colds, cholera, and other diseases. Some people believed that water weakened the body, making a person more vulnerable to illness. Failure to bathe could also be a matter of laziness: taking a bath entailed extra work.

During the mid-1700s, attitudes about bathing began to change in western societies. The well-known clergyman John Wesley stated, "Cleanliness is next to godliness." Early Americans washed themselves beside an outdoor pump or they brought in water from a well, river, or rain barrel into metal bathtubs placed beside indoor fireplaces. People also heated their bath water in a kettle placed over the fire. After they finished bathing, they had to remove the water from the tub.

During the nineteenth century, cleansing products changed a great deal. Before about 1840, many people made their own soap by mixing fats with homemade lye. Cooking soap was a smelly chore that often lasted a whole day and produced a substance that was harsh on the skin. The same soap, stored in barrels, was used all year round to wash laundry and clean the house, as well as for bathing. By the mid-1800s, manufactured soaps were available in most places. Americans could also buy soap in stores or from traveling salesmen. This soap smelled better and was gentler to the skin than homemade lye soaps.

Modern Times

By the mid-nineteenth century, regular bathing was becoming more common. In 1842, a wealthy citizen in Cincinnati, Ohio, had a bathtub with fittings built for his home. The design, which included a mahogany case and lining made from sheet lead, was based on a tub owned by Lord John Russell of Britain. The tub weighed nearly 2,000 pounds, and the fittings were connected to a cold water pipe and a hot water pipe. More well-to-do Americans installed bathrooms in their homes during and after the 1850s. In more remote parts of the country, the arrival of the first manufactured bathtub was often greeted with great interest.

Although most people bought soap and other bath products in general stores or drugstores, a few companies specialized in bath products. In England, the Yardley Company produced luxurious items for the bath in various scents. In America, James R. Caswell founded a bath products company that grew to include hundreds of stores in various countries. The first Caswell-Massey store was built in Newport, Rhode Island, in 1752.

The first hot water shower appeared in 1883 at the Berlin Hygiene Exhibition, where it was presented with the slogan, "Die Douche als Volksbad"—the rainbath is the people's bath. The new showers became popular in England, too, where military officers returning from tropical areas brought the idea home with them. Americans who visited England took the idea of the overhead sprinkler home with them.

By the mid-nineteenth century, well-to-do people in England were installing bathrooms in a small room of their homes, often an unused bedroom. These bathrooms might contain a fireplace, metal tub, and sometimes a shower-bath combination. During the Victorian era (1837–1901), wealthy people had grand bathtubs that featured paneled or embossed wood and ornate brass fixtures. Towels were warmed beside the fireplace for use after the bath. The less affluent people of the time bathed on Saturday night. Tubs were made from tin and copper, then later from cast iron. Apartment-dwellers sometimes used a bathtub that folded out from the wall.

By the turn of the nineteenth century, bathrooms in grand homes were truly luxurious. They contained not only a tub and shower bath but a sitz bath, foot bath, pedestal lavatory, and decorative rugs and windows. As time went on, smaller bathrooms were built to fit in the smaller homes that provided housing for growing numbers of middle-class and working-class families. Sinks with storage cabinets beneath them became more popular than pedestal sinks.

The plumbing industry expanded greatly during the early 1900s when more bathtubs, sinks, and toilets were manufactured. Indoor bathrooms became standard features of new homes. Bathrooms were also built in schools, hospitals, hotels, and factories. In 1920, the plumbing industry in the United States, which published *Domestic Engineering Magazine*, promoted a booklet called "The Story of the Bath" that described the many benefits of personal cleanliness, including the prevention of infectious diseases.

Bathtubs, sinks, and other plumbing fixtures were first made in the color white, but by the late 1920s, consumers could also buy fixtures in ivory, blue, green, lavender, gray, pink, or tan. By the end of the twentieth century, baths were widely regarded as a pleasant, relaxing experience as well as a way to clean the skin. Advertisements for bath products emphasized their soothing qualities. One popular ad campaign for scented, moisturizing bath products portrayed a harried mother who escapes from a stressful day by soaking in the tub.

Consumers could enjoy numerous bath products, including soaps scented with flowers, fruits, spices, and made in diverse shapes and sizes designed to fit any bathroom décor and appeal to bathers of all ages. Bath salts, powders, oils, gels, lotions, and bubbling products could be found in hundreds of scents, often matched to one's perfume or cologne. Products made with herbs, vitamins, moisturizing agents, and with aromas to suit or change the bather's mood were also available in regular stores, health food stores, and specialty shops.

In Asia, some bathing traditions have continued to the present day. Like their ancestors, modern Japanese take baths both for cleansing purposes and to relax. The relaxed warm state of the body is called "yudedako"—boiled octopus. This custom reflects the Japanese view of beauty as a reflection of inner balance as well as external appearance. In many places around the world, the use of oils in baths is popular. During the late twentieth century, affluent people in developed nations often built luxurious, multipurpose bathrooms. Consumers spent thousands of dollars for special oversized tubs with a whirlpool or for showers with special steam attachments and other features. Bathrooms contained exercise equipment, televisions, sound systems, and saunas. Luxurious fixtures included gold and silver faucets, hand-painted tiles, marble, stained glass, crystal, and custom-designed basins.

In contrast to the developed countries, regions of the world remain where people lack continuous access to clean water, as well as the resources to build indoor bathrooms. Simple bathrooms and even running water are luxuries in these places—a situation that has a negative impact on health and cleanliness. *See also* ADVERTISING (U.S.); BODY ODOR; COLGATE-PALMOLIVE CO.; FRAGRANCE; SOAP; SPAS, BEAUTY AND HEALTH.

Further reading: Geoffrey Bibby, *Four Thousand Years Ago: A World Panorama of Life in the Second Milennium* (1963); Katherine Graves Busby, *Home Life in America* (1910); George Duby and Michelle Perrot, eds. *A History of Women in the West* (1993); Donald R. Dudley, *The Civilization of Rome* (1960); Leigh, Michelle Dominique. *The New Beauty: East-West Teachings in the Beauty of Body and Soul* (1995); Elisabeth Donaghy Garrett, *At Home: The American Family 1750-1870* (1989); James Walter Graham, et al., *The Palaces of Crete* (1977); Jack Lindsay, *The Ancient World: Manners and Morals* (1968); Susan McKeever, *Ancient Rome* (1995); Marjorie Quennell, *Everyday Things in England: 1851-1914* (1937); Jay Stuller, "Cleanliness Has Only Recently Become a Virtue," *Smithsonian Maga-*

zine, February 1991, 126–134; Rebecca Weaver and Rodney Dale, *Machines in the Home* (1992).

Baudelaire, Charles Pierre (1821–1867)

Nineteenth-century French author Charles Baudelaire, best known for his poetry and art criticism, also wrote a book called *Eloge du Maquillage* (In praise of makeup, 1860). This book about cosmetics gave Baudelaire the title "father of modern cosmetic theory." It contained specific ideas about how to apply makeup. For instance, Baudelaire suggested that women use black eyeliner, because "It makes our look deeper and more particular, converting the eye into a window open to infinity." In his writings, Baudelaire also celebrated the beauty of women of color.

As a poet, Baudelaire was considered original and romantic, sometimes morbid, with a gift for lyrical language. His most famous book of poetry was *Fleurs de Mal (Flowers of Evil)*, published in 1857 after he returned from a two-year visit to India. The French government attacked the book as immoral and fined the poet, ordering that six of the poems be omitted from future volumes.

Baudelaire was also known for his meticulous personal grooming and attire. He was part of a group of European men including Beau Brummell who were known as "dandies."

Further reading: Charles Baudelaire, *Eloge du Maquillage* (1860); "Biography" in *The Lincoln Library of Essential Information* (1961), p. 1723; Jean-Paul Sartre, *Baudelaire* (1950).

Beards *See* FACIAL HAIR, MEN'S.

Beauty Industry (U.S.)

A beauty industry offering commercial cosmetics, hair care products and related services began to develop in America during the 1800s. In earlier decades, a few cosmetics and skin preparations were commercially available , but most women made their own creams and makeup at home, if they used makeup at all. Recipes for beauty preparations were handed down from one generation to another and could also be found in printed books, including cookbooks and beauty manuals, as well as personal recipes that people concocted on their own. Most recipes were for face creams, skin creams, face powders, lip balms (sometimes tinted), and cheek color.

During the early 1800s, wealthy American women who traveled abroad brought cosmetics back from other countries, primarily France. Some women who traveled to the Orient also bought rice powder and rice powder papers that Asian women used. A few entrepreneurs made and/or sold cosmetics in the United States. Peddlers made soap and certain other products and sold them in their regions. One of these entrepreneurs was Theron Pond, who sold his Pond's Extract skin cream in the 1840s. In Cincinnati, Ohio, Solon Palmer developed powder, cologne, perfume, and hair oil, then hired people to sell them. He shipped products as far as California via the Pony Express. Some manufacturers produced catalogues that described their beauty products. One of the most successful of these manufacturers was A. Simonson, who imported and sold cosmetics and hairpieces.

Ellen Demorest was another highly successful beauty entrepreneur.. A fashion designer based in New York City, she developed a nationwide distribution network for paper dress patterns, then began selling cosmetics through this same network in the 1860s. She employed chemists to create formulas for her "Madame Demorest" line of products, including perfumes, skin cream, and hair curling lotions. During these years, French perfumers also established themselves in America and marketed scents they manufactured.

In 1886, a company called Colonial Dames was founded in San Francisco. A stage actress, Marietta Bosworth Willats, decided to develop a line of skin care products for women on the West Coast. The company soon moved its headquarters to Los Angeles, where the products became popular among actresses. Because of their elegant packaging, Colonial Dames products have also been used as props for women's dressing tables in films and television shows. The company remains in business and is still operated by the same family.

Some women did not trust the quality or safety of commercial products, so they continued to make their own. However, many homemade cosmetics for the face were too white and thick in consistency to appear natural. Face whiteners often appeared chalky and could crack on the face if a woman smiled too broadly. Some of these preparations were less detectable at evening events.

As women became more interested in skin and hair preparations and more willing to artificially enhance their looks, new companies sprang up, founded by both men and women. Two African-American women, Madam C. J. Walker and Annie Turnbo Malone, were among the most successful. Door-to-door sales of beauty products increased, as did the number of hair and face care salons, notably in large cities and along the east coast. Avon Products, which began as a door-to-door perfume business, expanded into cosmetics.

The first beauty salons in North America appeared near the end of the nineteenth century. Women operated most of the early salons. One of these operators was Anna B. Adams, who founded a chain of beauty parlors. Adams, a physician, left medicine because of the barriers posed by male colleagues who opposed women physicians.

By 1925, the beauty industry in America had grown so much that women were spending about $6 million each day buying beauty products and paying for services in hair and beauty salons. The average American woman spent about $150 a year on beauty products and services, while wealthy women might spend a few hundred dollars each week. (Peiss, 1998)

Some Americans deplored these practices and urged women not to devote time and money to their appearance. Some institutions and companies banned the use of cosmetics among their students, staff, and employees. Clergymen preached sermons warning against vanity and artificial means of changing a woman's looks. They claimed that natural looks were more honest and appealing as well as more pleasing to God.

Attitudes about cosmetics changed during World War I, along with women's jobs and social roles. After the war, during the 1920s, careers in cosmetology opened new opportunities for women in the workplace. Men began to join them because they could earn more money in this field than in some of their former jobs as salesmen, clerks, or mechanics. A beginning beauty operator or cosmetics salesperson could earn between $20–$30 a week plus about $15 in tips, an income that often doubled by the end of the first year. Some beauty operators earned hundreds of dollars each week, far more than in other jobs then open to women, which paid around $17 a week. (Peiss, 1998)

Statistics for the year 1927 showed that the American beauty business netted $2 billion a year. The business continued to grow, and product sales alone totaled $500 million in 1928. At the end of 1929, when the Great Depression began in America, that total reached $750 million. Business did not diminish greatly during the Depression. In an article in a 1932 issue of *Ladies Home Journal*, beauty industry giant Elizabeth Arden told American women they should uphold high standards for their appearance during these hard economic times. She suggested that, if necessary, women could substitute fruits and vegetables for more expensive foods so that they could afford beauty products. Arden said that maintaining an attractive appearance was good for morale. (Lewis and Woodworth, 1972).

In 1932, the U.S. government passed a luxury tax that levied 10 percent on the sale of cosmetics. People in the beauty industry agreed to pass the tax on to their consumers. Women protesters wrote letters to their legislators, and some marched on federal buildings decrying the new tax and claiming that makeup was too important to be taxed. The passage of this new tax did not affect sales. Women also continued to go to hairstylists. In 1936, the middle of the Depression,

American women spent $4 million having their hair styled.

The beauty industry experienced tremendous growth after World War II. New products and sophisticated advertising techniques brought more consumers to department store beauty counters and beauty salons. Companies began advertising their products on television as well as radio, and ads became more expensive and sophisticated. More cosmetology schools sprang up to train people in hairstyling, nail care, skin care, and makeup application so they could work as beauty professionals.

During the late twentieth century, companies that sold beauty products increasingly looked at demographics and the purchasing patterns of different population groups. For example, an increasing number of women buying beauty products were over 40 years old, part of the Baby Boom generation. Another statistic showed that African Americans were the number one consumers of beauty products. In 1997, African Americans bought $576 million worth of Clairol products, about 40 percent of that company's annual $1.4 billion in sales. These statistics sparked the National Association for the Advancement of Colored People to state that the beauty industry has an obligation, in return, to give back to the community that accounts for such a large percentage of its profits. ("NAACP Targets Beauty Industry for Failure to Empower Blacks," 1997)

Statistics from the early 1990s showed that women in America were buying 1,484 tubes of lipstick every minute (cost: $4,566); 1,324 eyeliners, eyeshadows, and mascaras per minute (cost: $6,849); 2,055 jars of skin care products a minute (cost: $12,785). (Rodin, 1992; Etcoff, 1999) Americans spend more on beauty products each year than they do on education and social services together.

The beauty industry is also a major source of employment. In the United States alone, by the 1990s, hundreds of thousands of people were employed in the multibillion dollar industry as cosmetologists, hairstylists, salon owners and managers, teachers in beauty schools, and in merchandising. Other careers in the industry included product representatives, researchers, chemists, product developers, cosmetics' demonstrators, beauty editors, facial specialists, wig stylists, manicurists, and film and television makeup artists.

As was true during the Great Depression, sales of cosmetics and personal care products do not seem to suffer as much as some sectors of the economy in times of recession. The largest companies in the household and personal care products industries include some that manufacture or distribute cosmetics and toiletries, either exclusively or as part of a broader product mix.

Companies that deal more with cosmetics include Avon, Estée Lauder Companies, Revlon, Alberto Culver, Coty, Gillette, Mary Kay, Inc., Nu Skin Enterprises, French Fragrances, John Paul Mitchell Systems, Renaissance Cosmetics, Inc., AM Cosmetics, Nexxus, Conair Corporation, Dep Corporation, Liz Claiborne Cosmetics, Soft Sheen Products, L'Oreal, Shiseido, Chanel, Clarins, and The Body Shop.

Companies that have a broad product mix include Unilever, Procter & Gamble, Colgate-Palmolive, Bristol-Meyers-Squibb, Johnson & Johnson, and the Dial Corporation.

As more American women attempt to maintain youthful appearances as they age, the industry seems likely to continue flourishing. *See also* ADVERTISING (U.S.); AGING AND APPEARANCE; ARDEN, ELIZABETH; ASH, MARY KAY; AVON PRODUCTS, INC.; AYER, HARRIET HUBBARD; COSMETICS; EYES; FACE; HANDS; LAUDER, ESTÉE; LIPS; PERFUME; AND NAMES OF INDIVIDUAL COMPANIES.

Further reading: Margaret Allen, *Selling Dreams* (1981); Lois W. Banner, *American Beauty* (1983); Thomas Beer, *Mauve Decade: American Life at the End of the Nineteenth Century* (1926); Nancy Etcoff. *Survival of the Prettiest: The Science of Beauty* (1999); Alfred Allan Lewis and Constance Woodworth, *Miss Elizabeth Arden* (1972); Kate Mulvey and Melissa Richards, *Decades of Beauty* (1998); "NAACP Targets Beauty Industry for Failure to Empower Blacks," *New Amsterdam News*, 17 May 1997, p. 3; Kathy Peiss, *Hope in a Jar* (1998); Kathryn Perutz, *Beyond the Looking Glass* (1970); Judith Rodin, *Body Traps* (1992); "What Price Beauty?" *Glamour*, April 1991, p. 297; Paul W. White, "Our Booming Beauty Business," *Outlook*, 22 January 1930, 133–135.

Beauty Pageants. *See* CONTESTS; CONTESTS, CHILDREN'S.

Beauty Patches *See* FACIAL PATCHES.

Beauty Regimens

The term "beauty regimens refers to programs and approaches people use routinely to attain a certain appearance. These regimens gain popularity as people read about them in books or hear about them in other media. Some regimens develop into businesses, and people can hire consultants to help them develop a special look.

During the 1970s, the author John T. Molloy promoted a look for women in the workplace called *Dress for Success.* During these years, increasing numbers of women were entering professions that had once been primarily or exclusively males.

In *Dress for Success,* Molloy described the clothing, accessories, makeup, and hairstyles he considered most appropriate for businesswomen. He suggested that women who followed these guidelines would be taken seriously and were likely to be more successful in their careers. Molloy advised women to base their work wardrobes on conservative two-piece suits in navy blue, gray, black, or shades of brown with knee-length skirts, adding a tailored blouse and perhaps a neat bow at the neck as a feminine alternative to a man's necktie. Subdued, natural-looking makeup and conservative hairstyles were also part of the look. Molloy's latest book, *The New Women's Dress for Success,* published in 1996, suggests that women can now wear more traditionally feminine attire to work.

Another popular regimen comes from an organization called Color Me Beautiful (CMB), which gained popularity after the publication of a book by the same name. CMB now offers many services and products designed to help people choose flattering colors in makeup and clothing. The book was first published in 1980 and rose to the top of The *New York Times* best-seller list. The paperback edition of the book was on the list for five years, setting a record that had not been broken as of 1999.

The "Color Me Beautiful" system is based on a personal analysis of an individual's hair, eye, and skin coloring. Trained consultants help clients to choose the colors that suit them best. Colors for makeup and clothing are grouped into warm and cool groups that correspond to the four seasons: winter (cool), spring (warm), summer (cool), autumn (warm).

The CMB group's most recent book was *Looking Your Best.* The various CMB books have sold more than 11 million copies worldwide. The organization has expanded its operations to include training programs on style, esthetics, stress reduction, career coaching and personal health and wellness techniques and now does business in numerous countries.

Further reading: Carole Jackson, *Color Me Beautiful* (1980); Jackson, *Color For Men* (1984); Jackson, *Color Me Beautiful Makeup Book* (1988); John T. Molloy, *Dress for Success* (1975); Molloy, *New Women's Dress for Success* (1996).

Beauty Standards

Cultures develop standards by which they evaluate people's appearance. Along with other social, political, and economic changes, these standards may shift. They are communicated and passed down to new generations in various ways, including personal example, through story-telling, poetry, fiction, art, and, in modern times, the mass media. Children become aware of these often unspoken standards and grow up aspiring to meet them. Each culture's standards include certain physical traits, but they are also associated with things people want: love, happiness, power, success, security, respect, attention, and admiration.

Myths, folk and fairy tales are one of the ways in which cultural attitudes about appearance are transmitted from one generation to another. Appearance has often played a significant role in traditional tales, where feminine beauty may be associated with purity, goodness, and other virtues. Handsome men are portrayed as royal ("the handsome prince") and/or powerful; they are often clever and talented besides. Jealousy over the beauty of another character in the tale is a common theme, as in the tales of Cinderella and Snow White. In the latter story, a wicked stepmother plots to murder her rival when her mirror tells her that the maiden Snow White is more beautiful than she. Beautiful women must be modest, however, not vain; vain women are usually punished or taught a lesson along the lines of "Pride goeth before a fall." Vanity has traditionally been regarded as a character flaw, unbecoming to a heroine.

Different cultures have vastly different standards. Among the Mende people of the Sierra Leone in Africa, women aspire to be as beautiful as Tingoi, a mermaid in Mende mythology, who is regarded as perfection. The female form in general is considered to be the ultimate beautiful creation and is highly valued in Mende communities; however, women try to enhance their inherent beauty to reach the ideal. The ideal woman, in this culture, has long, thick, strong hair, an important focus of appearance for Mende women, as well as some other feature—eyes, head, breasts, hands, legs, or buttocks—approaching that of the mythical Tingoi. Men who are considered attractive are told they are "like a woman," a great compliment.

A look at European history shows examples of specific beauty standards in western cultures and how they have changed over time. In the tenth through the thirteenth centuries,, the "ideal woman" was portrayed as slender and pale, with small hips and breasts. A medieval cavalier described a much-admired young baroness in these words:

> She has fair blond locks and a forehead whiter than lilies. Her laughing eyes change color with her mood. Her nose is straight and firm. Her fresh face outvies the white and vermilion of the flowers. Her mouth is small and her teeth are white like snow on the wild rose. White are her fair hands, and the fingers are both smooth and slender. (Davis, 70)

Weight and build standards also change. Different cultures expressed a preference for slender figures versus fuller figures, and these trends changed from one era to the next. Although in Europe, a thin female figure was the medieval ideal, by the sixteenth century, plumper women with full breasts and full hips were more in vogue.

Renaissance Europeans—thirteenth through sixteenth centuries—admired these traits in women: red lips and cheeks, white skin, blond hair, dark eyebrows, a long slender neck, firm, round breasts with pink nipples, small feet, and a slim waist. In his 1536 publication, *El costume de la donne (Women's Dress),* Italian author Morpurgo listed 33 traits of the "ideal woman." They were long hair, hands, and legs; short teeth, ears, and breasts; wide forehead, chest, and hips; narrow waist, knees, and vagina; large height, arms, and thighs; thin eyebrows, fingers, and lips; round neck and arms; small chin, mouth, and feet; white teeth, throat, and hands; red cheeks, lips, and nipples; and black eyebrows and eyes.

The emphasis on pale skin that prevailed through the sixteenth century in Europe reflected the view that this pallor was more delicate and feminine compared to darker or more vivid tones, which were regarded as masculine. Skin color also reflected class-consciousness, because sheltered, affluent women could stay out of the sun and need not labor outdoors. White as a color was also linked to the idea of purity, a female virtue. Women were so eager to attain this look that they used cosmetics that contained harmful ingredients, including mercury and lead, and doctors joined the clergy in condemning their use. Women who applied certain formulas for long periods of time developed black teeth and, ironically, more vivid complexions.

Asians also favored pale skin and rosy cheeks for many centuries. Women used rice powder as a skin-lightener and rouge to lend color to their complexions. Delicate painted eyebrows were important, although precise styles in brows changed from one era to the next.

In China, tiny feet were for centuries a key measure of a woman's beauty. Women's feet were bound from early childhood so that they would conform to this standard, and

Madame de Pompadour (Jeanne Antoinette [Poisson] Marquise de) was considered an ideal beauty of the eighteenth century. *Library of Congress.*

nic and racial prejudices toward people of color and, later, immigrants from southern Europe, Mediterranean countries, Asia, and Latin America.

During the 1920s, in a movement known as the Harlem Renaissance, African Americans celebrated their own beauty as distinct from the narrow white European ideals. Black writers praised women's charms, comparing their skin colors to cinnamon, honey, ginger, and other appealing things. The Black Pride of the 1960s again reinforced the ethnocentricity of standards of appearance based on a white European ideal, which excluded the beauty of other cultures. This movement spread to other ethnic groups, and Native Americans, Asian Americans, and Latinos celebrated their uniqueness and beauty, too.

Modern beauty standards are spread through the media—magazines, newspapers, books, movies, and television. Television and magazines may influence attitudes about appearance in traditional cultures as well as media-saturated cultures. For example, in India, people practice many traditional customs that convey certain messages about appearance. They receive other messages, however, from watching western movies and television shows, such as shown on MTV.

Certain people have come to represent looks that were popular during different decades of the twentieth century. The actress Clara Bow was the "It Girl" of the 1920s; Jean Harlow was the glamour girl of the 1930s; and Marilyn Monroe became the "sex symbol" of the 1950s.

In the 1960s, voluptuous figures fell out of favor, and the British teenage fashion model Twiggy, with her large eyes and short, short hair, typified the "Mod" or "Carnaby Street" look that became popular. Thin bodies and brightly colored miniskirts were in vogue. Not all men found this look appealing, however, as *Playboy* and other "men's magazine" centerfolds continued to feature a particular look that included large breasts, a small waist, trim hips, and shapely legs.

During the twentieth century, scientists and others have studied attitudes about appearance and conducted research to see how

their entire futures depended on preventing their feet from growing beyond a certain size.

Eighteenth-century standards of beauty in Europe shifted to a more natural, fuller-figured look. Smallpox was no longer endemic, which meant that a woman's natural complexion was less apt to be scarred. Simplicity in art and appearance was more valued than it had once been.

Across the Atlantic, in colonial America, European settlers brought their ideas about appearance with them. Some of these standards, however, changed to suit life in a new and different land. For example, many men (and women too) stopped wearing wigs in the mid-1700s because they saw wigs and certain cosmetics as symbols of the hated British monarchy. Simpler styles in dress, hair, and personal adornment reflected the changing political attitudes of a society that aimed to be egalitarian instead of class-conscious. They also had less access to consumer goods, and in many cases, dressed in clothes in which they could work.

Nonetheless, Americans' prevailing standards of beauty favored a white European appearance. These standards reflected eth-

cultural standards on appearance affect people. Some researchers found that standards for male appearance usually stress dominance traits found in a more mature appearance, while standards for women emphasize looks that most resemble the infantile stage of development—full red lips, pink cheeks, smooth soft skin, and wide eyes. They concluded that these attitudes were instinctive and reflect the genetic imperative to reproduce. Men would tend to look for a partner who seemed young (thus fertile) while women would tend to seek men who appear to be good providers.

Authors, particularly feminists, have also explored topics related to beauty standards, their origins, and how they affect women. Some, including Nancy Friday (*The Power of Beauty*), Susan Brownmiller (*Femininity*), Susan Faludi (*Backlash*), and Judith Rodin (*Body Traps*), have explored the psychology of personal appearance and its influence on human relationships. In her book *When and Where I Enter*, Paula Giddings discusses views of African American beauty and the impact of white-based standards of beauty on women of color.

In her essay "Why Is Beauty on Parade?" author Deck Clarke contends that beauty and politics are closely intertwined. Clarke says, ". . . beauty, like wealth, becomes a method of ranking people, dividing them along lines of power." (Clarke, 1983) She says, "By being beautiful, women not only increase their market value as commodities. They become consumers of an amazing array of devices and substances to build beauty. Beautiful women are used two ways—to sell themselves and their femininity (and masculinity), and to sell all the technology of beauty. . . . in the form of many millions of dollars' worth of cosmetic chemicals, diet regimens and drugs, and reams of printed instructions." Clarke concludes that the western beauty ideal shows a preference for a woman who is pre-adolescent, not mature or grown-up, and hence not powerful. She describes this ideal as a Caucasian, preferably blonde, between 5'3" and 5'8" tall between the ages of 16 and 25 with no visible hair on her legs, thighs, underarms,

or face (except eyebrows), large eyes, abundant shiny hair, red lips, poreless skin, small white teeth, small nose, small ears, no body odor, toned slim body with long legs. In contrast, men who look adolescent are viewed as less attractive because mature looks in a man might reflect greater power.

Beauty standards can have a strong impact on social attitudes and interpersonal relations. Studies have shown that people tend to hold certain attitudes toward those they find attractive. They may describe attractive people as more friendly, intelligent, capable, and popular on the basis of looking at their photographs. One study showed that beautiful men and handsome women were perceived as being "warm, sensitive, kind, interesting, poised, sociable, and outgoing, [who] have good jobs and fulfilling lives." (Goleman, 1986) In some studies of families, parents were observed to spend more time talking with and cuddling babies they considered good-looking.

In other studies, college men were given photographs and told to select the women they would be most likely to do various things for, such as help move furniture or save from a fire or drowning. Their responses showed they were most likely to aid a beautiful woman. The one thing they were less likely to do for the beautiful women in the photographs was lend them money. (Etcoff, 1999) Some studies have shown that people are less likely to ask good-looking members of the opposite gender for help.

Reflecting on the way beauty standards affect women's views about their own appearance, makeup artist and author Victoria Jackson wrote,

> For the last several decades, women, for whatever reasons, have been denying their unique good looks, preferring to copy the image of a select few beautiful women. In the 1940s they wanted to look like Rita Hayworth and Betty Grable, 10 years later like Marilyn Monroe and Elizabeth Taylor, later like Audrey Hepburn and Natalie Wood. As models became the benchmarks of allure, the faces of Lauren Hutton, Cheryl Tiegs, Christie Brinkley, Brooke Shields, and Claudia Schiffer established

more impossible standards. None of them set out to become paragons of perfection, yet suddenly, women all over the world were trying desperately to look like them instead of themselves. . . ." (Jackson, 1997)

Reflecting a trend toward more inclusive and diverse standards, Jackson says, "As we approach a new century, redefining 'beauty' is a must. . . . When fashion dictates facial features, something is terribly wrong. . . . We should be able to look at ourselves realistically and appreciate what we see, not deprecate the reflection in the mirror because it doesn't meet a certain standard." (Jackson, 1997)

During the late twentieth century, more people challenged beauty standards, especially those that prevailed in western cultures. More men and women of different ethnic and racial groups became well-known models and actors, as did people whose features and body builds did not conform to the norm, including "oversize" and older models. Numerous books and articles opposed traditional ideas about beauty and its importance.

Paddy Calistro, co-author of *Redesign Your Body*, reflected these changing views when he wrote, "Good looks transcend race and ethnicity. When Cher, Shari Belafonte-Harper, Victoria Principal, Isabella Rosselini, and Sade are referred to as the new classic beauties, it's obvious that there's no one way to be beautiful. It's an emerging acceptance of beauty that goes beyond blond. And when *Harper's Bazaar* has named Whitney Houston, Barbara Carrera, and Lisa Bonet as three of the country's 10 most beautiful women, it's clear that standards of beauty apply across—not within—racial lines." (Calistro, 1986) *See also* AFRICAN AMERICANS; AGING AND APPEARANCE; BODY IMAGE; CRITICS OF COSMETICS INDUSTRY; FEMINISM; "LOOKS."

Further reading: Bruno Bettelheim, *The Uses of Enchantment: The Meaning and Importance of Fairy Tales* (1997); Paddy Calistro, "Shades of Meaning," *Los Angeles Times,* 26 October 1986; Carroll Camden, *The Elizabethan Woman: A Panorama of English Womanhood, 1540 to 1640* (1952); Davis, William Stearns. *Life On a Mediaeval Barony* (1932); De Clarke, http://www. igc.apc.org/nemesis/ACLU/Nikki/BeautyClarke2.html; Nancy Etcoff, *Survival of the Prettiest: The Science of Beauty* (1999); Paula Giddings, *When and Where I Enter* (1996); Daniel Goleman, "Equation for Beauty Emerges in Studies," *The New York Times,* 5 August 1986; Sara Halprin, *Look at My Ugly Face* (1995); Victoria Jackson, *Redefining Beauty* (1997); Robin Tolmach and Raquel L. Scherr, *Face Value: The Politics of Beauty* (1984); Susan R. Sulieman, ed., *The Female Body in Western Culture* (1986).

Begoun, Paula (b. 1953)

Paula Begoun, a reporter and author who covers the cosmetics industry for consumers, has become known as the "Cosmetics Cop." She investigates cosmetics and other grooming products to give consumers more accurate information—or, as she has said, "to get beyond the hype and chicanery of the cosmetics industry." In addition to writing and publishing several best-selling books, Begoun writes a syndicated column and newsletter called "Cosmetics Counter Update."

Begoun began her career as a freelance makeup artist and skin care consultant. During the late 1970s, she also worked part-time at department store cosmetics counters. Her supervisors criticized her for recommending less expensive alternatives and for steering customers toward products she thought would perform well for them when these were not sold in the product lines she was hired to promote.

In 1978, Begoun began reading more about cosmetics production and advertising and studied the techniques the industry used to attract customers. As she later said, "I wasn't anti-makeup—just the opposite—but I was (and am) anti-hype and anti-misleading information." (Begoun, 1997)

Begoun set out to learn as much as possible about the cosmetics industry and the properties and effects of different ingredients and products. Because there are so many products and manufacturers make so many claims, Begoun decided consumers needed much more information to make sound choices and spend their money wisely. In 1981, she founded her own cosmetic stores in the Seattle area, staffing them with well-trained salespeople, and began working as a consumer reporter on television. She was also featured in the national and international media.

To reach more consumers, Begoun has written several books on beauty and cosmetics. *Blue Eyeshadow Should Be Illegal* was published in 1986. In response to the many letters she received, Begoun wrote two new guides reviewing hundreds of individual cosmetics, skin care products, and hair care products. They were *Don't Go to the Cosmetics Counter Without Me* and *Don't Go Shopping For Hair Care Products Without Me.* Begoun analyzed the claims different companies made about their products and evaluated their performance, while also looking at the costs. She also publishes the *Cosmetics Counter Update* newsletter, writes a newspaper column, and runs a web site on the Internet to keep consumers informed about new products, research, and developments in the industry.

To obtain information about different products, Begoun says that she buys about $6,000 worth of cosmetics each year, watches numerous commercials, and studies ads and makeup displays at stores. (Begoun, *Don't Go to the Cosmetic Counter Without Me,* 1997) She gets other information from cosmetics chemists and other scientists, by reading research abstracts on various ingredients, and from consumer feedback. Her newsletters address questions from consumers, who also share their experiences with different products, and include responses from companies whose products Begoun has critiqued. *See also* BEAUTY INDUSTRY (U.S.); COSMETICS; LAWS AND REGULATIONS (U.S.); SAFETY.

Further reading: Paula Begoun, *The Beauty Bible* (1997); Begoun, *Don't Go to the Cosmetics Counter Without Me* (1997); Begoun, *Don't Go Shopping For Hair Care Products Without Me* (1998); "Paula Begoun," http://www.cosmeticscop.com

Bishop, Hazel (1906–1998)

Hazel Bishop, chemist and entrepreneur, founded a cosmetics company that featured her own lipstick formulas. Her Lasting Lipstick line was marketed as the world's first "kissproof lipstick."

When Bishop graduated from Barnard College, a prestigious all-women's school, she planned to study medicine. However, after the U.S. stock market crashed in 1929, followed by the Great Depression, Bishop could not afford to do so. A skillful chemist, she entered the workforce and developed high-altitude fuels for airplane engines.

During these years, she began experimenting with different cosmetic formulas in a laboratory she set up in her apartment. Some of her initial experiments with cosmetics did not succeed. Bishop sought to find a lipstick formula that would not rub off but would also not dry out or irritate the skin. She tried adding larger than normal amounts of colorant and was able to produce a lanolin-based cream that left a long-lasting stain on the lips. Starting in 1950, consumers could buy Hazel Bishop's Lasting Lipstick for $1 a tube. Ads for the lipstick called it "revolutionary" and proclaimed, "It stays on you . . . not on him." Bishop's product was called an indelible lipstick, and other companies hurried to develop indelible products of their own. Women liked the idea of makeup that did not have to be reapplied and also the idea that they could "wake up beautiful."

Hazel Bishop, Inc., was a financial success, as Lasting Lipstick attracted a 25 percent share of the lipstick market. By 1954, Bishop had sold her company, which went on to produce new cosmetics, including a blusher called Fresh and Bright that was introduced in the early 1960s and sold well into the 1980s. These were modestly priced cosmetics compared to some other brands, such as Revlon, Estée Lauder, and Elizabeth Arden. Hazel Bishop products were available in drug stores and variety stores.

After selling her company, Bishop embarked on a new career as a stockbroker and financial analyst in New York City. Later, she accepted a position as adjunct professor at the Fashion Institute of Technology. Bishop was known for her intelligence and wit. Once, when commenting about the purpose of cosmetics, she said, "Women should accentuate their most attractive feature. After the age of 25 or so, personality becomes an increasingly attractive feature." ("Lasting Legacy," 1998)   Bishop died at the age of 92 on December 5, 1998.

Further reading: "Lasting Legacy," *People*, 11 January 1999, p. 138; Mulvey and Richards, *Decades of Beauty: The Changing Image of Women, 1890s–1990s* (1998).

Black, Shirley Temple *See* TEMPLE, SHIRLEY.

Bleach, Skin *See* SKIN COLORING AGENTS.

Blepharoplasty *See* EYES; PLASTIC SURGERY.

Body Decoration

Body decoration (or body art) refers to both temporary and permanent decoration of the body. People have added designs and ornaments to different parts of the body in ways that vary from culture to culture. The designs may be applied for esthetic reasons, spiritual purposes, or to show a person's social status or role. Different designs and colors on the face or body might signify special events, such as war or death, or life passages, such as puberty or motherhood.

The application of color designs to the face and body dates back to prehistoric times. Two hikers stumbled over definite evidence of this in 1991, when, walking the Alps, they encountered the amazingly well-preserved body of a Neolithic man, complete with skin decoration. People found pigments in the plants and minerals around them. The first colors came from earth pigments and included iron oxide, plant juices, white clay, red and yellow ochre, and charcoal.

Ancient Britons, among them Celts and Picts, were among the oldest known users of body paint. They colored parts of their faces and bodies blue with a substance called woad

to frighten their enemies in battle as well as for adornment. They continued to use this blue paint for centuries; it can be seen on warriors in the Oscar-winning feature film *Braveheart* starring Mel Gibson. Henna, a plant dye, has also been used since ancient times to decorate the face, hands, and other parts of the body in China, North Africa, and Turkey.

Body painting may be done for aesthetic reasons or to show group identity or social status. In some cultures, people paint designs on themselves as part of spiritual or ceremonial customs; some, too, consider a plain body with no form of paint or tattooing ugly and animal-like. Modern body paints include both natural materials and manufactured preparations that add color to the cheeks, lips, eyes, and fingernails. Paint may be temporary or permanent.

Face painting has endured since ancient times in one form or another. As with general body painting, in the past and in some contemporary societies, it has often indicated a person's role or position or been linked to religious or other ceremonies. In modern industrialized societies, women are the primary users of color cosmetics, and they use them to improve their appearance or to indicate their social status, as in India, with caste marks.

In ancient times and among some contemporary native cultures, face-painting has been key to some spiritual ceremonies. It may also be used to distinguish special people in the community, such as healers or magicians. Native Americans applied certain colors and designs to their faces to signify status, life passages, and for certain occasions, such as going to war or embarking on a hunt.

In the Congo, male Kota paint their faces a vivid blue color to show they have become men. Nuba people of the Southern Sudan create colorful facial designs to show their age, family, and clan membership.

Among some peoples, women paint themselves as part of a systematic seduction process. Sharanahua women in Peru paint their faces and legs red with achiote (a berry), then make delicate patterns of black lines over this

Samburu tribal dancer (Africa). © *Renee Lynn/Photo Researchers.*

red base coat. Wodaabe men of Africa also use paint when preparing for special ceremonies during which they hope to attract a mate. New Guinean males are also known for the liberal use of facial and body paint and ornamentation, including feathers.

Berries are often used to color the skin. In the Caribbean, at the time of European exploration, women used body paint and feathers. One red dye, which they used on the lips and body, was prepared from the annatto plant. Native peoples in Trinidad obtain red juice from the roucou (achiote) berries for body paint, using it to stain their cheeks and lips. The Indians of Twanke, an Amazonian group make red dye from these crushed berries mixed with nut oil. One use of the dye is to anoint the body of a widow whose mourning period has ended. Roucou also repels insects. The berries were still used in the twentieth century for cosmetic purposes and to tint foods a reddish-orange color. The bush on which they grow is sometimes called the "lipstick bush."

The Wayana, a tribe that has lived since ancient times on the northern coast of South America, also use body paint made from roucou. They make it into cakes by crushing the seeds of the plant and blending them with nut oil. One of its uses is to paint the body of a widow whose period of mourning has ended.

Many traditional forms of body decoration are still followed in modern times. The Bororo of Brazil, a hunting tribe, paint their bodies with red paint for ceremonial occasions. The indigenous peoples of Papua New Guinea are known for their vivid and elaborate body painting.

In contemporary Africa, the Wodaabe, a nomadic group, decorate their bodies extensively with paint. Before a special festival called Geerewol, young men adorn themselves with ochre makeup to enhance their attractiveness to the women who will select partners that evening. Among the Berbers who live in North Africa in the Atlas Mountains, women and young girls paint their faces before the annual festival where mates are chosen. Berber women have continued the tradition of painting an upside-down blue trident on their chins.

In Latin America, women of the Seri, who live in Sonora, Mexico, traditionally painted sacred designs on their faces for ceremonies. Some designs are geometric shapes painted with blue and red pigments. The Kaipo, an Amazonian group in South America, wear black and red paint for certain occasions, as did their ancestors. The Yanomami of the Amazon region wear designs made up of black dots in a pattern across the face. The Wayana, another Amazonian group, wear designs painted in red. Certain designs and colors are used for special occasions; for example, men apply black paint around their eyes and on their cheeks and bold red and black designs on their thighs and calves for the ceremonial Dance of the Flies.

Body decoration has remained popular with tribal groups in Africa, parts of the Caribbean, South America, Oceania, and certain other regions into modern times. However, in some places, new laws have banned the custom as people in parts of Africa, Oceania, and Asia adopted western modes of dress and grooming.

Body painting and decoration is performed on an Aboriginal boy in Australia. © *Richard Harrington/Archive Photos.*

Body decoration became more popular in western cultures during recent decades. People who embrace this trend have been called urban aboriginals, urban primitives, and modern primitives. A contemporary American artist, Keith Haring (1958–1990) called attention to the art of body-painting during the 1980s. Haring, who was known for his vivid, fanciful designs and murals, often influenced by graffiti, painted elaborate decorations on the bodies of performers. In 1987, he covered his naked body with painted designs, then had himself photographed in Times Square in New York City.

In the Middle East and India, henna art and the Indian skin art known as mehndi are still worn on special occasions and during certain ceremonies. Westerners sometimes have henna designs painted on their bodies as a way to experiment with temporary tattooing. Hollywood stars, including Demi Moore, Mira Sorvino, and Naomi Campbell, are among those who have worn henna skin art. Some young people also choose to wear henna skin designs, usually on their necks, arms, backs, ankles, and stomachs. Some people have henna tattoos placed on parts of their scalp.

Those celebrating such holidays as carnivale in Brazil or Mardi Gras in New Orleans might also paint their faces or bodies. *See also* BODY ORNAMENTATION; EGYPT, ANCIENT; HANDS; HENNA; SKIN MODIFICATION; TATTOOS.

Further reading: Robert Brain, *The Decorated Body* (1979); Center for Responsive Law, *Being Beautiful: Deciding for Yourself* (1986); Carole Devillers, "What Future for the Wayana Indians?" *National Geographic*, January 1983, 66–83; Victoria Ebin, *The Body Decorated* (1979); Angela Fisher, *Africa Adorned* (1984); David Frye, Nancy Frye, and Alan Okagaki, *Consumer's Guide to Cosmetics* (1979); Loren McIntyre,

"Amazon: The River Sea," *National Geographic*, October 1972, 456–495; Nita Quintero, "Coming of Age the Apache Way," *National Geographic*, February 1980, 262–290.

Body Hair, Men's and Women's

Body hair refers to hair on body parts other than the head: the legs, arms, chest, back, pubic region, nose, or other parts of the face. Body hair may be augmented or accentuated to suit the styles of the day, or minimized or removed if it is regarded as unattractive.

Patterns of hair growth depend on gender and genes. Some people inherit a tendency toward excess hair growth (hirsutism). Women may experience unwanted growth of hair on their upper lip, chin, or the sides of the face as a result of taking certain medications or when female hormones decline during and after menopause. Men have varying amounts of chest hair, which they may like or dislike, and some men have noticeable hair on their upper and lower backs.

Attitudes about body hair vary from place to place. Some societies have considered certain types of body hair unattractive or a sign of poor personal grooming. In some places and periods of history, people have removed the eyebrows and eyelashes as well.

Women in ancient Greece and Rome, as well as several African tribes, Trobriand Islanders, and Turks of the early 1900s typically removed all their body hair—leg, underarm, and pubic. Among native groups in the Americas, it was traditional to remove pubic hair, sometimes by plucking. Africans and Asians also regarded body hair as undesirable. However, ancient Caucasian peoples usually did not object to body hair. Some groups, such as the European Jews of the Middle Ages, considered dense body hair to be lucky.

In early Christian Europe (around the tenth century), body hair was more acceptable than it was in many ancient societies. However, after European Crusaders returned from the Middle East during the eleventh century, they brought back a preference for Middle Eastern-style baths and influenced European women to remove all body hair, as was customary among the Turks. The practice did not last long, because Catherine de Médici, a powerful queen of France, called for an end to it in the mid-1500s.

Hair on a woman's arms, legs, or underarms is viewed differently around the world. In the United States, obvious hair on the legs and underarms is regarded as unattractive, and women remove it or bleach it. Some women also bleach the hair on their arms, while a small number of women shave it off. In the United States, shaving is the most common way to remove underarm and leg hair, although waxing and cream depilatories are also used. Women may also get rid of hair on the nipples, the so-called bikini line (pubic area revealed by swimwear), and back, as well as underarms and legs. In Europe, waxing leg hair is more common than it is in America.

However, in some parts of the world, hair on women's legs and underarms may be considered either irrelevant or attractive and also sexually appealing. In these cases, women do not remove it. In Latin America, women did not shave their legs and armpits until North American media exerted its influence on them.

Facial hair on women, however, has almost universally been viewed as unattractive, probably because it appears masculine. According to some analysts, such hair also may suggest that a woman is older—since she does not have the smooth skin of a baby or child and therefore may be an infertile (thus less desirable) mate because of aging. Women in western cultures may remove hair on their upper lips and chins or use hair bleach on these areas. Women with noticeable or dense chin hair have been regarded as curiosities. Bearded women were featured in circuses and traveling exhibits during the nineteenth and twentieth centuries.

In contrast, modern men may usually choose whether to shave facial hair or not. Until recently, they were rarely concerned about hair on their arms, legs, or underarms unless it served some special utilitarian or esthetic purpose to remove it. For example, swimmers, cyclists and certain other male athletes may remove leg and arm hair to improve their speed and performance. Female impersonators may also remove leg and underarm hair and bleach or remove obvious arm hair. Some male bodybuilders have hair removed from their chests and backs in order to achieve a smooth appearance for competitions. Men who have unusually large amounts of hair on their backs may or may not have it removed. Some homosexual men also prefer to remove hair from their legs, underarms, and other parts of the body.

Hair Removal Methods

Early depilatories—substances used to remove hair—were devised to remove body hair for both men and women in ancient cultures that preferred a hairless appearance. Later, hair-removal methods for women focused on the upper lip area, referring to this hair as "beard." Author Sara Halprin writes about the cultural imperatives against facial hair on women that exist in many places:

> Women who have facial hair and allow it to grow are often objects of ridicule, even violence, and are criticized by other women at least as much as by men. Implicit in these criticisms is fear, the fear of blurring and transgressing boundaries assumed for so long to be morally right, the fear of being branded "unwomanly" . . . (Halprin, 1995)

Hair on the face or body was sometimes removed with an abrasive substance. One of the most common abrasives was pumice, which comes from ground volcanic glass. During the mid-1800s, a cosmetics manufacturer known as Dr. Gouraud promoted his depilatory product, "Poudre Subtile," by claiming that the formula had come from the famous beauty, the Queen of Sheba. Gouraud said that he had "re-discovered" this amazing powder that could effectively "remove every appearance of beard from the lips."

During the 1920s, ads for a product called "Zip" depilatory showed before and after pictures of a woman who had apparently removed the hair along the sides of her face in front of her ears. The ad implied that by removing this hair, she looked cleaner and more socially acceptable.

By the late twentieth century, consumers could choose from a variety of hair removal products and services. Numerous products for removing hair were sold in drugstores and at cosmetic counters or could be ordered through the mail. They included shaving creams, lotions, and gels, electrolysis devices, and chemical depilatories. Many of the chemical depilatories used to remove hair from skin contain the strongly alkaline substance calcium thioglycolate. In the United States, the Food and Drug Administration (FDA) Office of Cosmetics and Colors, in the Center for Food Safety and Applied Nutrition regulated chemical depilatories, as well as shaving creams, foams, and gels and waxes.

Women also use do-it-yourself preparations to remove unwanted hair at home. Cream depilatories are popular for removing unwanted facial hair, arm hair, leg hair, and hair on the "bikini line." Occasionally, depilatories are used to remove unwanted hairs on the brow, but usually these are plucked with tweezers. Both men and women usually trim obvious nose hairs with small scissors.

Professional hair-removal services include salon waxing, electrolysis, and laser treatments. In 1995, the first laser treatment for hair-removal use was approved by the FDA. Salons around the world offer hair-removal services, often through waxing. Waxing involves applying hot wax to the hairy area, letting it cool, and then pulling it off, bringing the hairs with it. The use of wax to remove hairs dates back thousands of years. Supposedly, Cleopatra used a coating of warm liquid wax to remove hairs from her skin. Another method used by Egyptians, now called "sugaring," involves the application of a formula containing sugar to the skin. More men and women are using waxing services currently. Salon owners report that women have treatments on their chins, upper lips, underarms, and "bikini line," while men have hair removed from their chest or back. Eyebrow waxing has became increasingly popular among women and some men. Stray hairs are removed to create a "clean" and shapely browline.

Electrolysis dates back to the late 1800s. Charles E. Michel, an ophthalmologist practicing in St. Louis, Missouri, devised a method for removing what were called wild eyelash hairs. In 1875, Michel attached a sewing needle to a battery in order to produce a galvanic or direct current. He wrote that his goal was "to pass a fine gilt needle into the hair follicle and allow the current to produce the electrochemical decomposition of its papillae." (Canadian Organization of Professional Electrolysists, http://www.electrolysis.ca) Michel developed improved methods of electrolysis. Women with unwanted facial hair and people with unwanted hair between their eyebrows came to Michel for treatments. Electrolysis developed into a regulated profession; professional associations set standards, particularly in terms of safety and prevention of infection through the use of sterile, disposable needles. Specialized training was available to electrolysists in the United States, Canada, and other countries. Electrolysis remains the most long-lasting and sometimes permanent way to remove unwanted hair but it may be uncomfortable, expensive, and time-consuming. An electrical current kills each individual hair at the root, moving from one follicle to the next. A certain amount of the hair regrowth is usually seen after the procedure because hair grows in cycles and some of the roots at the site of removal may have been inactive at the time of the treatment.

Women typically use electrolysis to remove unwanted hair on the upper lip, brows, cheek or legs. During the 1970s, a fad among some homosexual males was to have facial hair permanently removed through electrolysis to have a smooth, stubble-free complexion. Electrolysis operators in the United States said that women clients tend to use the service for removing hair from the face, bikini line, abdomen, breasts, forearms, and underarms while men have hair removed from the area between the eyebrows, outside of the ears, and shoulders.

By the 1990s, three types of electrolysis were in use. Electrolysis involving the use of direct current is the oldest method and destroys the hair by chemical action when the current reacts with the body fluids and salts at the target site. Thermolysis (also known as diathermy or electrocauterization) involves the use of high frequency alternating current to cause intense heat that destroys the hair follicle. A third method, called the Blend, combines both direct and alternating currents. They may be applied either simultaneously or sequentially.

Critics and Nonconformists

Like many other grooming practices, hair removal has been controversial. During the 1970s, some feminists in America rebelled against the idea of shaving hair on their legs and underarms. Some women claimed that they no longer felt compelled to remove this hair, since shaving it reflected oppressive demands from a male-dominated culture. However, the vast majority of teenage and adult women continued to remove leg and underarm hair on a regular basis. According to reports from the Food and Drug Administration, in America, "millions of women, and a growing number of men, spend millions of dollars each year on products and services that promise smooth, silky skin free of 'unsightly,' 'excessive' body hair." (Segal, 1996)

One notable exception was a twentieth century woman whose family tree included women with an inherited tendency to have chin hair. In the documentary film, *Keltie's Beard: A Woman's Story*, this Canadian-born woman describes her experiences when she decided not to remove this facial hair. *See also* EYES; FACIAL HAIR, MEN'S; LASER COSMETIC PROCEDURES; LAWS AND RGULATIONS (U.S.); PERSONAL CARE PRODUCTS, MEN'S.

Further reading: Paul J. Alexander, ed., *The Ancient World: To 300 AD* (1963); James Henry Breasted, *Ancient Times: A History of the Early World* (1944); Sara Halprin, *"Look at My Ugly Face!"* (1995); Marian Segal, "Hair Today, Gone Tomorrow," *FDA Consumer*, September 1996.

Body Image

Body image—how people think about their own bodies—attractive, fat, thin—influences both self-attitudes and behavior. The attitudes are often closely related to the beauty standards in a culture. In most cultures, women are affected more by these standards than are men. Spending time, mental and physical energy, and money on appearance is considered more normal and acceptable for women than for men.

Social scientists have found that people tend to compare themselves to images of how an "ideal" body should look. These images, in turn, are shaped by what the culture views as attractive in terms of height, weight, proportions, facial features, coloring, length of limbs, and other physical traits. They are also aware of messages the people around them give them—implicitly or explicitly—about the way they look. Individuals tend to be most concerned about their appearance in cultures that emphasize looks and transmit many images of "good looks" and messages about appearance. In some cultures, people emphasize their looks more than their achievements and personality.

In modern times, the mass media has become a powerful force in disseminating cultural attitudes about appearance. Beauty standards, which exist in all societies, are often relatively narrow. For example, for centuries, women in China bound their feet to achieve the cultural ideal—a foot that measured about 4 inches long. Failing to achieve that standard could profoundly affect a woman's self-image, because women whose feet were larger were not considered marriageable. During the 1950s and 1960s in the United States, society's stereotypically ideal measurements for a woman were a 36-inch bust, 24-inch waist, and 36-inch hips. In the 1990s, men are inundated with images of well-toned male models who have broad, muscular shoulders, well-defined back muscles, and firm abdomens.

The late twentieth century ideal in western cultures for both men and women is a slender, "fit" body. The standard of the "ideal" female body gradually became slimmer during the 1970s. Some observers believe this trend began in the late 1960s when an English teenager nicknamed Twiggy (who, at 5'7," weighed about 90 pounds) became a popular model.

American culture's pervasive model of beauty—Caucasian, pale skinned, often blonde, and light-eyed—has affected the body image of women who did not fit this standard. According to Rita Freedman,

> This fair image weighs most heavily on the brown shoulders of minority women who bear a special beauty burden.... looks-ism joins with sexism and racism to exclude those who are unwelcome in the dominant domain. All three combine to stigmatize nonwhite women as triply jeopardized, triply deviant.... the media constantly reminds minority women of their nonconforming features. (Freedman, 1986)

As different "looks" come and go, women face shifting and often contradictory beauty ideals. They may emphasize opposite traits, for example a sexy and erotic look versus an innocent or unsophisticated look. Sometimes these looks are combined in the beauty ideals of a culture at the same time. Women who fit none of the ideals may find it difficult to develop a positive body image.

Scientists have studied how appearance affects a person's development, social relationships, and self-concept. Studies showing the effects of body image on personal development appeared more often after 1930. Parenting magazines published the results of studies showing that young women who perceived themselves as unattractive were more likely to have a negative body image and low self-esteem.

Girls and young women began obsessing about body image in a major way in the 1920s. Studies of teenage girls in the United States have found that they are growing increasingly insecure and negative in their feelings about their appearance, an increase that correlates with low self-esteem. Teenage girls typically are more concerned about their appearance than are teenage boys, although more young men seem to be expressing such concerns in recent years. Girls worry about their general shape and size as well as individual features.

Researchers Linda Sanford and Mary Ellen Donovan conclude that women often regard their bodies as a problem because our culture teaches women that they must be pretty to be worthy, and sets up beauty standards that are unhealthy and unattainable. The poor body image that underlies a variety of adjustment problems is largely a product of social conditioning. (Freedman, 1986).

According to scientists, people who have a poor body image may be more prone to feelings of depression and a sense of helplessness, as with a woman who feels she cannot control a basic aspect of feminine identity. For that reason, some psychiatric facilities have started hair care and other grooming programs to improve patients' moods. Such programs have also been used in facilities for delinquent teenage girls.

Ideas about body image can show distorted thinking. Surveys conducted throughout the 1980s and 1990s showed that more than half of the American women questioned expressed dissatisfaction with their bodies, especially their weight. Statistics, however, showed that less than one-third of all women were above the normal weights for their height set by insurance companies. During the 1990s, statistics showed that at any given time, 70 percent of the women in the United States were on reducing diets.

According to many observers, the idea that a body must be thin to be attractive is a beauty "myth," a false idea that causes people to feel bad about themselves. Critics believe such standards can lead to low self-esteem and eating disorders in susceptible people, especially teenage girls. In her book *SchoolGirls*, author Peggy Orenstein writes,

> Study after study shows that girls know, in spite of the overt messages of success and achievement proffered them, that their body is their most valuable commodity; indeed, they believe it defines them. In *Shortchanging Girls, Shortchanging America*, for instance, confidence in 'the way I look' was the single most important determinant of self-worth for white middle school girls. Boys, meanwhile, were more likely to cite their abilities . . . (Orenstein, 1994)

Recent studies show differences in how various racial and ethnic groups view their bodies. Nikki Teufel, Ph.D., a nutritional anthropologist, has studied groups of teenagers from different cultures and ethnic groups. She has found that young African American and Native American women have different and more accepting attitudes about their bodies than do young Anglo women. Other researchers have found similar results. *Shortchanging Girls, Shortchanging America,* a study sponsored by the American Association of University Women, also concluded that black girls have higher self-esteem than do white girls and were more satisfied with their appearance.

In that same 1990 study by the American Association of University Women, 45 percent of the black women between 22 and 49 said they were "attractive," compared to 30 percent of the white women. Eighty percent of the black women said they were happy when they looked in the mirror. The investigators also reported that more white girls than black girls consumed levels of calcium that were below normal because they had eliminated dairy products from their diets to lose weight.

Analysts have concluded that the reason for the discrepancy may be found in the traditional roles of white and black women and the models of femininity they learn while they are growing up. Educator Mary Williams Burgher notes that, for white women, the model of European femininity—"delicacy, innocence, and an idealized helplessness"—was seldom part of the black woman's outlook. Her African American heritage stressed strength of character and "a tenacious sense of self" as key values for women. (Burgher, 1979)

Studies have been conducted to compare body satisfaction among women in the United States and women in countries where the media do not feature the American-style images of women. For example, in Iran, Western media are banned, and women on Iranian television typically wear clothing that conceals most of the body. A study comparing the attitudes of college women in these two countries found that Iranian women scored much higher in terms of body satisfaction. Psychology researcher Daisuke Akiba at Brown

University said, "Materials promoting difficult-to-achieve body types are largely absent in Iran." (Morris, 1999) She concludes that when women are rarely exposed to these ideal and unachievable images, they are more likely to be satisfied with their own bodies.

Studies of males show that they also have concerns about their physical appearance and may feel ashamed of certain body parts, and also that they are becoming more attuned to how they look. Comparisons of various studies concluded that men polled during the 1970s were more satisfied with their bodies than a similar group of men polled in the 1980s. In a 1972 survey 15 percent of the men polled said they were dissatisfied with their overall appearance, a number that rose to 34 percent in a 1987 survey. During the 1990s, more men expressed the desire to have a more "athletic" build.

One survey reported by Judith Rodin identified three primary male worries. Like women, men worry about their weight. Male bodies tend to accumulate weight in the abdominal area, so many men complained about heaviness in that region. Hair loss and balding are also on their minds. A third area of concern was excess body hair. Social scientists noted that men were less likely to talk about their appearance than are women. Some evidence suggests that more men are suffering from eating disorders than in earlier decades. Some experts feared that the number of men suffering from eating disorders was on the rise and would increase in the twenty-first century.

Physical appearance seems to be a growing issue for men today. Images of tall, lean, muscular men increasingly appeared on magazines and other mass media. More magazines devoted to men's looks, fitness, and personal appeal are being published, and companies are developing more personal care products and cosmetics and advertising being aimed at men. Feminist author Susan Faludi devoted a book to this subject. In *Stiffed: The Betrayal of the American Man*, Faludi points out that men are increasingly being subjected to the same pressure as woman have endured for many years. Faludi

says, "Manhood is being defined by appearance, youth, attractiveness, glamor—the same traits that women have shucked off as demeaning." (Faludi, "Male-ady," 1999)

Image consultants and other people in the beauty and grooming industries have pointed out that in fast-paced societies and in large communities, people have less time to get to know each other. Thus, they are more likely to form impressions based on looks than on more substantive qualities that become evident when people become acquainted. *See also* AGING AND APPEARANCE; BEAUTY INDUSTRY (U.S.); BEAUTY STANDARDS; CRITICS OF COSMETICS INDUSTRY; FEMINISM; WEIGHT.

Further reading: American Association of University Women Educational Foundation, *Shortchanging Girls, Shortchanging America: Executive Summary* (1991); Tom Branna, "Fragrance and African-American Women," *Happi*, July 1997; Joan Jacobs Brumberg, *The Body Project: An Intimate History of American Girls* (1997); Mary Williams Burgher, "Images of Self and Race in the Autobiographies of Black Women," in Bell, et al, *Sturdy Black Bridges: Visions of Black Women in Literature* (1979); Susan Faludi, "Male-ady," *People Magazine*, 25 October 1999, 143-146; Faludi, *Stiffed: The Betrayal of the American Man* (1999); Rita Freedman, *Beauty Bound* (1986); Anne Hollander, *Black Looks: Race and Representation* (1992); Lois B. Morris, "Body Appreciation," *Allure*, September 1999, p. 98; Peggy Orenstein in association with the American Association of University Women, *SchoolGirls* (1994); Judith Rodin, *Body Traps* (1992); Roberta Pollack Seid, *Never Too Thin: Why Women Are at War With Their Bodies* (1989); Nikki Teufel, *Roseanne* show, interview with Nikki Teufel, Fox Network, 29 March 1999.

Body Odor

In many cultures, people find body odors—odorous feet or armpits, human excrement, or bad breath—objectionable and try to get rid of or mask them. They have used and continue to use both natural and manufactured products to cover up, reduce, or eliminate body odors.

Attitudes toward body odor vary among cultures in part because different races have different numbers of sweat-producing glands, called apocrine glands, located under the arms and in the anal and genital region. The odor is produced not by the secretions themselves, but by bacterial action. People of Caucasian and African heritage have more sweat glands on their bodies than Asians. Chinese and Korean peoples have the smallest number of apocrine glands; Japanese people have more apocrines than Chinese but far fewer than whites and blacks. Hence, in Japan, underarm odor has been regarded as a sign of illness, and men with this condition were excused from serving in the armed forces. (Stoddart, 1990)

Bathing was customary in many ancient cultures, as was the use of fragrances and perfumes. These practices reduced or eliminated body odors that were considered offensive in those cultures. In other cases, people used fragrance to mask them.

However, during the Middle Ages and certain other periods in history, people rarely bathed. Some people used strong perfumes to cover up body odors and the smells of unwashed clothing. They carried flowers and used different types of fragrances to scent their possessions and surroundings. Bathing became more and more common during the 1800s as developments in plumbing and soap products made bathing more convenient and comfortable.

During the twentieth century, people in certain countries, including the United States, used numerous commercial products to get rid of body odors. The most common product was soap, and certain soaps were marketed using the claim that they would freshen and deodorize the skin, eliminating body odors, as well as cleaning it. Lifebuoy soap ads made during the 1940s informed consumers that people had more than 2 million sweat glands on their bodies and that tension or excitement could cause "nervous B.O. (body odor)." A "tangy Lifebuoy daily bath" would prevent this problem, the ad claimed.

Feet

Two feet have a total of about 250,000 sweat glands and can secrete up to 8 ounces of sweat daily. In the cultures that consider foot odor troublesome, people generally wear shoes for a significant part of the day, and the shoe is an ideal environment for the bacteria that make sweat smell. In a small minority of cases, excessive foot sweating or odor may be caused by some other condition that is affecting the entire body, such as hyperthyroidism.

Although in some cultures, the natural smell of feet is considered erotic rather than offensive, in others it is viewed as a social liability. As for other forms of body odor, bathing is the first step in eliminating the condition. Cosmetics and foot care companies have also developed multiple products, including powders, sprays, and shoe inserts that the makers claim "eat" odors.

Underarm Odor

During the 1920s, new products were introduced to deal with underarm odors. Called deodorants and antiperspirants, they were formulated to kill or slow the growth of the bacteria that give sweat its odor. They may contain an astringent called aluminum sulfate, which reduces perspiration by closing the openings of the sweat glands. Antiperspirants were made to stop sweating in certain parts of the body, especially the underarms. The Odorano Company, based in Cincinnati, Ohio, sold its Odorano, the "Underarm Toilet," in both cream and liquid form to help women achieve "personal daintiness." Ads for the product claimed that underarm odor was a problem one might not notice but that it could offend other people and stain one's clothing. According to the ad, 3 million people were already using the product; they realized that "The underarm must have regular care, just as the teeth and fingernails." The ad recommended that men also use the product and offered a booklet geared to men called "Perfect Grooming Consists of More Than Cleanliness." An advertisement for "Veto" deodorant in 1948 featured a woman wearing an evening gown with captions that read: "You can say 'yes' to romance because Veto says 'no' to offending!"

Critics questioned the safety of some products. Safety concerns prompted the FDA to ban the ingredient hexachlorophene from deodorants in 1972. During the 1980s, some consumer advocates warned that the aluminum products commonly found in many deodorants and antiperspirants might also be dangerous. They pointed to the fact that high levels of aluminum were found in the brains of people who had Alzheimer's disease; however, to date, no link has been found between exposure to aluminum and Alzheimer's Disease.

Through the years, new deodorant and antiperspirant products have been introduced for men and women under various brand names. They are widely advertised in print and on television. Deodorant products can be found in roll-on, gel, aerosol, or stick form. During the 1990s, researchers found that most consumers preferred clear products that did not leave a residue on the skin. (Dunn, 1998) A 1997 study found that about 104 million American women were using underarm deodorant products. About 53 percent of that total used a stick, 27 percent used a roll-on, 10 percent used aerosol, and 7 percent used a gel. Some 92 percent of American men used underarm products: 54 percent preferred sticks; 15 percent chose aerosols, 15 chose gels, 14 percent used roll-ons and 2 percent used other types of products. (Branna, 1997)

A general trend toward "natural" products also affected the deodorant market. A nonchemical product in the form of a crystal that could be moistened and applied was sold. Companies such as Tom's of Maine offered products that were free from aluminum.

By 1998, the antiperspirant/deodorant market in the United States was well over $1 billion in sales. The leading brands included Procter & Gamble's "Secret" ($233 million in sales), Gillette's "Right Guard" ($158 million), Colgate-Palmolive's "Mennen" ($143 million), Helene Curtis's "Degree" ($130 million), and Procter & Gamble's "Sure" ($109 million). The top-selling roll-on deodorant was Chattem's "Ban." (Hickey, 1999)

Intimate Odors

Women have practiced douching—internal cleansing of the vagina for reasons of hygiene and, at least in some times and places, because they were concerned about odor. A 1928 advertisement for Zonite douche liquid in *McCall's* magazine shows a picture of a dismayed young women, with the caption "Had she only known the truth . . . earlier—about feminine hygiene," and goes on to discuss the regret and suffering that women might escape if only they were aware of this hygiene problem. In 1966, the American cosmetics industry began marketing a new line of products designed to eliminate this odor. These feminine hygiene products included deodorant sprays, new feminine douches with special scents, and deodorizers. These products purported to eliminate smells in the vaginal area. Critics claimed that these products were unnecessary and that they were another way to make women feel uncomfortable about their bodies. They also can disturb the natural chemical balance of the vagina.

By 1972, sales of feminine hygiene products had reached about $40 million a year. Hundreds of consumers, however, had reported adverse reactions, including irritated skin, rashes, infections, burning, itching, and even inflammation of the lower urinary tract, after using these products. Physicians advised women that regular bathing was enough to cleanse the vaginal area and that aerosol sprays might disturb the normal bacterial balance in that area of the body or dry out the skin. An FDA regulation went into effect in September 1977 that required warning labels on feminine deodorant sprays. *See also* BATHS; BREATH, BAD; FRAGRANCE; MEN'S PERSONAL CARE PRODUCTS.

Further reading: Tom Branna, "No Sweat," *Happi*, March 1997; Carolyn A. Dunn, "The Antiperspirant and Deodorant Market," *Happi*, March 1998; James P. Hickey, "A Market Gelling Together," *Happi*, March 1999, http://www.happi.com.special; Museum of Menstruation, "Odor," www.mum.org; D.M. Stoddart, *The Scented Ape: The Biology and Culture of Human Odor* (1990).

Body Ornamentation

Beyond body decoration involving paint, tattooing, and/or skin modification, people have also ornamented their bodies with piercings, in which they wear jewelry, some worn at all times. In traditional cultures, body piercing usually served some function or showed a person's status. In ancient Arabia, for example, young men had their scrotums pierced as a rite of passage into adulthood. Guards assigned to the imperial household in Rome wore nipple rings, which symbolized their courage and masculinity; these rings also served to hold the short capes they wore. Ancient Egyptian women of royal birth wore certain types of rings in their navels to indicate their status. Likewise, members of the upper classes in India were entitled to wear certain kinds of nose rings.

Lip piercing and nose piercing also date back to ancient times. Groups in Africa, Asia, Oceania, and South America have pierced their septa (the membrane behind the central cartilage in the nose) and inserted ornaments made from animal teeth and bones, shells, and feathers. Later, they made ornaments from precious metals and stones. Some also pierced the side of the nostril. Both men and women have worn nose ornaments, and such piercings are still popular in certain countries, such as India. Some women in parts of India may wear an elaborate hoop, several inches in diameter, adorned with metalwork and gems, on one nostril.

Certain kinds of piercings held different meanings among different peoples. The Bella Coola tribe of the northwest Pacific Coast of the United States believed that a baby's ear must be pierced or the child would not live long. Among the Arapaho Indians, pierced ears were believed to help protect children against lightning. The piercing of women's lips was also sometimes performed when they were ready to be married. Among ancient Hindus, married women had their left nostrils pierced and a heavy gold ring was placed in them. In New Guinea, male warriors had their noses pierced as a sign of manhood. The children of aristocratic Mayans were pierced in several places during infancy. Large jade

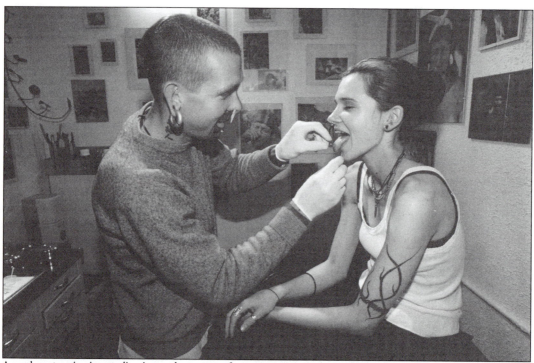

A worker at a piercing studio pierces the tongue of a customer. © *Catherine Karnow/CORBIS.*

spools were placed in their ears and lips. The nostrils and septum of their noses were also pierced, and the Classic Maya (300–900 B.C.E.) often created a beak-like sculpture on the bridge of the nose from a lump of clay or putty. Piercing of various body parts was also common in various parts of Africa and South America.

Piercings were stylish in Victorian England, the mid- to late nineteenth century. During the late 1800s, some women in Europe had their nipples pierced and wore gold "bosom rings" in each breast. Some women also wore a chain connecting the two rings. Some men of that era had a piercing called the "Prince Albert" through the head of the penis. This was done so the genitals could be bound firmly beneath their right or left pant legs at a time when men's trousers were especially tight-fitting. Many women also had their ears pierced for earrings.

Some of these practices continued into the twentieth century. At the same time, piercing became more widespread in industrialized nations. Young people in the United States and other countries, male and female, had been piercing their ears for decades and began piercing other areas, including the eyebrows, nose, breast nipples, navel, tongue, and genital organs. In the 1970s and the punk era in the 1980s, more young people pierced their bodies. By the 1980s, earrings on men had become more commonplace.

Piercing remains especially popular among young adults in their late teens and early twenties. On American college campuses, students can be seen with pierced noses (on the septum, bridge, or nostril), eyebrows, lips, necks, cheeks, chins, hand webs, and tongues. People wear various ornaments on the tongue, including rings, studs, and tongue bars. Navels, nipples, and genitals were also being pierced. Women are more likely to have their navels pierced than any other body part other than the ears.

Piercing any body part can lead to problems. Health professionals warn that these artificial holes may become infected with bacteria or viruses, including the HIV or the hepatitis virus. In a 1998 article in *Time*

magazine, dental professionals warned that tongue piercings can make people "vulnerable to cracked teeth, infection and other bodily danger." The piercing can cause the tongue to swell, which may interfere with normal breathing. Jewelry that becomes loose can cause choking. *See also* BODY DECORATION; EARS.

Further reading: Robert Brain, *The Decorated Body* (1979); Andrew Dunbar and Dean Lahn, *Body Piercing* (1999); Jean-Chris Miller, *The Body Art Book* (1997); Ronald D. Steinbach, *The Fashionable Ear: A History of Ear Piercing Trends for Men and Women* (1995); Beth Wilkinson, *Coping With the Dangers of Tattooing, Body Piercing, and Branding* (1999).

Body Paint *See* BODY DECORATION.

Body Piercing *See* BODY ORNAMENTATION.

Body Shop, The

The Body Shop was the first large cosmetics company known for its emphasis on consumer safety, fair trade, and a commitment to environmentalism. The company, which used traditional natural ingredients from around the world in many of its products, was started under a policy of "enlightened capitalism," which included using some of its profits and its commercial success to improve people's lives.

Anita Roddick, the company's founder, was born in 1944 to Italian parents who had settled in England. She became a teacher and anti-nuclear activist with strong concerns about the environment. After operating a guesthouse with her husband, Gordon Roddick, with whom she had two children, she decided to open a small cosmetics business.

In 1976, the first Body Shop store was opened in Brighton, a town in southern England. This store offered consumers a choice of 25 hair and face care products using natural ingredients, sold in five sizes. Customers were encouraged to bring the same containers back to the store for refills, thus avoiding unnecessary packaging. The business continued to grow, and by the 1990s, hundreds of Body Shops had opened world-wide. The company also has catalogue sales.

Roddick has said that beauty involves "vitality, imagination, energy, personality traits that have more to do with an individual's character than his or her age or some idealized arrangement of physical features." This approach led her to develop skin, hair, and body care products that she considers both useful and interesting, with multicultural roots. Roddick also stated that beauty products should be reasonably priced, safe to use, and not harm animals or the environment. The Body Shop shared information about how women around the world care for their bodies, and its products featured ingredients that had been used in various cultures for hundreds or thousands of years.

In keeping with the company's philosophy, the Body Shop purchases ingredients from people in developing countries who harvest and process certain ingredients. For example, members of the Kayapo tribe in Brazil provide nuts that the Body Shop uses in its Brazil Nut (hair) Conditioner.

After the business went public in 1984, the Roddicks made decisions about how to use their personal wealth to promote certain causes, including the environmental groups Greenpeace and Friends of the Earth. Roddick also worked to stop the razing of large areas of rain forest in South America. *See also* ANIMAL TESTING; CORPORATE STANDARD OF COMPASSION FOR ANIMALS; NATURAL PRODUCTS.

Further reading: The Body Shop Team, *The Body Shop Book* (1994).

Bound Feet *See* CHINA; FEET.

Bow, Clara (1905–1965)

Clara Bow, an American film star during the 1920s and early 1930s, was regarded as the original screen goddess. She personified the look of the liberated 1920s "flapper" girls.

Bow grew up in extreme poverty in Brooklyn, New York, where she was a tomboy—shunned by neighborhood girls because of her poor clothing. At age 16, the petite, auburn-haired Bow entered a movie magazine beauty contest, which won her the right to take a screen test. She was then chosen national winner and received a trophy, an evening gown, and a role in one movie.

That one movie led to many more. Between 1922 and 1933, Clara Bow made 56 films. The exuberant, wide-eyed actress was called the "It Girl" after her appearance in the film "It," which depicted her as an irresistible charmer. Women imitated her hairstyle, eye makeup, and bright red lipstick.

Bow retired in 1933, shortly after the advent of sound movies.

Further reading: Joe Morella and Edward Z. Epstein, *The "It" Girl: The Incredible Story of Clara Bow* (1976).

Brachioplasty *See* PLASTIC SURGERY.

Breasts

Women have long used cosmetics and special emollients on their breasts and have emphasized or de-emphasized them with clothing styles and foundation garments. During some eras, large breasts were regarded as a key part of female attractiveness and sexual allure; at other times, a straighter, more "boyish" silhouette has been popular.

When breasts are in fashion, women can wear garments that reveal a large portion of the breasts and also push them up, although some women have always been more willing to reveal more breast than others. At other times, such as the 1920s, women in some countries wore clothing that gave their torsos a flattened look. Western clothing styles during the 1940s and 1950s featured a well-defined waistline that highlighted the female shape by emphasizing the difference between the breast, waist, and hips. Foundation garments lifted the breasts and often had firm, pointed breast cups for emphasis.

Women have also resorted to artifice to change and particularly to enlarge their breasts. In Spain during the sixteenth and seventeenth century, women's garments compressed the breasts. Upper-class Frenchwomen of the sixteenth and seventeenth centuries massaged their breasts with herbs and had wet-nurses breastfeed their children so they could maintain small, firm breasts. During the late 1700s, clothing styles pushed the breasts together rather than keeping them separate. Styles changed again in the early 1800s when a metal device called a "divorce corset" was used to separate the breasts.

In some non-Western cultures, such as the Payagua of Paraguay, people distend the breasts to create a different look on the torso. In other less developed cultures, women may rarely cover their breasts, which at times are regarded more as functional than erotic.

Women have also used various methods to care for the skin of their breasts or to enhance the naked appearance of the nipples (for example, applying rouge) and surrounding breast tissue. Rouge has also been applied to the cleavage area, and during certain eras—late seventeenth century in England and the mid-to-late eighteenth century in the United States—women painted faint blue lines on their chests to give the appearance of translucent pale skin.

Traditional ways to moisturize breasts included oils, creams, and lotions made from ingredients found in the region. For instance, ancient Hebrews used almond oil on their skin. Women of the Taraipe tribe in Brazil have long used honey on their skin. The Magar of Nepal use apricot oil.

In earlier centuries when large breasts were fashionable, as in the nineteenth century, manufacturers identified a market for products that would purportedly enlarge or develop the bust and improve the skin on the torso. "Bore's Bust Food Cream," available by mail order in the United States for 40 cents a jar, claimed it would develop the bust and make it "firm and round." Ads for the "Vestro" method of breast enlargement appeared in American magazines and newspapers in 1899. Addressing "flat-chested and unattractive women," the ad claimed that by using this system, women could increase their bust-line by at least 6 inches.

During the mid-1900s, more sophisticated devices that purported to increase the size of the bust-line were marketed. Magazine ads for a product from Mark Eden contained testimonials by women who claimed the product had added inches to their bust-line. "Beauti-Breast of Paris," another product that purported to stimulate breast tissue and thus increase bust size, was marketed during the early 1970s. It operated by hooking up to a water faucet. The user turned the water on full blast and hooked up an electric stimulator attached to the "hydrotherapy water massage contour cups" of the device.

Critics claimed that the device caused trauma to the breasts, which led to engorgement rather than a permanent change. However, the ad featured an attractive, full-breasted blonde who claimed she had gained three inches in two weeks, which had "boosted my ego almost as much as my bust-line."

Women in the United States and other cultures are often confronted by media images of so-called ideal breasts. These images may affect their feelings about their own appearance. Studies of women's attitudes about their bodies have shown that many are not pleased with their breasts for various reasons, including size, shape, the degree of firmness, or lack of symmetry. In a 1973 poll conducted by the American magazine *Psychology Today*, 26 percent of the 62,000 readers who responded said they were "dissatisfied" with their breasts.

Breast Reshaping for Women

Women have breast surgery for three basic reasons: they think their breasts are too large; they need reconstruction following cancer surgery or some other trauma; or they want larger breasts.

Surveys such as the one cited above have found that it is much more common for women to consider their breasts too small than too large. Overly large breasts can cause back strain and other orthopedic problems. Breast reduction surgery, which became routine in the 1930s, was first considered reconstructive, and surgeons carried it out to relieve physical symptoms. Later, the purpose became more ambiguous; physicians acknowledged the physical problems, but also saw the surgery as relieving the psychological problems a girl or woman might experience from being overly buxom.

The first breast augmentation surgery was done in Heidelberg, Germany, in 1893, after a singer had had a growth removed from her breast. Because appearance was key to her profession, the surgeon reconstructed the breast using tissue from a fatty growth on her back.

Breast Implants

Although some breast augmentation surgery was done earlier, the surgical techniques were essentially developed during the twentieth century. Medical-grade liquid silicone was injected into the chest for this purpose during the 1950s. In 1965, the FDA banned the distribution of this material for use in the breasts. The agency said that liquid silicone, when injected into humans for cosmetic purposes, was a drug that had not been proved safe for this purpose. Critics of this procedure also said that injecting silicone into breast tissue might make it difficult for physicians to spot cancerous lesions growing in the breast.

After the banning of unencapsulated silicon, surgeons began using implants consisting of silicone inside a silicone shell, as well as other substances.

In April 1990, the Food and Drug Administration advised people not to use implants with polyurethane foam covers due to the risk that these implants might disintegrate and release TDA, a known carcinogen. The FDA began conducting tests of this type of implant.

According to the American Society for Aesthetic Plastic Surgery, by the 1990s, more than 130,000 women in America had breast implants each year. This figure included about 34,000 women who had breast reconstruction surgery after mastectomy (removal of a cancerous breast). Breast augmentation was the most popular form of cosmetic surgery among American women ages 19–34.

Silicone breast implants also became controversial as women claimed they experienced various complications. Some implants broke, and the silicone migrated to other areas of the body. Some women who had implants and developed certain autoimmune diseases (for example, lupus) contended that the implants had caused these problems. In 1992, the FDA (Food and Drug Administration) removed silicone implants from the market, and some women filed lawsuits against Dow-Corning, Inc., the manufacturer, contending that they had developed various diseases from the implants. The company's defense lawyers claimed that the implants did not cause the illnesses and that women who do not have implants also develop these conditions.

Both before and during the controversy over silicon, researchers were developing new types of implants. They contain saline (a salt-and-water based solution) rather than silicone, but critics maintain that the silicone shell around these saline implants is dangerous. During the 1990s, clinical studies using implants filled with soybean oil were conducted for possible future use.

Researchers continued to investigate the health consequences of silicone implants. In 1994, the Mayo Clinic conducted a study of 749 women in Minnesota who had received silicone implants. This study did not find a statistically significant connection between the implants and a connective tissue disease called scleroderma.

The lawsuits and side effects did not stop women from having the surgery. According to the National Clearinghouse of Plastic Surgery Statistics, surgeons performed 132,378 breast augmentations in the United States in 1998; during that year, they performed 32,262 breast implant removals. (However, about 68 percent of the breast surgeries performed on women 18 and younger were for the purpose of breast reduction.) The most common complication of this surgery was breast hardening, which affected about 44 percent of the women to some degree. Although plastic surgeons and implant manufacturers said that complication rates did not exceed 10 percent, public-health watchdogs and women who had problems with their implants claimed that the complication rates were much higher. They reported such problems as contractures of the breast, partial loss of sensation, implants migrating to the wrong place (such as the armpit), and various autoimmune diseases.

Other studies examined the possibility that breast cancer rates were higher among implant recipients but did not find a clear connection. Bruce Cunningham, M.D., director of the Scientific Research Committee of the American Society for Aesthetic Plastic Surgery, said that the study was good news for women who had implants. Cunningham pointed out that, "unlike previous reports, which were primarily anecdotal, this study was good science—well-designed and objective."

The debate over silicone breast implants continued during the late 1990s. Some scientists suggested that certain women might be sensitive to silicone, while others were not. Thousands of women chose to have their silicone implants removed or to replace them with saline implants during these years, rather than risk future problems.

During the late 1990s, a new kind of breast implant was developed and researched. These implants were made with a combination of saline and polyethylene glycol, commonly known as PEG. PEG is a colorless synthetic polymer that had been used safely in such products as skin moisturizers and eye drops. Implants made with this material felt more like natural breast tissue; they ruptured less often than the older implants; and PEG seemed to be completely and quickly excreted from the body if a rupture did occur. Scientists also noted that because PEG is translucent, the implants were not as likely to conceal cancer cells that might be growing in the breast. Such lesions could be detected more easily in translucent implants than in other implants during a mammogram of breast tissue.

Breast Reduction Surgery for Men

Men may have surgery to treat gynecomastia, a condition in which they develop abnormally large breasts. The condition, which may be the result of hormonal changes, the use of certain drugs or medications, and congenital problems, affects an unknown number of men. Mild cases may resolve themselves as hormones stabilize in the developing adolescent male. In extreme cases where breast size is persistently far larger than normal, surgery to reduce the breast tissue may be performed. Men may choose to have the surgery because they feel self-conscious on the beach or in other situations where their chest is exposed.
See also BODY IMAGE; IMPLANTS (COSMETIC); "LOOKS"; PLASTIC SURGERY.

Further reading: American Society for Aesthetic Plastic Surgery "Statistics" http://surgery.org/media/statistics; "Gynecomastia," University of Iowa, Department of Plastic Surgery; "Silicone Update: Safer Than You Thought?" *Longevity*, October 1994, pp. 14, 16; Sara Halprin, *Look at My Ugly Face!* (1995); "Implants, Dangerous Curves," *Mirabella*, August 1991, 104–108; Maggie Paley, "Scalpel Junkies," *Mirabella*, January 1991, 74–76; Plastic Surgery Information Service, National Clearinghouse of Plastic Surgery Statistics, "1998 Plastic Surgery Procedural Statistics," http://www. plasticsurgery.org/mediactr/trends92-98.htm; Janet Carlson Reed and Diane Guernsey, eds., "Comprehensive Guide to Cosmetic Surgery," *Town and Country*, March 1999, 144–162.

Breath, Bad

Around the world, sweet-selling or pleasant breath has been viewed with favor and methods for freshening breath and getting rid of unpleasant odors have existed for thousands of years. Many naturally occurring substances, including myrrh, cloves, and parsley have been used as breath fresheners in some cultures. In Africa, the Masai used a mixture of cow urine and ashes to eliminate bad breath. Chewing sticks were used in Mali and other Western African nations, made from bitter woods. These sticks are still sold in marketplaces. Medieval European women were advised to eat aniseed and fennel for breakfast to alleviate bad breath. Native

Americans traditionally used herbs, including sage, as did the Bedouin Arabs. Baking soda, which has a naturally deodorizing effect, was a favorite breath freshener among African Americans. Women in India may chew fennel or anise seeds after a meal.

Bad breath did not become a social problem until the company that sold Listerine mouthwash decided it was. The Lambert company ads played on people's social insecurity. One famous ad created for Listerine mouthwash contained the headline "often a bridesmaid but never a bride." The ad came out in the early 1920s and was the first time the subject of halitosis had been raised in an ad. The photo showed an attractive but weeping young woman, and the text claimed that the girl, named Edna, had the same primary ambition as any other girl "to marry." Although she was lovely and charming, she was nearing that "tragic 30-mark" and "marriage seemed farther from her life than ever." The ad went on to explain that Edna suffered from bad breath, called halitosis, which could be caused from food fermentation inside the mouth. Listerine mouthwash, said the ad, was an effective antiseptic for this problem.

Listerine was the first in a long line of anti-halitosis products. New commercial products were developed to eliminate bad breath and promote a pleasant taste and smell in the mouth. Advertisements for toothpaste, mouthwash, breath mints, and other breath-freshening products often link the use of these products to consumers' worries about offending other people or their desire to appeal to the opposite sex.

Breath mints and certain chewing gums have been promoted as ways to freshen breath. A product called Nullo contained chlorophyll, the ingredient found in green plants, and its manufacturers claimed this remedy was as safe as a vitamin pill. Clorets chlorophyll gum, widely sold beginning in the 1950s, promoted the idea of "kissing-sweet breath" in its ads. The ad invited people to do a "breath test." After first eating onions or garlic, smoking a cigar, and drinking alcohol, they were advised to chew one or two Clorets and ask a best friend to smell their breath. An ad for Certs breath mints posed the question: "If he kissed you once, will he kiss you again?"

A variety of products that claim to combat bad breath are steadily introduced and advertised to consumers. Along with mints, chewing gum, mouthwashes, and teeth-cleaning substances, there are now pills that claim to eliminate body odors and bad breath. Some of these nonmedicinal pills contain oil of parsley or parsley seed.

Researchers have concluded that bacteria in the mouth contribute to bad breath, and some products will be effective, at least temporarily, if they kill these bacteria. Careful cleansing of the mouth to remove food debris and bacteria is now regarded as a primary way to freshen breath. In China and some other Asian cultures, an implement called a tongue scraper has long been used to remove debris and bacteria that remain on that part of the mouth despite careful tooth brushing. Dentists in the United States are also now promoting tongue scrapers. *See also* BODY ODOR.

Further reading: William Stearns Davis, *Life On a Mediaeval Barony* (1932); James B. Twitchell, *Twenty Ads that Shook the World* (2000); Julian Lewis Watkins, *The 100 Greatest Advertisements, Who Wrote Them and What They Did* (1959).

"Breck Girl"

The "Breck Girl," a female model pictured in ads for Breck shampoo, became a recognized beauty symbol in the United States and Canada beginning in 1946 and extending into the 1970s. Delicate pastel paintings showing the heads of various models were featured in print ads that showcased shining, well-tended hair. For 15 years, the well-known American artist Rob Anders painted Breck girls after the company commissioned him for this work (1958–1973).

Most of the Breck models were blonde, but Anders also painted brunettes. Children and mother-daughter "Breck girls" appeared in some ads. As a child, the actress Brooke Shields was a Breck shampoo model; she was featured in a 1974 ad holding a baby doll.

Most of the 200 Breck girls were high-school age or younger. The company stopped featuring younger models in ads during the

Breck advertisement from 1951. *Breck Girls Collection, Archives Center, National Museum of American History, Smithsonian Institution.*

1970s for fear that women in the feminist movement would criticize the company for using young women to sell hair products.

Among the other celebrities who appeared in ads that lauded "beautiful hair" and "gold formula Breck" were models/actresses Jaclyn Smith, Erin Gray, Cybill Shephard, Cheryl Tiegs, and Kim Basinger.

Further reading: Charles Goodrum and Helen Dalrymple, *Advertising in America: The First Two Hundred Years* (1990).

Brinkley, Christie (b. 1955)

International supermodel Christie Brinkley was one of the best-known fashion and cosmetics models of the twentieth century. Brinkley was the only model to appear on the cover of the *Sports Illustrated* annual "Swimsuit Issue" for three consecutive years. She is known for her glowing "California blond" looks and sunny smile.

A native of California, Brinkley moved to France as a young woman to study art. While living in Paris, she caught the eye of a fashion photographer and was invited to pose for a French magazine. One modeling assignment quickly led to another, and Brinkley found herself in demand on both sides of the Atlantic. She suspended her art studies to pursue a modeling career and signed with the prestigious Ford Model Agency in New York City. Her representative on the West Coast was the Nina Blanchard Agency.

After her first *Sports Illustrated* swimsuit cover came out in 1979, Brinkley became a celebrity whose face was recognized by millions of people. She was the first model to appear on the cover a second time (1980) and again in 1981. By 1999, she had appeared on the cover of more than 500 magazines.

Brinkley's versatility and business skills led to a long, successful career. In 1981, she also became the first model featured in a *Sports Illustrated* swimsuit calendar, where she appeared in all 12 photographs. The calendar sold so well that she decided to produce her own calendars during the next two years. Brinkley set another record when she repre-

sented Cover Girl cosmetics (part of the Noxell Corporation) for 20 years.

As she pursued other interests, Brinkley came out with a line of eyewear, including sunglasses, and appeared in a hit movie, *National Lampoon Vacation*. She was also featured in a popular music video *Uptown Girl* with her first husband Billy Joel and created a vivid oil painting for the cover of Joel's 1993 recording "River of Dreams." During their 10-year marriage, Brinkley gave birth to daughter Alexa Ray Joel, the first of her three children. An accomplished horsewoman, Brinkley also won some awards for her riding skills. People who have worked with her praise her professional behavior, energy, and upbeat attitude about life. *See also* MODELING AND MODELS.

Further reading: "Classic Beauty," *Beauty Handbook*, June 1992, p. 29; Lifetime Network Biographies for Women: "Christie Brinkley."

Brown, Bobbi (b. 1957)

Bobbi Brown, a makeup artist, founded her own cosmetics company, Bobbi Brown Essentials, which specializes in natural-looking, subtle colors. Brown also advocated an efficient, "common sense" approach to makeup use that appeals to busy women and are unwilling or unable to devote much time to their appearance, yet want to look their best.

Brown grew up in Wilmette, Illinois, the eldest of three children born to a lawyer father and a homemaker mother. She became interested in cosmetics as a child, using her mother's old lipsticks and eye makeup on her dolls. In 1976, she left the University of Arizona and enrolled in Emerson College in Boston, where she pursued a major in theatrical makeup. She graduated in 1979 and worked as an assistant to a makeup artist in New York City.

As her reputation grew, Brown was hired as a makeup artist for models in photographic sessions for major fashion magazines, such as *Glamour* and *Vogue*. However, Brown was dissatisfied with the cosmetics that were available, especially the lipsticks, which she thought should look more natural in color and texture. Brown collaborated with a chemist to create lipsticks she liked better. She and Rosalind Landis, a friend who used and liked the lipsticks, worked together to market them to Bergdorf Goodman and other prominent New York stores. In 1991, Brown founded her own company. As the business grew, Landis became the president of Bobbi Brown Essentials.

Brown, a mother of three sons, settled in New Jersey where she wrote the how-to book *Bobbi Brown Beauty: The Ultimate Beauty Resource*. She continued to develop new products, including powders and foundations geared to match various skin tones and blend easily. Brown is known for formulations that have brownish tones and for avoiding undertones she considers too pink to look natural. As she developed her line, Brown also worked as a makeup artist for major fashion events and made television appearances.

In 1995, the cosmetics giant Estee Lauder purchased the cosmetics line. By 1997, Bobbi Brown Essentials was grossing $30 million a year. The company was operating stores in the United States, Canada, England, Ireland, France, Hong Kong, Taiwan, and Japan as of 1999.

Among the well-known people who patronized the company's products were members of the "Spice Girls" pop music group, television and film personality Oprah Winfrey, and the late Diana, Princess of Wales. Brown continues to work as a makeup artist for major fashion photographers, including Walter Chin, Irving Penn, and Arthur Elgort, at fashion shows, and for fashion and beauty magazine shootings. Her monthly column for *Seventeen* magazine called "Ask Bobbi" is popular with young women. In 1997, Brown was chosen as *Glamour* magazine's "Woman of the Year." Brown expresses this beauty philosophy:

"Develop your own style. Look for the traits that make you special, learn to accentuate them, and then build your personal style around them. And more than anything, strive to be positive and feel good about yourself. (Bobbi Brown Cosmetics Web site, May 2000)

Further Reading "About Bobbi," http://www.bobbibrowncosmetics.com/bobbi/bio; Sophronia Scott Gregory and Lan N. Nguyen, "Powder Broker," *People*, 7 July 1997, 91–92.

Brummell, Beau (George Bryan) (1778–1840)

Englishman George Bryan "Beau" Brummell was known for his sense of style both in his personal grooming and clothing. He was referred to as a "dandy," which came to mean, at the time, a man who was meticulous about his appearance.

After graduating from prestigious Eton College, Brummell became the intimate companion of George IV when the future king was the Prince of Wales. Among the members of the royal circle, Brummell was considered an authority on men's dress, grooming, and manners. He was also a compulsive gambler, and, in 1816, he fled to France to escape his creditors, never to return to England. Before being sentenced to debtor's prison in 1832, he was appointed to a diplomatic post. He was rescued from debtor's prison by friends, but after suffering a series of strokes, died in a mental hospital.

Brummell introduced the male fashionable world to the concepts of regular bathing, rejecting knee breeches for long pantaloons, and wearing suits of dark, monochrome shades, a trend that has lasted to the present day.

The words "Beau Brummell" are still used to denote a particular style of male appearance. For example, in 1996, an article called "Men Slowly Accept New Clothing Choices," quoted Jack Herschlag, executive director of the National Association of Men's Sportswear Buyers: "The survey [of men's clothing preferences] points to the return of the dandy, Herschlag notes. This fellow dotes on elegant, refined clothing in the tradition of Beau Brummell." (Associated Press, 8 February 1996). *See also* LOOKS.

Further reading: Associated Press, "Men Slowly Accept New Clothing Choices," 8 February 1996; Hubert Cole, *Beau Brummell* (1997); Ellen Moers, *The Dandy: Brummell to Beerbohn* (1960).

Byzantine Empire

The Byzantine Empire, centered in Constantinople (now part of Turkey), existed from C.E. 330 to 1453. Because the empire was previously the eastern half of the Roman Empire, Roman grooming practices and use of cosmetics remained influential. During the early years of the empire, men styled their hair like Roman men. They shaved their faces, except for the philosophers, who wore short beards. Men wore short straight bangs and sideburns halfway down the cheek. They wore a band of gold, sometimes with a central medallion, encircling the head.

After Roman influence waned, during the rule of Justinian (527–565 C.E.), men wore beards and mustaches and wore their hair long in the back and short on the front. Under Constantine IV (668–85 C.E.), men grew their beards long, sometimes all the way to the waist, and curled or plaited them. During his reign, Constantine V (741–75 C.E.) passed a law requiring men to shave. After the tenth century, long hair and beards came into favor once again.

Women parted their hair in the middle of the forehead and made coils up and down each side. They held it in place with gold, silver, and pearl bands or combs made from ivory or tortoiseshell. Their makeup included red rouge, worn on the lips and cheeks. Women took doses of the drug belladonna to make their pupils appear darker and rounder. Above the eyes, they plucked their eyebrows into a long straight line. Under these thin brows, women drew a black line.

Cosmetics were kept in ornate containers. A rouge pot that has survived since the sixth century was made of filigreed gold and glass. In the capital, Constantinople, wealthy and titled people wore jewelry made of gold, silver, carved ivory, and enameled designs. Earrings were often long pendants studded with gems.

People bathed often, sometimes two or three times a day, and wealthy people had their own bathhouses. Public baths were similar to those in Rome, with hot and cold pools and a steam room. Men were permitted to bathe during the days, while women could use the baths in the evening. One eleventh-century Byzantine princess surprised members of the German court when she brought the custom of bathing with her to her new home after she married a German emperor.

See also ARABIA (ANCIENT TO MIDDLE AGES); BABYLONIA; CHINA; EGYPT, ANCIENT; GREECE, ANCIENT; INDIA, ANCIENT; JAPAN; ROMAN EMPIRE.

Further reading: Tamara Talbot Rice, *Everyday Life in Byzantium* (1967); Stephen R. Lawhead and Steve Lawhead, *Byzantium* (1997).

C

Cellulite

The word *cellulite* (pronounced cell-u-leet) refers to bumpy tissue made up of fat, water, and what have been termed "toxic waste products" trapped in pockets of connective tissue just under the skin. It appears as rippled, rather than smooth, bulges on the thighs, hips, buttocks, arms, and abdomen, as well as the upper back and ankles. People who are otherwise thin or of normal weight may develop cellulite, as well as those who are overweight. Cellulite is more common in women than in men, evidently because of differences in their connective tissue. It also tends to run in families.

Studies have shown, however, that although cellulite does have a distinctive appearance, its composition is almost certainly virtually identical to that of other body fat. The subject, in fact, remains controversial in the medical community, as does the question of whether any of the various creams, tablets, or massage devices are effective.

A French dietitian has been credited with popularizing the word "*cellulite*" in 1970. Others, however, had noticed the condition much earlier. Swedish masseurs and doctors had been studying cellulite for decades and used the word *cellulite* too, as well as *panniculite* and *myocellulite* to describe lumpy, bumpy deposits right under the skin that did not respond to the usual treatments: exercise, diet, and massage. Special types of massage, along with diet and exercise, aimed at removing excess water and wastes from the body were then developed.

The American public became more aware of the existence of cellulite in the early 1970s. Nicole Ronsard, a body-shaping expert and the founder of a New York salon that specializes in cellulite treatment, published a best-selling book on the subject in 1973 (*Cellulite: Those Lumps, Bumps, and Bulges You Couldn't Lose Before*). Ronsard recommended a program she designed with three primary goals: to promote elasticity and suppleness of the connective tissue, to free substances trapped in these tissues, and to drain and remove those trapped materials.

Since these early efforts, various firms have introduced numerous products, diets, and treatments purported to reduce or eliminate the tissue. Companies continue to market creams, lotions, scrubbing mitts, and massage tools, sometimes in "cellulite kits." Hydrotherapy, herbal wraps, herbal capsules, muscle stimulators, and liposuction have also been promoted as ways to cure or lessen cellulite, and cellulite removal remains a popular subject for magazine articles. Salon operators sometimes offer massage treatments, and some dermatologists also provide treatments for cellulite.

During the 1990s, new "thigh creams" came onto the market. With these, according to the manufacturers, women could slim their stomachs and thighs and so reduce

71

cellulite effortlessly. Some manufacturers claim their products can actually dissolve fat and smooth out skin, although these claims have yet to be documented scientifically. One concern voiced by the Food and Drug Administration is that many of these thigh creams use aminophylline, used to treat asthma, and if people who have asthma use these products, they may be come "desensitized" to aminophilline, thus making it less effective as an asthma treatment.

In 1993, Ronsard published *Beyond Cellulite: Nicole Ronsard's Ultimate Strategy to Slim, Firm, and Shape Your Lower Body.* In 1998, Dr. Elizabeth Dancey's book *The Cellulite Solution* was reissued, recommending a variety of anti-cellulite strategies.

New products promoted as cellulite reducers continue to appear on the market. In 1998, the FDA approved the use of a massage tool in a procedure called Endodermologie. For best results, the manufacturer recommended 10 to 20 treatments. Herbal capsules, also introduced in the 1990s, also came on the market as cellulite reducers. The capsules, already available in Europe, started being sold in the United States in 1999. The herbs are supposed to work by improving the microcirculation right under the skin so that fat deposits are metabolized and leave the body. The manufacturer claimed that Italian women who used the treatment for a certain number of weeks got rid of cellulite deposits.

Critics say, however, that the capsules are not likely to eliminate cellulite if, as some studies have shown, the condition results from the effects of connective tissue on fat, not from fat itself. They note, too, that no product taken by mouth can affect only a specific part of the body. They contend that objective scientific studies are needed to evaluate the herbal product, as well as all other anti-cellulite treatments. Regulatory agencies in various countries are monitoring these products. *See also* LEGS; PLASTIC SURGERY.

Further Reading: Stephen Barrett, M.D. "Cellulite Removers." http://www.quackwatch.com, 7 April 2000; Paula Begoun *The Beauty Bible* (1997); Susan Bordo, *Unbearable Weight: Feminism, Western Culture, and the Body* (1993); Elizabeth Dancey, *The Cellulite Solution (1998);* Sander L. Gilman *Making the Body Beautiful: A Cultural History of Aesthetic Surgery (1999);* Elizabeth Haiken, *Venus Envy: A History of Cosmetic Surgery (1997);* Nicole Ronsard, *Cellulite: Those Lumps, Bumps, and Bulges You Couldn't Lose Before* (1973); Ronsard, *Beyond Cellulite: Nicole Ronsard's Ultimate Strategy to Slim, Firm, and Shape Your Lower Body (1993);* M. Rosenbaum, et al., "An Exploratory Investigation of the Morphology and Biochemistry of Cellulite." *Plastic and Reconstructive Surgery*, June 1998; U.S. Food and Drug Administration Center for Safety and Applied Nutrition *"Thigh Creams,"* Fact sheet, 24 February 2000.

Chanel, Coco (Gabrielle) (1883–1971)

Coco Chanel was one of the most influential modern fashion designers and the founder of a company that developed high-end cosmetics and perfumes, including the classic Chanel No. 5.

Born Gabrielle Chanel in rural Saumur, France, Chanel was raised in an orphanage after her mother died and her father abandoned the family. At age twenty, she was apprenticed to a tailor and also worked as a dance hall singer at night. Her nickname—

Gabrielle "Coco" Chanel in 1910. *Library of Congress.*

later to become her business name—came from a song she performed, "Qui Qu'a Vu Coco."

In 1910, a well-to-do lover set her up in a millinery business. Three years later, Chanel opened her first boutique, in Deauville, France, where she designed and hats, clothing, and accessories that were ingeniously suited to yachting and other sporting activities in this resort community.

Within a few years, Chanel had become known as a trendsetting designer of comfortable, elegant clothing, often made of wool jersey fabric. The Parisian couturier Poiret called Chanel's styles "Poverty deluxe" because of their simplicity. These styles suited women's changing roles and needs as they entered the workforce during World War I.

During the 1920s, Chanel created a "Total Look" for women that included accessories to go with her dresses and suits. Her designs, including trousers, were suited to women's increasingly active lives. She was also a leading designer of what became known as "the little black dress," a versatile garment that women could adapt for many occasions by changing accessories. Chanel's introduction of black garments for everyday use was revolutionary; black had previously been worn only for funerals or by people in mourning. Chanel's trademark accessories included sling-back pumps, a handbag with a gold chain handle, and multiple strands of pearls, often worn with gold or jeweled chains.

Chanel affected style not only through her clothing designs but also with her personal taste. Women did frequently copy her clothing, but they also adopted her hairstyles and mannerisms. For example, when Chanel was photographed with a suntan, tanned skin became more popular, breaking the long-standing beauty standard of delicate pallor.

In 1921, Chanel became the first couturier to launch a signature perfume. She worked with chemist Ernest Beaux, who had been devising ways to use aldehydes in scents. When he brought her a batch of numbered sample fragrances, Chanel chose the one labeled "5" and it became Chanel No. 5, one of the most successful fragrances in history. The fresh, modern scent contained jasmine and rose and several woodsy ingredients, such as sandalwood and vetiver—some 130 ingredients in all. Its scent lingered longer than those of other perfumes of the time.

Five years later, the designer introduced her Chanel No. 21, another Beaux creation, this time a perfume with a strong floral scent and citrus and fruity notes. Both scents came in simple bottles that echoed Chanel's fashion philosophy. Sales of Chanel No. 5 remained high decade after decade. During the 1950s, actress Marilyn Monroe gave the company more publicity when an interviewer asked her what she wore to bed. She replied simply, "Chanel No. 5."

Chanel's multifaceted business grew steadily, and by 1935, she employed nearly 4,000 people. She retired from the business during World War II but returned in the late 1940s with new, streamlined designs, including the Chanel suit, with its braid-trimmed, collarless jacket.

Although her romances were legion, Chanel was married only to her career. She was still working on new designs when she died in 1971. Sales dropped in the company's couture division after her death, but designer Karl Lagerfeld revived the business when he took over in the 1980s and created designs that often appealed to younger women.

The company Chanel founded continues to produce clothing and accessories, fragrances (including the successful Cristalle and Coco), color cosmetics, and skin care products. *See also* FRAGRANCE; PERFUME.

Further reading: Claude Delay (Barbara Bray, trans.) *Chanel Solitaire* (1973); Alice Mackrell, *Coco Chanel* (1992); Annette Tapert and Diana Edkins, *The Power of Style* (1994).

Charm Schools (U.S.)

During the 1920s, institutions known as charm schools began operating in the United States. The schools were designed to teach adolescent girls how to increase their feminine charm through grooming, makeup, appropriate attire, good manners, and a generally pleasing demeanor. As girls or adult women improved their appearances and developed social skills, they would become "ladylike," cultured, and attractive.

The intent of this training, whether stated explicitly or not, was to make the girls more ladylike and socially presentable.

The number of such programs increased steadily in the late 1940s and early 1950s, and they continued in various forms into the 1960s. Health classes for girls in high junior and senior high school also covered matters of grooming and hygiene. In addition to independent charm schools, other institutions—schools, department stores, girls' clubs, 4-H clubs, and such women's organizations as the Young Women's Christian Association (YMCA) sponsored classes in beauty, grooming, and etiquette.

Among the women who attended these classes were immigrants and upwardly mobile women. Some courses culminated in fashion shows, teas, or dances so that women could show off their new appearance and social skills.

Magazines for women and companies that made cosmetics and toiletries became involved in this activity by publishing booklets on grooming, makeup application, and charm. Some of these materials were used in high school and college home economics courses. Grooming and beauty classes became part of the freshman courses for young women at various colleges.

Many charm schools offered potential clients a free consultation, evaluating their hairstyles, figures, makeup, clothing, and other personal attributes. Clients who wished to take the course then paid to attend classes.

Some companies or organizations sent their employees to charm schools or beauty classes. During the 1940s, members of the All-American Girls Professional Baseball League (AAGPBL) received instruction on hair styling, makeup, posture, and etiquette so that the public would view female athletes as "feminine" and well mannered. Airline stewardesses (forerunners of today's flight attendants) also often completed a charm school program as part of their training. Modeling agencies ran their own programs or sent their models to specific classes designed to help them polish their appearances. Other charm school clients included women who hoped to win beauty contests or pursue careers in the entertainment industry.

Recent decades have brought new versions of charm schools and they cater to both men and women. Modeling schools continue to operate classes where people can learn techniques to improve their personal appearance, posture, and etiquette, and also choose the most flattering clothing styles. *See also* MODELING AND MODELS.

Further reading: Lois W. Banner, *American Beauty* (1983);Diana Helmer, *Belles of the Ballpark* (1993); Sue Macy, *A Whole New Ballgame* (1993).

Chemical Peels

Chemical peels are skin treatments in which a chemical solution is applied to the face or portions of the face, usually around but not on the eye and mouth areas, as well as other parts of the body (for example, neck or hands). The treatment peels away the top layers of skin, which causes the regeneration of new, smoother skin, thus reducing fine lines and wrinkles. The new skin is also usually more even in color and looks like the skin of a younger person. Face peels of various types have been used since the early decades of the twentieth century.

Today's peel solutions may contain alpha hydroxyl acids (AHAs), lactic acids, glycolic acid, phenol, or trichloracetic acid. The solutions differ in strength and penetrate to different depths, and so cause effects that vary. Initially, only plastic surgeons and dermatologists carried out skin peeling procedures. Now they are done by nonmedical professionals, although beauty experts advise people to have the treatment done by a physician or other highly trained professional. After the procedure, the skin is typically red and sensitive and requires time to heal completely. Complications may occur, too; the skin may be discolored or colored unevenly. Patients must remain out of the sun for a specified period of time because their skin is hypersensitive during the healing process.

Chemical peels have become increasingly popular. Women who want to reduce signs of aging on their skin but are not ready for a surgical face-lift sometimes choose this less invasive procedure. The effects are not permanent, but some people may nevertheless elect to repeat the procedure.

Many women opt for a less drastic approach to maintaining a youthful skin texture by using products that contain alpha hydroxyl acids in lower concentrations (AHAs). These products cause the shedding of surface skin, or exfoliation. They are marketed to improve skin texture and tone, as well as to unblock pores and improve acne. The extent of exfoliation depends on the concentration of AHAs in the product; most over-the-counter creams have concentrations of up to 10 percent. The FDA suggests that products with a concentration of 20 percent or higher be used by cosmetologists for "mini-peels."

Both the FDA and consumer groups have raised concerns about AHA products because they make the skin more sensitive to the effects of sunlight. The federal agency recommends that AHA users always wear a sunscreen when going outside. In two studies completed in 2000, the agency reported that using AHA on the skin did increase the number of "sunburn" cells as well as decreasing the amount of time it took for skin exposed to sunlight to become red. The studies also showed, however, that the skin will react normally within a week of discontinuing AHA use. (FDA, 7 March 2000)

See also PLASTIC SURGERY; SKIN.

Further reading: American Society for Dermatologic Surgery, Information sheets. (Schaumburg, IL, 1999); Paula Begoun, *The Beauty Bible* (1997); Elizabeth Haiken, *Venus Envy: A History of Cosmetic Surgery* (1997); David J. Leffell, M.D., *Total Skin* (2000); Nicholas Perricone, M.D., *The Wrinkle Cure* (2000); U.S. Department of Health and Human Services, "Skin Peelers," updated 30 March 2000; U.S. Food and Drug Administration, *Alpha Hydroxy Acids in Cosmetics,* 24 February 1998. U.S. Food and Drug Administration, *FDA Completes Two Clinical Studies on the Safety of Alpha Hydroxy Acid,* 7 March 2000.

China

More than 4,000 years ago, the Chinese became the first people to use cosmetics strictly for personal adornment. Their skin care routine was elaborate and included nightly treatments with tea oil and rice powder. Women normally wore heavy makeup as a part of dressing, and they regarded a pale complexion as ideal.

Fragrances were used on the body and hair. Chinese women wrapped flowers into their bun-style hairdos, causing the scent to linger around them for hours. After bathing carefully, they applied perfumed oils to their bodies.

Women in the upper classes followed the changing fashions in cosmetics and grooming. Each had her own cosmetic container with compartments that held her face powder, cheek color, and pigments for drawing on eyebrows after they plucked their own. From ancient through medieval times (C.E. 300–1300), women used white lead and rice powders to make the face and shoulders pale. Women also used rouge made from cinnabar and safflower to tint their lips and cheeks.

Men and women in ancient China paid particular attention to their hair. Both genders wore ornaments and fancy hairpins. Men shaved their heads except at the very top, which they let grow long and then twisted on top of their heads in a knot (topknot). They then adorned the knot with gold hairpins. Women wore jeweled gold crowns with little bells hanging from the edges.

Women painted their eyebrows with blue, black, or green grease. During the second century B.C.E., the Chinese favored brows with sharp-pointed arches. That style gave way to brows with curved arches. In the late Han period(202 B.C.E. to C.E. 220), women wore "sorrow brows"(possibly causing them to appear to have a sorrowful expression on their faces), while those of the T'ang period (C.E. 618–907) wore a brow design called "distant mountains." The designs were drawn onto foreheads tinted yellow with pigment that was brought from Cambodia.

As trade gradually brought more outsiders to China (although not Europeans until

Marco Polo in 1275), these visitors from other lands brought new ideas, including ones about fashion and cosmetics. During the eighth century, fashionable women adopted styles from Turkey and Iran. Court ladies wore a style called the *Uighur* chignon, which came from the Middle East. During the T'ang Dynasty, wealthy women favored a hair ornament called a *buyao*. The Empress wore golden buyaos surrounded with flowers and birds, all attached to a wig, when in full ceremonial dress.

Ancient Chinese tales celebrated women of great beauty. Three of the most famous beauties are Xiang Fei, Yang Kuei-fei, and His Shih. In some cases, legendary femme fatales, such as Daji, a princess who lived during the dynasty known as both Shang and Yin (1523–1027 B.C.E.) were said to have bewitched rulers and brought down kingdoms.

During the thirteenth century, wealthy women in Peking applied a thick paste called the "Buddha adornment" to their faces each winter to keep their complexions smooth. When spring came, they removed the hardened paste. Women in southern China enhanced their looks with white powder, called *meen-fung,* and applied reddish color to the lips, cheeks, nostrils, and tongue. Most women plucked their eyebrows and drew on new ones with a pronounced arch, using pencil or charcoal. Women abstained from makeup on two occasions: when they were in mourning and on their wedding day.

Chinese of both genders also carefully groomed their hands. Upper class Chinese men and women grew very long fingernails as a sign that they never needed to use their hands to work. Servants cared for these extremely long nails, which were often adorned with jewels or gold coverings.

Bound Feet

One of the best-known "beauty" traditions in China was bound feet. For more than a thousand years, the Chinese considered tiny feet essential to female beauty. The origins of this practice are unclear, but apparently started because temple dancers and courtesans generally had small feet that were considered beautiful, and women wanted to emulate them. Another possibility is that they wanted to resemble an empress of the Shang or Yin Dynasty, who was born with clubfeet (a birth defect) or because people were enamored with a Chinese court dancer (circa C.E. 900) who had unusually small feet. A ruler of Nant'ang had a dancing girl with bound feet who danced gracefully on a six-foot-high golden lily adorned with pearls and jewels.

To acquire this look, women began to force their feet into smaller and smaller shoes. Through the years, people began to bind the feet of female children at about age three so that although the rest of the girl would grow, her feet could not develop properly and remained small, although deformed. The process of foot binding was painful, as the four small toes on each foot were bent under the sole and tied in place with tight figure-eight bandages. As the child's foot bones tried to grow, the arch was bent upwards, and the heel and toes were pushed together. Binding broke the instep. Sometimes the flesh trapped beneath the bandages rotted because of the lack of circulation.

The tiny, bound foot was called a "golden lotus" or "little dumpling" and was considered extremely desirable and sexually alluring. Fang Hsien of the Manchu dynasty (1644–1912) wrote a book about foot-binding and described the ideal bound foot as fat, soft, and elegant, saying, ". . . fat feet are full and smooth to the touch, soft feet are gentle and pleasing to the eye, and elegant feet are refined and beautiful." (Yutang, 1939)

The result for the woman was less pleasing, although they too subscribed to this standard of "beauty." Walking on these stumps was painful and kept women housebound and often secluded. Many women who had endured foot-binding became so crippled they could not even walk upright and were forced to crawl as they grew older (see photo, page 120).

The pain notwithstanding, however, a girl was not considered marriageable unless she had small feet (three to four inches was considered the ideal). A man could annul his marriage if he discovered that his wife had led him to believe that her feet were less than five inches long, and they turned out to be larger. Often beginning in childhood, girls continuously wore tiny, pointed slippers that showed off their small, seldom used feet. Before they were married, they spent hours embroidering delicate shoes and slippers for their trousseau.

The fixation with tiny feet extended to Chinese brothels, in which women stood behind screens that revealed only their shoes. Male clients could pick the girl with the smallest feet. Beauty contests called "tiny foot festivals" were held in China.

As China became less closed to the rest of the world, people in other countries took note of the curious custom. In 1887, British newspapers described the feet of Madame Kuo ta jen, the wife of the Chinese ambassador to England, after she allowed a brief glimpse of her feet, which were wrapped in blue silk. A reporter called her the "Tottering Lily" and said the feet were about the size of "a lady's doubled fist."

By the early 1900s, Chinese officials began to take steps to stop the custom. In 1928, the government outlawed foot-binding throughout China.

Twentieth Century

During the early twentieth century, women continued to use rice powder as a popular cosmetic and to wear their hair in traditional upswept styles. Gradually, with advances in communication and more outsiders, they became more aware of western styles.

In the early 1900s, the Chinese began manufacturing a cream called "Royal Concubine Radiant Beauty Cream." Now made in the People's Republic of China, the cream has been popular since it was introduced. It contains ingredients women in China have used for centuries on their skin, including pulverized white jade, pearl powder, and ginseng.

The Chinese Revolution, which ended with the formation of the People's Republic of China in 1949, changed attitudes toward grooming and appearance among both men and women. Revolutionaries emphasized

The Chinese Fakien custom of triangular hairpins was banned in the 1920s. Traditionally, the pins and darts used to keep the style in place were originally used as self-defense weapons. *Archive Photos.*

simplicity in dress and personal grooming, and it was the collective, not the individual, that mattered. Communist leaders regarded cosmetics as a part of a materialistic culture and found them incompatible with their values. They praised people who practiced a natural look that allowed them to focus on their work and community service.

In the 1990s, as some aspects of Chinese life became more relaxed, men and women began to show more diversity in hairstyles and clothing. Chinese women are using more cosmetics and grooming products, and several successful companies in China produce and sell these products there and in other countries. *See also* ASIAN MARKETS (MODERN); HAIR, STYLING OF; HANDS; KAN, YUE-SAI.

Further reading: Rita Freedman, *Beauty Bound* (1986); David Frye, Nancy Frye, and Alan Okagaki, *Consumer's Guide to Cosmetics* (1979); Roy Genders, *The History of Scent* (1972); Howard S. Levi, *Chinese Footbinding* (1966); J.A.G. Roberts, *A Concise History of China* (1999); "The Sleeping Giant Awakes," *Soap, Perfumery & Cosmetics,* May 1997; Jonathan D. Spence, *The Chan's Great Continent: China in Western Minds* (1998); Lin Yutang, *My Country and My People* (1939).

Cleopatra (69–30 B.C.E.)

Cleopatra, queen of Egypt from 51 to 30 B.C.E., was renowned for her physical charms and ability to attract powerful men, as well as for her political skills, intelligence, and learning.

Cleopatra's beauty is legendary, as is her skill as a seductress. Her beauty routines, as recorded by contemporary historians, included staining her nails with henna, bathing in goat's milk, using bear grease to groom her hair, and wearing a personal perfume that contained sandalwood, patchouli, woodrose, myrrh, and other ingredients. Cleopatra used this mixture in incense, potpourri, and to scent her clothing and rooms. Like other Egyptian women, she probably also enhanced her eyes with kohl, derived from a powder of the mineral antimony.

In the end, neither her beauty nor her intelligence saved her, but she made ample use of both during her life. When she was 17, in 51 B.C.E., her father, Ptolemy XII, died and she ascended the throne as Cleopatra VII, ruling jointly with her 12-year-old brother Ptolemy XIII. Her brother, however, followed the suggestion of his advisors and exiled her.

Cleopatra managed to find her way back, an enterprise in which her beauty probably helped. Although Egypt had its royalty, the country was then under the control of Rome, and when the Roman ruler Julius Caesar came to Alexandria in 48 B.C.E., Cleopatra contrived to meet him. They became lovers, and she gave birth to his son, whom she named Ptolemy Caesar. Caesar helped her to amass an army that overthrew the Egyptian rulers (her brother), and he declared Cleopatra queen of Egypt in 47 B.C.E. The next year, she went to Rome, where Caesar gave her a villa and royal status. He had a golden statue of Cleopatra made and placed in the Temple of Venus as a tribute to her beauty.

Caesar was assassinated in 44 B.C.E., however, and Cleopatra returned to Egypt and ruled jointly with her young son, Ptolemy XIV Caesar (Caesarion). She later married another Roman, Marc Antony, and bore twins. The Roman emperor, Octavion, declared war on both Cleopatra and Antony. They lacked the military strength to triumph over him, and both chose death over defeat. Although accounts have been highly romanticized, historians generally agree that Antony died after he stabbed himself in the abdomen (or fell on his sword, in the usual dramatic description), and Cleopatra committed suicide by snakebite using an asp, or Egyptian cobra.

Cleopatra's image survives today. Paintings and other depictions of the Egyptian queen show her with elaborate eye makeup that Egyptian women of that era typically wore. The 1962 film *Cleopatra*, starring actress Elizabeth Taylor, may have been partly responsible for the renewed interest in dramatic eye makeup that took place around that time, including dark eyeliner and thick mascara.

Because the name "Cleopatra" symbolizes glamour and allure, it has often been used in advertisements for various beauty products. The Palmolive Company, for example, claimed that Cleopatra used palm oil, which was part of their soap formula, on her skin. Pictures of the Egyptian queen have also appeared on labels and containers for perfumes and eye-makeup, some of which were named after her. *See also* EGYPT, ANCIENT.

Further reading: Michael Foss, *The Search for Cleopatra* (1997); John Romer, *Valley of the Kings* (1981); Sir John Gardner Wilkinson, *The Manners and Customs of the Ancient Egyptians* (1878).

Colgate-Palmolive Company

Colgate-Palmolive Company is a major producer and distributor of personal grooming and health care products, as well as other items. The $9-billion-dollar-a-year-in-sales company is based in New York City, where it got its start in 1806.

William Colgate, a soap and candlemaker, ran a store in New York City on Dutch Street, where he sold starch, candles, and soap. Today it operates in 200 countries in Asia, Europe, and North and South America.

During the 1860s, Colgate introduced perfumed soap and also manufactured perfumes. The company produced the first milled perfumed toilet soap, "Cashmere Bouquet," in 1872. The company also began making dental products, offering a scented toothpaste in jars in 1873. By 1896, the paste was packaged in collapsible tubes. In 1908, Colgate introduced the first modern toothpaste in a tube, called Colgate Ribbon Cream. By then, the company was making hundreds of kinds of perfumes and 160 kinds of toilet soap.

Colgate & Company merged with the Palmolive-Peet Company in 1928. Palmolive-Peet grew from a soap company that the Peet brothers started in Kansas City, Kansas, in 1872. This company joined the B.J. Johnson Soap Company, which had developed the formula for its Palmolive soap in 1898. Palmolive became the best-selling soap in the world. One popular ad for the soap claimed that it would give users "That Schoolgirl Complexion." The ingredients included palm oil and olive oil.

The company continued to grow, with sales reaching $100 million in 1939. In 1953, the company was renamed Colgate-Palmolive. Sales passed the $1 billion mark in 1967. During the next 20 years, Colgate-Palmolive offered new dental care products, including fluoridated toothpaste (1968) and Ultra-Brite, a cosmetic toothpaste designed to brighten teeth. The company also introduced its "Irish Spring" deodorant soap. Another innovative product, Colgate Winterfresh gel toothpaste, was introduced in 1981.

The company added to its deodorant line in 1992 when it acquired Mennen Company, known for its successful stick deodorant/antiperspirants and Baby Magic products.

Among Colgate-Palmolive's largest community projects is the "Bright Smiles, Bright Futures" health education program, which has expanded to include 50 countries and more than 35 million children. The program provides materials for teachers and students in preschools and elementary schools with activities, quizzes, and games about dental health. It also has online activities through the company's home page on the Internet. *See also* BATHS; BEAUTY INDUSTRY; SOAP; TEETH.

Further reading: "Our History," "When It Happened," and "Kids' Place" from Colgate-Palmolive http://www.colgate.com/html

Collagen Injections *See* IMPLANTS (COSMETIC).

Colognes, Men's *See* FRAGRANCE.

Color Additive Amendments *See* LAWS AND REGULATIONS (U.S.).

Color Additives

Coloring agents, or color additives, have been used in cosmetics as far back as 5000 B.C.E. Then, as now, coloring agents were used to tint products to make them more appealing to people or as primary ingredients in cosmetics that added color to the face and body, in some cases for adornment and in others for ritual face or body painting.

The first colorants used in cosmetic pigments were derived from nature—from plants and minerals. Turmeric and saffron, with their reddish-brown hues, both were used as coloring agents. Cosmetics makers—or women themselves—continued to use these substances and others into modern times.

During the 1800s, chemists developed processes that allowed them to create a greater range of colors from different sources and to create synthetic dyes. The colors could be produced more cheaply and easily.

Some of the colors used in the late 1800s contained poisonous substances such as arsenic and were unsafe if used improperly or in excess. Arsenic is a naturally occurring substance known to be poisonous; at the same time, however, artificial coloring agents used at the turn of the century were not tested for safety. Some chemically synthesized colors that were used in the early 1900s contained aniline, derived from petroleum, and known to have toxic effects in its pure form.

Cosmetic chemists today still derive modern color additives from petroleum (coal-tar dyes, now with toxic substances removed), minerals, plants, and animals. Laws in the

United States and other countries state that government agencies must approve substances used to color foods, medications, cosmetics, and medical devices. In the United States, when medical professionals or consumers report possible health problems from a particular coloring agent, the Food and Drug Administration investigates the allegations.

Americans use and consume color additives constantly. They are part of personal grooming products and cosmetics, including deodorant, shampoos, toothpaste, mouthwash, lipstick, eyeliner, mascara, body lotion, and cologne. *See also* HAIR COLOR; FACE; LAWS AND REGULATIONS (U.S.); SKIN COLORING AGENTS.

Further reading: John Henkel, "A Colorful History," *FDA Consumer*, December 1993; Henkel, "From Shampoo to Cereal: Seeing the Safety of Color Additives," *FDA Consumer*, December 1993; U.S. Food and Drug Administration Center for Food Safety and Applied Nutrition, "Color Additives," Office of Cosmetics Fact Sheet, 7 February 1995.

Consumer Product Safety *See* SAFETY.

Consumer Protection *See* LAWS AND REGULATIONS (U.S.); SAFETY.

Contests

Beauty contests, or pageants, in which people are judged on the basis of physical appearance and named "best-looking," "most handsome," or "most beautiful," date back to ancient times. Some historians cite the Greek myth in which Paris gives a golden apple to Aphrodite, choosing her as the most beautiful goddess because she promised him the most beautiful woman in the world, as the earliest known version of a beauty contest. May Day celebrations, local festivals, fairs, carnivals, expositions, and athletic contests often included a parade or contest to choose a queen or other female standard-bearer, who might play a special role in the events or simply be admired by the spectators.

According to the historian Michel Chevalier, festival queens have served to symbolize community ties and fruitfulness, especially at sports events. Other historians point out that beauty contests provide a way to promote certain traditional ideas about women's roles and to reward women who pursue beauty and try to please men rather than competing with men in other areas of life.

Beauty Contests in the United States
The first organized annual beauty contests in America were probably the selections of Mardi Gras queens in New Orleans, a tradition that began during the 1600s. Circus impresario P.T. Barnum is credited with organizing the first modern beauty contests during the 1850s. He invited women throughout the United States to send photographs of themselves. The winner would receive a diamond tiara if she was married or, if she was single, a dowry. Barnum got only a small response to his invitation mainly because most Americans thought that displaying women's bodies that way was immoral and immodest. In 1888, however, another circus owner, Adam Forepaugh, received more than 11,000 photographs from women who wanted to be chosen as his "$10,000 Beauty" and star in a dramatic spectacle that he planned to produce. The winner was a chorus-girl-turned actress, Louise Montague. (Banner, 1983)

By the twentieth century, beauty contests had become a regular feature of carnivals and regional fairs. In subsequent years, newspapers, magazines, and beauty product companies also sponsored beauty contests, which became more structured and elaborate.

Beauty contests in the United States were segregated by race. In response, in 1914, the *New York Age* newspaper sponsored a beauty contest for African American women. When the first Miss America pageant was held in 1921, the national Miss Bronze contest was organized for women of color, and the first Miss Bronze title was awarded in 1927. A Miss Black America Pageant was also organized and held annually. Racial and ethnic groups continued to hold pageants and contests when their members were excluded from contests or when those contests gave preferential treatment to white women. New pageants, such as the Miss Black Swimwear contest, expanded opportunities to showcase African American beauty.

By the 1930s, more contests were being held in towns and cities across the country, including schools, where students might vote on "queens" and "kings" for various athletic events and formal dances, including the annual proms. In some schools, student bodies also voted on the most attractive or beautiful student(s) in the class. The bestowal of beauty titles to attractive women contestants was a stock feature at American events ranging from automobile shows to the Rose Bowl football game. Such contests were also popular around the world and could help a young woman develop a career as a model, actress, or performer. For example, after she appeared in an Italian beauty contest, a judge encouraged Sophia Loren to have a screen test, which led to her successful acting career. Actress-singer Cybill Shepherd won a Model of the Year beauty contest before embarking on her successful acting career. Former Miss Miss Americas Mary Ann Mobley, Lee Meriweather, and Phyllis George also went on to careers in show business.

Various companies also sponsored beauty contests to promote their products. Manufacturers of soaps, such as Woodbury and Dove, and face-cream manufacturers were among the sponsors of contests to select women with beautiful skin who used their products.

By 1999, more than 80,000 pageants were being held annually in the United States alone.

Teen Contests

The number of beauty contests for teenagers in the United States also increased after the 1950s. The Miss Universe organization had sponsored the Miss Teen-USA pageant for decades. Other teen pageants were America's Junior Miss, Miss National Teenager, Miss Teenage America, Miss United Teenager, and Miss American Teenager. Teen pageants often included talent competitions and emphasized a contestant's academic achievements, extracurricular activities, and community service. Observers of local beauty contests for teenagers near the end of the twentieth century noted that contestants are more diverse, representing more of the different races and ethnic groups in America, and that contestants often show individuality in their clothing and personal style.

Beauty Contests in Other Countries

By the 1990s, national beauty pageants were being held in most countries around the world. The People's Republic of China instituted an annual competition for men and women. There was no swimsuit event. Contestants, who were judged on their patriotism and knowledge of history and politics, were awarded the title of Miss Canton and Mr. Canton. However, some governments expressed negative attitudes toward beauty contests. In 1992, officials in Canada announced that there would be no national sponsorship of beauty contests in the future because these events were considered demeaning to women. Contests in Canada are still held for contestants of different ages. They are sponsored by corporations and organizations, sometimes aiming to promote tourism. The first Miss Moscow contest was held in 1988, two years before the breakup of the Soviet Union.

International Contests

International beauty contests have competitors and winners representing many different races and ethnic groups. They include specialty contests, such as the "Miss Hawaiian Tropic International" title, and larger-scale pageants, such as "Miss World," held in London, "Mr. World," "International Modeling and Talent Association Male and Female Models of the Year Awards,' and the "Miss Universe Pageant," held in the United States. The winner of the Miss USA pageant, held each April, represents the United States at the Miss Universe pageant in July along with national winners from all over the world.

Miss Universe is one of the largest and most elaborate international pageants. Unlike the Miss America pageant, which is non-profit, the Miss Universe organization is a for-profit business. It was first held in 1952 and was sponsored by Catalina, a swimsuit manufacturing company. Catalina had been a major sponsor of the Miss America Pageant but left that event in 1951 after the winner that year, Yolande Betbeze, refused to pose for photographs in a swimsuit because she wished to emphasize her singing talents rather than behave as a pin-up.

In 1996, business mogul Donald Trump bought the Miss Universe organization for $10 million, sold half of it to CBS (Columbia Broadcasting Company) and hired an accountant, Maureen Reidy, as president. Reidy worked hard to gain prominent sponsors and enhance the fashion appeal of the pageant.

In 1998, Miss Universe was Wendy Fitzwilliam, Miss Trinidad and Tobago, and the pageant was held in Hawaii. The cost of putting on the pageant was estimated at between $8-$10 million. Reidy said of the pageant: "It's all about health and fitness. It's not about being tall or thin. It's not about perfect measurements. And we do not encourage plastic surgery." (Bussmiller, 1999, 29)

In recent years, some of the contestants competing in international pageants have come from countries that previously criticized these kinds of events as frivolous and demeaning to the idea of equality between the sexes. Among the nations that began taking part in the Miss Universe Pageant during the 1980s and 1990s were Cuba, Russia, Bulgaria, and the People's Republic of China.

Other Competitions

Different competitions feature African Americans and Asian Americans. The Miss Mundo Latino International Pageant is the analogous competition for Latina women.

In still other pageants, the contestants are older women or women that belong to specific groups. The Mrs. America Pageant debuted in 1938 in Palisades Park, New Jersey, and continues today.

Mother-Daughter pageants, pageants for grandmothers, and pageants for models or other professions are among the other beauty contests held.

Contests to choose new models are also held. The Coppertone Company, maker of tanning products and other products to use in the sun, sponsors a Coppertone Model Search. The three finalists of this annual contest receive modeling assignments and are featured in ads in *Cosmopolitan* and other magazines.

Some of the newer competitions are for petite women, plus-size women, senior citizens, and married couples. Other contests include the Miss Wheelchair America Pageant, the Miss Deaf Virginia Pageant, and the Miss Rodeo Kansas Pageant. A parody of beauty contests, called the "Miss Ugly Contest," is also held annually in the United States.

A winner of a "Hunk of the Year" contest, a competition for men. ©*Stewart Mark/Globe Photos, Inc.*

Magazines and other media have conducted surveys in which readers select the most beautiful or handsome celebrities. An annual feature of *People* magazine is "The 50 Most Beautiful People in the World." The same magazine names a "Sexiest Man Alive" and runners-up each year. Winners of this title have included actors Mel Gibson, Tom Cruise, Denzel Washington, Brad Pitt, Richard Gere, and the late John F. Kennedy Jr., son of the late President John F. Kennedy and founder of *George* magazine.

Contests for Men and Boys

Men's contests, which include Mr. America, Mr. Universe, Mr. Olympia, and other such competitions as "Hunk of the Year," are not like women's beauty pageants. Rather, they focus the results of body building and strength. Appearance matters in the sense that the competitors go through a series of standard poses, followed by a short routine of poses that each competitor choreographs. There are also pageants for young boys, including the "All American Girl and Boy," "All Star Kids," "Tropical Kids," and "Universal Master." *See also* CONTESTS, CHILDREN'S; MISS AMERICA PAGEANT.

Further reading: Lois W. Banner, *American Beauty* (1983); Elisabeth Bussmiller, "Ms. Universe," *Equity,* February 1999, 29-30; Frank Deford, *There She Is* (1971); John L. Jennings, *Theatrical and Circus Life* (1882); David Levinson and Karen Christensen, ed., "Bodybuilding," *The Encyclopedia of World Sport from Ancient Times to the Present* (1997); John William Ward, ed., *Society, Manners, and Politics in the United States* (1961).

Contests, Children's

Beauty contests, (or pageants, as their organizers prefer to call them) became increasingly common during the late twentieth century, particularly in the United States. Thousands of children's contests are held at local, regional, and national levels and are most common in the southern United States. Pageants are held for babies as well as for older children and for both boys and girls.

The first organized, large-scale American children's beauty pageant was "Little Miss Universe," held in Miami in 1960. During that decade, interest in pageants rose following the first televised broadcast of the Miss America Pageant in 1954. Watching the pageants at home, many girls imagined that they might grow up to be Miss America, too. Children's dolls featured beauty pageant outfits that included gowns, chest banners, tiaras, and sceptres.

Other well-known children's pageants, all held annually, include Our Little Miss, Little Miss La Petite, the Universal/Southern Charm National Pageant, and The Sunburst International Pageant.

In many pageants, young girls wear elaborate dresses and accessories, pantyhose, makeup, false eyelashes, and hair extensions. Some parents color their children's hair. They may hire special consultants, clothing designers, and makeup artists to help them prepare

A mother kisses her daughter, who has won a children's beauty pageant in South Africa. © *David Turnley/CORBIS.*

for the pageants. Pageant organizers earn money from the fees the entrants pay and from sponsors and business advertisers.

Critics claim that such contests have many negative effects on children. Children learn to focus too much on their appearance, they contend, and place too much importance on their looks and how they compare to others. They may also spend too much time competing and preparing for contests instead of focusing on the usual activities of childhood. Opponents of the contests also warn that children who lose these competitions may develop low self-esteem. In addition, critics oppose letting children perform sexually provocative talent routines and say they should not be encouraged to wear makeup or sophisticated clothing and accessories at such a young age. *See also* CONTESTS; MISS AMERICA PAGEANT.

Further reading: Lise Hilboldt-Stolley, "Pretty Babies," *Good Housekeeping*, February 1999, p. 102ff.

Corporate Standard of Compassion for Animals

The Corporate Standard of Compassion for Animals was put together by a coalition of animal protection groups in the United States, including The Humane Society, People for the Ethical Treatment of Animals (PETA), and the Doris Day Animal League. Their goal was to help consumers identify cosmetics and other products developed without using animal testing of a type that they consider cruel or inhumane. The coalition will provide interested consumers with a list of items developed by companies that follow these guidelines.

To be identified as "cruelty-free" under the coalition's standard, companies must meet certain criteria. The standard recognizes that companies may have tested ingredients on animals in the past but states that they must set a date after which they will not conduct or commission new animal testing on their products or ingredients. Companies must submit an annual statement of their continued commitment. The standard also includes information about testing methods

that do not use animals and shows how manufacturers can comply with their criteria while still maintaining their safety standards for products. Consumers can support this initiative by buying only those products that comply with the standard and by boycotting products that involve animal testing or that the coalition states harm animals in any way.

The coalition also urged consumers to ask stores to stock "cruelty-free" products and to write letters to companies that continued to use animal testing, informing them that they will not use their products until they replace animal testing with different methods.

Among the companies that have adopted the standards are The Body Shop, Kiss My Face, Borlind of Germany, John Paul Mitchell, Island Dog Cosmetics, and Tom's of Maine. *See also* ANIMAL TESTING.

Further reading: Christine Canning, "Animal Testing Alternatives: The Quest Continues," *Happi* February 1997, http:www.happi.com/special/febmain97.htm.

Cosmetic Executive Women (CEW)

Based in New York City, the Cosmetic Executive Women, Inc. (CEW) was founded in 1954 as a nonprofit organization for women executives from the cosmetic, fragrance, and related industries. The association's goal is to teach CEW members more about their profession and promote the contributions of women in the cosmetics industry. By the 1980s, it was also carrying out more educational and philanthropic activities. As of 1999, the CEW had more than 1,200 members, and associated organizations had been formed in France and the United Kingdom.

Each year, the CEW gives Beauty Awards to the beauty products that association members select as the best new products of the year. The awards include best new hair product, best new cosmetics product in limited distribution, best new bath, body, or sun product in mass distribution; best new cosmetics product in mass distribution, best new skin care product in limited distribution; and the best new bath, body or sun product in limited distribution. In 1997, CEW president Jean Zimmerman said, "The CEW Beauty

Awards provide a great service to women across the country, who, until now, have had no way of knowing what insiders in the beauty industry consider to be the very best products. Award winners in 1999 included Chanel Triple Color Crayon (best new cosmetic product, limited distribution); Pond's Soothing Cucumber Eye Treatments (best new skin care product, mass distribution); Helene Curtis ThermaSilk Moisturizing Shampoo (best new hair product, mass distribution).

Through its Cosmetic Executive Women Foundation, the CEW assists homeless women and children and funds the Women's Venture Fund, which aids inexperienced entrepreneurs from low-income communities.

Further reading: "About CEW," "Cosmetic Executive Women 1997 Beauty Awards," "Cosmetic Executive Women 1999 Beauty Awards," Cosmetic Executive Women (CEW) http://www.cew.org and http://www.beautyawards.com

Cosmetic Surgery See PLASTIC SURGERY.

The Cosmetic, Toiletry, and Fragrance Association (CTFA)

The Cosmetic, Toiletry, and Fragrance Association (CTFA) was founded in 1894 in the United States as a trade association for the personal care products industry. The CTFA defines its purpose as providing "a full range of services to support the industry's needs and interests in scientific, legal, regulatory, legislative and international fields." The organization operates at the local, state, national, and international levels in pursuing its mission: "to protect the freedom of the industry to compete in a fair and responsible marketplace."

As of 1998, the CTFA had about 600 members, which included active members—manufacturers and distributors of finished personal care products—and associate members—suppliers of ingredients, raw materials, and packaging materials and services used to produce and manufacture retail goods.

The CTFA informs members about pending legislation that could affect them and has promoted voluntary industry self-regulation. It works with chemists and their professional organizations to study the effects of cosmetic ingredients and publishes the *Cosmetic Ingredient Review*. Although published by the association, the CIR evaluation of cosmetics' safety is conducted by independent scientists who, as with those who evaluate products for the FDA, must be free of conflicts of interest. Available online, the CIR lists safety alerts and updates on products.

The CTFA is also a political organization that promotes members' interests. It monitors new or pending regulatory legislation that would further regulate the agency or require companies to add new warnings or labels on products. In 1998, the CTFA opposed some state environmental laws that would limit the amount of certain plastic packaging materials.

Internationally, the CTFA worked in Japan to help members abolish the pre-market approval process required before new products could be marketed. If successful, Japan will adopt a system like that used in the United States and the European Union. In December 1998, the CTFA also completed its International Legal and Regulatory Database, an electronic service for members that includes information on hundreds of cosmetic laws and regulations in 60 countries. The association had already created a database with information about United States laws and regulations.

CTFA publishes *The International Cosmetic Ingredient Dictionary and Handbook, CTFA Scientific/ Regulatory Reference CD-ROM, International Buyers' Guide, Microbiology Guidelines, The CTFA List of Japanese Cosmetic Ingredient, Safety Testing Guidelines, Labeling Manual*, and *The International Regulatory/Resource Manual*. These publications are updated regularly. With the American Cancer Society and National Cosmetology Association, CTFA sponsors a program called "Look Good . . . Feel Better" for women recovering from cancer.

Further reading: "CFTA Annual Report," The Cosmetic, Toiletry, and Fragrance Association (CTFA), New York, 1998, http://www.ctfa.org; www.cir-safety.org.

Cosmetics

Cosmetics—from the Greek word *kosmetikos*, which means "skilled in adorning or arranging"—refers to preparations used to cleanse, beautify, condition, and protect the skin, hair, lips, nails, or eyes. The word comes from the Greek word *kosmos*, which means "order." According to the Food, Drug, and Cosmetic Act of 1938, the term "cosmetics" encompasses any "articles to be rubbed, poured, sprinkled, or sprayed on, introduced into, or otherwise applied to the human body or any part thereof for cleansing, beautifying, promoting attractiveness, or altering the appearance."

People have used cosmetic substances since primitive times. The earliest were substances used to apply color and designs, most often to the face. At different times and in various lands, both men and women painted their faces and other parts of their bodies. People also used tattooing, scarification, and permanent ornaments, such as lip plugs, to change their appearances. Historians believe that our early ancestors used face and body paint to ward off evil spirits, disguise themselves, frighten strangers, and identify themselves to fellow tribal members. At the same time, although their ideas of beauty may not coincide with contemporary standards, the cosmetic use practiced by primitive people may nevertheless have been considered beauty enhancing.

Archaeologists have learned about early cosmetics by excavating tombs, studying artifacts, and examining ancient pictures on cave walls. Ancient Egyptian women emphasized the contours of their eyes with various natural products, especially a substance called kohl, which was made from a powder of the mineral antimony. Egyptian women applied black kohl to their eyelids and used green or blue powders above and below the eyes. They also used kohl was also used to thicken eyelashes and eyebrows. Archeologists have found unguent jars and signs of scented unguents in Egyptian tombs, along with tools to apply cosmetics.

Women's graves found in the ancient ruins of Catal, located on what is now Asia Minor, contain cosmetics sets. As did the ancient Egyptians, these people sent beauty products along with the dead to the next life.

The Romans were close to enthusiastic about the use of cosmetics. Ovid, the poet, advised women to "rouge a pale cheek, a red one powder. Each maiden knows that art's allowed." (Lefkowitz and Fant, 1982).

Roman women who wished to lighten the color of their faces used mixtures that contained white lead, a custom that persisted for centuries in various countries. Because lead is highly toxic, women died from lead poisoning as a result of this practice.

After the decline of the Roman Empire and the spread of Christianity, cosmetic use declined. Christian leaders promoted a simple way of life and spiritual values, rather than material and worldly ones. They regarded the way that the ancient Romans lived as self-indulgent. Europeans continued to disapprove of cosmetic use into the Middle Ages, when a pale, natural look was the beauty ideal.

During the Renaissance, royalty and nobility used cosmetics widely. Women were offered suggestions and advice on ways to achieve a better appearance that conformed to the ideals. Writers also gave them tips on how to hide their shortcomings. Many books gave recipes for making cosmetics and hair-care products. Cosmetics were as much a part of appearance as clothing and jewelry. To help women who had less money for cosmetics, Italian author Caterina Sforza, who wrote *Esperimenti* in the late 1400s, suggested cheaper ingredients for making creams, face whiteners, and red paints for the lips and cheeks.

During the 1500s, women and men in England wore a great deal of makeup. Both men and women used a powder called ceruse, made of lead, carbon, and oxygen, whose lead contents at times proved lethal to the wearer. Their desire for beauty had damaging effects for others: Dutch workmen also suffered many ill effects from lead poisoning as they produced quantities of ceruse that was exported to other countries.

Men wore powder, and some wore masks outdoors to keep the sun off their faces. Both sexes also commonly used perfume during this century. When talc, a mixture of magnesium, silicon, and oxygen, came into use, it was a big improvement over lead powders, both in terms of safety and appearance.

Religious leaders criticized cosmetic use. They said that using cosmetics was wrong; they altered God's work and went against his will. Religious leader Thomas Tuke rebuked women who used cosmetics, asking them how they could pray to God, "with a face, which he doth not owne?" (Camden, 1952)

In Italy, women of all classes were using cosmetics, including creams, powders, and paints, during the 1700s. Women tried to lighten their hair by exposing it to the sun and using lemon juice or mixtures made with rhubarb, saffron, or sulfur. Women also used depilatories or plucked the hair along their foreheads to raise their hairlines. After thinning their eyebrows, they colored them black.

Customs varied throughout Europe, and that they did was often linked with the morality of the time and place. During the 1700s, the English parliament passed laws against the use of cosmetics. The law declared that women could be punished for witchcraft and have their marriages annulled if they used "perfume, paint, artificial teeth, wigs, stays, hoops, high-heeled shoes" in order to find a mate. (Camden, 1952)

Colonists brought these attitudes with them to America. The Quakers (Society of Friends), as well as the New England Puritans banned the use of cosmetics, and the practice was frowned upon throughout the colonies, some of which also enacted laws against them and declared them immoral. Women did use homemade preparations to soften their skin, and some surreptitiously added a bit of color to their cheeks or lips by rubbing them with pieces of red ribbon or with flowers, leaves, or other plant materials that contained reddish stains.

The French were the pioneers of new cosmetics research during the 1800s. These chemists produced new and improved versions of various cosmetics and more and more women used them. Usage increased as mass production made it possible to buy less expensive products. In America, negative social attitudes toward cosmetics still prevailed, so manufacturers and salespeople usually advertised them as products to improve the health of the skin rather than as beauty preparations. Women had long exchanged recipes for mixtures to beautify the complexion, and had concocted some cosmetics, as well. By the mid-nineteenth century, they augmented their home ingredients with ones they purchased at pharmacies to add color or fragrance.

In America, the first lipsticks (based on formulas containing lanolin or cocoa butter) and eyebrow pencils were being mass-produced around 1915. Their production coincided with the time when metal tubes became available as lipstick cases, which made it possible to produce lipsticks in tubes. However, few women admitted to using lipstick, and they were careful to apply cosmetics so that they looked natural.

World War I brought more changes in the status of women as they gained more political rights and moved into the workplace in increasing numbers. The use of makeup became more acceptable, and variety stores carried larger selections of products, some of which were inexpensive enough for women with limited budgets. Some women were harshly criticized for using cosmetics, and some even lost their jobs because of it. Young women who worked as servants, clerks, or office workers were advised not to wear any obvious makeup. Nurses and teachers were also expected to abstain. Women who chose to break these social rules taught themselves to apply makeup subtly that it was not easily detected; they otherwise might face the disapproval or censure of employers or others.

By the 1920s, society had become more accepting of cosmetics, although parents, husbands, and employers continued to voice their objections. The main products sold in America during the 1920s and 1930s were moisturizing skin creams and powders, which were formulated from talcum (powdered magnesium silicate) and zinc oxide. Skin cream companies tried to present an appealing image for their product. For example, in 1927, the Ponds Company ads for its cold cream and vanishing cream (what "vanished" were wrinkles) featured excerpts from a complimentary letter written by Queen Marie of Romania. The queen supposedly said that the cream gave her great "satisfaction." The ad also stated that the queen of Spain and various other royal women and socialites used Ponds' cream. (Watkins, 1959)

To meet a growing demand, the cosmetics industry developed new products and offered women more choices. Face powders came in natural flesh tones, as well as lavender and green. Lipsticks were made in different shades of red, pink, rose, or peach, and there was rouge to brighten the complexion, Formulas for nail polish changed to provide more coverage, more colors and easier application. Soon, women could match their nail polish to their lipstick.

Cosmetics companies continued to bring out new and improved products and to offer consumers more choices, different price ranges, and greater convenience. The fragrance industry also expanded greatly, offering hundreds of different scents in new forms. The mass media and advertising industries exerted a tremendous influence on cosmetics use.

As motion pictures carried images all over the world, people looked to actors and actresses as role models for appearance. Some makeup artists developed their own cosmetics companies. For example, Max Factor, a well-known makeup artist in Hollywood, developed a commercial business that offered the first pancake makeup, a foundation that provided heavy coverage.

Women's makeup use in the 1950s was almost certainly influenced by the glamorous stars of the movies, as well as by their return to more traditional female roles following World War II. Applying lipstick—often in bright colors—powder, and rouge were integral to many women's daily routines; many did not consider themselves "dressed" without their makeup.

As the 1950s ended and the 1960s began to take shape as a distinctive era of rebellion against authority, many—although not all—young women began to spurn makeup as unnatural and unnecessary. For those who still wanted to use cosmetics, companies marketed more products labeled "natural." The feminist movement also influenced women's use of cosmetics. At least some women saw cosmetics use as yet another way that women spent time on their appearance at the expense of more serious pursuits.

By the mid-1970s, however, as these young women were entering the formal workforce, many again began using cosmetics. In contrast to the bright and unsubtle makeup of the 1950s, however, the makeup that came into vogue was more natural, intended to enhance rather than to obscure a woman's appearance.

Cosmetic companies also focused on certain groups of consumers, specializing, for example, in expensive lines sold only in department stores or boutiques or on products that were available in drugstores and variety stores. They also became aware that women of color represented an important market, and began targeting these groups. Companies that featured products especially for African Americans included Fashion Fair and Johnson Products. Other companies were emerging to provide more and better products that were especially suited for people of Asian and Latino ancestry.

Recent innovations in cosmetics include products that claim to give skin extra benefits, such as "time-released" moisture, lipsticks and other cosmetics that have more "staying power" and do not rub off on clothing, and glittery creams, gels, and sun blocks for the face and body.

Teen and Youth Markets

Before the twentieth century, children were usually not encouraged to use cosmetics, but did learn certain grooming rituals, depending on their culture. Throughout history, in many cultures, cleanliness has been children's most common grooming practice and was emphasized as a virtue. Clean, clear skin, neat hair, and well-kept nails were—and still are—considered signs of good grooming.

During the 1940s, cosmetics company executives began targeting specific groups of consumers by age and other demographic factors. Ads for cosmetics were placed in magazines that teenagers read, including *Charm, Young Miss,* and *Seventeen.* Marketing experts helped the industry to gear certain products to that young market, package them in ways that would appeal to teens, and offer them at prices young people could afford. Inexpensive lipsticks were among the first of these products.

By the middle of the twentieth century,, teens in the United States had more money to spend, and a "teen culture" developed that promoted various products on which they should spend it. Ads and commercials were aimed at teens and encouraged girls to use makeup geared to their tastes. Special skin care products for teen acne also appeared in increasing numbers, and some companies sold cosmetics just for teens.

New magazines for teenage readers developed, and they contained ads that promoted cosmetics, hair-care products, and various grooming products, as well as clothing, shoes, and other goods. The use of makeup was seen as a rite of passage as girls moved through adolescence and into adulthood. Starting with lipstick, girls used more products as they grew older until they were using the same kinds of products as adult women.

The editorial content of these magazines supported the notion that teens should use cosmetics. Articles on the use of cosmetics, reports on the latest fashions in cosmetics, and the illustrations in the magazines all reinforced the notion that teenagers should use cosmetics to improve their appearances.

Teenagers who wore makeup were encouraged to use a light touch and natural colors and not to appear too mature or sophisticated. At slumber parties, girls experimented with makeup, trying new looks on themselves and each other. The ways teenagers used makeup and other grooming products and styled their hair often showed that they belonged to a particular socio-economic group or clique or club within their schools or communities.

Grooming products for children were first developed and sold in the United States in the 1950s. Most were bath products, such as bubble bath in floral fragrances and lip gloss and light pink fingernail polish. Early on and today, products for children and preteens encourage them to play "dress-up" with single items of makeup or kits containing products that resemble those that adult women used. Girls who grew up in the 1950s may recall the Tinkerbell kits with pretend cosmetics and colognes. Today's kits are more extensive: they may include nail polish, lipstick, powder, cheek color, cologne, and scented bath products. Lipsticks and flavored lip gloss are geared to appeal to young girls. Stores also offer teen fashion dolls, such as Barbie, and toys that include makeup kits and wigs, hair-styling tools, and dolls with hair that can change color or "grow." Children can buy nail kits with press-on fingernails and nail decals.

By the 1960s, more teenagers used eye makeup than in previous decades. Teens developed special makeup looks of their own and sometimes started trends that were adopted and at times modified by older women. One survey conducted during the mid-sixties showed that American teenage girls, who made up 11 percent of the population, bought about 25 percent of all cosmetics and beauty preparations.

After the 1960s, cosmetics companies aimed more ads at preadolescents and teenagers, whose purchases support an industry that generates billions of dollars annually. Pond's, Noxzema, Yardley, Maybelline, Bonne Bell, and Cover Girl are among the companies that have sold skin care products and cosmetics especially designed to appeal to teens. Through clever, targeted advertising, cosmetics companies also created fads in makeup and cologne, so that a particular fragrance became a must-have for every teen-

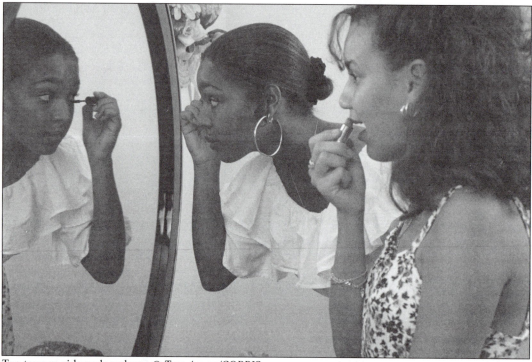

Two teenage girls apply makeup. © *Tony Arruza/CORBIS.*

age girl. Some entire lines, such as "jane" from the Estee Lauder Company, are aimed at teenagers.

Statistics show a steady rise in the amount of money teenagers spent on cosmetics, and companies spent more money on ad campaigns aimed at teens. By the 1980s, teenagers in America were spending about $20 billion each year on various products. A survey by Teenage Research Unlimited, in Northbrook, Illinois, found that in 1999, teenagers (boys and girls) spent $141 billion, a 16 percent increase over 1998. The survey did not report what percentage of this they spent on cosmetics, but the amount is likely to be substantial. "The teen consumer is obsessed with Hollywood, glamour, and celebrity," according to Kristin Penta, creator of Fun Cosmetics, as quoted in the August 1999 issue of *Happi* magazine. She notes, too, that trends are changing faster, and girls will spend more on cosmetics to keep up with these trends. teen models, including popular celebrities, were and are featured in ads for these products. Girls as young as ten were wearing lipstick, blush, eye makeup, fragrances, and

nail polish, while younger girls used nail polish, fragrances, and tinted lip gloss. Teenagers used various cosmetics and hair products, including hair color.

In their quest to assert their individuality, however, some teenagers are using makeup not to "enhance natural beauty," as did their earlier counterparts, but to make themselves stand out in other ways. They use black or purple nail polish and lipstick and color their hair bright colors. Novel cosmetics are extremely popular, such as the nail polish that changes color when exposed to sunlight that SolarFX makes. Sales increased 400 percent from 1998 to 1999. (*Happi,* August 1999) Teenage boys, too, are bleaching their hair, and some use the same brightly colored hair dyes that girls use.

To encourage teenage girls to buy and use these products,, some cosmetics manufacturers and clothing companies feature preteen girls wearing makeup in advertisements that show them in provocative poses, looking "sexy." Music videos feature young people wearing heavy makeup, as does the mass media, where an increasing number of shows are targeted at young audiences and a growing number of magazines are published for this group

Critics of the cosmetics industry claim that this advertising to young people exploits their youthful insecurity. At this age, they are especially vulnerable to such pressure and are eager to fit in, gain social acceptance, and achieve cultural ideals of beauty.

Age and Cosmetics

The cosmetics industry now is confronted with another shift that will change consumer behavior: the aging of the Baby Boom generation, whose members would like to maintain a youthful and hip appearance. The cosmetics industry has responded by producing makeup specifically labeled "anti-aging," often pictured on older models. They also market a virtually endless array of skin creams to retain or restore youthful skin tone and texture. Men, too, are offered various anti-aging skin products.

Cosmetic use still varies enormously according to age, where a woman lives, and what kind of life she lives. The allure of being able to change one's appearance, however, is likely to remain unchanged. *See also* ANIMAL TESTING; BEAUTY INDUSTRY (U.S.); BEAUTY STANDARDS; BODY IMAGE; CONTESTS; CONTESTS, CHILDRENS; EYES; FACE; HANDS; LAWS AND REGULATIONS (U.S.); LIPS; MEN'S PERSONAL CARE PRODUCTS; MODELING AND MODELS; SAFETY.

Further reading: Laura Bradford, "On the Teen Scene: Cosmetics and Reality," *FDA Consumer*, May 1994; Joan Jacobs Brumberg, *The Body Project: An Intimate History of American Girls* (1997); Carroll Camden, *The Elizabethan Woman: A Panorama of English Womanhood, 1540 to 1640* (1952); Richard Corson, *Fashions in Make-up: From Ancient to Modern Times* (1972); Michael Grant, *A Social History of Greece and Rome* (1969); Fanjet Gun, *The Artificial Face: A History of Cosmetics* (1973); Joan Liver-sidge, *Everyday Life in the Roman Empire* (1976); Maggie Angelo Lou, *A History of Make-up* (1970); Kathy Peiss, *Hope in a Jar* (1998); Kathryn Perutz, *Beyond the Looking Glass: America's Beauty Culture* (1970); "Seventeen Survey," *Cosmetics Fair*, July 1967, 17-18; Toni Stabile, *Everything You Want to Know About Cosmetics, or What Your Friendly Clerk Didn't Tell You* (1984); University of Michigan Research Center, *Adolescent Girls*, 1957; Julian Lewis Watkins, *The 100 Greatest Advertisements: Who Did Them and What They Did* (1959).

Cosmetics, Men's *See* PERSONAL CARE PRODUCTS, MEN'S.

Coty Company

Founded as the House of Coty in Paris in 1905, this company initially specialized in perfumes and expanded to produce a wide variety of cosmetics and fragrances. Thirty-two-year-old Francois Spoturno, a native of Corsica, launched the company after studying perfume-making for two years in Grasse, France, the center of the world's perfume industry. He was inspired to develop his own cosmetics firm after watching a neighbor concoct toilette water and after visiting exhibits at the 1900 World's Fair in Paris.

With some financial help from his grandfather, Spoturno was able to open his first store on the Rue de la Boitie in Paris. His first commercial offering, "La Rose Jacqueminot," was a success. Spoturno, who has been called the first great perfumer of modern times, commissioned Baccarat and Lalique, the famous crystal-makers, to create elegant flagons for his early perfumes. He believed that packaging was a key part of enticing customers to buy perfumes and various cosmetics. He thought, too, that women would buy better quality products that were presented in tasteful and beautiful containers at a reasonable price.

Coty (the name he assumed) was also known for his bold efforts to promote his products. It was said that when a department store refused to give him counter space for his line, he deliberately broke a bottle of perfume on his way out the door so that customers could sample the scent and try to buy some. However, other accounts state that the bottle fell and broke by accident. In any case, the smell from his "La Rose Jacqueminot" perfume attracted hundreds of new customers within days of the incident.

Coty moved his business to a spot near the Bois de Bologne, a stylish section of Paris. He went on to create more than fifty scents, including the popular Oriental fragrance "L'Origan" (1927) and the modern floral "L'Aimant" (1927).

The Coty Company later expanded its product lines to include makeup. Its founder devised the idea of selling a line of goods in a specific fragrance. The company was bought by Pfizer Corporation during the 1960s, a decade when it launched new fragrances called "Imprevu," "Masumi," and "Wild Musk." In 1980, Coty became part of the Colgate-Palmolive Corporation and, later, part of Beauty International, a division of European Brands Group, Ltd. Nevertheless, the company continues to have an independent identity and to produce various color cosmetics, and it remains a strong competitor in the fragrance market. Two of its most successful lines for women and men have a vanilla scent. "Raw Vanilla," for men, contains Brazilian mint, South American spruce, bamboo and musk.

During the 1990s, Coty conducted research to determine how and why women select perfume and found that they chose scents to suit themselves more than to attract men. The survey showed that women were seeking lighter fragrances. In response, the company launched "Celebrate," a light scent developed by perfumers at Givaudan-Roure. *See also* COSMETICS; FRAGRANCE; PERFUME.

Further reading: Diane Ackerman, *A Natural History of the Senses* 1991; Christine Canning, "Fine Fragrances," *Happi,* November 1996, 12-19; William F. Kaufman, *Perfume* (1974); Kate Mulvey and Melissa Richards, *Decades of Beauty: The Changing Image of Women, 1890s-1990s* (1998).

Crawford, Cindy (b. 1966)

Cynthia Ann—Cindy—Crawford is one of the best-known international "supermodels" and has appeared on hundreds of magazine covers across the globe. Crawford grew up in Dekalb, Illinois, where she graduated first in her high school class, and was studying chemical engineering at Northwestern University on a scholarship when she began mod-

Cindy Crawford at a 1997 event. © *Henry McGee/Globe Photos, Inc. 1997.*

eling in Chicago. As she received more modeling assignments, Crawford left school to devote all of her time to her flourishing career. In 1983, she was a finalist in competition for the Elite "Look of the Year Award," sponsored by the Elite modeling agency, which her brought widespread attention and higher paying jobs around the world.

In addition to runway work for top couturiers, Crawford appeared on the covers of the most prominent magazines, including *Vogue, Cosmopolitan,* and *Glamour.* Her dark eyes, long dark hair, and distinctive mole set her apart from the blue-eyed blond models who often dominated the modeling business. She signed lucrative contracts with Revlon and the Omega watch company, among others, and was prominently featured in Revlon's "Colorstay" cosmetics line. Among her colleagues, Crawford was known for her professionalism and even temperament.

Moving beyond modeling, Crawford, like many models of her era, became a television and film personality, hosting the successful MTV program "House of Style" for six years during the early 1990s and acting in some movies. She also produced two best-selling workout videos (*Cindy Crawford/Shape Your Body* and *The Next Challenge*) and appeared in the 1995 feature film *Fair Game.* While continuing to model, she appeared in television series and on awards programs. She wrote the beauty book *Cindy Crawford's Basic Face.* In May 1998, *Business Age* estimated that Crawford was the second wealthiest supermodel in the world, after Australian Elle MacPherson.

Crawford was married to actor Richard Gere for four years; in 1998, she married Los Angeles businessman Rande Gerber and gave birth to their son in 1999. *See also* MODELING AND MODELS.

Further reading: "About Cindy," Cindy.Com, The Official Cindy Crawford Web site http://www.cindy.com/about/biography; "Cindy Crawford," *Cosmopolitan,* October 1990, p. 42; "Who's Who: Cindy Crawford," *Vogue* biography http://www.vogue.co.uk/content/ie4/295/357491-0-1-1.html

Creed, House of

The House of Creed, founded in Paris in 1760 by James Henry Creed, is a perfume company that has supplied fragrances to royalty and other prominent people throughout its long history. The company uses mostly natural ingredients and imports flowers, fruit essences, and oils from around the world.

The company managed to survive the French Revolution and went on to provide scents for Napoleon II, Queen Victoria, and the Shah of Iran, among others. In 1956, as a gift to his bride, actress Grace Kelly, Prince Rainier of Monaco commissioned a fragrance for her that was named "Fleurissimo"; it later became a favorite of First Lady Jacqueline Kennedy. Among the celebrities who have bought customized fragrances are actress Julia Roberts and actor Harrison Ford. After five years, the fragrances become the property of the company. The House of Creed remains a family-run company, with the fifth-generation Olivier Henry Creed serving as master perfumer.

Today, besides the more than 200 fragrances sold in retail outlets, the House of Creed still creates individual scents, albeit at considerable cost. A customer who wants Creed to design a scent must travel to meet with Olivier Creed. The cost of one liter, including travel, meetings, and the perfume itself, now ranges from $5,000 to $20,000; the minimum order is 10 liters. For a more modest amount—$3,000 to $4,200—Creed will revive a "vintage" scent, one that the company is not at the time producing, and mix up 3 to 5 liters.

Further reading: Anne-Marie O'Neill et al. "Custom-Made Cachet," *People,* 22 February 1999, 107–108; Janet Carlson Freed, "Signature Scents," *Town and Country Weddings,* http://tncweddings.women.com.

Critics of Cosmetics Industry

"Beauty," as applied to human appearance, is a relative term whose interpretation changes over time and in different cultures. As the beauty industry has grown throughout the twentieth century, it has attracted multiple critics. Many have spoken out and/or written critiques of the beauty industry as a whole, as well as of individual products.

One of the first books to criticize the industry was published in 1934. *Skin Deep: The Truth About Beauty Aids—Safe and Harm-*

ful was written by consumer advocate and author, M.C. Phillips, and sponsored by a group called Consumers' Research. The book has been credited with helping to increase public demand for the regulatory laws that came a few years later in the form of the Food, Drug, and Cosmetic Act of 1938.

Phillips criticized the cosmetics industry for deceptive advertising practices and for peddling unrealistic dreams to women. She exposed unsafe ingredients and described cases in which women had been disfigured and even died from using unsafe products. Phillips said that consumers had the right to use cosmetics that were safe and did what they were advertised to do. She recommended some products that she regarded as safe, effective, and worth the cost.

The book sparked a great deal of debate, and Phillips received hundreds of letters from people who agreed or disagreed with her. Some women thanked her for helping them to understand the beauty industry better; some wrote that they had been duped into buying expensive products that cost up to a week's salary and as a result had become careful not to spend money on useless products. At the same time, however, women also told Phillips that cosmetics had become an important part of their lives and said they would continue to use them.

The Beauty Trap, Exploring Women's Greatest Obsession, a 1984 book by Nancy C. Baker, was one of the first postfeminism books to discuss how American culture and the beauty industry affect women. Baker discusses how women are conditioned from birth to value beauty and seek to reach certain physical standards that are essentially out of reach of most women. After interviewing women around the world, she concluded that the "beauty trap" is universal: "There are women everywhere who are overly concerned about physical appearance and its impact on their lives." (Baker, 1984) The book suggested how women could break out of the "beauty trap" and focus instead on developing inner beauty that would last a lifetime.

In *The Beauty Myth: How Images of Beauty Are Used Against Women* (1991),

feminist author Naomi Wolf discusses how social attitudes about female beauty and economic pressures to conform to accepted standards of appearance can undermine women psychologically and politically. The author describes how policies about appearance have affected women through the years; for example, airline stewardesses had to quit their jobs at age 32—the year when they evidently stopped being sufficiently attractive. She analyzes, too, how women's jobs are affected by what Wolf calls "the beauty myth." Standards of appearance—perhaps implicit and not acknowledged—can nevertheless have an impact on a woman's progress up the corporate ladder. The book became an international bestseller.

One of Wolf's major assertions is that societal pressure to "look beautiful" has become a way to control women, because this quest absorbs time, money, and energy that they could otherwise spend on their jobs or other activities. In turn, this limits the time and energy that they have to compete against men in the workplace, where they could threaten male supremacy and economic control. Wolf voiced the concern that images of thin, glamorous-looking fashion models are too prevalent and offer too narrow a vision of mature womanhood. She also said that "ad pressure forces women's magazines to center readers' anxieties on the scale and the mirror, at the expense of real coverage of the wide world of women." Furthermore, Wolf contended, women often receive incomplete or misleading information about the products that they are urged to buy to make themselves look better.

Wolf, who was 29 years old at the time her book was published, is a graduate of Yale University and former Rhodes Scholar at Oxford University. She made guest appearances on televised news programs and talk shows to discuss these issues. Responding to the controversy over her book, she pointed out that she did not advise women to either use or avoid makeup, nor did she object to "images of glamour and beauty in mass culture." Rather, Wolf said, "The harm of these images is not that they exist, but that they proliferate at the expense of most other images and stories of female heroines, role models, villains, eccentrics, buffoons, visionaries, sex goddesses, and pranksters." (Wolf, 1991) In late 1999, Naomi Wolf was the center of some controversy when it was revealed that she had been hired at a high fee by Vice President Al Gore, in his campaign for the presidential race of 2000, to be an image consultant. *See also* ADVERTISING (U.S.); AGING AND APPEARANCE; BEAUTY INDUSTRY (U.S.); BEAUTY STANDARDS; BODY IMAGE; FEMINISM; LAWS AND REGULATIONS (U.S.); PLASTIC SURGERY; SAFETY.

Further reading: Nancy C. Baker, *The Beauty Trap, Exploring Women's Greatest Obsession* (1984); Kate Mulvey and Melissa Richards, *Decades of Beauty* (1998); Kathy Peiss, *Hope in a Jar* (1998); M.C. Phillips, *Skin Deep: The Truth about Beauty Aids—Safe and Harmful* (1934); Naomi Wolf, *The Beauty Myth: How Images of Beauty Are Used Against Women* (1991).

D

Daché, Lilly (1904–1989)

Lilly Daché, one of the most famous hat de-signers in history, founded a company that produced millinery, clothing, jewelry, and cosmetics. At her New York building, Dache operated beauty salons where clients could receive hair, skin care, and makeup services for head-to-toe glamour.

At age 14, the French-born designer left school to work as an apprentice to her aunt, a hat-maker in Bordeaux. She then worked for a famous milliner in Paris before moving to New York City in 1924. While employed as a salesclerk at Macy's Department Store and later at a small milliner's shop, Daché built up her hat business. She created cus-tom-made hats at night, using the small de-posit she collected for each hat to buy the materials. Within a few years, she saved enough money to buy the shop where she worked. In 1952, she married Frenchman Jean Despres, who worked in New York for Coty, Inc., a well-known cosmetics and per-fume company.

Daché was known for her innovative de-signs and uses of materials. She designed turbans, the cloche hat, and the swagger hat, which was often associated with one of her most famous clients, actress Marlene Dietrich. Daché's business grew to include lingerie, dresses, jewelry, and cosmetics, as well as beauty and hair salons for her cus-tomers. Her line of cosmetics included a face cream made with jelly that came from the queen bee. In 1965, she published *Lilly Daché's Glamour Book*, which expressed her philosophy about fashion and beauty and gave specific advice about hair and skin care. She retired in 1968.

Further reading: Lilly Daché, *Lilly Daché's Glam-our Book* (1965).

Dandridge, Dorothy (1922–1965)

Singer-actress Dorothy Dandridge was one of the first African American women to achieve leading roles in motion pictures. A native of Cleveland, Ohio, Dandridge was regarded as one of the most beautiful women in Hollywood, and she was also one of the first black women to be featured on the cover of *Life* magazine (1954).

Dandridge began her career as a singer, mostly for church audiences, in a trio that included her sister Vivian. Her mother relo-cated to Los Angeles to boost her daughters' careers. Dorothy and Vivian broke away from their mother to perform with a friend named Etta as "The Dandridge Sisters." Besides appearing in nightclubs throughout the United States and Europe, the group was fea-tured in some films, where they performed musical numbers.

Dandridge broke new ground as the first black woman to appear in nonstereotypical film roles in leading, romantic roles. Audi-ences were dazzled by her glamour and sex appeal. Her most famous film role was in the musical *Carmen Jones* (1954), for which she was nominated for an Academy Award for the best female performance of the year. She was also praised for her performance in Otto Preminger's film version of *Porgy and Bess*.

Dandridge endured many hardships during her life. Besides the racism that she had to overcome in her career, her two marriages failed and her second husband was an abuser who exploited her financially. Her only child, a daughter, was born with serious disabilities, and Dandridge worked hard to care for her. She suffered from depression throughout her life.

Dorothy Dandridge helped to open doors for other black performers. The dazzling dark-skinned brunette beauty helped to change racist attitudes that regarded white skin and Anglo-Saxon features as more attractive than the physical traits of people of color. *See also* AFRICAN AMERICANS

Further reading: Donald Bogle, *Dorothy Dandridge: A Biography* (1997); Earl Conrad, *Everything and Nothing: The Dorothy Dandridge Tragedy* (2000).

Dermabrasion *See* SKIN

Dermatologists

Dermatologists are medical doctors who treat various conditions affecting the skin, hair, and nails. They prescribe treatments for acne and other problems that affect the appearance and health of the skin, and may prescribe treatments and perform cosmetic procedures, such as facial treatments that reduce the signs of aging.

Hair transplants, botox (derived from the pathogen botulism) injections, collagen injections, fat injections, eyelid surgery, chemical peels, dermabrasion, removal of varicose and "spider" veins with lasers or injections, laser hair removal, and laser treatments of the skin are among the cosmetic procedures dermatologists may perform. A well-known New York City dermatologist, Norman Orentreich, M.D., was a pioneer in hair-transplant procedures. In recent decades, dermatologists have also been prescribing creams and lotions intended to reduce the signs of aging on the skin, such as Retin-A.

The American Academy of Dermatology, founded in 1938, is the largest of all dermatology professional associations and is the one that certifies medical doctors who specialize in this field.

Further reading: American Academy of Dermatology Web site, http:/www.aad.org; American Society for Dermatologic Surgery, Fact Sheets; "Norman Orentreich, M.D.," interview, *Cosmopolitan*, February 1990, 122,124.

Diana, Princess of Wales (1961– 1997)

Celebrated for her beauty, sense of style, and humanitarian work, Diana, Princess of Wales, influenced beauty and fashion trends around the world for more than a decade. She also raised consciousness about eating disorders after publicly discussing her problems with bulimia.

Lady Diana Spencer, one of four children born to the fifth Earl of Spencer, grew up on Althorp, the family's ancestral estate in England. She was working as a kindergarten teacher when, at age 19, she became engaged to the Prince of Wales, Charles, heir to the British throne. The royal wedding in July 1981 was televised around the world, and

Diana, Princess of Wales, in 1985. © *Archive Photos*.

millions of people noted every detail of Diana's appearance, including her radiant smile. One author noted that by her wedding day, "Lady Diana had slimmed from a size 12 to a size 10, and her plump cheeks had vanished to reveal high cheekbones, a good bone structure and an elfin-like face." (Owen, 1983) By 1983, reporters noted that the 5'10" tall Diana often wore a dress size 6.

The young princess quickly became the most photographed woman in the world. She appeared on more magazine covers than any person in history, and her appearance and behavior were discussed in numerous articles, news stories, and on television. People were interested in the style and color of her hair, favorite fragrances, makeup and beauty routines, shopping habits, and growing interest in fitness. They discussed every feature of her appearance, including her fluctuating weight, highlighted blonde hair, facial features, and jewelry. Tabloids covered these matters regularly, and several books focusing on Diana's appearance were published during the 1980s. She became perhaps the most photographed woman of the twentieth century. Her hairstyles and fashions were also widely copied around the world.

When it became known that Diana had been seeing a psychiatrist, she discussed her eating disorder publicly. Her openness helped to remove the stigma from this health problem, and it encouraged more people who suffered from it to seek professional help.

As Princess of Wales, Diana supported various charities and social causes. She spoke out for land-mine reform and visited people who were suffering from AIDS and other diseases and disabilities, especially children. Diana's warmth and ability to communicate with people from all walks of life won her the affectionate nickname "The People's Princess." She and Prince Charles divorced in 1996, but she retained her popularity in Britain and elsewhere. Her death in a car crash in 1997 brought an outpouring of grief and tributes from people throughout the world.

Further reading: Anne Edwards, *Ever After: Diana and the Life She Lived* (2000); Andrew Morton, *Diana: Her True Story* (1997); Jane Owen, *Diana, Princess of Wales* (1983).

Dieting *See* WEIGHT.

Dreadlocks

The term "dreadlocks" originally referred to twisted, matted, or tangled clumps of hair that becomes this way because the hair is not combed, brushed, trimmed, or otherwise groomed. In contemporary western cultures, dreadlocks are usually deliberately cultivated according to certain hair fashions rather than resulting from a lack of combing or styling.

The word originated in Jamaica, where the style has been popular with men in modern times. The late Jamaican reggae musician Bob Marley is one of the people who brought the style to the attention of people around the world.

Dreadlocks have apparently been worn since ancient times and before, when prehistoric peoples did not use grooming implements or shampoos on their hair. Old Sanskrit texts show that the ancient people living in India wore their hair in "twisted locks" or "matted hair." This style was linked with to women in mourning and holy men,

Singer and actress Erykah Badu in a type of dreadlocks. © *John Barrett/Globe Photos, Inc., 2000.*

among others. They are still worn today by Sadhus (holy men) in India.

Versions of dreadlocks have also been worn by tribes in Africa, including people in Ethiopia, Senegal, Kenya, and Ghana. Tribes whose members have worn different versions of dreadlocks include the Pokot, Kau, Shonja, Ashanti, and Fulani. Short dreadlocks have been seen on the heads of Borneo natives.

In western societies, dreadlocks have been seen on African Americans and Jamaicans who preferred this natural style, as well as on some white people, often those who work in the music business or the arts. Young people in different regions of the United States have also embraced the style. Both male and female high school and college students can be seen wearing versions of dreadlocks. *See also* AFRICAN AMERICANS.

Further reading: Nekhana Evans, *Hairlocking: Everything You Need to Know: Africa, Dread and Nubian Locks* (1999); Wanda Johnson and Barbara Lawson (illus.) *The Art of Locks* (1991); Francesco Mastalia, *Dreads* (1999).

du Barry, Madame (Jeanne) (1743–1793)

Madame Jeanne du Barry began her career as a high-priced prostitute and ended up wielding great power as the mistress of King Louis XV and one of the most famous beauties of her time.

Jeanne du Barry was the illegitimate daughter of a seamstress and a monk. At age 6, she went to live in a Paris convent. When her education ended at age 15, she found work as the companion in the home of a prominent widow, but was fired when her employer learned that she was receiving male visitors. She found work as a salesgirl and spent her nights as a high-priced prostitute.

In 1765, a family named Count du Barry invited the 20-year-old Jeanne to live in his apartment, where he introduced the young beauty to socially prominent male clients who taught her etiquette and social skills. She began calling herself Madame du Barry and appeared at the opera and other social events in Paris. When she visited Versailles, the king's lavish estate near Paris, the 58-year-old King Louis XV became enamored of her. After a sham wedding was arranged with du Barry's brother, she was installed in luxury apartments near the king's. Many prominent Parisians were shocked when she was officially presented at court in 1769. She was the subject of jokes and obscene songs.

These critics aside, other people were captivated by her beauty, and one admirer wrote that du Barry was ". . . one of the prettiest women in a court where beauties were legion, was the most seductive of all because of the perfection of her entire person. Her hair, which she often dressed without powder, was the most beautiful blond, and so abundant that she hardly knew what to do with it. Her wide open blue eyes had a frank and caressing look. . . . Her nose was adorable, her mouth very small, and her skin of a dazzling whiteness." (Bernier, 1981)

Du Barry was also known for her lovely bust line, which she accentuated with low-cut gowns.

As the king's favorite mistress, she received lavish jewels and gowns, rode in gilded carriages, was attended by hundreds of servants, and received a large annual pension, part of which she used to amass valuable porcelains.

After Louis XV died in 1774, his son became king and his wife, Marie Antoinette, who disliked du Barry, became queen. Du Barry was exiled to the French provinces, but returned two years later and moved to a rural estate where she was known for her charitable activities in the surrounding area.

During the early years of the French Revolution, du Barry managed to avoid arrest, although she was denounced several times as an anti-Republican. She kept her property until 1793, but late that year, she was again denounced and was sentenced to death by guillotine.

Du Barry's reputation lived on after her death. Her life was the subject of two feature films made in 1919 and 1930. In 1935, the Hudnut Company introduced a line of products including face creams, lotions, facial toners, cotton balls, and powder in its Madame Dubarry set. Each container was adorned with a cameo style portrait of the famous courtesan. A line of color cosmetics named Dubarry was also available during the late twentieth century.

Further reading: Olivier Bernier, *The Eighteenth-Century Woman* (1981); Vincent Cronin, *Louis and Antoinette* (1974).

E

Ears

Ears have long been decorated and altered for reasons of appearance. In some cultures, people paint decorations on their ears. Ornaments are also used to enhance the ears' appearance and to show social or professional status or affiliations. Both men and women have adorned their ears, although ornaments for women are more common.

Ear ornaments date back to ancient times and include earrings, earplugs, and ear flares. Many are worn through holes that have been pierced in the earlobe.

Earrings

Earrings have been worn as ornaments since antiquity times and are mentioned in the Old Testament of the Bible. In most cases, holes were pierced in the ear lobes to hold earrings; clip- and screw-type earrings appeared in modern times. Earrings have been made in a wide range of sizes, and designs range from elaborate to simple. The earliest earrings were rings, sometimes with pendants attached with simple hooks. Ornate ancient Greek and Etrurian earrings, in the form of studs, pendants, and rings, were crafted from precious metals. Egyptian earrings often featured filigree work and were made of gold and gemstones. The ancient Romans made simpler ear ornaments from pearls and other stones and gold. In ancient Egypt, Israel, and western cultures, women wore earrings. In Asian cultures, both men and women wore earrings, as was true of the Ainu, aboriginal people of Asia.

Earrings made and worn in India have often been singled out for their creative and complex designs. Many earrings are large and skillfully crafted of gold or silver and studded with gems. Lavish ornaments have remained popular in India into modern times, and people living in other countries collect antique and modern Indian jewelry.

Earring styles varied from one period to another. For instance, pearl drops were popular among European and American women during the seventeenth and eighteenth centuries. Beginning in the late 1700s, earrings became more elaborate, and sparkling gems were used more often, as were pendant designs.

During periods when ears were covered by elaborate hairdos and wigs, earrings were either out of fashion or were small and less significant. Ear ornaments became more obvious when hairstyles were swept back from the face. In Victorian times, for example, upswept hairdos revealed various styles of earrings made with cameos, carved ivory, gold filigree, jet, and bright-colored gemstones, such as garnets.

In most cultures, people have worn earrings in both ears. However, wearing a single earring was popular during the Renaissance and the Baroque periods in Europe. Some people still favor only one earring today. In

Latin America, the ears of baby girls are routinely pierced at birth.

Earrings that were screwed or clipped onto the ear lobe became popular in the twentieth century. Costume jewelry—imitations of precious metals and real gemstones—was also mass-produced during the 1900s. During the 1960s, young women led the trend back toward pierced ears. They were joined by women of all ages who chose to pierce their ears. Women claimed that they were less likely to lose an earring this way. Since the 1970s, it has been fashionable in the United States and some other countries to pierce more than one hole in the ear and to wear multiple earrings, a custom that may have originated in West Africa. Models and celebrities, including tennis star Chris Evert, could be seen wearing multiple pierced earrings. Ears were pierced in the cartilage and tragus (prominence in front of the opening of the ear canal) as well as the lobe, although surgeons have reported serious infections that can result from pierced cartilage because the blood supply that is needed for healing is poor. (Armstrong, 1998)

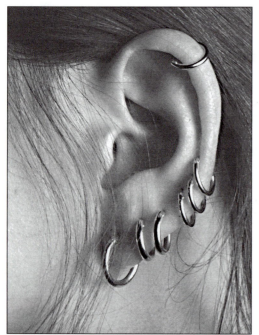

Multiple earrings are currently common. © *Photo Researchers.*

Pierced ears have become so popular in the United States that people can easily get their ears pierced in places other than physicians' offices. Teenagers sometimes pierce each other's ears or their own, using ice to numb the lobe and a needle passed through a flame. A scene in the popular Broadway musical and feature film *Grease* contains an ear-piercing scene among teenagers of the 1950s. Jewelry stores also offered customers ear-piercing services and "starter" earrings.

Health professionals warn that these procedures might be dangerous when performed by untrained people or in unsterile conditions, leading to infections, even hepatitis. Complications can also occur when people do not care for the newly pierced ear properly. Earring-wearers sometimes develop sensitivity or allergic reactions to materials in certain earrings. This has been blamed on the type of metal in the jewelry, usually nickel.

Before the twentieth century, pirates were known to wear large hoops, and sailors could be recognized by the earring they wore in one ear. Motorcycle club members also frequently wore an earring in one ear, as did some homosexual males. More men around the world are now wearing one earring in one pierced ear, a trend that gained more acceptance during the 1980s and does not necessarily indicate sexual orientation. Many male athletes and performers wear gold hoops, diamond studs, or other earrings. Well-known men who wear an earring include basketball superstar Michael Jordan and actor Harrison Ford.

Earplugs

Earplugs are another type of ornament worn on the ears, outside western countries. They are essentially objects placed in a hole in the earlobe that is much larger that the holes made for traditional ear piercing. Among the Suya tribal group of Brazil, ears are traditionally pierced at puberty. The earplugs worn by the Suya also serve as a symbol of how important it is to hear well in their culture. The Botocudo, a native group living in the forests of southeastern Brazil, wear wooden plugs in their ears. Portuguese invaders gave them their name, from a Portuguese word, botoque) that means "wooden plug." In Polynesia, the people of the Marquesas Islands make earplugs of ivory, embellished with carvings.

Ear flares were worn by the high-ranking ancient Mayans and native peoples of present-day Costa Rica (C.E. 500). These large, rounded ornaments were often made of gold, sometimes with jade or turquoise trimmings.

Cosmetic Surgery

Cosmetic surgery may be performed to change the shape and position of the ears. A procedure to flatten protruding ears is called otoplasty and is performed by surgeons who specialize in cosmetic or reconstructive procedures. Otoplasty may be performed to improve ear functioning as well as appearance. Children are among those who have surgery to "pin back" protruding ears. Some have been the victims of teasing and name-calling as a result of their ears' appearance. Because the ear usually completes 85 percent of its growth by age 3 and is completely grown by around age 10, the surgical procedure can be done early in life. *See also* BODY ORNAMENTATION.

Further reading: Myrna L. Armstrong, RN, "A Clinical Look at Body Piercing," www.rnweb.com; Angela Fisher, *Africa Adorned* (1983); George Gerster, "River of Sorrow, River of Hope," *National Geographic,* August 1975, 152-189; Timothy Kendall, "Kingdom of Kush," *National Geographic,* November 1990, 96-125; Julian Robinson, *The Quest for Human Beauty* (1998); Anthony Seeger, "The Meaning of Body Ornaments: A Suya Example," *Ethnology,* July 1975.

Eating Disorders *See* WEIGHT.

Eber, Jose (b. 1945?)

Jose (Joe-zey) Eber is a hair stylist who became famous during the 1970s. He has written books on hair styling and has made numerous guest appearances on television, where he discusses and demonstrates his techniques. He also created a line of women's hairpieces and a chain of hair-styling salons that bear his name.

Eber was born and raised in Nice, France, where he decided on his future career at the age of 13. He discovered he had a talent for styling the hair of his mother and sister, even though he had never had any training. After the Eber family moved to Berlin, Germany, 15-year-old José began working at the beauty salon in the Berlin Hilton Hotel. He then moved to Paris where he studied his craft and gained a reputation as the best stylist at a prestigious salon.

While vacationing in the United States, Eber decided to move to Los Angeles, where he took a job in a Beverly Hills salon. His clientele soon included models, actresses, and other celebrities, along with women who admired his work. Eber opened a salon called Maurice/Jose a block from the famous shopping street, Rodeo Drive, in downtown Beverly Hills. Later, he added three more salons. Among his famous clients were actresses Jamie Lee Curtis, singer/actress Cher, and television journalist Barbara Walters. Eber became known to a wider audience as he appeared on television shows and performed hair "makeovers."

In his 1982 book *Shake Your Head, Darling!* Eber described his approach to hair styling, which included analyzing a woman's way of life and personality, as well as her features and hair type. He is known for creating individualized styles and "touchable" hair that does not look stiff or overly styled. Some of the hairstyles he has created for his clients have influenced styles across America and around the world. His second book was called *Jose Eber: Beyond Hair.*

During the 1980s, Eber promoted a line of human hairpieces called "Secret Hair," which were designed to blend with a woman's natural hair. These products were introduced through a television infomercial featuring Eber. Jose Eber hair salons, franchised, were also opened throughout the United States.

Eber has dedicated time and money to helping victims of domestic violence. Joining forces with an organization called Sojourn, he helps battered women by raising money and by performing beauty makeovers to help these women feel more empowered. He continues to work as a stylist in his Beverly Hills salon, called Jose Eber, where clients from around the world seek his expertise.

Further reading: Jose Eber, *Beyond Hair: The Ultimate Makeover Book,* (1990); Eber, *Shake Your Head, Darling!* (1982).

Egypt, Ancient

Both men and women in Egypt used a variety of cosmetics at least as early as four thousand years ago as evidenced by their artwork, excavated tombs, and writings. Ancient texts contain directions for making different preparations for the face, hair, and body, including "cures" for baldness. As early as 2000 B.C.E., they appear to have used processes involving wet chemistry to formulate their cosmetics.

In the fourteenth century B.C.E., Egyptians also sought to change the body itself to meet the beauty standards of the day. They considered a long, oval-shaped head attractive and used boards and cloths to bind the heads of young children when the bones were still soft enough to mold.

Egyptian gravesites yield further information about the grooming habits of wealthy Egyptians, because makeup was buried with mummies for use in the afterlife. Makeup was kept in containers made of reed, stone, wood, and ceramic. Cosmetic ingredients were mixed on bronze plates; pigments were stored in alabaster jars or reed containers, and powders were mixed with animal fats or oils when it was time to apply them. Perfume jars and mirrors with elaborate handles in the shapes of animals, flowers, and people have also been found in Egyptian tombs. The tomb of Thutu, the wife of a thirteenth century B.C.E. ruler, held a case containing makeup, implements, and special cushions on which she could rest her arms while servants applied eye makeup.

Both men and women used rouge, lipstick, and nail colorings. They moisturized their skin with substances made from almond, palm, sesame, and olive oils. Oil of fenugreek, a plant that was widely available, was applied to freckles and wrinkled skin.

Women used numerous preparations on their skin. These included facial masks containing egg white, face creams, unguents, often perfumed, and creams just for the hands. They used pumice stones to smooth rough skin and to remove unwanted body hair.

Eye makeup was especially elaborate and was designed to create a look like that of the Egyptian sun god, Re. During damp weather, shadow powder was applied to the eye with pencils made from wood or ivory. Colored liquid protected the eyelids during hot, sunny days. Women frequently wore green shadow made from powdered malachite on the eyelids, outlined with dark gray lead ore and designed with "wings" at the corners. Eyeliner, mascara, and eyebrow darkener were made from kohl, a mixture of powdered antimony, carbon, and oxide of copper. Dark lines of color started at the outer corners of the eye and eyebrows, then met in front of the earlobes. Kohl was a major cosmetic item, and small kohl pots were made in various shapes, such as monkeys (which the ancient Egyptians kept as pets). Kohl pots were made from limestone and other stones, which were then painted and/or glazed.

As the final touch to their makeup, women used a mixture of red ochre and oil to tint lips and cheeks. Sometimes they painted their lips with a bluish-black color. They achieved a frosted look on their skin by using face paint to which pulverized ant eggs had been added. Gold paint was sometimes applied to the nipples. Some women also outlined the veins on their temples and breasts with blue paint. Tattoos were a popular form of body art, and certain designs appear on the bodies of ancient Egyptian brides.

Perfumes were widely used and often contained myrrh, frankincense, thyme, cedar, sandalwood, and/or musk. The Egyptians used herbs and flowers that were brought from Arabia, Persia, India, and Palestine. Frequently, they made the scents by steeping flowers and herbs in an oil base, then adding a fixative. Usually, the fixative was balanos, derived from the fruit of the Egyptian Plum tree, which grew in the Nile Valley. Scents containing balanos seemed to keep their fra-

Ancient Egyptian women chat. From the tomb of Nebamun, Dra Abu el-Naga, West Thebes, 18th Dynasty. © *Werner Forman/Art Resource, NY.*

grance for a long time, so Egyptian perfume-makers regarded it as an effective fixative. Some fragrant essences were considered more valuable than gold. Wealthy Egyptians used scents made from the rarest materials and prized their myrrh, spices, extracts of lily, and a perfume called kyphi, which was used by King Tutankhamen.

Egyptians wore wigs as sun protection as well as adornments. A smooth hairstyle, worn fairly close to the head, prevailed during the early kingdoms. As time passed, Egyptians began to favor longer and more arranged hair, with curls and braids becoming popular during the New Kingdom period (1539 B.C.E.–30 B.C.E.). Beeswax was used to set hairstyles, as were combinations of mud and water, after which the hair was exposed to the hot sun. Hair was dyed with henna, cow's blood, and a substance that combined warm oil and crushed tadpoles.

The use of henna to tint nails, palms, soles, and hair remains popular in the Middle East today, and henna hair coloring is used in other countries as well. *See also* BATHS; BODY DECORATION; BODY HAIR, MEN'S AND WOMEN'S; BODY ORNAMENTATION; CLEOPATRA; COSMETICS; EYES; FACIAL HAIR, MEN'S; FRAGRANCE; HAIR COLOR; HAIR, STYLING OF; HENNA; PERSONAL CARE PRODUCTS, MEN'S.

Further reading: Amy Adams, "Ancient Egyptians Make Up Chemistry," *Academic Press, Daily InScight,* 13 February 1999 http://www.apnet.com/inscight/02121999/grapha.htm; Paul J. Alexander, ed. *The Ancient World: To 300 AD* (1963); James Henry Breasted, *Ancient Times: A History of the Early World* (1944); Alice J. Hall, "Dazzling Legacy of an Ancient Quest," *National Geographic*, March 1977, 293-311; William F. Kaufman, *Perfume* (1974).

Elizabeth I (1533–1603)

As the ruler of England from 1558 to 1603, Queen Elizabeth I influenced fashions in clothing, cosmetics, and hairstyles during her long and prosperous reign. During this era, women used skin moisturizers, perfumes, white powders on their faces, and lip and cheek color derived from geranium petals. They grew their hair long, although they wore it pinned up in various styles and covered with various types of cap or "coif."

Elizabeth herself was once described as being "comely rather than handsome." The queen was tall and slim with pale skin and faint eyebrows. Like many people of her era, Elizabeth had been stricken with smallpox, which left many victims with scars called pock marks on their faces and bodies. To cover these marks, Elizabeth used heavy makeup, as much as an inch thick, according to some observers. Her cosmetic lotion was made of egg white, powdered eggshell, alum, borax, and white poppyseeds, all ground up with water to form a paste. This was actually a bleaching lotion, which could be used no more than three times a week. She also applied pale blue marks on the temples of her face and on her chest to make her skin look more translucent. The queen removed hairs at the hairline to give herself a higher forehead, which was the style of that era.

Elizabeth had flaming red-gold hair, and many of her subjects dyed their own hair to various shades of red as a way of flattering the monarch. Some of her closest advisers, all male, also dyed their beards red. The hair dyes people concocted were made from lead, sulfur, and quicklime—substances that could be harmful to the scalp.

Although rumors circulated that the queen had gone bald sometime around age 30, historical sources indicate that she did not wear wigs specifically to cover hair loss until the last twenty years of her life.

The queen enjoyed wearing perfume and used rose water from Antwerp, as well as a personal scent made from marjoram. Writers of the day indicate that she preferred light scents.

Further reading: Elizabeth Jenkins, *Elizabeth the Great* (1958); Alison Weir, *The Life of Elizabeth I* (1998).

Exercise *See* FITNESS MOVEMENT; WEIGHT.

Eyeglasses *See* EYES.

Eyes

Throughout history, eyes have often been adorned with various cosmetics and regarded as a focal point of the appearance and "the windows of the soul." People have altered and painted their eyelids, eyebrows, and eyelashes, as well as the undereye area.

Styles in the shape and thickness of eyebrows have been part of the changing fashions. At times people preferred thick brows over thin ones, have shaved or plucked out their brows, and have added color with natural materials or synthetic pencils, powders, liquids, or permanent dyes.

People also modify their eyes to fit a culture's ideas about beauty. The Mayans, who flourished until C.E. 900 then experienced a rapid decline in population, are one example. They preferred crossed eyes, so they hung objects between a baby's eyes so the child would develop a cross-eyed gaze. Usually, this object was a ball of pitch that was hung from a headboard placed between the baby's ears.

Eyes have been more or less emphasized depending on the culture. At other times, for example, during the Elizabethan period in England (1558–1603), people did not pay particular attention to the appearance of their eyes. In contrast, the ancient Egyptians and modern Indonesians are among those who have strongly made eye makeup central in their beauty rituals.

For thousands of years, people have applied various substances to the eye area to add color, depth, and definition. The ancient Egyptians were renowned for dramatically emphasizing the eye. The Egyptians colored their eyelids, often using a sparkling shadow, which was made from malachite and ground beetle shells. Men and women lined their eyes with kohl, as did children. This substance not only beautified and enhanced the eyes, it protected them from the harsh Egyptian sunlight.

Women in the Roman Empire (27 B.C.E–C.E. 395) used burnt cork to darken and thicken their eyelashes. They shaped their eyebrows by plucking them.

In addition to changing the shape of eyebrows through hair removal or makeup, people have also changed the color with bleaches or dyes. Ancient Greek women used soot (*asbokos*) or powdered antimony to darken their brows.

In western cultures, people have tended to prefer a wide space between the eyebrows, but in some Asian cultures, people admire eyebrows that form a continuous line across the bridge of the nose.

Indeed, eyebrows have been a major focus of appearance in certain Asian cultures at various times. At different periods in history, women plucked their eyebrows to resemble shapes that had special names, such as "distant mountain." In Japan during the Heian era (C.E. 794–1185), both women and men of noble birth plucked their brows and penciled on new brows higher on the forehead. Plucked eyebrows during the Edo period (1603–1876) was a sign that a woman had married and borne a child. Later in that era, some women did not pluck their brows and chose more individualized shapes and styles. Women preferred thicker brows that were not shaved or plucked during the Meiji era in the late nineteenth century.

In western cultures, two distinct brows have been considered most attractive. Both men and women who have obvious hairs connecting the brows across the middle choose to remove them by plucking, chemical depilatories, or electrolysis.

Eyelashes were regarded as unimportant and unattractive in Renaissance Europe, from the fourteenth through the sixteenth centuries. Women with dark or obvious lashes sometimes pulled them out to achieve the blank-eyed look popular during that era.

During Elizabethan times, English women plucked their eyebrows into thin lines, or sometimes completely removed them. Breasts were a focal point of the female body at this time, so women also shaved off the hair at the top of their forehead. All this was done to give the face a plain, empty appearance so that people would direct their gaze lower, to the bosom.

During the 1800s, most western cultures discouraged cosmetic use as a manifestation of vanity. Nevertheless, women found noncosmetic ways to enhance their eyes. Some women ingested belladonna, a substance that comes from the leaves and roots of the deadly nightshade plant. One of its effects was to make the eyes look larger, brighter, and sometimes darker. A long-standing natural treatment for irritated eyes was to place damp teabags or sliced cucumbers on the eyelids to soothe them.

During the eighteenth and nineteenth centuries, kohl remained popular with some groups in Africa and the Middle East. It was customary among the Berber women who live in North Africa's Atlas Mountains to use kohl to line their eyelids and to mark each corner with a large black dot. The substance became popular in western societies during the nineteenth and early twentieth centuries. Singer Josephine Baker (1906–1975) and actresses Sarah Bernhardt (1844–1923) and Theda Bara (1885–1955) used kohl around their eyes. The 1960s, with its emphasis on natural cosmetics, brought renewed interest in using kohl eye pencils.

Eye makeup was among the last cosmetics to win public approval in modern times, perhaps because it was more obvious than face powder and certain other cosmetics. Mascara appeared during the eighteenth century, but the average woman did not use it until after the 1930s. By the 1950s, women's use of eye shadow and eyeliner was more widespread. Eyes received more attention during the late 1960s, when dark eyeliner and thick eyelashes, including false lashes, became popular. Heavy eye makeup and pale lipstick were part of a popular look that originated in England and could be seen on popular models such as Twiggy and Jean Shrimpton, a look known as the "Carnaby Street" look after a fashionable street in London.

Modern cosmetic items used to dramatize the eyes include eyebrow pencils and brush-on powders, eyeshadows in different colors and textures, mascara, eyeliner, undereye concealer, and false eyelashes, both in strips and in individual clumps. Both men and women use various creams and lotions on the skin around the eyes to condition and moisturize and to diminish the signs of aging.

Consumers' choice of eye-enhancing products is truly enormous. Eyeliners can be applied from liquid, pencil, cake, or powder formulations, and mascaras can lengthen and thicken lashes, along with changing their color. Eyeshadow is available in a large number of colors; what colors are considered fashionable changes from season to season. Many of these cosmetics are waterproof or water-resistant. Products that remove eye makeup are also available.

Recently, Americans of both genders have been purchasing more eyebrow grooming kits. One of the most popular kits is called "Eliza's Eyebrow Essentials" and was created by eyebrow designer Eliza Petrescu The kit contains tools for grooming eyebrows, along with a booklet explaining how to plan a flattering shape for the brows and pluck them accordingly.

Permanent makeup—dye—is a way to darken existing eyelashes and add extra "hairs" to the brows through a tattooing process. People who don't want to reapply makeup regularly may opt for permanent makeup. A beauty professional usually does these procedures.

Corrective Lenses

Methods for correcting vision affect appearance. The oldest known vision aids were handheld, such as magnifying glasses or rock crystals held up to printed material that enlarged the text. The Chinese had a form of eyeglasses about 2000 years ago, but these did not correct vision; rather, they were meant to ward off evil spirits. Eyeglasses to aid vision appeared in Italy sometime in the thirteenth century. They can be seen in frescoes painted in 1352. The earliest eyeglasses were for reading, and they included two eye-pieces attached to a v-shaped piece of metal that was placed over the nose. During the mid-1400s, technology advanced to create lenses

to aid people who were nearsighted. In the 1600s, Spanish spectacle makers used silk ribbons worn over the ears to hold the glasses in place. Other early eyeglasses had metal frames and were made in a limited number of sizes and styles.

Some people, such as the French, wore their reading aids in only private and preferred not to be seen in them. Some societies viewed spectacles as a sign of weakness or aging. However, in Spain, people of various socioeconomic classes thought eyeglasses gave them more status. Upper-class men in Europe and England wore an eyeglass for just one eye, called a monocle, during the late 1800s until around 1914.

Lorgnettes—two lenses mounted on a frame and held with a handle—became a form of jewelry for the women whose vision needed correction during the eighteenth century. They were frequently made from gold and studded with gems. Women who did not like the look of glasses could use the lorgnette as needed.

Some people regarded eyeglasses as unattractive, particularly on women. At the turn of the nineteenth century, an optician named Norburne Jenkins wrote, "Glasses are very disfiguring to women and girls. Most tolerate them because they are told that wearing them all the time is the only way to keep from having serious eye trouble." This stigma did not seem to apply to sunglasses, which gained in popularity during the 1930s. Through the years, eyeglass manufacturers created more styles and colors, and manufacturers began to produce different styles eyeglasses for males and females.

Fashions in lens shape also changed from time to time as well, and continue to do so. Round lenses were made during the mid-1700s to about 1820. This shape made a comeback in the late twentieth century. Oval lenses were most common in the 1800s, although oblong and rectangular shapes were also made during that century. Currently, very small oval lenses are considered chic.

A person who wears eyeglasses may be the victim of stereotypes. They may be regarded as more intellectual, restrained, quiet, or serious than people who don't wear them.

Women in particular have been exposed to negative social messages toward wearing eyeglasses, as expressed in line from the writer Dorothy Parker: "Men seldom make passes at girls who wear glasses."

However, attitudes change, and some actors and actresses and other well-known people have worn glasses as a fashion statement, even when they do not need them to improve vision. Many people consider sunglasses an appealing fashion accessory, as evidenced by the hundreds of styles and colors to choose from. Some people have trademark styles; for instance, Jacqueline Kennedy Onassis was known for her large dark sunglasses and author and feminist Gloria Steinem for her "aviator style" wire-rimmed eyeglasses. Actress Audrey Hepburn also made large sunglasses a trademark, especially in the film *Breakfast at Tiffany's*. Sales of Ray-Bans increased after actor Tom Cruise wore them in the feature film *Risky Business*.

Contact lenses

Contact lenses, which are plastic corrective lenses worn on the eyeball itself, were first tried without much success during the late nineteenth century. With the development of new plastic materials during the 1900s, manufacturers were able to produce hard contact lenses, which became available in 1938. Later, bifocal contact lenses and hydrophilic (water-absorbent) lenses came into use.

Contact lenses allow people to correct certain kinds of vision problems without wearing eyeglasses, which may be less convenient. Many contact-lens wearers prefer them for reasons of appearance. The first contact lenses were made from clear plastic methyl methacrylate. By 1964, over six million people in the United States were wearing contact lenses. About 65 percent of them were female.

Later, soft lenses made from plastic material that conformed even more closely to the shape of the cornea were developed and became more popular than hard lenses. Soft lenses felt more comfortable and seldom fell off the eye. Another development was extended-wear lenses, which could be worn for longer periods of time; some people could even wear them overnight.

As contact lenses became easier to wear and more colorful, more people opted for them, sometimes purely for cosmetic reasons. For the first time in history, people could change their eye colors cosmetically. A person with with light-colored eyes could deepen the natural color by wearing blue or green tinted lenses. Some dark-eyed women chose lenses in shades of pink or yellow to alter their eye color slightly. By the 1980s, the Wesley Jessen Corporation offered colored lenses that could change dark brown eyes to various shades of green, blue, blue-green, and violet. People who did not need vision correction bought colored lenses because they wanted a different color of eyes.

More innovative designs in contact lenses emerged during the 1990s. Lenses became more colorful and featured decorative and unusual designs. By 1998, people could wear lenses that gave their eyes an unnatural "whited-out" look that became a trademark of "shock-rock" star Marilyn Manson. Lenses in the "Wild Eyes" line, sold by Wesley Jessen, featured stars, eight balls, flames, and spirals. *See also* COSMETICS; PLASTIC SURGERY; PERMANENT MAKEUP.

Further reading: Advertising materials from the Wesley Jessen Company; Richard Corson, *Fashions in Makeup* (1972); David Frye, Nancy Frye, and Alan Okagaki, *Consumer's Guide to Cosmetics* (1979); Kathy Peiss, *Hope in a Jar* (1998); Herbert Solomon and Walter J. Zinn, *The Complete Guide to Eye Care, Eyeglasses, and Contact Lenses* (1977); Ellen Tien, "Brow Tools for Him and Her," *The New York Times*, 11 April 1999, 3.

F

Face

The face is the focus of appearance for both men and women, and they have gone to great lengths to make their faces match the beauty standards of their time and culture. Numerous substances, products, and objects have been used to treat facial skin or alter or adorn this part of the body. In modern times, people have turned to cosmetic surgery to change features or to reduce the signs of aging.

Particular facial shapes and skin coloring have been regarded as attractive throughout history, particularly for women. For instance, in ancient Ireland, an oval face, more narrow in the chin than the brow, and fair skin were considered the signs of an aristocratic and beautiful woman.

An oval face is still often considered the "ideal," and numerous beauty books and articles describe ways to shade and highlight other facial shapes to make them appear more oval. For men, more rugged, masculine facial contours have been admired in western cultures during recent decades, although the recent emphasis on fitness has smoothed some of the rough edges off the male ideal.

Facial Coloring

Fashions in cheek color have varied greatly during different historical eras and from one culture to another. A blooming appearance on the cheeks was frequently regarded as a sign of health and youth and thus pursued as a beauty ideal in various cultures. Women have used various shades of pink, red, coral, and copper on their faces, particularly on the cheeks, to give the impression of a rosy or glowing complexion.

At other times, a pale, translucent complexion was regarded as ideal, and women used white or pale powders and other substances to subdue their natural face color or the tanning effects of the sun. A pale look was popular in the Roman Empire (27 B.C.E.–C.E. 476) and Elizabethan England (1558–1603) and in Asian countries for thousands of years. In ancient Ireland, a pale face with a blush across the cheeks was prized. Women used material from the plant ruam to heighten that blush.

A preference for a pale appearance has sometimes reflected class-consciousness. For instance, from the time of the Renaissance (founteenth century) through the nineteenth century, a pale complexion was considered desirable for upper-class women in Europe. and the 1800s. High color or a sun-tanned look gave the impression that the person spent time outdoors doing physical labor rather than enjoying a life of privilege.

At times, however, women wanted both rosy cheeks and an otherwise pale complexion. They achieved this various ways. During Elizabethan times, women made a kind of cheek color from geranium petals. A rosy complexion became more desirable during the Romantic era (late eighteenth and early nineteenth centuries) and eighteenth-century Age of Enlightenment in Europe, both characterized by a renewed interest in nature. The art of the period features subjects who are often rosy cheeked and robust. During the late 1700s, almost every Frenchwoman wore rouge, so called for the French word for "red," on her cheeks. The British viewed matters differently. Makeup was considered to be in bad taste in England, at least during the Victorian and Edwardian periods, and women who used obvious color on their cheeks were criticized or regarded as disreputable. Women who wanted a rosy glow would sometimes pinch their cheeks or apply a hint of color that could not be detected as fake. Other women risked using cheek color they made from recipes containing berry juice, cochineal, carmine, or beetroot. Stores sold balls of cream rouge packaged inside silk or gauze packages, which were fastened to a stick. Users dipped the ball into water, then applied it to the face or cleavage. Men known as "dandies" used cheek color during the late 1800s.

More shades of rouge paste were available in the early 1900s, and some women used theatrical makeup to give color to their cheeks. Along with face powder and lip salve, rouge was one of the three best-selling color cosmetics.

During the 1920s, the fashionable young women in America and England known as flappers rebelled against much conventional female behavior, including the prohibition against makeup. They reddened their cheeks with manufactured rouge, applying two high, round areas of color.

By the 1930s, women were able to change their faces in many ways, as cosmetics of all kinds became more acceptable. Cosmetic companies offered consumers a considerable choice of products. Women who did not want to appear made up could choose subtler shades of cream or cake rouge.

As women's roles and occupations changed during World War II, they gave themselves new faces to match their new image. The intense colors in rouge and lipstick became more popular. Women held jobs that had been male-only, working in defense plants and other factories and driving trucks, operating machinery, delivering mail, and running streetcars. The new, brighter image of women emphasized health, energy, and independence, rather than a fragile or sedentary appearance that would be associated with pale skin.

But as women faded back into the domestic scene of the 1950s, so did their complexions, and cheek coloring became more subtle.

The later 1960s, however, with the emphasis on individualism, allowed women again to use makeup to use their faces as a kind of self-expression. Cosmetics again became colorful. The Revlon Company introduced a popular product called "Blush-On," a powdered cheek color that came in a compact with a brush applicator. Other companies also produced powdered blush products, which their makers claimed could be blended easily to give a natural look. Numerous shades of powdered blushers became available in matte and frosted finishes, and this type of blush remains popular today.

During the 1970s the natural look was popular, and women's cosmetic alterations to their faces reflected this. More brownish shades of blush were best sellers. Companies introduced new products for applying color to the cheeks or all over the face for a "natural glow." Products made from plants and other materials found in nature also became increasingly available.

What constitutes an attractive face varies from place to place. In India, for example, golden cheek colors are preferred, and some women use powdered turmeric, a spice with an orange color, on their cheeks. In some parts of the world, women have continued to use non-manufactured sources of color. Berries and certain roots also provide color in places where women do not buy or choose not to use manufactured blushers or other cosmetics. Berber women used strong cheek coloring, applying a round stain of akkar. Small pots of this reddish stain are sold in marketplaces. In Haiti and other places, women have created powder for blusher by smashing red-clay bricks.

Face Powder

Powder has long been used as a means of altering the look of faces. Asian women were among those who used light or white colored powders on their faces. Using a wet cloth, they applied dried rice powder, which was made into cakes women kept in their homes. Later, talc was used to make face powder.

Powder was also a means of signaling that one was a lady. The appearance of an oily complexion was considered unladylike and coarse looking, a sign of overexertion or manual labor not in keeping with the refined ideal. Young ladies were warned not to perspire in any obvious way with an old adage: "Men sweat, women glow."

Sheer powders that allowed women to look natural and unmadeup were developed in the 1970s. These, although made of synthetic materials, were in keeping with the natural look of the face favored at the time. Face powders were available in loose form or in compacts that could be carried for use during the day or evening. Powders were applied with brushes or powder puffs made of cloth or foam. As time went on, manufacturers developed powders in hundreds of shades to match women's complexions.

Although most women who use face powder buy a manufactured product, this cosmetic can also be made from household ingredients. In Cuba and some other countries, women make a powder called *cascarilla* from pulverized eggshells.

Faces of Modern Youth

In the 1980s and 1990s, some young people made up their faces to make visible their rejection of mainstream society. Black lipstick, flat white makeup, and heavily made up eyes, as well as facial piercings, said, in effect, that they regarded themselves as separate. These once-extreme forms of makeup, particularly the nontraditional colors of lipstick, have now entered the mainstream.

Cosmetic Procedures

A face-lift, known medically as a rhytidectomy, is a form of cosmetic surgery performed to tighten the sagging skin of the face, neck, and jaw that results from aging or weight loss. The desired outcome is a smooth, firm appearance that is not too tight and unnatural looking. A face-lift may be done along with other procedures, such as a chin tuck, forehead lift, and eyelid surgery.

The surgery is done under anesthesia and nearly always as an outpatient procedure. During the surgery, incisions are made in the hairline near forehead down to the ears. The surgeon tightens sagging muscles, removes excess fatty deposits as needed, and cuts away excess folds of skin before sewing the incision. During a surgical face-lift, incisions are made around the ear and sometimes behind it so that the skin of the face and neck can be lifted off the underlying muscles and bones and tightened for a younger look. Excess skin and fat are removed and the surgeon contours the remaining tissue. Complications of a face-lift may include swelling, bruising, and numbness in the face and neck, scabbing, scars.

A procedure may also be done to repair neck muscles and alter the line of the neck and jaw line. The scars eventually fade and cosmetics and hair styling are used to cover any scars that remain.

Face-lifts are most common in western cultures, particularly in the United States. Women make up the overwhelming majority of people seeking face-lifts, usually during or after their late 50s. Since about 1990, if they didn't want a full-scale facelifts, people were also choosing more limited procedures called "mini-lifts" and less invasive procedures, including laser surgery and endoplasty. Thirty-seven percent of all facelifts are being done on people between the ages of 35 and 50, and 2 percent are performed on people aged 19 to 34.

The number of people having face-lifts and other kinds of cosmetic surgery on the face continues to rise each year. Although most are women, the percentage of men continued to rise during the 1990s. *See also* AFRICAN AMERICANS; BEAUTY STANDARDS; COSMETICS; FACIAL PATCHES; "LOOKS"; PLASTIC SURGERY; SKIN; SKIN COLORING AGENTS.

Further reading: Paula Begoun, *The Beauty Bible* (1997); Janet Carlson Freed and Diane Guernsey, eds., "Town and Country's Comprehensive Guide to Cosmetic Surgery," *Town & Country*, March 1999, 144–162; Kate Mulvey and Melissa Richards, *Decades of Beauty* (1998); National Clearinghouse of Plastic Surgery Statistics, "1998 Plastic Surgery Statistics," and "As 'Boomers' Age, Cosmetic Surgery Increases," http://www.plasticsurgery.org/mediactr/trends92-98.htm.

Face-Painting *See* BODY DECORATION.

Facial Hair, Men's

Men's facial hair—on the chin, known as a beard, and above the lip, called a mustache—has been a focus of grooming practices throughout history. At times, beards and/or mustaches have been fashionable, although styles in both changed.

Beards—unshaven facial hair stretching across the chin, sometimes from ear to ear—have been grown long or trimmed and arranged according to local customs and the fashions of the times. Laws and religious customs have required or banned beards or limited them to certain men. In some places, such as ancient Egypt, men and/or women wore false beards.

Men did not wear beards at all in some ancient cultures, such as the Sumerians (5000 B.C.E.–1950 B.C.E.), who occupied what was ancient Mesopotamia, the land above the Tigris and Euphrates Rivers. Men in ancient India also shaved off their body hair and usually shaved off their facial hair every four days. In the ancient Americas, the Incas of Peru had laws banning beards. The Aztecs, who lived in present-day Mexico, also did not wear beards. Other Native Americans in North America and Central and South America also scorned facial hair, including beards. Ancient peoples living in what are now Wales and Brittany shaved their beards, but grew mustaches. Soldiers in Assyria (900 B.C.E.–612 B.C.E.) wore short beards.

Men in some regions added decorative elements to their beards. Assyrian men curled their beards and added dyes and gold dust on occasion. Kings of ancient Persia laced their beards with gold threads, as did the long-haired, long-bearded Merovingians, who lived in present-day France during the sixth to mid-eighth centuries C.E.

Among the ancient Egyptians, men considered body hair disagreeable, and some men shaved their whole bodies. As a result, as early as 500 B.C.E., barbers, who performed shaving services, were prominent members of Egyptian society. During the period known as the Old Kingdom (3110–2000 B.C.E.), men did grow some hair on their chins, which they might dye or frizz. Some men added gold threads to their beards. Later, Egyptians attached false beards to their chins for ceremonies. A sign of royalty was a beard made of metal; Egyptian queens wore gold beards. Long false beards were a sign of rank and were considered fashionable for both men and women. After they fastened their beards in place around their heads, they put wigs on their shaved heads. Egyptian kings, queens, and priests wore these long beards.

Men living in Imperial Rome grew long beards, often with elaborate waves and curls, and adolescent men followed the custom of dedicating their beards to the gods. Barbers first arrived in Sicily around 299 B.C.E., and they cared for beards as well as hair growing on the head. The custom spread to Rome and other parts of the empire. However, under Caesar, who was clean-shaven, fashions changed again. Beards became popular again during the reign of Hadrian (C.E. 117–138), who wore a beard to cover his facial scars and blemishes.

In ancient Greece, men wore beards, and the first sign of chin growth on young men was dedicated in a temple according to religious customs. The custom of wearing beards declined when Alexander the Great rose to power in 323 B.C.E. and sent Macedonian troops into Asia, where they lost several battles to Persian troops. The Persians were able to capture many Greek soldiers by grabbing their beards and pulling them off their horses. As a result, Alexander banned beards in the military and other Greek men followed suit.

Religious customs governed the growth of beards in some societies. In the Middle East, followers of the Prophet Mohammed had to trim their mustaches and beards in a certain way to show they were Muslims. Bedouin Arabs also had beards, which they groomed to a point. Ancient Jews were expected to wear beards, which were regarded as a sign of manliness. Men trimmed their beards but let them grow longer during times of mourning. Some modern Jews of the Hasidic group and other Orthodox Jews follow this custom.

At times, conquerors or dictators forced people to shave, and the cutting of a man's beard against his will was sometimes done as a way to humiliate conquered peoples. Christian leaders ordered Celts and Teutons to shave off their beards. When Japan conquered the Ainu, a tribe that lived in the north of the archipelago, they ordered the Ainu men to shave. (Modern Ainu men never shave their faces.) As they took power in Austria, Poland, and other countries, Nazi German soldiers forced orthodox Jewish men to shave their beards, which were worn for religious reasons.

From the ninth century to the present, styles in beards have continued to vary with time and place. Beards and mustaches were worn during the reign of Henry VIII, who had his own red beard. Some styles were used to designate rank and group affiliation; others were decreed by law; some were grown to imitate fashionable figures.

When beards were fashionable, they were often regarded as sign of manliness, health, and honor. In places where shaving was the norm, the growth of a beard could be viewed as a sign that something was amiss in a man's life. Perhaps the man was in mourning, lacked time to spend on his appearance, or did not care about social conventions.

Clean-shaven faces were common in America during the 1700s, when the most prominent politicians and respected "frontier" men, such as Davy Crockett and Daniel Boone, did not have beards. When he took office, Abraham Lincoln was the first bearded U.S. president.

Sideburns came into fashion during the Civil War in the United States. General Ambrose Everett Burnside, a Union commander of the Army of the Potomac, wore bushy side whiskers known as "burnsides." By the turn of the nineteenth century, the name had reversed to become "sideburns."

Other men in mid-nineteenth century America also favored full beards. A more portly and mature appearance for men was popular during the years following the Civil War, and most American males of the 1860s wore whiskers, which were thought to impart a wise and responsible look. While men in the east wore their sideburns and chin whiskers according to fashions, some western men, such as army scout William "Buffalo Bill" Cody, claimed they wore beards for practical reasons: shaving was not convenient. The same reason probably applied to the many bearded men who pioneered the western United States.

Another style of beard, the goatee, has also cycled into and out of fashion. Goatees are tufts of hair on the chin, trimmed to look like the beard of a male goat, which gives them their name.

Some men wear a mustache along with this type of beard. Variations of this look include the Van Dyke beard, which was named for seventeenth-century Flemish artist Anthony Van Dyck (1599–1641), whose portraits showed men wearing goatees. The Imperial, popularized by Napoleon III who reigned from 1852–1871, came to a sharp point. To achieve this effect, men applied wax or pomade to their chin hairs and brushed them into the pointed shape. In the United States, this style was popular during the Civil War era. "Bohemians" was the name given to the artists, writers, and intellectuals in Paris who wore this style during the late nineteenth century.

At the start of the twentieth century, the neatly trimmed beard of King Edward VII of England (1841–1910) typified the style that was considered tasteful for a gentleman in many western cultures. The king influenced fashions during the late 1800s when, as Prince of Wales, he was the leader of the fash-

King Charles of England (1600–1649) wore a Van Dyke beard. *Archive Photos.*

ionable "Marlborough House set" in London society.

In 1910, ads from the Gillette company urged men to stay clean-shaven in order to appeal to women, whom they called "the great civilizer. . . [who] admires a clean, healthy skin." A clean-shaven look, said this ad, gave men a healthy look that suggested "the outdoor rather than the indoor man." (Atwan, McQuade, and Wright, 1971)

In the mid-twentieth century, after several clean-shaven decades, the beard again became a statement. The so-called "beatnik" "Beat Generation" men in the 1950s often wore goatees. During the 1960s, youths who identified themselves as part of the counterculture (known as "hippies") adopted beards and long hair as one means of free expression.

In the 1980s, some celebrities and other men opted to wear a light growth of beard, left deliberately unshaven. The actor Don Johnson on a television series *Miami Vice* regularly had a light growth of beard. The Palestinian leader Yassar Arafat was also known for what appeared to be a permanent three-day stubble.

A few religions still use beards to indicate membership in a particular group. The Amish men grow beards, but not mustaches, when they get married. Orthodox Jewish men also wear beards.

The Mustache

Mustache, or moustache, refers to hair growth above a man's upper lip. As with beards, men have worn mustaches since prehistoric times for religious, social, personal or practical reasons. Facial hair was a source of warmth in cold climates.

Men with thin mustaches appear on pottery and other artifacts from ancient Egypt. The Gauls also wore mustaches but not beards, a custom that the Roman conquerors regarded as barbaric ("barba" is the Latin word for beard). During the mid-1400s, men in England were required by law to shave off mustaches. Later, British soldiers were expected to keep theirs. Mustaches were popular among soldiers in France, Prussia, and England during the early 1800s, but Bavarian rulers at the time outlawed mustaches among their troops.

Shaving

The first shaving tools used to remove human body hair were made from sharpened flints and shells. Cave drawings dating back more than 20,000 years show pictures of men both with and without beards. The Egyptian pharaohs used bronze razors, which have been found in their tombs. In ancient Greece, the men apparently shaved daily. To keep their cheeks and chin smooth, Roman legionnaires rubbed them with pumice, a volcanic rock, rather than shaving every day.

In some other cultures, men plucked out their chin hairs. Native Americans used pairs of clam shells for this purpose, and men in the South Seas used flint.

Shaving was more common during the Middle Ages in Europe and men often shaved weekly. Few people could shave daily; self-shaving required soap, and this was scarce, expensive, and often uncomfortable for use on the face. Razors were primitive, and left stubble on the face.

A French barber invented the first safety razor in 1762. His invention was a marked improvement over the straight razors that swordsmiths had fashioned. Jean Jacques Perret created a metal razor with a metal guard along one edge of the blade. Other people tried to improve on the straight razor.

During the 1800s, American men used shaving brushes, dipping them into a cup of soap lather, and hand-held straight razors. They sharpened the blades on leather bands called "strops."

The idea for a disposable razor blade came from a traveling salesman named King Gillette. Working with a professor from the Massachusetts Institute of Technology, he developed the blade that went on the market in 1903.

Gillette's business expanded greatly during World War I. The government ordered 3.5 million razors and 36 million blades for servicemen. Allied soldiers in Europe learned about the invention from American soldiers. A soldier named Jacob Schick wanted to improve on the safety razor and developed a dry razor powered by an electric motor that did not require water, soap, or shaving cream. The Schick electric razor went on sale in 1931 and cost 25 dollars. Between 1931 and 1937, sales rose from 3,000 to almost 2 million a year.

During the mid-1900s, men were encouraged to shave daily for a well-groomed appearance, and beards were generally viewed as either bohemian or intellectual. New equipment and technology made this grooming task easier.

One of the best-known ad campaigns of the twentieth century was for a shaving cream called Burma Shave, which came in tubes and jars and could be spread on the face with the fingers. Innovative billboard ads for this product appeared in 1925 and ran till 1963 . The owners of the company, the Odell family, decided to place a group of four sequential three-foot long signs on Route 65 in Minnesota. The signs read: "SHAVE THE MODERN WAY/FINE FOR THE SKIN/ DRUGGISTS HAVE IT/BURMA-SHAVE. The idea caught fire, and the company began using six boards for its ads, which became more and more creative. They appeared along the side of the highway so that motorists would read them in sequence as they drove along. The signs told a brief "story" and ended with the words "Burma Shave." Within a few years, they had spread throughout the country in all but a few states. The ads aimed to be clever and intriguing. An example: A SILKY CHEEK/SHAVED SMOOTH AND CLEAN/IS NOT OBTAINED/WITH A MOWING MACHINE/ BURMA-SHAVE. This ad was a response to the growing number of electric shavers after they became available in the 1920s.

During the late 1920s, Burma Shave began sponsoring contests for new advertising slogans. People could send in their ideas for new billboard "stories" to advertise this product. The company received thousands of entries each year. The winners received $100. Burma Shave signs became part of the landscape in America. Some of the signs contained public interest messages, such as: PAST/SCHOOLHOUSES/TAKE IT SLOW/LET THE LITTLE/SHAVERS GROW/BURMA-SHAVE.

Sales of Burma-Shave rose until 1947, remained level for about seven years, then started to decline. The company realized that motorists were driving so fast they no longer had time to read the ads along the highways. They sold the business to Philip Morris and Burma Shave became part of its American Safety Razor Products. Sets of Burma-Shave signs are displayed in the Smithsonian Institution in Washington, D.C., and the American Advertising Museum in Portland, Oregon.

Shaving offered cosmetics companies another big opportunity to create men's toiletries. Ads for personal razors stressed the convenience of shaving in one's own home, as well as the privacy and money-saving aspects. Gillette ads featured men other men might admire—athletes, soldiers, and professional men. A Gillette ad from 1910 equates the man who shaves himself a with the "American spirit" and initiative. Another ad by the same company claims that using a Gillette razor daily helps a man develop regular habits and self-respect. Men with clean-shaven faces could be seen "in the store, the counting-room, the classroom, the office— in work and sport out of doors . . ."

As more shaving equipment and supplies were developed and marketed, companies emphasized the importance of a man's face and appearance in the modern job market. More and more men in western nations became convinced that shaving was important to their appearance, hygiene, and social status. Today, most men in western societies shave daily. They also use a wide array of grooming products associated with shaving: aftershave lotion, skin toners, shaving cream, shaving gel, and others. *See also* BABYLONIA; BODY HAIR, MEN'S AND WOMEN'S; BYZANTINE EMPIRE; EGYPT, ANCIENT; GREECE, ANCIENT; MEN'S PERSONAL CARE PRODUCTS.

Further reading: Robert Atwan, Donald McQuade, and John W. Wright, *Edsels, Luckies, & Frigidaires: Advertising the American Way* (1971); Charles Goodrum and Helen Dalrymple, (1968), *Advertising in America: The First 200 Years* (1990); Michael Grant, *A Social History of Greece and Rome* (1992); James Laver, *Taste and Fashion: From the French Revolution to Today* (1937); Jack Lindsay, *The Ancient World: Manners and Morals*; Ellen Moers, *The Dandy: Brummell to Beerbohn* (1960); Reginald Reynolds, *Beards* (1950); James B. Twitchell, *Twenty Ads that Shook the World* (2000).

Facial Patches

Facial patches are ornamental cut-outs made from various fabrics and applied to the face. Some patches were small and subtle, while others were quite elaborate. They were worn at various times in history to draw attention to certain facial features, such as the lips or eyes, or to hide scars. Before smallpox vaccine became available in the late 1790s, smallpox was prevalent throughout Europe and left many people with scars on their faces and bodies.

Facial patches were popular during the seventeenth century in Europe. The patches were made in the shape of stars, suns, crosses, moons, birds, and other objects, and were created from black fabrics, usually silk, velvet, or leather. Most of the patches were worn to hide scars or other disfigurements of the face or to highlight attractive features. As time went on, people sometimes wore several patches, even a dozen at a time, and patches became larger and more elaborate. People expressed their personalities and sense of style by wearing particular types or combinations of face patches. The patches also had social meanings. A patch on the right cheek meant that a woman was married, while a patch on the left cheek meant she was engaged. Flirtatious women placed a patch at the right corner of their mouths; passionate ones applied a patch to the corner of the eye.

In England, Oliver Cromwell (1599–1658), who had overturned the monarchy, forbade face patches as an aristocratic affectation. The fashion was revived during the subsequent reign of Charles II but faded out during the later 1700s.

Under the name of "beauty patches," facial patches have made comebacks in Europe and North America from time to time. During the mid-twentieth century, for instance, women could purchase kits with small black patches in assorted designs, primarily hearts and stars. *See also* FACE.

Further reading: Olivier Bernier, *The Eighteenth-Century Woman* (1981); Christopher Falkus, *The Life and Times of Charles II* (1972).

Fawcett, Farrah (b. 1947)

During the 1970s and 1980s, the actress Farrah Fawcett became famous for her distinctive hairstyle, dazzling smile, and "all-American" look. She endorsed cosmetic and hair products and posed for a swimsuit poster that sold a record-setting 12 million copies and established her as a pop culture icon. Her hairdo has been called the most frequently copied style in American history and *Time* magazine has called Fawcett the "epitome of '70s glamour." (*Time*'s 100 Most Influential Women of the Century," November 1999)

Fawcett, a native of Texas, attended the University of Texas in Austin as an art major. During her freshman year, she was chosen as one of the ten most beautiful women on campus, and her picture caught the attention of a Hollywood publicist who urged her to pursue an acting career. Two years later, Fawcett moved to Los Angeles and quickly found work in television commercials, appearing in ads for Noxzema men's shaving cream, Ultra-Brite toothpaste, and Mercury-Cougar automobiles, among other products.

Fawcett appeared in two feature films, then starred with Kate Jackson and Jaclyn Smith in the hit television series *Charlie's Angels*, which was shown around the world. The "angels" were featured on numerous magazine covers and interviewed about their lives and beauty regimens.

After one season, Fawcett left *Charlie's Angels* and performed in feature films and on stage. She later won critical acclaim for her dramatic performances on stage and in various television movies and feature films. She continues to act in television and films and appeared in *Playboy* magazine pictorials in 1995 and 1997. She has also exhibited her artwork and sculpture.

Fawcett embodied the trim, glowing look that was popular in America during the 1970s, when fitness and a natural look were especially admired. Fans requested her advice on hair and makeup and asked what exercises she did to stay fit. Magazine articles described her daily routines, makeup, hair care, and favorite foods and sports, which included tennis. Her long, casual, layered hairstyle, which was created by stylist Hugh York, was widely copied, and she endorsed Wella Balsam hair products in television and print ads.

Nevertheless, Fawcett viewed her looks as a mixed blessing and once said, "People want to see me in a certain way. I understand this. Still, I think deep down every actress would like to do a role where she doesn't wear any makeup, where she is accepted on her acting alone." (Burstein, 1977)

Further Reading Patricia Burstein, *Farrah* (1977); Steve Friedman, "The Importance of Being Farrah," *Mirabella*, March/April 1998, 122ff; *Time*, "Time's 100 Most Influential Women of the Century," November 1999.

Feet

The appearance of the feet has been and still is a matter of cosmetic importance in various cultures and times, usually for women more than men, and more so in places where the feet are not encased in footgear year-round. In certain places, such as India and parts of Africa, the skin on the top or bottom of the feet is painted with designs. Elsewhere, only the toenails receive much ornamentation.

Unadorned Feet

An attractive foot is also ideally, in the west at least, smooth and free of flaws or problems. In past centuries, the same oils used to smooth the skin of the rest of the body were applied to the feet. Today, various products are also available to soften the skin of the feet. Creams and lotions are used all over the foot, and special products contain pumice and other abrasives to remove dry skin and dead cells from the skin of the feet. Pumice stones and large-sized emery boards are also used to remove dead skin.

Feet, perhaps because they are subject to much hard use, are also susceptible to problems such as calluses, corns, and plantar warts, and other conditions that are considered unhealthy or unattractive and are possibly painful as well. Over-the-counter products are sold to treat these ailments, or a person may seek help from a dermatologist.

Foot odor, too, is viewed as a problem at least in many western cultures, although perhaps not a medical condition. To ward off or alleviate foot odor, manufacturers have developed a variety of spray and powder foot deodorants.

Decorated Feet

Adornment of the toenails dates back to ancient times. In Turkey, women in the sultan's harems applied henna, a plant extract used in other cosmetics and hair colorings, to draw symbols on their toenails that spelled out special messages for the sultan. Egyptian women also painted their nails with henna, which imparted a reddish color

Most women who adorn their toenails in recent times have used nail polish. Nail polish was apparently invented by the Chinese about 3000 B.C.E. During the Ming Dynasty (1368–1644), the Chinese combined egg whites, gelatin, beeswax, vegetable dyes, and Arabic gum to make polish.

The first manufactured polishes came in shades of pink, red, coral, and peach. Manufacturers produced an increasing range of colors, and began to sell matching lipstick and nail polish. In the 1980s and 1990s, young women who rejected the cosmetics standards of the time favored nontraditional colors: black, eggplant, and the like. In 1995,

the Chanel company brought these colors into the mainstream with its black-red "Vamp" nail polish. That set in motion a widespread trend that made nail polish in virtually any color acceptable. Toenail polishes now come in shiny or frosted finishes and in a wide range of colors, including blues, greens, purples, black, and metallics. Some polishes contain built in decorations, such as tiny metallic stars. Decals and other decorative trimmings are available for use on the toenails.

Salons offer pedicure services where they treat the skin of the feet and groom the cuticles and nails. Toenails may be painted with a variety of colors, using the same kinds of polishes that are applied to fingernails.

Another form of adornment, jewelry, including toe rings, may be worn on the foot. Ankle bracelets have also been popular, in some cultures since ancient times, and, more recently, in westernized countries. Women in modern India wear ankle bracelets, usually made from silver and in the form of bangles. In western cultures, ankle bracelets are more likely to be made from thin chains or tiny beads, and favored by teenage girls.

Shaping the Foot

The creation of an attractively groomed foot, for women, has also included practices that reshaped feet to conform with the beauty standards in effect. Perhaps the most well-known example of this comes from China, where the practice of foot binding prevailed for hundreds of years. Very small feet were considered beautiful, and women aspired to have tiny feet, like those of many courtesans and dancers. They went to extremes to achieve this; the feet of Chinese girls were bound tightly from infancy onward to change their shape and size. This process was painful and caused some women to become permanently disabled. Feet were considered so important that in Chinese brothels, women stood behind screens that revealed only their shoes. Customers could pick the girl with the smallest feet. Beauty contests called "tiny foot festivals" were held in China. During the early 1900s, Chinese officials began to try to halt the custom of foot-binding, and the government outlawed it 1928.

Less extreme but also potentially disabling are high or stiletto heeled shoes. High heels for women are a relatively modern invention. They are believed to have originated with the Italian noblewoman Catherine de Médici (1519–1589), a petite Italian woman who wanted to make a grand impression when she arrived in France in 1533 to marry Henry, son of King Francis I and future king. A Florentine shoemaker designed shoes with raised heels for the future queen, and this style gained popularity. High heels on modern women's shoes range from low—perhaps one inch—to the three or four inch spike heels that periodically become fashionable. Platform shoes are a variation that are raised under the front of the foot as well.

High-heeled shoes, which often featured sharp, pointed toes, forced the foot into quite unnatural positions. Women endured—and some still endure—the discomfort and limitations on their mobility caused by these kinds of shoes to achieve a certain appearance and stature. Some observers have said that men enjoy the way women walk in high heels because it emphasizes and elongates the appearance of their legs and causes their hips to sway.

Women are no longer as willing to subject their feet to potentially damaging fashions. During the 1990s, actress Cybill Shepherd made a personal fashion statement with her feet when she wore bright-colored sneakers with glamorous formal gowns to the Academy Awards presentations. Shepherd stressed the value of comfort and later became a spokesperson for "Easy Spirit" shoes, which emphasized a woman's right to be herself and to "live comfortably." *See also* BODY ODOR; CHINA.

Further reading: Jean Kilbourne, *Deadly Persuasion* (1999); Kate Mulvey and Melissa Richards, *Decades of Beauty: 1890-1990* (1998).

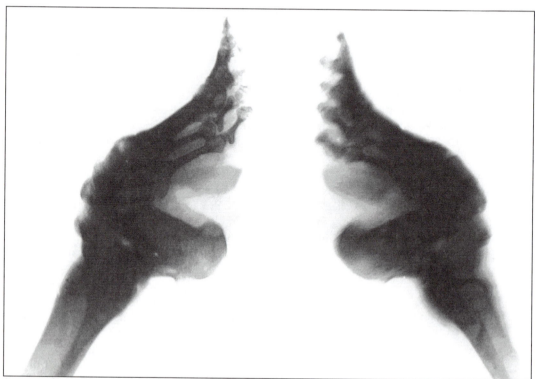

An x-ray of bound feet, which have become permanently disabled. The x-ray was probably taken in the early twentieth century. *Library of Congress.*

Feminism

Feminism is a social movement that has its roots in longstanding and widespread efforts to gain more rights for women. Feminism as such accelerated in the 1970s, under the name of "women's liberation." The philosophy challenges political, economic, and social power structures, which feminists declare are dominated by white males. Although most widespread in western countries, feminism has made small incursions into societies in which women are subject to male domination, such as Islamic and Hindu countries.

Feminists have sought to ensure that women have equal rights at home and in the workplace. They say that a more egalitarian society also has a liberating effect on men, who may be limited by social expectations about appropriate roles and behavior for men.

Along with their quest for political and economic power, many feminists say that women should understand how male-determined beauty standards and consumerism affect women's lives. They urge women to refuse to accept limiting standards that have a negative impact on their self-esteem and personal development. Some feminists refuse to use cosmetics or accept the idea, promoted by a consumer-driven society, that their faces and bodies are not acceptable in their natural state. They reject the narrow definitions of beauty that dominate cosmetics advertisements in the mass media and its traditional slant toward women who fit into a white European-based mold of appearance.

In books and magazines, especially the feminist magazine *Ms.*, which was founded in 1972, authors of both genders discussed the social pressures that propel women to pursue beauty ideals, showing how that pressure can become a weapon used to keep women "in their place." Feminist Kate Millett spoke for many women when she declared, "The image of woman as we know it is an image created by men and fashioned to suit their needs." (Quoted in Jackson, 1993)

In her book *Look at My Ugly Face!* author Sara Halprin discusses some of these issues. Halprin says that social forces work "to diminish our power, limiting us to a deco-rative role in the lives of men." (Halprin, 1995) She continues, "Hardly any woman can sustain these standards over time without sacrificing her need to express many diverse parts of her being. Pressed to fit whatever model of femininity is currently in vogue, women spend precious time and energy straining to meet impossible ideals, ignoring our own needs for growth and development." (Halprin, 1995)

Besides criticizing the consumer-driven beauty industry, feminists have also registered strong objection to beauty contests as shallow and demeaning to women. Some critics say that these kinds of competitions reinforce the idea that women are of value chiefly for their outward appearance. Contest sponsors have addressed these criticisms by placing more emphasis on talent and achievement, although clearly, looks are still a major determinant of who wins. *See also* BEAUTY STANDARDS; BODY IMAGE; CONTESTS; CRITICS OF COSMETICS INDUSTRY; STEINEM, GLORIA.

Further Reading: Sara Halprin, *"Look at My Ugly Face!"* (1995); Victoria Jackson, *Redefining Beauty* (1993); Jean Kilbourne, *Deadly Persuasion* (1999).

Fingernails *See* HANDS.

Fitness Movement

A modern physical fitness movement arose in response to a desire for better health and a trim, toned body that meets social standards for attractiveness. The movement is an extension of nineteenth-century physical culture movements that arose in western countries, in which girls were encouraged to participate in various physical activities. In recent decades, the movement gathered momentum during the 1970s when women regarded a thin body as ideal, and fashion and beauty ads featured extremely thin supermodels.

Both men and women, however, have become increasingly interested in physical fitness, as modern transportation and conveniences made their lives more sedentary, resulting in weight gain and poor physical condition.

In the United States, Charles Atlas (1894–1972), an Italian immigrant who changed his name to fit his image, was one of the first fitness experts to market a bodybuilding system for men. Atlas claimed his system would create a strong, muscular appearance. Atlas said he had been a "spindle-shanked, scrawny weakling" during his youth and had developed a program he called "dynamic tension" to build the muscles in his chest, arms, legs, and stomach. In 1922, *Physical Culture* magazine won the body-building title of "The World's Most Perfectly Formed Man." He then went on to promote his exercise system as a way for other men to achieve a muscular body. Atlas claimed his program required only 15 minutes of exercising a day. Ads for Atlas's booklet, "Everlasting Health and Strength," featured a cartoon entitled "How Joe's Body Brought Him Fame Instead of Shame." In the pictures, Joe and his girlfriend are sitting on a beach when a muscular bully kicks sand in their faces. Joe, who is thin and looks weak, feels helpless. He decides to send for the Atlas book and uses the program, which makes him fit and muscular. Back on the beach, he demonstrates his new strength against the bully, while his girlfriend says, "Oh, Joe! You are a real man after all."

Marjorie Craig became one of the first and best-known fitness experts in the United States during the 1950s through the 1970s. She wrote several best-selling books on exercise. Born in 1912 in Bangor, Maine, Craig received a B.S. degree in physical education from Arnold College (later Bridgeport University) in Connecticut, then did postgraduate work in the field of physical therapy at Columbia University in New York City. Beginning in the 1950s, Craig was in charge of the fitness department at the elegant Elizabeth Arden beauty salon on Fifth Avenue. She helped individual clients firm and tone their figures and urged all women to follow her own regimen by exercising at least one-half hour each day.

Her popular work was one of the first best-selling fitness books. She later wrote *Miss Craig's Face-Saving Exercises* and *Fit After Forty*. Her own trim, youthful appearance and exuberant energy inspired other women.

One key development in the fitness movement was the publication of *Aerobics,* written by an Air Force physician named Kenneth Cooper. Although Cooper's aim was to promote aerobic exercise as a way of preventing coronary heart disease, others quickly adopted it as a way of achieving the standard slim body. Cooper's book was translated into many languages. During what became known as a "fitness craze," Americans and others who had been sedentary or relatively inactive began walking, jogging, attending exercise classes, and embarking on personal fitness programs. A trim, fit body became an ideal for men and women living in cultures that equated fitness with beauty.

New health and fitness clubs were built to accommodate people interested in exercise classes or one-on-one sessions. Membership in health clubs increased substantially during the 1980s, and as did sales of exercise videos, exercise clothing, exercise shoes, and other equipment. Celebrities and others also hired personal trainers to plan a fitness regimen for their particular needs. More magazines devoted to health and fitness were published for both men and women.

The actress and political activist Jane Fonda is strongly associated with the fitness movement in the United States, and was nicknamed the "shape-up queen of the eighties." She influenced untold numbers of people to exercise regularly. Beginning in 1983, Fonda appeared in her own fitness videos, which eventually numbered 23. She also founded a chain of fitness centers and endorsed a treadmill that was marketed during the early 1990s. Fonda also wrote a cookbook that emphasized healthful, low-fat meals based on natural, whole foods.

Other fitness experts who became prominent during the 1980s and 1990s included Tammilee Webb, Denise Austin, Kathy Smith, Callan Pinkney, Susan Powter, and Richard Simmons. All of them have written books on fitness and exercise, and several appear regularly on television. Their exercise videos help people to exercise at home. Austin, the author of *Hit the Spot!* and other books, appears regularly on American television, where she demonstrates a daily workout routine that

Jane Fonda doing the splits (1979). © *Douglas Kirkland/CORBIS.*

includes a warm-up, aerobics, toning, and stretching. Simmons has been a popular guest on various interview and talk shows, where he encourages people with serious weight problems and has been the host of his own shows in the 1980s and 1990s. In 1999, he became the host of a weekday morning program. He has developed a multifaceted program designed to help people exercise, eat a healthful diet, and maintain a positive attitude toward life.

Numerous actresses and models known for their slim, toned bodies have produced exercise books and videos. They include Raquel Welch, Debbie Reynolds, Ali MacGraw, Jaclyn Smith, Stefanie Powers, Dixie Carter, Cindy Crawford, Claudia Schiffer, and Kathy Ireland.

A 1996 study conducted by American Sports Data, Inc., showed that between 1987 and 1995, the number of Americans aged six and older who regularly take part in sports, fitness, or outdoor activities rose by 31 percent, a figure that exceeded the 10 percent population growth rate by 20 percent. More people over the age of 45 were engaging in fitness activities, and walking was the first choice for people over 50. Several research studies showed more adults were taking part in strength-training exercise. Two university

Richard Simmons exhorts a group to exercise more often. © *Stan Gelberg/Globe Photos, Inc.*

researchers of the School of Nutrition Science and Policy at Tufts University found that even modest weight training could reverse some of the physical debilitation associated with aging. Their work helped to spark women's increased interest in weight training, also favored because women found that working out with weights and resistance machines could help them to develop a leaner and stronger body without bulky muscles. *See also* BODY IMAGE; CELLULITE; WEIGHT.

Further reading: David Levinson and Karen Christensen, eds., *Encyclopedia of World Sport from Ancient Times to the Present* (1997); Miriam E. Nelson with Sara Wernick, *Strong Women Stay Young* (1997); Julian Lewis Watkins, *The 100 Greatest Advertisements, Who Wrote Them and What They Did* (1959).

Food and Drug Administration
(FDA) *See* LAWS AND REGULATIONS (U.S.); SAFETY.

Fountain of Youth

The Fountain of Youth was a legendary place that was said to contain a magical spring with the power to give humans eternal youth. European explorers attempted to find the fountain, which they expected would bring them great power and riches, along with eternal life.

Among these explorers was Spaniard Juan Ponce de Leon (1460–1521), who heard the legends from Indians who lived in what is now Puerto Rico. According to these native peoples, a place called Bimini, supposedly north of Puerto Rico, had a spring of water that could restore youthfulness. In 1512, the king of Spain authorized Ponce de Leon to search for, and then colonize, Bimini. When the Spaniards reached the coast of Florida, they believed they had reached Bimini, but did not find the fountain there. Because he arrived at this place on Easter Sunday, Ponce de Leon called it "Florida," from the Spanish words Pascua Florida—"flowery Easter."

Although others sought the fountain, they never found it. The phrase "fountain of youth" has been used in modern times on labels and advertisements for cosmetics and as a name for companies or stores that sell various beauty and health products. The fantasy that there are places where people never age has also been kept alive in books and films, notably James Hilton's *Lost Horizon* and Aldous Huxley's satire on the quest for eternal youth, *After Many a Summer Dies the Swan. See also* AGING AND APPEARANCE.

Further reading: Anthony Q. Devereux, *Juan Ponce de Leon, King Ferdinand, and the Fountain of Youth* (1993); Sean Dolan, *Juan Ponce de Leon* (1995).

Fragrance

The use of fragrance to enhance personal attractiveness dates back thousands of years, as humans recognized that scents can powerfully affect emotions and interpersonal relationships, as well as disguise or cover up less agreeable odors.

The human nose can distinguish around 10,000 different odors. The olfactory nerves transmit these odors go to the limbic region of the brain, which is the emotional center. Smell is a vital sense in evoking memories, and scientists believe that it plays a critical role in sexuality and attraction. Certain scents may evoke strong personal memories and feelings, but they can also affect many people in a similar way. For instance, lavender tends to relax the brain by increasing alpha waves. Jasmine, rosemary, and peppermint stimulate beta waves. Vanilla and green apple scents seem to help people relax; other scents have been used to reduce insomnia.

The use of scents on the body can be traced back to millennia, when humans derived fragrances from plant oils. Personal fragrances made from flowers and plants were named according to their source, such as rose water, almond essence, or musk. Ancient Indian, Chinese, Arab, and Egyptian civilizations extracted the essential oils from plants. Several thousand years ago, Indians were using the scent of these oils medicinally. People used powders made from dried leaves, spices, and flowers in religious festivals and also rubbed them on their bodies. Some of the early fragrances have retained their popularity for centuries, for example, orange flower water, which is worn in Morocco and Latin America.

Ancient Egyptians also used fragrances on their bodies for religious purposes. Women in ancient Egypt found that their scent lasted longer if mixed the powder with bits of fat, which would melt from their body heat. Plant resins, plant roots, flowers, and tree saps were sources of aromatic materials. Musk, secreted by the male musk deer, was among the animal products used in fragrances. The Egyptians burned sweet-smelling fragrances to their gods and used cedarwood oil to help preserve corpses about to be buried. Each part of a mummy was uniquely scented so that any part of a dead person could recognize another if the parts were accidentally separated in the next world.

Throughout the Middle East, scents were prized as gifts and in trade. Arabia became the center of a lively trade in perfumes and their raw materials. Alexander the Great scented his clothing by burning incense nearby. In Persia, kings scented their crowns with myrrh, and wealthier people applied musk to their bodies after bathing, while men used civet (secreted by the animal of the same name) on their beards.

Legends and stories circulated about the power of fragrance to seduce members of the opposite sex. According to the Bible, in 800 B.C.E., King Solomon became romantically attached to the Queen of Sheba when she brought him gifts of fragrances.

After traveling to the court of Genghis Khan in 1275, the Italian explorer Marco Polo returned to Europe with herbs and fragrant essences. They included patchouli, previously unknown in the region. The Portuguese explorer Vasco de Gama (1460–1524) found sandalwood in India. Trees are rare, and today the government owns and controls all the sandalwood trees.

During medieval times and the Renaissance (from the eighth through the mid-seventeenth century), people bathed infrequently, and they seldom cleaned their clothes. To mask the odors, people wore scented balls of wax called pomanders around their necks. They sewed small bags of dried lavender and other flowers or spices into their stale clothing. Scented handkerchiefs were brought out to cover the nose when passing a smelly sewer.

A type of liquid fragrance that was the forerunner of modern perfumes was created in the thirteenth century for Queen Elizabeth of Hungary. Fragrant oil was mixed with alcohol, which allowed the scent to evaporate slowly on the skin. This was the predecessor of eau de cologne.

As European explorers traveled to the Americas, some brought back materials that could be used in fragrances. One of the Italian noblemen who visited the West Indies with Christopher Columbus brought back the plumeria alba, which was distilled for perfume-making.

Royalty used scents in numerous ways to enhance themselves and their surroundings. King Louis XIV (1638–1715) had his shirts scented with toilet water that included aloewood, rosewater, orange flower, musk, and spices. The concoction was called "heavenly water" and was made by simmering spices and other substances in rose water, then adding the other ingredients, along with a few grains of musk.

Soap was manufactured in England as of 1649 and had spread to most parts of the world by the 1800s. Manufacturers added fragrances to soap formulas to increase their appeal. These soaps were usually too costly for the average person.

Josephine, first wife of Napoleon Bonaparte (crowned Napoleon I in 1801), bathed daily and used manufactured soap, which was uncommon in the early 1800s. She mixed rosewater and brandy into her bath. Apparently, after her divorce she sprayed her scents, which contained her favorite odor, musk, all over the house to remind Napoleon of her. In turn, Napoleon had the wallpaper changed and used a lemon fragrance to cover up the scent.

Napoleon himself used more than 150 bottles of cologne during a three-month period, and had been known to order 60 bottles of cologne every month. His favorite soap was called Brown Winsor and was made from bergamot, caraway, cassia, cedarwood, clove, lavender, rosemary, thyme. The emperor also favored Jean Marie Farina, produced by the oldest perfumers in the country, Roger & Gallet, founded in Paris in the 1700s. This fragrance was also used to scent soap.

Synthetic sources of scents were first used during the 1700s. This led to new types of fragrances and an expansion of the fragrance industry, which was centered in France. France was long a prominent producer and exporter of fragrances. Modern techniques in perfume making led to the development of an array of fragrances for men and women. The perfume industry produced concentrated scents, mostly geared for women.

The 1900s saw more fragrances and scented products for men produced around the globe During the 1920s American men used more scented talcum powder then before. During the late 1930s, ads for the new product Aqua Velva described the product in terms of sexual attractiveness. Ads read, "She noticed the difference in your skin."

As men's colognes were heavily promoted during the 1930s, fragrances were linked to shaving products and ads tried to dispel the idea that fragrances were "feminine." Men were expected to be more rugged and not especially prone to vanity or interested in artificial adornment. Men's colognes gained acceptance and were given masculine names and packaged accordingly. They contained lime, spices, woodsy notes, bay leaves, and bayberry associated with sailors (Spanish Main). New men's colognes were described as manly, virile, or invigorating. Manufacturers also gave them masculine sounding names, such as "fine tobacco," "Cedar forest" or "leather." They contained such substances as sandalwood, musk, pine, and lavender, fragrances that appealed to men and also to women. The Mennen Company brought out an after-shave lotion called Skin Bracer in the 1940s. Ads called it "100 percent male."

In the latter twentieth century, advertising campaigns for men's fragrances have often emphasized the power these scents have to attract women. Sexual appeal is promoted in ads that portrayed the virility and masculinity of the men who use the product. During the 1960s, an advertisement for the cologne "Hai Karate" cautioned, "Be careful how you use it," implying that the fragrance would have an overpowering effect on women. Attractive women were featured in ads. A series of ads for English Leather showed a beautiful woman who said, "My men wear English Leather, or they wear nothing at all." The 1961 ad for King's Men After Shave Lotion described its "subtle, manly fragrance." The photo that accompanied the ad showed an attractive woman sitting on a man's lap as he reads the morning paper at the breakfast table with a caption reading: "Why don't you take the 8:45 [train] instead?"

The names of men's colognes may contain references to sports, power, and prowess. An example is "Eau Savage" by Dior (1966).

Other popular fragrances for men include "Hallmark" by Lentheric, a company that was founded in 1875 by hairdresser Gillaume Lentheric, who began producing both fragrances and cosmetics. The company also made "Tweed" for women, which was introduced in 1933. (Lefkowitz and Fant, 1982) Another best-seller, "Aramis" (from the Italian company Aramis that later became part of the Esteé Lauder group), came out in 1965. Dior's "Eau Savage" (1966) and "Fahrenheit" (1988) were best-selling men's fragrances.

Since the 1970s, more fragrances designed for both men and women—called unisex formulations—have been made. An early unisex fragrance was Dior's "Eau Fraiche" (1955); later, Calvin Klein introduced "One." One company, Human Pheromones Incorporated, incorporates human pheromones, which they synthesize, into various fragrance products under the brand name "Realm" perfumes. Humans (and other mammals) produce pheromones, which are linked with sexual attraction.

Consumers can select fragrances made with natural versus synthetic fragrances or combinations of the two. The first totally synthetic fragrance was created in France in 1983 and was an almond scent. By the late 1990s, perfumes contained between 60 to 100 percent synthetic ingredients. Some companies also offer consumers individual essential oils so that they can mix their own fragrances.

Fragrances are used not only in perfume and cologne but also in nearly all toiletries and cosmetics, including soaps and other bath products, talcum powders, face powders, lipsticks, deodorants and antiperspirants, hand and body lotions, depilatories, mouthwash, and nail polish.

A new trend has emerged in the area of designer fragrances. In earlier decades, top couturiers and high-priced fashion designers lent their names to fragrances. In the 1990s, companies that produced more casual and less expensive clothing came out with their own signature fragrances. They included The Gap, Tommy Hilfiger, Jones New York, Burberry's, Perry Ellis, and Eddie Bauer, a sports-clothing manufacturer. These fragrances are displayed and marketed in stores and also sold through catalogs.

Marketing Fragrance

Fragrance companies study market trends and the buying habits of different sectors of the population to market their products. In 1997, the Fragrance Foundation held a seminar, sponsored by *Heart & Soul* magazine and Yankelowich Partners. Speakers at the conference presented the results of a study showing that African-American women are twice as likely to shop in department stores, twice as likely to spend money on personal appearance products, and more than twice as likely to spend money on fragrances. About 72 percent of the women in one study said they own a wardrobe of, on average, six scents, and tend to be loyal to certain brands. The scented products they used most often included scented body lotions, perfumes, cologne, soap, bath oil, potpourri, candles, and essential oils. *See also* ARABIA, ANCIENT THROUGH MIDDLE AGES; FRAGRANCE FOUNDATION; FRAGRANCE INGREDIENTS; GRASSE; INTERNATIONAL FLAVORS AND FRAGRANCES (IFF); MÉDICIS, CATHERINE DE; NEW AGE COSMETICS; "NOSES"; PERFUME.

Further reading: Diane Ackerman, *A Natural History of the Senses* (1991); Tom Branna, "Fragrance and African-American Women," *Happi,* July 1997; Christine Canning, "Fine Fragrances," *Happi*, November 1996, http:// www.happi.com/special/ novmain.htm; Roy Genders, *Perfume Through the Ages* (1972); Mary R. Lefkowitz and Maureen B. Fant, *Women's Life in Greece and Rome* (1982); A. Hyatt Verrill, *Perfumes and Spices* (1940); Julian Lewis Watkins, *The 100 Greatest Advertisements: Who Wrote Them and What They Did* (1959).

Fragrance Foundation

Based in New York City, the Fragrance Foundation was established in 1949 by representatives from six leading cosmetics firms—Elizabeth Arden, Chanel, Coty, Guerlain, Helena Rubinstein, and Parfums Weil—as a nonprofit and educational institution for the fragrance industry. It is an international source of historic, cultural, scientific, and industry-related reference materials on the subject of fragrances. In 1982, the board of the foundation set up the Olfactory Research Fund, which supports scientific and psychological research at leading universities and hospitals around the world relating to the sense of smell and benefits of fragrance. The foundation also sponsors National Fragrance Week each November, maintains its research library and educational programs, and holds exhibitions, seminars, and symposia.

Members of the foundation included retailers, packagers, designers, manufacturers, suppliers, advertising and public relations industries, and the media. Each June, the foundation sponsors National "FiFi" week in connection with the FiFi awards, which honor creative achievement in the field of fragrance. The awards were first given in 1961, after Fragrance Foundation President Annette Green proposed the idea. The award itself is a crystal sculpture designed by Pierre Dinand and produced by the French company Pochet. The first fragrance named as the "Most Successful Introduction of a Fragrance" honor was Chanel No. 19. Fragrances that are considered classics, having achieved a distinctive status at least 10 years after they were introduced, may be elected to the "FiFi" Fragrance Hall of Fame. A permanent display of "FiFi" winners is set to be on permanent exhibit at the Musee Parfum in Oita, Japan.

In 1999, the U.S. Women's "Fragrance Stars of the Year" included Yves Saint Laurent's "Baby Doll," Gucci Parfums' "Gucci Rush," Coty's "April Fields," Demeter Fragrances's "Snow," and Victoria's Secret's "Dream Angels Heavenly." Men's winners included Fragrances Exclusive's "Salvatore Ferragamo Pour Homme," Ralph Lauren Fragrances' "Ralph Lauren Romance Men," Coty's "Adidas Moves," Demeter Fragrances' "Snow," and Banana Republic's "Modern for Men." Men's European Fragrance Star of the Year for 1999 was Chanel's "Allure Homme," and the Women's European Fragrance Star of the Year was Christian Dior's "J'Adore."

Hall of Fame winners in the women's fragrance category include Poison (Christian Dior, 1999); First (Van Cleef and Arpels, 1998); Giorgio (1997); Coco (Chanel, 1996); Youth Dew (Estee Lauder, 1994), Oscar de la Renta (1992); Opium (Yves St. Laurent, 1993); Joy (Jean Patou, 1990); Shalimar (Guerlain, 1989); L'Air du Temps (Nina Ricci, 1988); and Chanel No. 5 (1987). Men's winners include Canoe (Dana, 1997); Drakkar Noir (Cosmair, 1996); Aramis (Aramis, 1995); and Old Spice (Procter & Gamble/ Noxell, 1991). *See also* CHANEL, COCO (GABRIELLE); FRAGRANCE; PERFUME.

Further reading: The Fragrance Foundation, http:// www.fragrance.org.

Fragrance Ingredients

A variety of natural and synthetic ingredients have been used to produce fragrances that people wear to enhance their personal appeal. They include spices and herbs such as cinnamon, bay and rosemary; tree oils such as cedar, pine, frankincense, and eucalyptus; fruit extracts, such as bergamot, lemon, and orange; and grasses such as vetiver. Some animal products are also used, including musk, secreted by the male musk deer, civet,

from the animal, and ambergris, believed to be produced by sperm whales.

Gum Resins

Among the most popular of the gum-resin based fragrances are frankincense, sandlewood, and myrrh. Frankincense comes from a small tree that is native to North Africa and Arabia whose gum-resin is distilled to produce the oil. The scent is rich, mellow, and somewhat peppery. People have harvested the tree for thousands of years for this valuable material, which was used in religious ceremonies, to make cosmetics, and to treat illnesses. Frankincense was valued so highly that workers at the processing center in Alexandria had to remove their clothing before they could leave each day, according to the Roman historian Pliny the Elder (23–79 C.E.). Today, Southern Arabia contains the best of these trees and produces a few tons of frankincense each year.

Sandalwood, too, has a long history as a fragrance ingredient. It has been used in fragrances that were applied to the body as well as in incense to perfume the air. The oil comes from the roots and inner wood of an evergreen tree native to India and Indonesia called *Santalum album*. When the nineteenth-century French perfumer Septumus Piesse devised his "musical scale" of fragrances, he included sandalwood as one of the basic "notes." Sandalwood is often used in perfumes as a fixative or blender. It appears frequently in quality modern perfumes.

Myrrh is a fragrant gum resin from trees that has long been used in perfumes, chiefly as a fixative. The Egyptians also used it for embalming. It can be found in Arabia, Africa, and Ethiopia. A Biblical reference to myrrh—as well as frankincense—appears early in the New Testament when the three kings brought the two perfumes and gold as gifts for the Christ Child. In modern perfumes, myrrh oil is an ingredient in Yves St. Laurent's popular perfume Opium (1977), an Eastern-style scent that was created by the Roure-Bertrand firm.

Animal Sources

Musk has been used in perfume-making for thousands of years. About one-third of the fragrances produced for men contain some amount of musk. Musk is also widely used as a fixative—ingredient in perfumes that helps the fragrance as a whole to endure. Musk deer live in the Himalayan Mountains and were hunted in China, Afghanistan, and other countries; the highest quality musk, Tonquin musk, is found in Tibet and China. The sac containing the musk can be removed without hurting the deer. When musk is first extracted from its sac, it has a pungent, disagreeable odor and must be diluted before it can be used cosmetically. Small amounts may produce the desired effect. A reference to the use of musk in perfumery was recorded in the sixth century, when an Arabian, Cosmas, describes it as a material originating in India and used by Arab and Byzantine perfumers. Arabians regarded musk as a luxurious and regal substance that also acted as an aphrodisiac. Because it was such a long-lasting scent, the Arabs added musk to the mortar of important buildings as well as using it in their personal fragrances. They believed that the fragrance would continue to waft from the building, perfuming the air.

The first synthetic musk fragrance was patented in 1888 by German chemist Albert Baur. He went on to develop other formulas for synthetic musk, including musk ketone and musk ambrette. Since the 1970s, a variety of musk-scented perfumes, colognes, and bath products have been produced by different companies, including Coty, Max Factor, and Jovan. Musk fragrances continue to sell well and are available in scents for both men and women.

Ambergris was long used as a fixative in expensive perfumes. Natural ambergris comes from the excreted material of the sperm whale. It was first discovered in ancient times floating in the form of gray lumps on the sea or on shore, mainly in and around the Indian Ocean. Lumps of ambergris ranged in weight from one to seven pounds or even larger. Its natural odor can be offensive until the ambergris has been aged for several years and diluted with alcohol. The substance may have been first used during early Arab times, and some Arab rulers sent it to Persia as a form of tribute during the sixth century C.E. Ambergris was also used by people in Byzantium. Because the scent is so durable and can withstand washing, it was used to perfume gloves during the sixteenth and seventeenth centuries. During the 1800s, the whaling industry killed millions of whales for their oil, whalebone, and ambergris, and these sea mammals became endangered. Since the mid-1900s, perfume makers have used synthetic ambergris instead of the natural form. *See also* ARABIA, ANCIENT; FRAGRANCE; JOSEPHINE BONAPARTE; PERFUME; PERSONAL CARE PRODUCTS, MEN'S.

Further reading: Thomas J. Abercrombie, "Arabia's Frankincense Trail," *National Geographic*, October 1985, 475–512; Elisabeth Barille, *The Book of Perfume* (1995); Roy Genders, *Perfume Through the Ages* (1972); *International Cosmetic Ingredient Dictionary* (1997).

G

Genioplasty *See* PLASTIC SURGERY.

Grasse

Grasse, a city in Provence in the south of France, has been the center of the French perfume industry since the 1500s. Before that time, the region had been known for its fine leather-tanning industry. People in that industry began making perfume for leather goods, including scented gloves, a custom

A woman checks a distilling vat, which is full of rose petals, at the Molinard perfume factory in Grasse, France, in 1955. © *G.W. Hales/Archive Photos.*

that was introduced to France by Catherine de Médicis, wife of the French king, Henry De Médicis set up a laboratory in Grasse to study perfume with the goal of creating high-quality perfumes equal to those that the Arabs produced. The warm, consistent climate in the region, and its coastal location, made Grasse an excellent site for growing plants and shipping fragrant products to other countries.

By the end of the 1600s, the Grasse region was producing oils from jasmine, narcissus, orange blossom, violet, hyacinth, and jonquil plants, as well as from a variety of roses. More fragrant plants were cultivated in the years that followed. Factories processed thousands of tons of flowers and plants, which were used to make perfumes in France and another countries.

During the next two centuries, dozens of perfume factories built located in the Grasse region. Grasse became known as the perfume capital of the world.

Land prices and labor costs rose in this region during the 1900s. By the 1980s, Grasse producers were cultivating less, and the center of rose and jasmine production shifted to Egypt and Morocco. However, the Grasse region remained the center of perfume manufacturing, with perfume experts and factories that produced materials for major fragrance labels, including Chanel, Fragonard, and Houbigant. Grasse is also the home of the Musee International de la Parfumerie, where visitors can learn about the 3000-year history of perfume making and the process of distilling fragrances. *See also* MÉDICIS, CATHERINE DE; FRAGRANCE; MUSEÉ INTERNATIONAL DE LA PARFUMERIE; PERFUME.

Further reading: Elisabeth Barille, *The Book of Perfume* (1995); Roy Genders, *Perfume Through the Ages* (1972).

Gray, Dorothy

Dorothy Gray was one of the first proprietors of a modern beauty salon, establishing her first New York salon in 1916. She went on to develop a leading cosmetic and beauty products company based in Chicago, Illinois.

One of her successful lines of facial creams and tonics was called "Russian Products."

During the 1920s, Gray added manufacturing plants and a marketing operation for her products. In 1928, the company erected the Dorothy Gray Building on Fifth Avenue in New York City to house its New York offices and a large beauty salon.

Between 1910 and 1950, the Dorothy Gray Company was one of the three most successful cosmetic companies in America. Elizabeth Arden and Helena Rubinstein were Gray's chief competitors. As the three companies vied for the top position, Elizabeth Arden complained that Gray imitated her products. For instance, a few years after Arden introduced "June Geranium Bath Salts," Gray brought out "June Geranium Bath Soap." Gray also produced a travel makeup case similar to one that Arden was selling. During the 1920s, all three companies produced foundation makeup for the face. These foundations were somewhat sticky in texture.

In 1926, Gray sold her skin-care line to Lehn and Fink, a company that made household products and toothpaste. In the years that followed, Gray's cosmetics and skin care products appeared in drugstores and other less exclusive stores. *See also* ARDEN, ELIZABETH.

Further reading: Alfred Allan Lewis and Constance Woodworth, *Miss Elizabeth Arden* (1972); Kate Mulvey and Melissa Richards, *Decades of Beauty* (1998); Kathy Peiss, *Hope in a Jar* (1998).

Greece, Ancient

Ancient Greece refers to the historical periods in Greece known as the Archaic, Ionian, Classical, and Hellenistic periods, which began in about 1200 B.C.E. and ended with the death of Alexander the Great in 323 B.C.E., Information about bathing, grooming practices, and cosmetic uses has been derived from historical writings and the arts of ancient Greece. Mirrors, combs, and perfume bottles are among the artifacts that have been found in ancient Greek ruins. Ornate gold or jeweled studs and pendant earrings were worn.

The Greek sculptor, Phidias (c490–432 B.C.E.), is a good example of classic Greek male beauty. *Archive Photos.*

Greek women took pride in their appearance and devoted time to styling their hair and beautifying their faces and bodies. They may have spent most of the morning bathing and completing their beauty and grooming rituals. Wealthy women had slaves and servants to help them with these rituals.

Women in Athens and certain other places used cosmetics to emphasize their eyelashes, eyelids, and cheeks. A whitening substance called *psimythion,* made from powdering and then heating corroded lead, was applied to the face. The skin below the eyes was colored with a powder tinted the color of flesh. Cheeks were rouged with a variety of substances. One, called *phykos,* was made from the juice and roots of the alkent plant. Women also used ox tongue, cinnabar, crushed mulberries, and dye from a flower called paideros to redden their cheeks. They dyed their eyebrows with pulverized antimony or soot, and removed unwanted hairs with tweezers, razors, or plasters.

Oil and brushing and massage were used to soften and style the hair, while fragrant spices and oils were applied to perfume it. Women usually parted their hair in the center and pulled it back into a chignon or knot. Experienced hairdressers created curls and braids. The first known ponytails also originated in Greece. Greek women used ribbons, metal hoops, and metal and cloth bandeaus in their hair during the Hellenistic period, as well as wood and ivory combs to hold hair in place. Both men and women bleached their hair blond when light hair was in vogue, using a concoction made from potash water and yellow flowers. Women also wore colored wigs. Different kinds of oils, pomades, and lotions were applied to the hair to style it and make it smell fragrant.

Hairstyles could indicate a person's age, social position, and marital status. Young girls wore their hair in pigtails or cut short, while unmarried young women wore their hair down loose. Women in mourning colored their hair with powders or pomades rather than cutting it short, as was the custom in some cultures.

Women of ill repute altered their grooming habits to suit their line of work. One Greek historian described how prostitutes in Athens altered their appearance in the fourth century B.C.E. He wrote that they stuffed cork into their shoes to make themselves taller or wore thin slippers and walked with their heads lowered to seem shorter—whichever they needed to do to attract clients. To increase the size of their hips, they put on bustles, and enlarged their breasts with false breasts. He continues: "Eyebrows too light? They paint them with lamp-black (soot). Too dark? She smears on white lead. Skin too white? She rubs on rouge. If a part of her body is pretty, she shows it bare. Nice teeth? Then she is forced to keep laughing, so present company can see the mouth she is so proud of. . . ." (Lefkowitz and Fant, 1982).

In contrast, according to historians, Spartan women shunned cosmetics. They engaged in physical exercise, which, along with fresh air, they believed to be the best methods for attaining a radiant complexion. Men took pride in their physiques and exercised to achieve a muscular and well-balanced form. The naked male form was considered to be a work of art and male beauty was valued even more than female beauty in this culture.

Greek men patronized the forerunners of modern barbershops, where they could socialize and exchange ideas while getting massages, haircuts and stylings, shaves, manicures, and pedicures. They usually wore their hair long and curled in an arranged manner, except for Spartan men who kept their hair shorter.

After he defeated Darius III of Persia, Alexander the Great brought fragrances into Greece. Alexander used scents, including some containing the valuable ingredient myrrh, on his clothing. Once introduced to the idea, Greek scientists studied plants and designated which part of a plant produced certain categories of scents. Scents also had religious significance; the Greeks believed that they were sent by the gods. The Greeks also anointed the bodies of the dead with scented oils.

Greek women wore perfume once they knew of it, and hostesses welcomed gifts of perfume from their guests. They learned to make perfumes by boiling flowers and herbs down to a concentrated essence that was mixed with olive oil. Myrrh and frankincense were imported from the Middle East beginning in the eighth century B.C.E. Women rubbed on these scents after bathing. In contrast, Greek homosexual men rejected the use of perfume and claimed that a natural body odor was most appealing. *See also* BABYLONIA; BATHS; BYZANTINE EMPIRE; COSMETICS; EGYPT, ANCIENT; FACIAL HAIR, MEN'S; HAIR COLOR; ROMAN EMPIRE.

Further reading: H. Blumner, *The Home Life of the Ancient Greeks* (1966); E. Fantham et al, *Women in the Classical World* (1994); Michael Grant, *A Social History of Greece and Rome* (1992); Ian Jenkins, *Greek and Roman Life* (1986); Mary R. Lefkowitz and Maureen B. Fant, *Omen's Life in Greece and Rome* (1982); Marjorie Quennell, *Everyday Things in Ancient Greece* (1954).

Grooming Products, Children's

Toiletries and hygiene products, including soap, skin lotions, bubble bath, toothpaste, shampoo, lip balm, and sunscreen products, are made for the use of babies and children. Fragrances for children are also marketed, often in fruit or floral scents. In addition, "play make-up" is sold either as separate items or in kits, in packaging designed to appeal to children or encourage them to play "dress-up." Many products tie in with other popular children's toys, such as "Barbie."

In previous centuries, children often used the same cleansing and grooming products as adults. Among the first modern grooming products created especially for children were shampoo and soap. Shampoo formulas for infants usually do not contain sulfates, which are used in adult formulas. These shampoos usually do not lather as heavily as those for adults. One of the best-known shampoos is Johnson and Johnson's gold-colored "Baby Shampoo" ("no more tears"), a product the company promoted as being mild enough for young children. Ivory Soap, from Procter and Gamble, was also recommended as a "pure" soap product that was suitable for infants and children. Skin-care products for infants were also manufactured and new brands were introduced over the years. These include baby powder and lotion, including products to deal with diaper rash. Although some baby powders have been made with talc, during recent decades, many consumers preferred cornstarch powder.

Some children's products were designed to suit children's special needs. For example, children's toothbrushes were designed with smaller heads and softer bristles. The brushes were made in child-pleasing colors and contained the images or shapes of popular cartoon, movie, or television characters. Because many children disliked the taste of adult toothpastes, companies brought out special brands for children. These pastes were flavored with various fruity or bubble gum flavors to appeal to children (and repel adults). Combs and hairbrushes are also made in sizes that are suitable for infants and children.

Many personal care products are linked to popular children's toys, television programs, and movie characters and themes. Disney productions are a perennial favorite as are "Sesame Street" characters. Manufacturers also use characters from fairy-tales, folk tales, and popular children's books and movies on the packaging and design of children's products.

Soaps have been made in a variety of fanciful shapes, colors, and scents to appeal to children. There are also soaps in the form of "bath crayons" that children can use to draw designs on the tub while they are bathing.

Consumer advocates have expressed concern about certain products that are made for children. Physicians warn parents who use powder on infants to use cornstarch powders, not powders containing talc, because of the hazards associated with talc inhalation. Parents are also advised to be careful when using bubble baths, because some children develop skin irritation and rashes as a result of the fragrances and colors in these products. The *Safe Shopper's Bible* states, "Physicians have found that bubble baths strip away the mucous lining of the genito-urinary tract and make the area vulnerable to infection, especially in young girls." (Steinman and Epstein,1995) *See also* BARBIE DOLLS; "BRECK GIRLS"; SAFETY.

Further reading: David Steinman and Samuel S. Epstein M.D., *The Safe Shopper's Bible* (1995).

Grooming Products, Men's *See* MEN'S PERSONAL CARE PRODUCTS.

Guerlain

Founded in 1828 by Pierre Guerlain, a chemist, the firm of Guerlain has become one of the most famous perfume companies in the world and is known for both its innovative and classic fragrances. Pierre Guerlain made his first perfume in 1850, and the first Guerlain shop opened in Paris, offering scents and toiletries. As the business grew, Guerlain opened factories in Courbevoie, outside Paris, and in Chartres to manufacture perfumes, cosmetics, and beauty preparations. Empress Eugenie was one of their best-known clients.

In 1889, Guerlain introduced a startling new fragrance called "Jicky," which used the essences of sandalwood and fern, rather than the florals that predominated during that era. It became popular with women who considered themselves avant-garde.

During the early 1900s, Jacques Guerlain, one of Pierre's descendants, created some of the company's best-known fragrances. In 1911, as he was walking home from work at dusk on a summer evening, Guerlain paused on a bridge over the River Seine in Paris and was inspired to create a perfume that captured that peaceful time of evening. The resulting scent was called L'Heure Bleu—"the blue hour." It quickly became popular and remained a best-selling perfume for more than 50 years. His second big success was Mitsouko, which was introduced in 1921. Vol de Nuit ("Night Flight"), brought out in 1933, was described as a fragrance full of "excitement and adventure."

Currently the company, which has remained in the Guerlain family, has introduced more than 120 different scents. Its most popular perfumes include "Jicky" (1889), "L'Heure Bleu" (1912),"Shalimar" (1925), "Chant d'Aromes" (1962), "Parure" (1975), and "Jardins de Bagatelle" (1984). Famous men's fragrances from Guerlain include "Habit Rouge" (1964) and "Derby" (1985). *See also* FRAGRANCES; PERFUMES.

Further reading: Roy Genders, *Perfume Through the Ages* (1972); A. Hyatt Verrill, *Perfumes and Spices* (1940).

H

Hair Care

Hair care has been an important aspect of grooming rituals since primitive times, when humans used natural plant and animal substances to wash, condition, and groom hair. They made implements to comb, brush, and style hair from wood, plant fibers, and metals. Early methods of caring for the hair included the use of plant extracts. For example, natives of North America used yucca for a shampoo and they treated dandruff with the plant chaparral, which also served as a hair tonic. For some tribes, hair cleansing was part of rituals and ceremonies. The Hopi of the American Southwest still follow a wedding tradition that includes shampooing the hair of the bride and groom together, intermingling their hair while it is being washed.

As people found ways to make lye-based detergents from ashes and fats, they often washed their hair with the same kind of soap they used on their bodies. The soaps did clean the hair, but they often left it looking dull, with a residue that the water could not seem to remove. Early manufactured cake soaps, which became widely available during the 1800s, were also used to cleanse the hair. Coal-tar soap, one type of soap used for shampooing, did not have a pleasing fragrance.

Shampoos to be used exclusively on hair came into use during the 1930s. They contained water, detergent, and other ingredients, such as fatty material, coloring, herbs, fruits, and proteins. Manufacturers added fragrances to increase their sensory appeal, and some customers selected their shampoos on that basis. Companies advertised widely in the mass media to increase their market share. Models with shining, carefully styled hair appeared in advertisements for different shampoos and conditioners.

For people who could not wash their hair in the regular way, dry shampoos were created. Most of them contained absorbent powder and a mild alkali.

Manufacturers also worked to develop special shampoos and other products to treat dandruff—a scalp condition characterized by itching and flaking. White flakes on the hair and clothing was regarded as a grooming problem, and ads for antidandruff shampoos, lotions, and creams promoted the idea that dandruff was a social liability.

Today, the hair care products industry has grown to become one of the largest in the world. New products to cleanse, condition, protect, and improve the hair appear regularly. Research chemists also seek new ingredients and formulations that will improve the condition and texture of hair or even restore hair growth and thickness.

During the 1990s, the trend toward "natural" ingredients led to the use of more plant substances in hair-care products. A number of hair care products now offer shampoos, conditioners, and styling gels that contain botanical ingredients (ingredients that come from plants).

At the same time, manufacturers researched the negative effects of sun exposure and made products with sunscreens and other ingredients designed to protect hair from the elements. These are available for athletes and other people who spend a great deal of time outdoors. Swimmers can purchase shampoos and conditioners that purport to remove or neutralize chlorine and other pool chemicals from their hair. *See also* ADVERTISING (U.S.); ALBERTO CULVER COMPANY; BATHS; EGYPT, ANCIENT; HAIR COLOR; HAIR, STYLING OF; L'OREAL; MICHAELJOHN; SASSOON, VIDAL.

Further reading: Wendy Cooper, *Hair, Sex, Society, Symbolism* (1971); Richard Corson, *Fashions in Hair* (1965); Nancy Etcoff, *Survival of the Prettiest* (1999).

Hair Color

Fashions in hair color and preferences for certain hues have changed throughout history, and the use of various substances to alter hair color dates back thousands of years. Men and women both have colored their hair to give a more youthful appearance after it turned gray or white. The earliest dyes were made of plant products, including such fruits, flowers, and vegetables as chamomile, indigo, logwood, henna, and walnut hull extract.

People living in the ancient societies of Mesopotamia and Persia dyed their hair, which was usually worn long.

In ancient Greece, around 400 B.C.,E. women dyed their hair or dusted it with color. Blonde hair was favored in ancient Greece as a feature common to Greek male gods. The ancient Greeks used a liquid made from potash water and yellow flowers as a hair coloring agent. The early Romans preferred dark hair, but began to favor light hair after the legionnaires brought in fair-haired slaves from Gaul. Roman women tried to lighten their hair, but the substances often caused hair loss, so they resorted to wigs made from the captives' hair, or they sprinkled gold dust on their hair to give it a blond look. Some Roman men also dyed or lightened their hair. During this same era, Saxons dyed their hair blue with a substance called woad.

Ancient Egyptian women sometimes dyed their hair with henna, derived from the dried and ground leaves and stems of the henna shrub, which grows in the Near East and North Africa. When combined with hot water and applied to the hair, it imparted different reddish shades to the hair. People had to be careful when using henna, because they could also inadvertently dye their fingernails and skin.

Like other styles, fashions in hair color change regularly. From the eighth to the thirteenth centuries, blonde hair was greatly admired on women. Some people tried to lighten their hair with mixtures containing henna, gorse flowers, saffron, eggs, and calf kidneys. A coppery red hair color was popular in sixteenth-century Venice, Italy. To obtain this hue, women applied caustic soda to their hair, then sat outside in bright sunlight. In France, Marguerite de Valois, the first wife of Henry IV (1553–1610) , is believed to have introduced more advanced hair-bleaching techniques to France.

Red hair was popular during the reign of red-haired Elizabeth I of England, from the mid sixteenth to the early seventeenth century. In an effort to duplicate this color, Englishwomen used saffron and sulfur powder, which caused numerous side effects, such as nausea, headaches, and nosebleeds. Some male members of the court also dyed their beards red as a sign of loyalty to their queen. High-ranking men in Elizabethan England dyed their hair auburn. A popular style was to grow one long strand, which they tied on one side with a ribbon.

During the 1600s, people used lead combs on their wet hair to darken the color to black. At the time, they did not realize that lead was poisonous and could cause kidney failure and death.

Other natural, more benign products, such as lemon juice and chamomile, were used to lighten or highlight the hair. People continued to experiment with various common substances, including wine, plant extracts, and roots. During the late 1800s, people discovered that the chemical hydrogen peroxide would remove pigment from the hair shaft, leaving it a yellow or sometimes orange-yellow color. Using this substance straight from the bottle also tended to dry hair.

The first chemical hair color was patented in France in 1883. A Parisian company, Monnet et Cie, developed a formula that contained paraphenylenediamine, a dye that was previously used on textiles. People reported various ill effects after using manufactured hair dyes. In 1909, Eugene Schueller, a French chemist, tried to alleviate fears by naming his new business the French Harmless Hair Dye Company.Changing the name, however, did not change the effects of hair colorings. During the early-to-mid-1900s, bleaching products were harsh, and colors often looked unnatural. Bleaching was done with peroxide, ammonia, and soap flakes. These chemicals sometimes caused burning and blistering of the scalp.

Dying hair was still regarded as daring and "low-class" in America until after the 1930s. The film actress Jean Harlow, popular during the 1930s, bleached her hair to a pale platinum blond using dime-store hair coloring. Other women copied her hair color.

Blonde hair, although considered desirable at some times and places, also had negative connotations. For instance, in ancient Greece and Rome, female prostitutes wore blond hair. From late seventeenth century through the early 1900s, women in America and most other countries were discouraged from changing their color in any obvious way. Bleached hair was the sign of a prostitute or "fast" woman.

Although blond hair has had negative connotations in some times and places, in others, and in much of the twentieth century,, light shades of hair have been considered attractive. These colors are associated with gold and light, a mark of innocence and youth and appeal to the opposite sex. The author Anita Loos put the phrase "gentlemen prefer blondes," in the popular idiom with her 1925 book by that title, which later was made into a Broadway musical and 1953 feature film starring Marilyn Monroe and Jane Russell. The Clairol Company ran a successful ad campaign in 1956 using the phrase "Is it true blondes have more fun?" Another Clairol ad said, "If I have only one life, let me live it as a blonde." Blonde hair is often regarded as youthful looking, because although many children have blond hair, only 5 percent of the women who are born blonde (one in four in the United States) keep that hair color into adulthood.

In the 1950s, coloring the hair became more socially acceptable as new and improved products made it possible to lighten hair without first bleaching it. The new dyes looked more natural, and they also covered gray hair more effectively. In 1950, a survey of American women showed that 7 percent of them dyed their hair. Today, an estimated 75 percent of American women have used some kind of coloring agent. Most of them use color to conceal gray hairs associated with aging. So many women change their hair color that in 1969, the designation "hair color" was deleted from U.S. passports.

Consumers can choose from a variety of products that produce permanent, semipermanent, or one-time color that washes out immediately. Some products add highlights or enhance a person's natural color. Around the world, far more women and men use hair-coloring kits than have their hair colored at a salon. Increasing numbers of women choose to enrich or change their natural color with any of the hundreds of shades of blond, brown, red, black, and gray.

Although modern chemical hair dyes are far safer than their predecessors, critics have questioned their safety. Some consumers are allergic to them, and package instructions always advise that users test the dye on a small area to see if they have a negative reaction.

More serious health concerns arose during the 1960s, when consumer advocates claimed that certain materials used in dyes were associated with increased rates of cancer. In 1975, researchers conducted tests on some common commercial hair coloring products. They showed that certain permanent hair dyes contain mutagenic substances—that is, substances that are capable of causing mutations in the genes of laboratory animals. Further testing showed that as many as 89 percent of the chemical hair dyes on the market might cause genetic mutations. In 1994, a study reported an increased risk of two types of cancer, non-Hodgkin's lymphoma and multiple myeloma, for women who had used black hair dye for more than 20 years. In 1998, however, a study conducted at the University of California at San Francisco found no association between dye use and non-Hodgkin's lymphoma. Hair color manufacturers maintain that the chance of becoming ill or being seriously harmed from these dyes is extremely low.

Scientists have warned pregnant women to avoid hair color to prevent any possible damage to their babies. They have also told consumers that, because studies have not been conducted over long periods of time, consumers should weigh cosmetic effects against safety when deciding if they should color their hair. (Center for the Study of Responsible Law, 1986)

Covering Gray

Hair color is often used to cover gray hairs associated with aging. When and how much hair turns gray varies greatly among both men and women. In general, however, most people get their first gray hairs when they are around age 30; the proportion of gray becomes about 50 percent by age 50. In many cultures, white or gray hair has been considered undesirable as a sign of aging, while in other countries, gray hair is considered not only acceptable but attractive. In India, for instance, it is regarded as a sign of grace and charm.

The practice of coloring gray hair dates back thousands of years. In Roman times, a mixture made from ashes, boiled walnut shells, and earthworms was believed to keep hair its natural color. The Romans also used a lead-coated comb dipped in vinegar; the lead salts on the comb darkened the hair over time.

This was the forerunner of modern hair-coloring products, such as the brand "Grecian Formula" that gradually darken the hair as metallic salt dyes deposit color on the hair shaft without penetrating the shaft. Men who wished to color their gray hair often preferred these products, which worked gradually, so that the change would not be so sudden or noticeable. In 1998, the Food and Drug Administration issued a regulation permitting the use of lead acetate in these products. The agency reported that studies have shown that those who used dyes containing this ingredient showed no increased lead levels in their blood, nor was lead absorbed into the body. (FDA, 1998)

Since the 1970s, more hair-coloring products have been developed for men. They include permanent and semipermanent dyes, made with the same ingredients as hair colors marketed for women, but with different, masculine-sounding names. Sales of men's hair color products reached $113.5 million in 1998, according to a report cited in the June 1999 *American Demographics.* This is three times the figure of 10 years ago. According to another study cited, 1 in 12 American men dye their hair. Many are in their 30s and 40s and actively seek to retain a youthful appearance in other ways, such as exercising frequently. Manufacturers suggest that men color their hair for two principal reasons: "the boardroom and the bedroom." A youthful appearance has become increasingly important in professional advancement, and single men also want to maintain a competitive edge in the social scene. Hispanic men are 50 percent more likely to color their hair than other men. (Weiss, 1999). The article also reports that geographic patterns of men's use of hair coloring mirror those of other products and processes whose use increases with age, including Viagra, the drug used to treat erectile dysfunction, and the same age group of men who color their hair, those aged 30–50, are also those most likely to undergo cosmetic surgery. *See also* ADVERTISING (U.S.); EGYPT, ANCIENT; ELIZABETH I; GREECE, ANCIENT; HENNA; ROMAN EMPIRE; SAFETY.

Further reading: Paula Begoun, *Don't Go Shopping for Hair-Care Products Without Me* (1998); *The Body Shop Book* (1994); Center for the Study of Responsible Law, *Being Beautiful* (1986); Margie Pollak, "Hair Dye Dilemmas," *FDA Consumer,* April 1993; Michael J. Weiss, "Father's Day Special: Guys Who Dye," *American Demographics,* June 1999.

Hair Loss

People who experience hair loss, sometimes resulting in total baldness, may regard this as a problem that detracts from their personal appearance. This is especially true in cultures that place a high value on youth, if hair loss is viewed as a sign of aging.

People often have strong feelings about their hair. Social scientists have said that a full head of hair is associated with youth, which, in turn, signifies health and vigor, while hair loss reminds people of mortality. Jerome Shupack, M.D., professor of clinical dermatology at New York University medical center in New York City said, "It's one of the leading ways people can establish their individuality and express their style. Hair has had sociological importance throughout history." (Pine, 1991)

Hair has also been a plot element and symbol in myths, folklore and literature. In the Bible, for example, Samson's hair was connected to his physical prowess. The fairy tale character Rapunzel used her long hair to gain freedom and love. Because hair symbolized power in some cultures, warriors collected the scalps of their victims and attached them to their shields as a protection during battle. Cutting a woman's hair off was a punishment and could brand the woman as a prostitute, slave, criminal, or traitor. In some cultures, cutting off the hair signified mourning.

Both men and women may develop a receding hairline and thinning hair, especially on top of the scalp, as a result of changing hormones and the aging process. Stress, genetics, diet, malnutrition, and medications, or a specific disease, may cause thinning hair or baldness.

Myths about what can cause and cure hair loss still exist. Wearing a hat will not bring on hair loss, nor will vigorous toweling of the head. Hair loss will not be cured by standing on your head, massaging your scalp, or brushing your hair. The notion that hair will regrow once the follicles are cleared of trapped sebum (secreted by the follicles) is completely untrue; surgeons report that there is no "trapped hair" to be found. (*FDA Consumer*, April 1997)

In men, one form of hair loss is genetic, inherited from one or both parents. Male pattern baldness (MPB) causes men to lose hair on top of the head and develop receding hairlines at the forehead. Age and male hormone production, as well as genetics, probably contribute. Statistics suggest that male pattern baldness affects about 12 percent of all men aged 25, 37 percent of men by age 35, 45 percent of men by age 45, and about 65 percent of those aged 65, with a slight increase in the years thereafter. Baldness of this type tends to be more severe the earlier in life it begins. (Hudson, http://www.phudson.com)

Dr. Gary Hitzig, speaking for the American Hair Loss Council estimates that the percentage of men who have lost hair roughly matches their ages. For example, 50 percent of men aged 50 have experienced hair loss. For women, the figure is between 20–25 percent. Some 2.5 million Americans experienced hair loss from other causes, such as illness or radiation therapy.

Both men and women have dealt with hair loss in various ways. These include accepting hair loss, or trying different ways to grow hair, such as topical treatments, massage, dietary changes, nutritional supplements, prescription drugs, and medical treatments. Some people replace missing hair with hairpieces, wigs, or hair extensions, or they have non-removable hair replacements attached to their remaining hair or scalp.

During the mid-1900s, methods were developed for implanting artificial hairs in the scalp, but the Food and Drug Administration banned this procedure in 1983. These hairs were made from polyester, modacrylic, and polyacrylic. Some men were permanently disfigured when the fibers could not be removed from their scalps. Hair transplant techniques, however, have become increasingly popular for some types of hair loss.

Hair tonics, lotions, and other products, including scalp massagers and other devices, have long been promoted as ways to prevent, postpone, or stop hair loss or restore hair growth. The ancient Egyptians put lettuce on their heads to encourage hair growth. In

Mongolia, men used yogurt. Some of the men's hair tonics that appeared in the 1800s purported to increase hair growth, but no product lived up to that claim. The American Medical Association contends that consumers waste millions of dollars each year buying shampoos and other products that purport to retard hair loss. In 1989, the FDA banned all nonprescription hair creams, lotions, or other external products claiming to grow hair or prevent baldness.

Nonetheless, new preparations continue to appear in the marketplace as part of the billion-dollar-a-year hair products business. Some claim to make hair look thicker or fuller, but all they do is coat the hair with chemicals called polymers that stick to the hair. They do give it a thicker appearance until a person's next shampoo.

Researchers have worked to develop chemical products capable of promoting hair growth. During the 1960s, a group of physicians experimented with ointments containing testosterone, a major hormone for males, to treat baldness, but the results were disappointing.

In 1988, the FDA approved the topical solution of minoxidil, sold under the trade name Rogaine, for use in men as a medically prescribed treatment for hair loss. The drug had originally been approved to treat high blood pressure, but scientists were not sure through what mechanism it combated hair loss. They speculated that it either increased circulation, which stimulated nourishment of the hair follicles, or that it increased the size of certain hair follicles so they produced hair of normal rather than very small diameter. Three years later, the drug was approved for use in nonpregnant women. In the late 1990s, Rogaine became available over the counter and was packaged in different strengths and containers for male and female consumers. Clinical tests showed that consistent use of Rogaine did encourage hair growth in some people, but the results continued only as long as they used the product. Another prescription formula, Propecia, is available as a medical remedy for hair loss.

While some men are going to great lengths to keep their hair, others are opting to remove theirs voluntarily. This group shaves their heads for a fashionable "no-hair" look. Former basketball superstar Michael Jordan is among the men who popularized this look, which is also seen on top models and actors. New products have been designed for men who choose to divest themselves of their hair (or lose it involuntarily). They include "Bald & Bold," from Supreme Beauty Products based in Chicago. The line includes a cleanser and soothing lotion for men whose heads are shaved. A moisturizer contains sunscreen to protect the bare head. The company estimates that about 35 million bald male consumers who might use their products. Spokesperson Cheryl Patterson said, "Instead of telling men to just grow some hair, we're saying it's okay. to be bald. And many women find these men very sexy." (Dunn, 1997) *See also* HAIR, STYLING OF; HAIR TRANSPLANTS; WIGS AND HAIRPIECES

Further reading: American Hair Loss Council. http://www.ahlc.org; Carolyn A. Dunn, "The Ethnic Hair Care Market," *Happi*, April 1997; Larry Hanover, "Hair Replacement: What Works, What Doesn't, *FDA Consumer*, April 1997; Patrick Hudson, M.D., "Causes of Male Pattern Baldness," at http://www.phudson.com; E.A. Olsen et al., "Five Year Follow-Up of Men With Androgenetic Alopecia Treated with Topical Minoxidil," *Journal of the American Academy of Dermatology*, April 1990, 643–646; Devera Pine, "Hair! From Personal Statement to Personal Problem," *FDA Consumer*, December 1991; Edmund Van Deusen, *What You Can Do About Baldness* (1978).

Hair, Styling of

The styling of hair has major part of personal grooming for millennia, for both men and women. People have combed, brushed, cut, augmented, ornamented, and arranged their hair in various styles, ranging from simple and natural to extremely elaborate. Hairstyles may show social and economic status, express individuality, or symbolize rebellion against prevailing styles or society in general. They may also be adopted for practical reasons that reflect the climate or geography of a region.

In most societies, hairstyles also show gender differences. Exceptions include the men and women of the Orinoco-Amazon Basin region, who have traditionally worn the same hairstyle, cut in a bowl shape. In developed areas, during the 1960s, both men and women wore long, natural hair at a time when unisex hair salons became commonplace in the United States and certain other countries.

Hairstyles may signal a person's social status or eligibility for marriage. When a bald Julius Caesar covered his bare head with a crown of laurel, this became a sign of nobility. About 100 C.E. Jewish women began a custom of shaving their hair at the time of marriage and wore wigs; today, married orthodox Jewish women still cover their hair. Among the Fulani in West Africa, a hairstyle bedecked with small amber beads and coins was a sign that a girl was unmarried and a member of a nomadic family. Married women wore large amber ornaments. During the 1800s, young women in America began to wear their hair in an upswept style when they were ready to marry. Toposa women of the Sudan wear their hair in many small pigtails to show they are married. Among Native Americans, unmarried Hopi women traditionally wear a distinctive whorl, or "butterfly," hairstyle characterized by a twist of hair on each side of the face.

Hairstyles can indicate other important events or transitions in life. The Tchikrin of the Brazilian rain forest, shave their heads after the death of a spouse, child, or sibling. Cutting off all the hair is one that marks the "coming-of-age" for female Wayana Indians, who live on the northern coast of South America. The shorn head is a sign that this is to be a period of fasting and seclusion. Hindu boys also traditionally shaved off their hair when they reached adolescence. An ancient Greek custom involved cutting the hair of widows and burying the hair with their husbands. Among the Rendille of Kenya, women have adopted a cockscomb hairstyle after the birth of a first son. The style is created using mud, animal fat, and ocher. Women shave their heads at the time their son is circumcised or to show that a close male relative has died.

Hairstyles may reflect religious beliefs. During the eighth century, men who joined Catholic monastic orders adopted a distinctive hairstyle called the tonsure. The top of the head was shaved, leaving a ring of hair around the bald crown. This practice was continued into the twentieth century. Women who join certain religious orders have their hair cut very short as a sign that they are renouncing worldly ways and vanity in order to serve God. Women and men living in Islamic cultures have a tradition of covering their hair in public. Strict followers of the Muslim faith require women to cover their heads in public with a cloth called the Hijib.

The loss of one's hair could be a mark of shame, as when adulteresses were punished by having their heads shaved. This was an ancient custom among some Native Americans, Hindus, Teutonics, and Jews. In the Bible, after Samson's hair was cut, he lost his physical strength. The hair of slaves was sometimes cut as a sign of their status. Manchu conquerors of China demanded that their subjects shave their entire heads except for one long queue, which was left hanging down the back of the head. The Mandarins resented this coercion, which was another way their enemies humiliated them by depriving them of their traditions.

At times in history, women have worn short haircuts to signify rebellion against the social order or membership in a particular social groups. The flappers of the 1920s, tomboys, nuns, lesbians, suffragettes, and others adopted short hair when long hair was considered to be a hallmark of femininity and a symbol of traditional female roles.

Ancient Styles

Archaeologists have found wooden combs made dating back to the Stone Age, which began about 2 million years ago and ended between 40,000 and 10,000 years ago, depending on location. Curly styles and plaits were popular among the ancient Assyrians and Persians. Egyptians of both sexes often shaved their heads because of the hot climate, adding wigs made from human hair or sheep's wool on occasion. To style and set their hair, Egyptians sometimes used wet mud. Later, they found that soaking quince seeds in water produced a thick jelly that they could use for that purpose. Religious laws forbade the ancient Hebrews from cutting their hair or beards. In Northern Europe, Celtic and Germanic peoples wore their hair long. Men's styles were more elaborate and longer in prehistoric societies.

Greek men in Sparta wore their hair short and curled, while men in other parts of Greece under age 18 kept their hair long. Women had long hair that was parted in the center, then brought behind the neck into a chignon or knot.

In India, women traditionally styled their long hair in braids. Over time, Indian women developed the custom of having young women show that they are no longer children by switching from two braids to a long single braid. The Sikh refrain from cutting their hair, which they wind around their heads and cover with a turban. In Islamic countries people traditionally covered their heads, men with turbans and women with head cloths and veils.

Japanese women preferred long, loose hair until the 1600s, when they began wearing ornate upswept styles or buns at the back of the neck. They used ribbons, pins, and ornaments on these pomaded styles. The famed geishas of Japan devised special styles on different occasions and for events and holidays. A traditional Japanese wedding hairstyle was an elaborate upsweep adorned with peach blossoms and silk ribbons. Chinese women traditionally wore their long hair twisted into a low knot.

Hair cutting and styling is a group activity in some cultures. Sioux women and some other Native Americans may schedule their haircuts at the same time. Members of the Samburu tribe of Northwest Kenya may spend as long as 12 hours a day braiding their long hair and coloring it with yellow ochre. This group places great importance on hairstyling. Samburu warriors do not normally

A Walpi girl (American Indian), with hair tied in a traditional style (1900). *Library of Congress.*

cut their hair, but are required to shave it off completely after the death of someone close to them or to show respect when a prominent tribe member dies. In East Africa, Masai warriors spend hours styling their hair and talking about hair care.

Traditional hairstyles in Africa, island societies, and Asia have often been decorated or held by combs made of horn, shell, bone, ivory, or wood. Tribesmen in West Irian and Indonesian New Guinea wear curly hair in twisted strands that hang to the ear on the sides of their heads and reach the eyebrows in the front.

Senegalese women wear braids with gold or gold-coated metal stars and other designs worked into them. Mexican women may braid colorful ribbons into their hairstyle.

In the Americas, native peoples styled their hair differently in different regions. In some places, people wore their hair long in plaits; other groups preferred loose styles. Still other styles were more dramatic. In a style for men that became known as the Mohawk, after the tribe that wore it, the head was shaved except for a ridge of hair that ran from the front of the head to the back. Hairstyles were ornamented with feathers, shells, beads, animal hair, and other items. Men of a certain rank could wear elaborate headdresses made up of many feathers and buffalo horns. Women usually wore simple long hair, often plaited, and held in place with a headband.

Middle Ages

European men wore simple hairstyles during the Middle Ages and let it grow longer than in earlier centuries. During the ninth century, upper class men wore their hair about neck length, and the pageboy and bowl-cut styles were dominant.

European women, especially those of the higher social classes, had long hair, often worn in plaits. After they were married, women were expected to wear a veil over their hair as a sign of modesty, because a woman's hair was considered erotic—a practice that continued for several centuries.

Long braids for women remained popular from 1000 to 1200, and some women grew their hair down to their knees. They parted their hair in the center and wore two braids. Some women added false hair to make their braids longer. They adorned their hair with circlets or chaplets of real or jeweled flowers, worn around the head. Golden hair was regarded as the most beautiful.

Men's hairstyles were short, with a roll of hair at the neck or above the ears. Plaited hair remained in fashion for women during the thirteenth and early fourteenth centuries, but they coiled their plaits in the back or above their ears. Wealthier women covered their hair with linen or netting made from gold.

The Renaissance

By the end of the mid-fourteenth century, generally considered the start of the Renaissance, noblemen were wearing their hair cut at the neck, then curled under around the ears and neck. Women continued to wind their long braids over their ears, then binding them in the back, covered by gold net or linen. Veils were also popular.

Styles varied throughout Europe during the 1400s. Italian women wore bands or caps, sometimes studded with jewels, over their curled, plaited, or coiled hairstyles. French, Dutch, and Flemish women covered their heads with large wimples attached to veils.

In the 1500s, some women plucked their hairlines because high foreheads were fashionable in Elizabethan England, for example, and at some courts in France and Holland.

The 1600s brought new styles for both men and women. Long, waving hair was popular for men, who also curled, powdered and scented their hair to achieve the "cavalier look" during these years. For stylish women, short bangs, called a fringe, were arranged across the forehead, and they wore the sides in long curls or in puffs. They attached pearls, ribbons, and other ornaments to their own hair and the false pieces that they often added to make their hair look thicker.

Trends sometimes began in unusual ways. During the late 1600s, Marie, the Duchesse de Fontanges, was briefly a mistress of the French King Louis XIV (reigned 1643–1715), who wore a tall wig to add height and conceal his bald head. The very young duchess sparked a new trend when, during a hunting outing, she toppled off her horse, and her hairdo fell apart as the pins scattered. She used one of the garters from her stocking to pile her hair loosely back up on her head. The "Fontanges," as this style was called, became popular with young Frenchwomen for the next three decades.

Eighteenth Century

Other notable Frenchwomen,, including Queen Marie Antoinette (1755–1793) and the Marquise de Pompadour (1721–1764), mistress to the French king Louis XV, set style trends for women, who had started wearing larger and more ornate arrangements in the late seventeenth century and early eighteenth century. Women decorated their hair with figurines and replicas of objects, such as windmills, and even historical scenes. They added false hair and used wires, padding, and stuffing to create hairdos that might soar three feet high. Englishwomen took up this fad and added their own touches. An English widow was seen wearing a replica of her husband's tombstone on her hair.

Soaring hairstyles created problems as women moved through entryways and entered and got out of carriages. Doorways were raised to accommodate high hairstyles. An inventor named Beaulard came up with a mechanical hairdo that could be raised and lowered at the touch of a spring. Sleeping posed other problems, and women often used wooden neck supports at night.

Hairstyles were shortened and greatly simplified in France during the French Revolution (1789), when the common people denounced the opulent aristocratic ways of life. Women wore their hair in a simple chignon style pulled to the back of the neck. As a symbol of the nobles and other wealthy French people who were being guillotined, revolutionaries wore a blood-red ribbon around their hair at the back of their necks.

Men's hairstyles remained fairly short after that time. Then and later, however, some men spurned conventions or wore exaggerated versions of popular styles. Late in the nineteenth century, the artist Aubrey Beardsley (1872–1898) wore his hair short with a sharply defined center part that created a gap between the sides of his straight cut bangs.

European women stopped wearing towering wigs during the 1800s, but often adopted elaborate hairstyles with curls, fringes, and ringlets. Victorian women sometimes added false hair in the form of a "switch" or "fall."

In the North American colonies, European settlers brought with them the hairstyles and fashions that were popular in their homelands. Some colonial Americans continued to follow the more elaborate European fashions of powdered hair, wigs, and ringlets, but others gradually adopted simpler styles. On the eve of the American Revolution, patriots such as Benjamin Franklin openly opposed the use of wigs or other hairstyles associated with the aristocracy or with England.

Many enslaved African women in America also retained hairstyles from their homeland. Some followed an old custom of wrapping their hair in bunches with strings or cords, a style that is still popular in certain parts of Africa, including Togo.

Twentieth Century

In western societies, many early twentieth-century hairstyles were influenced by French fashions. After World War I, daring young women cut ("bobbed") their hair, and short haircuts were identified with women called "flappers" during the 1920s. Actress Louise Brooks (1906–1985) strongly influenced this trend by wearing her dark, shiny black hair in a short bob with straight thick bangs.

Beauty parlors and hair salons became more numerous during the 1900s, and women of all classes used professional hair services. Wealthier women patronized salons regularly, sometimes once a week, to have their hair styled as well as cut. It was common for European and American women to have their hair washed and set once a week, and the style was expected to last for seven days, until their next appointment. The beauty salon had a social as well as a cosmetic function; women met their friends there and exchanged and gathered news.

The growth of the mass media during the twentieth century gave public figures even more influence over hairstyles. Movie magazines featured the hairstyles of the stars, and magazines devoted to beauty and hairstyling showed how to duplicate these styles at home. During the 1930s, many women adopted the style of the actress Veronica Lake, who wore long hair with a side part that fell over one eye—so many that at the advent of World War II, government officials asked her to cut it because female factory workers were getting their hair caught in equipment (she complied). Women read with interest that Marlene Dietrich sometimes sprinkled gold dust in her hair for some film roles.

The Veronica Lake look notwithstanding, many women in the 1930s and 1940s wore carefully constructed styles that featured waves and curls. New hair styling products were also developing. Some evolved from the lacquer materials Japanese women had traditionally used to keep their hairstyles in place; this contained a form of shellac. After the 1930s, hair sprays were changed and improved so that they were lighter in texture and easier to wash off.

The permanent wave was invented in the 1930s. The solution used in the permanent wave actually changed the structure of the hair shaft. The chemicals used in these waves were heat-activated, and the hair would be wound around curlers attached to an electric heating device. During the early 1940s, "cold-wave" permanents became available, and women could give themselves relatively simple home-permanents, although the results were not entirely predictable. Permanents became easier and more pleasant to use and more natural looking during the 1950s. More women bought kits to use for themselves and their children. One permanent manufacturer promoted the natural appearance of its product in an ad featuring twins that asked: "Which twin has the Toni?"

During the 1950s and early 1960s, the bouffant hairstyle was quite popular in United States and Europe. Women wore curlers or rolled their hair around rags or used hairpins to produce waves and curls. In the early 1960s, First Lady Jacqueline Kennedy wore a widely copied bouffant hairstyle. Women kept these styles—the bubble cut, beehive, the flip and the pageboy—with hairspray. They achieved height by backcombing, also called "teasing."

Wigs and artificial hair, in the form falls and switches, were also popular during the late 1960s and 1970s. The "hippy look" featured long straight center-parted hair for women.

For women, both very long and very short hairstyles were popular during the 1960s, and shorter styles with more natural movement became popular in the latter part of that decade. Connecticut-native Dorothy Hamill (b. 1956), the 1976 Olympic gold-medallist in women's figure-skating, popularized the short "wedge" haircut that she wore as a com-

petitive skater. Journalists wrote about her natural good looks and shining, dark brown hair cut in a "wedge," a style that was originally created at a Vidal Sassoon salon. It was adapted for Hamill by the hairstylist Suga, who worked with the skater to design a cut that would enhance her "line" without inhibiting her movement. Before that time, most female figure skaters wore their hair in a ponytail, French twist, bun, or other controlled style.

In the years that followed, female athletes wore more diverse styles. In some cases, a well-known stylist was appointed as the "official" hair-stylist of a particular Olympic Games, and cut the athletes hair in a way designed to work with their athletic event and appearance. After the Olympics, Hamill became a commercial spokesperson for a successful line of hair-care products.

Since the mid-1970s, women have continued to follow various hair fashions, but at the same time have had more freedom to choose the style that best suited them. Fashion magazines continue to print articles that illustrate the latest styles, but the social pressure for women to conform has eased considerably.

Men's Hair

Men's hairstyles also changed regularly during the twentieth century. The style known as the crew cut—in which hair was cut very short and combed straight or upright—may have originated with the German military (hence the "crew"). During World War I, the U.S. Navy adopted this as the regulation haircut for seamen, and other branches of the military followed. Under the first regulations, the hair on the top of the head could be no longer than one inch. In the mid-1920s, the rules changed to permit a length of two inches.

As men's hairstyles changed, manufacturers began creating products for whatever look was fashionable, notably, at first, hair creams to give shine and stability to slicked-back hair or hair that was combed in an unnaturally upright position, as with the crew cut. One of the best-known of these creams for men was Brylcreem, created in 1928 by the Birmingham County Chemical Compan in Great Britain, and advertised with the phrase, "Brylcreem/a little dab'll do you/Or watch out/the girls will all pursue you." In 1940 when Britain was at war, this hair cream was issued to men in the military as part of their personal care kits. At that time, it was known as Elite Hair Dressing Cream. During the 1930s, at least five million British men used Brylcreem, and the product was also quite popular in the United States and numerous other countries. The well-known cricket star, Dennis Compton, was featured in a popular ad campaign for the product.

Brylcreem retained its popularity with the advent of the "ducktail" haircut, in which young men slicked their hair back into a "tail" at the back. During the late 1930s, young, male Mexican immigrants living in coastal cities in California, sported their distinctive ways of dressing and hairstyles. These young men, called Pachucos, wore a hairstyle called an Argentine duck-tail.

The late 1940s and 1950s brought more variety in men's hair styling. In 1948, the Marine Corps rejected the two-inch haircuts in favor of a more closely cropped head. A number of celebrities, including film star Steve McQueen, wore crew cuts, and the crew cut was also popular among clean-cut high school and college boys of the time. Another short haircut became fashionable among a different crowd when a jazz musician named Gerry Mulligan influenced men's hairstyles by cutting his hair short and combing it forward into a distinctive style. This look, which often included wearing sunglasses and turtle neck sweaters, was considered to be modern and "hip."

During the same period, however, some men favored a more styled look. The popular haircut called the D.A. (duck's ass) was apparently a variation of the Argentine ducktail, and became popular during the 1940s. Large numbers of British and American young men adopted this style. The singer Frank Sinatra wore a variation of this style, which again required that men use hair creams to slick back their hair. Subsequently, the singer Elvis Presley made the style even more popular.

A well-known men's hairstylist, Joe Cirello of Philadelphia, claimed to be the man who developed this hairstyle in United States. He later said, "I invented the D.A. in 1940 at 6th and Washington Avenue, on a blind kid. I was just playing around, I had something in mind — they figured this kid can't see what I'm doing, so I kept on practicing. And then the kids started coming in from Southern High (the neighborhood school), they said 'Hey, that looks great, try it on me.'" Cirello went on to work at Warner Brothers film studios in Hollywood, where he cut and styled the hair of film stars, including Humphrey Bogart, Wallace Beery, James Dean, and other well-known performers, including Frank Sinatra and Elvis Presley.

Brylcreem lost favor during the 1960s when a wet-hair look became less fashionable. The company went on to develop other products, such as gel and water-based hair creams. Other companies did likewise; the Gilette company introduced "the Dry Look."

The transition from the 1950s to the 1960s was helped by the "English Invasion" of pop singers, most notably the Beatles, whose tidy but longer hair quickly caught on both sides of the Atlantic. This haircut in essence broke the barrier that stood between the 1950s short, if styled, hair and the longer men's styles that followed.

The 1960s and 1970s were for men, like women, decades when they ignored conventions and did as they pleased with their hair. Some chose to retain conventional short haircuts, but many young men opted for long hair that signaled their alliance with the counterculture and their rejection of mainstream society. Others just liked the look of long hair.

Gender-Neutral Hair

In western cultures, the 1980s brought "punk styles," which originated in Europe. Some people cite French artist Yves Tanguy as the first man to wear a spiked haircut. Short, short hair and spikes of hair, colored with purple and hot pink, and even rainbow colors, were part of this look. Androgyny was also a part of the alternative styles. Followers of these trends sometimes shaved their heads or adopted the Mohawk—a partially shaved head with a band of hair running from the forehead to the back of the neck. Gels, mousses, styling gels, and glazes were used to style the hair. Punk styles persist into the present.

Pop music as seen in concert and on television channels continues to exert a strong influence on hairstyles, as well as cosmetic use. Among the celebrities who have influenced trends have been Elton John, Madonna, Boy George, David Bowie, Prince, Michael Jackson, Brandy, Britney Spears, and Jewel.

Hairstyle and Group Affiliation

Many modern hairstyles have symbolized membership in a particular group or cult, or protested existing social standards. The Afro style—left natural, without chemical or any other sort of straightening—symbolized black pride during the 1960s. Angela Davis and Jesse Jackson were two activists who promoted this style, which many black people still favor. At the opposite end of the spectrum, skinheads are generally white males who can be recognized by their shaved heads. Military haircuts are also identifiable on men, and among those who are not in the military, sometimes symbolize an alliance with so-called traditional values.

In modern times, traditional African cultures continue to decorate their hair with feathers, flowers, and other objects. The Songhai people of Mali wear beads, coins, and lumps of amber and other stones in their hair. In Namibia, Himba women twist sheep's wool around their hair, stretching it out, and then apply a mixture of mud, fat, and ochre to hold the style in place. They then adorn the hairstyle with ornaments made from cloth and plant materials. Women in Mauritania also prefer intricate hairstyles, adorning their plaited hair with various colored glass beads, amber, golden balls, and shells. Japanese geisha continue to use hair ornaments that cor-

A Turkana woman from northern Kenya, Africa, has an intricate hair style, incorporating beads. © *Des Bartlet/ Photo Researchers.*

respond to different seasons and months of the year, such as peach blossoms or chrysanthemums.

Products and Style

In more developed countries, both women and men spend billions of dollars annually on hair-stylists and hair care products, such as shampoos, rinses, conditioners, lotions, gels, hairsprays, straighteners, and hair coloring products for home use.

Manufacturers also produce numerous styling products for hair, including creams, gels, mousses, and products to reduce frizziness or relax curl. They have also developed new and improved implements to style, wave, and curl hair. To produce curls and waves, stores offer hairpins for winding pincurls and hair rollers made from cloth, mesh, metal, rubber, foam, and plastics. Electrical appliances include helmet hair dryers, blow-dryers, hot rollers, and machines that dry and curl or wave hair simultaneously, as well as curling, crimping, and straightening irons.

Different implements have also been used to style and hold hair in place. Early implements were combs and hairpins. The Romans had a primitive version of the modern curling iron. Modern electrical appliances are used to dry hair, add curls, straighten, wave, and condition hair. Chemical processes are used to straighten, curl or wave, or color hair.

During the 1990s, manufacturers developed new products to calm frizzy hair and flyaway ends and to treat dry and damaged color-treated hair. John Frieda launched the Frizz-Ease line of products, featuring mousse, hair serum, and sprays; other companies introduced similar lines.

During the twentieth century, products for men were among the fastest growing segments of the hair products industry. Grooming preparations for men's hair had focused on cleansing, holding styles in place, conditioning the hair and scalp, and giving hair shine. During the 1970s, more men began using hairspray and other products that had once been associated with women's hair care. Men's hairsprays had masculine containers and scents and did not stiffen the hair. In western societies, more men used mousses, hair gels, and other products, and an array of these products could be seen on the shelves of drugstores and variety stores. More men also used hairdryers to blow-dry after shampooing.

During recent decades, companies continued to add men's products to their lines. For example, the men's line from Vidal Sassoon, a well-known hairstylist, was launched in 1985 and featured gels, mousse, and hairspray. Men were encouraged to express their personality and style, instead of stopping at being merely well groomed. By the 1990s, more men than ever were having hair styled in salons and receiving color and permanents.

Today's Trends

During the late 1990s, trendy women in New York City and Los Angeles tried a new unkempt look in hair. Runway models could be seen wearing stringy and uncombed or deliberately matted hair at fashion shows, and some actresses adopted the look as well. New York salon owner Renato Vasconcelos said of the "proletarian look": "It works best in extreme situations: a fashion runway, music video, awards ceremony, soap opera or movie." During a New York fashion show with a sea theme, models decorated their messy hairstyles with pieces of seaweed and driftwood.

Certain styles are popular in the United States with young people, those in their late teens to 30s. Celebrities have made some of these styles popular, such as Jennifer Aniston, who plays the character Rachel on the hit television series *Friends*. Another popular style is a short pixie cut with bleached ends. Other styles feature strands of loose hair at the crown or sides. Some young men and women use vivid colors on their hair, sometimes in combination. Basketball star Dennis Rodman is known for his short curled hairstyle and propensity to change his hair color. Keith Flint, a member of the British band Techno, has worn spiked extensions dyed green. People from all races and ethnic groups can be seen wearing dreadlocks, cornrows, and other styles that originated with people of color.

New hair accessories have also been introduced. They include a variety of small-to-large-sized clips in different colors and styles. Small glittery or metallic ornaments that can be placed anywhere on the hairdo and stay put with Velcro are also selling well in American stores. *See also* EBER, JOSE; HAIR COLOR; HAIR LOSS; HAIR TRANSPLANTS; MICHAELJOHN; PERMANENT WAVE; SALONS, BEAUTY; SASSOON, VIDAL; WIGS AND HAIRPIECES.

Further reading: Richard Corson, *Fashions in Hair* (1965); Wendy Cooper, *Hair, Sex, Society, Symbolism* (1971); Carole Devillers, "What Future for the Wayana Indians?" *National Geographic*, January 1983, 66–83; Angela Fisher, *Africa Adorned* (1984); Michael Grant, *A Social History of Greece and Rome* (1992); James Laver, *Taste and Fashion: From the French Revolution to Today* (1937); Jack Lindsay, *The Ancient World: Manners and Morals* (1968); Kate Mulvey and Melissa Richardson, *Decades of Beauty* (1998); Esther Pan, "Scary Hair," *Newsweek*, 30 November 1998, 72.

Hair Straightening

People who dislike their naturally curly or frizzy hair have tried different methods to straighten it, primarily with pomade, heat, and chemicals.

Naturally curly or frizzy hair has gone in and out of fashion for centuries, if not longer, and women, in particular, have spent as much time trying to curl their hair as to straighten it. Frequently, fashion calls for hair that is part straight and part curly, as in the latter half of the nineteenth century, when women smoothed and pinned up their long hair, then curled the "fringe," or bangs.

Hot pressing or hot combing was first used to straighten hair at the turn of the nineteenth century. Pressing oil was applied to clean hair, then a metal comb heated to 300–500 degrees Fahrenheit was quickly run through a strand to straighten it. The effects were temporary, and the curl might return if the hair became damp or was exposed to humidity. The process sometimes damaged hair or burned the scalp. Chemical straightening products produce more lasting results.

These products were widely used by young women in the 1960s, when the "hippie" look called for long, straight hair parted in the center. Some used chemical straighteners, while others resorted to such home remedies as ironing their hair, or wrapping it around empty 32-ounce cans so that it would dry straight. Older women, who had spent their youth trying to attain curly hair, found this ludicrous. Soon after, however, a more natural look came into vogue, and young women and men with curly hair took pride in leaving it in its original state.

Race and Straight Hair

People of color used hair straightening products and equipment for decades. During times when African Americans accepted white cultural ideas about how hair "should" look, they straightened their hair with pomades, creams, and hot combs, as well as chemical straighteners. These chemicals, however, could also damage hair and cause it to break and fall out.

During the early 1900s, advertisements and prevailing social attitudes urged African-American women to change the texture of their hair to make it straighter and smoother. Some women also preferred straighter hair because it gave them more styling options. Ads for hair-straightening products sometimes featured well-known African Americans. For example, a 1955 ad for Perma-Strate claimed the product was "proved by over 1,000,000 happy users" and showed photographs of singer Sarah Vaughan and musician Count Basie, as well as a musical trio that included Sammy Davis Jr.

Even during these periods, however, some African American hairdressers and cosmetics manufacturers did not encourage women to straighten their hair, but rather to focus on cleaning and conditioning. They urged women to take pride in their natural appearance. This attitudes prevailed during the 1960s when a Black Pride movement encouraged African Americans to appreciate their heritage and beauty. Many blacks chose hairstyles that did not require straightening, such as the Afro, also called the "natural" hairdo. Products designed to enhance these natural styles and to appeal to black pride appeared in the marketplace. Actors, athletes, and other celebrated African Americans wore these styles.

Some of these hairstyles carried political connotations during the 1960s, but they later became more a reflection of personal style and ease of care. More hairstylists and salons offered hairdos that worked with, rather than against, the natural texture of African American hair.

Controversy over African American hairstyles erupted in 1998 over a children's book written by an African-American author, Carolivia Herron, called *Nappy Hair*. Some African Americans protested that the word "nappy" was insulting and they asked that the book not be read in school classrooms. The author, however, responded that her intent had been to celebrate natural African American hair, not to denigrate it. *See also* AFRICAN AMERICANS; BARBERS; BEAUTY INDUSTRY (U.S.); DREADLOCKS; HAIR, STYLING OF; MALONE,

ANNIE TURNBO; WALKER, MADAME C.J.; WIGS AND HAIRPIECES.

Further reading: Carolyn A. Dunn, "The Ethnic Hair Care Market," *Happi,* April 1997; Lola Ogunnaike, "Some Hair Is Happy to be Nappy," *The New York Times,* 27 December 1998, 9-1, 9-3; Noliwe Rooks, *Hair Raising: The Roots of a Black Dilemma* (1996).

Hair Transplants

Hair transplants became available during the 1970s. Early efforts used synthetic hair and did not work; the hairs fell out, and men developed infections and scarring. Since that time, techniques have become much more sophisticated, and the results look far more natural. Some men start transplant treatments soon after they begin losing their hair, which can occur as early as the 20s. Most men require more than one treatment to fill in the bald spots on their scalps. Women are poor candidates for hair transplantation because when they lose hair, they tend to lose in all over, rather than in localized areas.

Men, in contrast, generally continue to have thick hair around the back and sides of their head after the top hairs have fallen out. In transplanting hair, surgeons take hair from the sides or back of the head and implant them at the hairline and on top of the head. During the procedure, done on an out-patient basis, the surgeon uses local anesthesia on both the donor and recipient sites. In one form of the procedure, plugs of skin about 3–5 mm. in diameter, containing active hair follicles, are cut out from the side and back of the scalp and into places where cylinders of skin of the same size had been cut out. In the process of grafting, between 250 to 750 small plugs of hair called mini or micro grafts may be inserted. Surgeons also use plugs of between 7 and 10 hairs, as well as "line grafts" that shift strips of 9 to 12 hairs. (*FDA Consumer,* 1997)

After the procedure, sterile dressings are placed over the surgical areas, and the patient is advised to be careful not to disturb the transplants while they began to heal. In transplants involving plugs of scalp hair, scabs form on the area, which tend to be sore. New hair growth is expected within two to six months. *See also* HAIR LOSS.

Further reading: American Medical Association, *The AMA Book of Skin and Hair Care* (1976); Larry Hanover, "Hair Replacement: What Works, What Doesn't," *FDA Consumer,* April 1997; Patrick Hudson, M.D., "Hair Transplant," Devera Pine, "Hair! From Personal Statement to Personal Problem," *FDA Consumer,* December 1991; Edmund Van Deusen, *What You Can Do About Baldness* (1978).

Hands

Care and adornment of the hands has been part of human activity for thousands of years and in all cultures. Besides using different substances to soften and condition the skin of the hands, people have painted designs on them and worn finger rings, bracelets, and other jewelry. Fingernail ornamentation and polish is also widely used.

People living on several continents follow the ancient tradition of using the plant-derived substance henna to paint designs on the hands. In the Middle East, some women have elaborate henna designs painted on both the backs and fronts of their hands. Intricate henna designs are painted on the hands and feet of brides in traditional ceremonies in North Africa, the Middle East, Egypt, and India. Designs on the palms are thought to bring good luck. It is also said that the prophet Mohammed wanted women to wear hennaed designs on their hands, particularly so that their hands would not look like men's.

Small hearts and other designs are created on the palms at certain ceremonies in Tunisia. Intricate designs of black, some of them words or verses, are traditionally used in North Africa, India, and parts of the Middle East. The designs are often made with stencils. Artists who specialize in the application of designs for the hands can be found in local marketplaces in the Middle East and in Africa.

Fingernails

Fingernails are also specially groomed and embellished in various ways. Coloring agents for the nails have varied from simple plant dyes or animal substances to nail lacquer to colored artificial nails and press-on nails. Nail extensions are used to increase nail length. Other contemporary nail decorations include decals, stamps, and stenciled designs.

Nail care dates back thousands of years. Egyptians stained their nails shades of orange with henna, a substance derived from a plant that grew in that region. The ancient Romans painted their nails with a mixture of sheep fat and blood. Ancient Turkish women devoted hours to caring for their hands and nails. They created a pink tint for the nails with boiled rose petals. The Romans used sheep's blood mixed with fat as a dye for their nails.

Nail polish may have been invented by the Chinese in approximately 3000 B.C.E. In the Ming dynasty (1368–1644), they created a nail polish made from egg whites, beeswax, vegetable dyes, and Arabic gum.

The Chinese were known for their extraordinarily long fingernails. Some ancient Chinese also wore gold, jewel-adorned nail guards to protect their nails. Women of the Ming Dynasty grew nails that measured 8 to 10 inches long. Chinese noblemen also grew long nails, and some had to rely on servants to feed, dress, and perform other personal chores for them because they could not use their hands without risking breaking a fingernail.

Eighteenth-century upper-class English women colored their fingernails. At the turn of the nineteenth century, women in western cultures used nail-polishing pastes to add shine to their nails, but these did not contain lasting color. Colored nail polish was uncommon in the western hemisphere until the twentieth century. An article describing liquid nail polish, newly invented, appeared in *Vogue* magazine in 1907. The polish came with a separate camel-hair brush. The first modern nail polish, a clear gloss, appeared in the 1920s.

In the 1920s, young women called "flappers" buffed their nails to produce a shine, a look that they preferred to colored nail-polishing pastes. Their style was boyish and casual; painted nails did not go with that mood.

In 1930, Charles Revson and his partners found a method to add opaque pigments to nail lacquer/polish so nails could be coated evenly with color. Revlon, Inc. was founded two years later and became a leader in the nail care field. Other companies developed colored nail polishes in different price ranges. In addition to more natural tones of pink and peach, customers could buy different shades

Manicure: Applying nail polish. © *Capucine/Explorer. Photo Researchers.*

of red, wine, purple, orange, and coral, among others. Frosted polishes added another dimension.

The last few decades have brought new developments and fashions in nail polish and decorations. Manufacturers brought out quick-drying nail polish to suit the fast-paced lives of modern women. During the 1990s, brightly colored polish in shades of blue, purple, green, and other colors were popular. Unusual colors, including black and gunmetal gray, appeared along with ice cream pastels, citrus shades, and glittery metallics. Cutex, a company that specialized in nail care products, introduced sheer pastel colors that could be applied over a French manicure, which features white-tipped natural colored nails. Some polishes contain built-in decorations, such as tiny metallic stars. Decals and other decorative trimmings are also put on the nails.

Innovations in nail polish continue. In 1998, American Jenai Lane created "mood nail polish." Her line of polishes, called P.M.S., changes color according to body temperature. Lane said, "It's heat-based, and heat is a reflection of your mood." With this polish, nails can change color from minute to minute—from blue to pink, orange to melon, violet to silver, and vice versa. Similarly, the company FXSolar introduced nail polish that changes color when exposed to sunlight.

Sales of nail polish rose sharply during the late 1990s. Between February 1996 and February 1997, sales of nail polish in drugstores, grocery stores, and mass outlets rose 18.8 percent. Out of total sales of $267.2 million, Revlon was the leader, with sales of $65.9 million. The Sally Hansen company sold $42.1 million and L'Oreal reported sales of $26.9 million. Sales of nail polish and polish removers for that same period totaled $378 million. (*Happi,* May 1997)

New technology and materials have also resulted in more realistic-looking artificial fingernails and nail tips. Acrylic nails are available either as full-length nails or extensions that are sold with glue adhesives or glue tabs. Salons offer professional applications of false nails or nail-tips with nail wraps of linen, silk,

and fiberglass materials. Consumers can also buy kits to use at home. The Food and Drug Administration cautions, however, that no one should wear artificial nails for longer than three months at a time, and that artificial nails should not be used if a fingernail area shows any sign of infection.

Salon operators note that the number of male customers continues to rise as men viewed well-kept hands and nails as an important part of their personal grooming and professional image. *See also* COSMETICS; FEET; HENNA; "LOOKS;" REVLON COMPANY.

Further reading: Angela Fisher, *Africa Adorned* (1984); "It's Not Your Mother's Nail Polish Anymore," *Happi,* May 1997; "Moody Hues," *People,* 7 December 1998, 111; Kate Mulvey and Melissa Richards, *Decades of Beauty* (1998);

Head

Grooming of the head usually focuses on hair, both its color and style. However, some cultures have modified the shape of the head itself. The custom of head flattening or elongation was practiced by certain peoples in parts of Africa, Melanesia, North, Central, and South America, and the Middle East. Some cultures regarded a pointed and/or elongated skull as more attractive than the natural, more rounded shape. To achieve the elongated shape, a person's head was bound starting early in life when the bones are still soft enough to change shape. Wooden busts made in the image of the Egyptian King Tutankhamen (reigned about 1350 B.C.E.) show that the boy's head may have been bound to develop a slender point.

Several Native American groups practiced head-flattening. They included the Catawba, Choctaw, and Waxhaw of the present-day southern United States, and the Chinook, who lived on the Northwest Coast. Cradleboards and headpieces were designed to press against the back of infants' heads so they would develop an elongated shape that rose to a peak. For instance, the Choctaw strapped infants to cradleboards that pressed against the bones to create a flat forehead. For many tribes, this flattened head shape was a sign of a person's rank.

The ancient Maya of Mexico also regarded a pointed slender head and sleek straight profile as a sign of good looks and privilege. The Classic Mayans (C.E. 300–900) bound the heads of infants between two boards for a period of several days. This pressure created a long, backswept shape. Historians believe the Mayans sought to achieve the shape of an ear of corn, which was their principal food. Sculptures of the Mayan Corn God show an elongated head. *See also* LATIN AMERICA, ANCIENT.

Further reading: Michael D. Coe, *The Maya* (1987); George E. Stuart and Gene S. Stuart, *The Mysterious Maya* (1983).

Height, Men's

Modern standards of appearance for men promote a taller stature as more attractive. Although being taller than average was also viewed as good for women during the late 1900s, height still tended to be more important for men. A height of six feet or more was considered desirable. Phrases like "tall, dark, and handsome" summed up one standard. Through the years, actors like John Wayne, Clint Eastwood, Cary Grant, Sean Connery, and Will Smith personified the appeal of tall, attractive men.

The tall-is-better stereotype can affect men's careers. During the late 1900s, research studies showed that a man's height could affect his job opportunities. Taller men were perceived as being more intelligent and stronger leaders. In some studies, shorter were less likely to be hired for management jobs than taller men who had similar qualifications and experience.

Remedies for short stature in adult males have been tried. Various products and techniques have been offered to increase men's height. In the early 1900s, the Cartilage Company of Rochester, New York, claimed it had developed a method to help men increase their height without drugs, surgery, hard work or great expense. In its ad, entitled "Every Woman Admires a Tall Man," the company offered a free booklet to men who wanted to learn more about its scientific and physiologic methods for expanding the car-

tilage, which would also increase a person's health, nerve force, and life-span, according to the ad. Men have also placed lifts in their shoes in order to appear taller or have worn other special kinds of shoes.

Neither ancient nor modern medicine has found a way to make an adult actually grow taller. As a result, both men and women have found ways to make men look taller. The "physically ideal" couple is regarded as one in which the man stands taller than his female partner. To make men appear taller, some tall women wear low-heeled shoes or slouch when standing beside their mate. Observers noted that when Lady Diana Spencer became engaged to Britain's Prince Charles, they posed for their engagement pictures so that Charles stood on a step above his fiancée, who was 5'10," about the same height as her future husband. After their marriage in 1981, Princess Diana usually wore low-heeled shoes when the two appeared together in public.

Film makers also find ways to help male actors appear taller on film. In some cases, men stand on boxes or platforms when doing scenes with significantly taller actresses.

However, attitudes about appearance have become more flexible, and diversity is appreciated more than in the past. Significant numbers of male celebrities who are not taller than average—among them Robert Redford, Tom Cruise, Henry Winkler, and Michael J. Fox—are recognized for their talents and strong physical appeal. Taller women with shorter mates are also more common. Tom Cruise and his 5'10" wife Nicole Kidman are regarded as a strikingly attractive couple. *See also* BEAUTY STANDARDS; BODY IMAGE.

Further Reading: S. Ellyson and J. Dovidio, *Power, Dominance, and Nonverbal Behavior* (1985); National Education Association, "Report on Size Discimination Due to Physical Size," http://www.lectlaw.com/files/con28.htm

Henna

Henna, which is derived from the dry leaves of the Lawsonia inermis plant, has been used as a hair coloring agent, hair conditioner, and body-paint for more than 5,000 years. The shoots and leaves of the plant are crushed and made into a paste that is red in color and is often mixed with water. A black color can also be extracted from the henna plant.

Women in India and Arabia have used henna to create designs on the skin, often in connection with marriage ceremonies or other occasions. The designs can be applied in such a way that they last one to two weeks. At a special party for the bride after a traditional wedding ceremony, women are painted with intricate henna designs on their feet and hands. Red henna is usually used on the tips of the fingers and toes, while the black color is used to paint designs on the soles of the feet and on the hands.

The first recorded use of henna as a dye for the hair can be traced to an ancient Egyptian queen named Ses, who also used henna preparations to cure baldness. The color and depth of henna hair dye depends on the strength of the henna and the length of time it remains on the hair.

Many people who had never heard of henna became acquainted with its hair-coloring properties while watching the popular 1950s American comedy series *I Love Lucy*. On her weekly television show, actress Lucille Ball, who played the main character, Lucy Ricardo, regularly referred to the fact that Lucy used henna hair color to turn her brown hair red.

Through the years, henna paste has been used to tint hands, feet, breasts, navels, and hair. It is still used for body painting in parts of Africa, India, and the Middle East. In the Middle East, women use henna to condition their hair. Afterwards, they may apply a paste made of crushed indigo leaf and water to impart a bluish-black shine.

Henna tattoos have also remained popular. Examples dating back to 2800 B.C.E. have been found on mummies of Egyptian royal children and pharaohs. The art spread to countries in other parts of the Middle East and to Asia. Today, men and women in various countries have revived the practice. Henna body art is not permanent like a tattoo and can be changed.

Henna kits for do-it-yourself body art can be bought in specialty stores, drugstores, and toy stores and from mail-order sources. *See also* BODY DECORATION; EGYPT, ANCIENT; HAIR COLOR; HANDS.

Further reading: Thomas J. Abercrombie, "Arabia's Frankincense Trail," *National Geographic*, October 1985, 474–513; Aileen Marron, *The Henna Body Art Book* (1998); Norma Pasehoff Weinberg, *Henna From Head to Toe* (1999).

Hispanic Americans

Hispanic Americans are a diverse mix of people from approximately 22 countries in Latin America, including Mexico, Cuba, Puerto Rico, and various other countries in Central America and South America, as well as Spain. During the late twentieth century, Hispanics became an increasingly influential minority in the United States and numbered about 30 million in 1999. They are expected to become the most numerous minority by the year 2005. Latinos have relatively recently experienced the surge of ethnic pride that characterized the Black Pride movement of the 1960s. At times, they have sparked new trends in fashion and grooming. Many have also adopted prevailing styles in cosmetics and grooming and hair-styling or blended their own "look" with popular styles. Latinos have been a strong force in politics, sports, music, art, cuisine, the media, and other areas of American life.

During the early 1940s, one small group of young Hispanics started a fashion trend that had a political impact. The "zoot suit" and the look and mannerisms associated with it became popular in Chicano communities in southern California, although some historians say that African Americans in Georgia or Harlem may have worn the style first. The zoot suit consists of a long, loose broad-shouldered jacket and very wide trousers that fit snugly at the ankles. "Zoot-suiters" also carried pocket watches on long chains and wore broad-brimmed, feather-trimmed hats. The look was popular among Mexican-American youths, who were called *pachucos*, a term affluent Mexican Americans used in a derogatory way. Some black youths also adopted the look. The Mexican-American youths usually also wore an Argentine Ducktail haircut. Young women associated with the pachuco subculture adopted an all-black outfit, consisting of zoot-suit jackets, short skirts, and fish-net stockings. They were called Black Widows or Slick Chicks.

Because America had entered World War II in 1941, cloth was being rationed, so some Americans regarded the suit as "unpatriotic." The zoot suit youths were also labeled as delinquents. During the "Zoot Suit Riots" of 1943, U.S. servicemen on shore leave attacked Mexican-American youths and stripped off and burned their clothes. The police moved into the areas to arrest "zoot-suiters." Some were badly beaten. Although these youths were labeled as gangsters, many claimed that pachucos belonged to clubs, not gangs and that they were not hoodlums. They asserted that racism and fear of people from a different cultural group had led to the attacks. Edward James Olmos, a well-known actor who performed a lead role in the 1978 play *Zoot Suit,* said that the outfit "became the statement of the Chicano and their identity, pride and self-esteem." (Aguila, 1998)

The zoot suit was worn by entertainers, including Louis Armstrong, Cab Calloway, Dizzy Gillespie, and the Mexican comedic actor El Gran Pachuco. It was also popular among people who enjoyed the "swing" dance craze of the 1940s and was worn to swing clubs. (When this dance style was revived during the 1990s, people bought zoot suits to wear for dancing.)

During the mid-twentieth century, many Americans grew more familiar with people from Hispanic cultures through the entertainment media. Male Latino actors, including Cesar Romero, Gilbert Roland, Antonio Moreno, Ramon Navarro, Ricardo Montalban, and Fernando Lamas were popular leading men in romantic roles. Cuban-American Desi Arnaz became one of the most popular actors in America during the 1950s and early 1960s when he co-starred with his wife Lucille Ball on the TV series *I Love Lucy.* Singer Carmen Miranda was a popular Latina performer of stage and screen. Later, award-winning singer and actor Rita Moreno starred on Broadway, in films, and on television. Erik Estrada co-starred on the popular television series *Chips.*

More recently, an increasing number of Latino celebrities have become extremely popular. They include pop singers the late Selena Perez, Jon Secada, Ricky Martin, Marc Anthony, Gloria Estefan, Paula Abdul, Lysa Flores, Shakira, and Jennifer Lopez, who has also been featured in films. Other well-known Latino actors include Andy Garcia, Benjamin Bratt, Jimmy Smits, Antonio Banderas, Maria Conchita Alonso (Miss Venezuela, 1975), Daisy Fuentes, Freddie Prinze, Jr., Penelope Cruz, and Selma Hayek.

Beauty contests that feature Latina women include Miss U.S. Latina, which is open to single women and provides scholarships among other prizes. Other pageants include Latina National Look, Teen Latina National Look, and Ms. Belleza Latina. As of 2000, Laura Harring was the only Latina to win the Miss USA Pageant (1985). She became an actress and earned a leading role on the daytime soap opera *Sunset Beach.*

Hispanics are a major consumer force. According to figures from the 1995 U.S. Hispanic Market report from Strategy Research Corporation and Simmons Market Research, Hispanic women buy about $1.6 billion worth of cosmetics, fragrances, and personal-care products each year. (Thomas, 2000) Companies that produce cosmetics and personal-care products pay attention to the needs and desires of these consumers. Some have developed products especially suited to the skin tones and hair coloring of Hispanics. In 1993, Avon Products, Inc. began holding a Latina Model of the Year contest. The winner becomes a spokesperson and professional model for Avon and appears in their sales brochures. She also receives an educational scholarship. Thousands of young women have entered the contest each year.

Hispanic models of both genders have become more common since the 1980s. They appear on runways, in print ads, and on television, among other places. Christy Turlington, whose mother was born in El

Salvador, is a top international supermodel. Turlington, who has represented Calvin Klein, among others, contributes time and money to charitable organizations, including groups that help Salvadoran children.

Daisy Fuentes, born in Cuba to a Cuban father and Spanish mother, is another well-known model who moved into television where she hosted *MTV Internacional* for seven years. She also hosted MTV's "House of Style". Her workout video marks the first time a woman has starred in a total body workout that is available both in English and Spanish. Fuentes has appeared in several feature films. She represents Revlon cosmetics, as does actress and model Selma Hayek. Model Astrid Munoz, whose heritage is Puerto Rican and Dominican, has appeared on the covers of high-fashion magazines such as *Elle* and *Marie Claire*. She once said, "I don't feel I am a role model to Latinas, but I definitely can be an inspiration to little girls in South America who have big dreams." (Thomas, 2000)

Singer-dancer-actress Jennifer Lopez (b. 1970), who grew up in a Puerto Rican family in New York City, has appeared in the TV comedy series *In Living Color* and in a number of feature films, including the film biography of the well-known singer Selena. She is equally well known as a singer and has performed to sold-out crowds around the world. Lopez is known for wearing revealing and eye-catching clothing and her stunning appearance. When she received a fee of $8.9 million for her performance in the film *The Wedding Planner*, Lopez became the highest-paid Latina actress ever.

Magazines that target Hispanic readers include *Latina, Latina Style, Que Linda,* and *Generation N. Latina* Magazine offers articles on fashion, beauty, career, celebrities, and health and fitness. Latin Girl is published for teens and features material on beauty, fashion, relationships, school, and other topics. Beauty and fashion websites for Latinas are also available online.

More salons with a distinctly "Latin" feel have also emerged in recent decades. Nelson Barreto, the owner of Ene, a successful beauty salon in New York City, serves Sangria wine and aims for a relaxed environment. Early in 2000, he described the latest styles among trendy Hispanics: "[Women] love those reds! For 20 years, they've been doing the red lipstick. Scandalous red! But now, the red is spread all over. It's red dresses, red hair, red everything. I've seen orange-red dresses at the clubs. Latinas, for many years, did the blonde thing, and when it didn't work, their hair turned that funky yellow. Now red is where it's at . . ." Latino men, said Barreto, were using silver and blonde hair-color and some men in the East Village were dying their eyelashes blonde. Barreto praises the Latina woman who has "pride in herself and her body." (Latinos on the Beauty Beat: February 2000: Nelson Barreto, East Village, NYC at http://www.holachicas.com/latino_e.html). *See also* HAIR COLOR; LATIN AMERICA, ANCIENT.

Further Reading: Justino Aguila, "Zoot-Suiting Up," *Seattle Times,* June 7, 1998, at http://www.seattletimes.nwsource.com/news/lifestyles/html98/zoot_060798.html; Patti Davis, *"Life in Tune* [Gloria Estefan]," Editors of *Latina* Magazine and Belen Aranda-Alvarado, *Latina Beauty* (2000); Carolina Gonzales, "The Making of Selena," *Swing* magazine, March 1997, pp. 76-77; Christy Hauberger, "The Legacy of Generation N," *Newsweek,* July 12, 1999, p. 61; [Latinos on the Beauty Beat: February 2000: Nelson Barreto, East Village, NYC] at http://www.holachicas.com/latino_e.html; John Leland and Veronica Chambers, "Generation N," *Newsweek,* July 12, 1999, pp. 53-58; Maria Conchita Alonso, "A Conquering Heroine," *People,* August 21, 2000, pp. 69–73; Johanna Schneller, "Drama Queen [Jennifer Lopez]," *Premiere,* August 2000, pp. 56-63; Irene Middleman Thomas, "Models and $$$," *Latina Style* magazine 11/2000 at http://www.mnbglobal.com/latinaju.htm. Other websites: http://www.misslatina.com/; http://www.hollywoodfactory.com/magazines/title/latin_girl.htm; http://www.magazinecity.net/magazinecity/7000-12.html

Houbigant

Houbigant is the oldest of the great French perfume houses and the second-oldest perfume house in the world (after Floris, established in London in the 1730s).

Twenty-three-year-old Jean-Francois Houbigant founded the House of Houbigant in 1775 in Paris to sell gloves and perfume to wealthy French people and the nobility. During that era, gloves, worn on almost all occasions, were scented, and French glove-makers were usually perfumers as well.

Within seven years, the House of Houbigant had become the official supplier to Marie-Antoinette, wife of King Louis XVI, and her court. They provided these clients with powders, scented gloves, and toilet waters, including scents called Eau de Millefleurs and Eau de Chypre. The flowers and plants used to make the scents came from Grasse, a town in southern France that has been the center of the French perfume industry since the 1500s.

During the French Revolution, the firm managed to survive. In the years that followed, the business continued to serve wealthy people in France and from abroad as Houbigant's son took over, followed by his business partner. The House of Houbigant became the official *parfumeur* to Emperor Napoleon, who ordered gloves, toiletries, perfumes, and scented pastilles from the firm. In 1838, Queen Victoria of England selected the firm as her official perfumer, as did Emperor Napoleon II (1870) and the Tsar and Tsarina of Russia in 1890. Houbigant sometimes created special fragrances just for its clients, who included celebrities and industrialists, as well as titled people.

In 1880, Paul Parquet, an expert perfumer who was one of the first to add synthetics to perfume recipes, took over Houbigant. Among his creations was a scent called "Fougere Royale," which made its debut in 1882. "Ideal," a scent Houbigant sold in 1900, has been called the first true composite perfume. Robert Bienaime' joined Parquet at the turn of the century. His 1912 creation, "Quelques Fleurs," often called the first true multifloral bouquet, was popular for decades. This classic perfume was regarded as a trendsetter, increasing the market for light florals. The famous crystalware company, Baccarat, designed bottles for several Houbigant scents, including "Ambre," "Etude," and "Essence Rare."

The company was also one of the first modern cosmetics firms. They produced color cosmetics, including lipstick and rouge. During the 1930s, one of their most popular products was a triple compact containing powder, rouge, and lipstick.

Other well-known scents from Houbigant include the best-selling "Chantilly," which came onto the market in 1941 and remained popular throughout the second half of the twentieth century. The scent was named for the Chantilly lace that royal brides traditionally used in their wedding veils. Orange blossom, rose, jasmine and several spices, along with sandalwood and amber, were part of the formula. The company also produced "Ciao" (1980), "Les Fleurs" (1983), and Lutece" (1986). "Monsieur Houbigant" (1969) and "Musk Monsieur" (1977) were among its men's fragrances. *See also* FRAGRANCE; GRASSE; MARIE ANTOINETTE.

Further reading: Roy Genders, *Perfume Through the Ages* (1972); Kate Mulvey and Melissa Richards, *Decades of Beauty* (1998).

I

Iman (b. 1955)

Born in Mogadishu, Somalia, Iman became one of the first black "supermodels," as well as an actress and the spokesperson for her own line of cosmetics. The daughter of a diplomat and a gynecologist, Iman Abdul Magid was studying political science at the University of Nairobi when American photographer Peter Beard encouraged her to become a model and featured the tall, elegant young beauty in a series of photographs.

After Iman signed with the prestigious Wilhelmina Modeling Agency in 1977, her first assignment was for *Vogue* magazine. She became a top runway model for the world's most famous fashion designers and appeared in numerous magazine layouts and ads during the 1980s and early 1990s. Her success encouraged other black models and prompted magazine editors to feature more women of color as cover girls.

In 1992, Iman worked with the BBC to produce a film about the devastating civil war in her homeland and the suffering it had caused. She also appeared before the U.S. Congress, seeking their help in the form of economic aid to Somalia.

Iman was married to basketball star Spencer Haywood, with whom she had a daughter; they divorced, and in 1992 she married rock musician David Bowie.

By the late 1990s, Iman had also appeared in several feature films. Iman developed a line of cosmetics for women of color that was marketed by Johnson Products. In the past, Iman said she had to mix her own products "Because in all my years of modeling, and with all the products I've used, I had never been able to find a foundation to match my skintone without mixing a variety of shades. Then there were the eyeshadows, blushes, and lipsticks not rich enough or true enough for

Iman. © *Steve Finn/Alpha/Globe Photos, Inc.*

women of color." ("Iman: All You Want, All You Need," p. 1) In 1999, Iman introduced a line of fragrance products called "Essence of Iman," which contained sandalwood and spices, among other ingredients. *See also* JOHNSON, BEVERLY; JOHNSON PRODUCTS; MODELING AND MODELS.

Further reading: "Iman: All You Want, All You Need," http:// www.sheen.com/iman/iman.htm; Eric Levin, ed. "Iman" in *Unforgettable Women of the Century* (1998).

Implants (Cosmetic)

Implants used for cosmetic purposes are made of different natural and synthetic materials. The most common sites for implants are the chin, cheek, pectoral area (on men), breasts (on women), and calves (most commonly on men).

Some people seek cheek augmentation, which was originally used only to correct certain kinds of birth defects. In 1990, more than 2,000 cheek-augmentation surgeries were performed in the United States. Nearly 13,300 chin implants were performed on people who wished to increase the prominence of their chins. In some chin implant surgeries, the bones of the chin were also repositioned. Implants to augment the calves are more popular with men, especially body-builders who want to achieve a balanced look. Buttock augmentation, rarely done in North America, is more common in South America.

A small number of men have had implants to increase the size of the penis, a process called penile augmentation, in which surgeons graft fat from the thighs or buttocks into the penis. According to author Claudia Kalb, "Critics call the surgery unsafe and unethical since if can result in permanent dysfunction." (Kalb, 1999)

Implants to augment the calves were more popular with men, especially body-builders who wanted to balance their well-developed arm muscles with their legs. The practice of calf augmentation apparently began in Japan in the 1950s, when surgeons injected silicon into the withered legs of polio victims. (Haiken, 1997) Buttock augmentation was rarely done in North America, although more common in South America.

Collagen injections are a form of cosmetic surgery called soft tissue augmentation. The collagen used for cosmetic injections is a natural protein derived from the purified deep layers of cow skin. (Human collagen is a protein found naturally in connective tissue, bone, and cartilage.)

During the process, a very thin needle containing the collagen is inserted into superficial layers of the skin. During the 1980s and 1990s, progress in the use of collagen injections led to the development of collagen that could be used in needles that had a diameter fine enough for use in the eye area to fill in "crows-feet" and other lines around the eyes and between the eyebrows. People who might have had traditional eyelift surgery opted for these less invasive injections, which did not leave scars and could be performed in a doctor's office in about 10 minutes with little or no anesthetic. One possible complication of this procedure is swelling, which may last up to about 10 days. Unlike eyelift surgery, the effects of collagen injections are temporary, usually lasting from six months to about a year, because the body eventually absorbs the collagen. Some people have repeat injections, from twice a year to every 18 months or so. Collagen may also be used to create fuller lips.

Some researchers have expressed concerns about the potential health hazards of injecting collagen into the body. Scientific studies predict that about 3 percent of the population will have an allergic reaction to collagen. Some patients have reported that they developed autoimmune diseases after receiving collagen injections, but, as of 1997, research studies were inconclusive. (FDA, 1991)

Fat implants (also called microlipo–injections) are medical procedures in which fat is removed from one area of the body, such as the buttocks, and injected into the lips, hands, face, or other places to plump out wrinkles. The procedure, which may be done by dermatologists or cosmetic surgeons, involves three steps: cutting the fat out, processing the fat, and inserting it into a new site. Some people who have this procedure choose to have extra fat removed and frozen for use in future procedures. However, some critics say that frozen fat cells are less effective than fresh because they tend to dissolve in the body more quickly.

As with collagen, the results of fat implants are temporary, since the fat is eventually reabsorbed into the body. Side-effects may be minimal because the body is unlikely to reject an implant that is made up of its own tissue, but potential side effects include the formation of scar tissue or lumps when the fat is absorbed into the body at an uneven rate. *See also* BREASTS; EYES; FACE; LIPS; PLASTIC SURGERY.

Further reading: American Society for Dermatologic Surgery, "Soft Tissue Augmentation," Fact Sheet #006, 1995; Paula Begoun, *The Beauty Bible* (1997); Elizabeth Haiken, *Venus Envy: A History of Cosmetic Surgery* (1997); Claudia Kalb, "Our Quest to Be Perfect," *Newsweek*, 9 August 1999; U.S. Food and Drug Administration (FDA), "Collagen and Liquid Silicone Injections," http://www.fda.gov/opacom/backgrounders/collagen.html, August 1991.

India, Ancient

Grooming practices in ancient India included bathing and the use of cleansing tools and cleansing substances, as well as scented oils and powders, cosmetics, and ornate jewelry.

The country is rich in scented flowers, resins, woods, and sources for musk, and fragrances were made for religious purposes, as well as for household and personal use. It became customary for women to bathe daily in perfumed water for a month before their wedding day. An old Hindu custom, still followed today, dictates that a handmaiden will rub the bride with fragrant ointments on the day of her wedding. The bridal couple sits underneath a canopy that is scented with sandalwood.

Indian women used a variety of cosmetics, including perfume ointments and a mascara-like substance for their eyelashes. They applied color to their hair, nails, and bodies. Directions for making cosmetics appear in the Kama Sutra, written by Vatsyayana. Both men and women used a paste made from ground-up sandalwood on their skin. This paste was sometimes tinted and used to paint designs on the body. Men and women of all social classes reddened their lips and used eyeshadow.

High-ranking women and the king's mistresses were carefully groomed. Their clothing was perfumed with incense, and their bodies were massaged with fragrant oils and ointments. Colored designs were applied to their skin, and their eyelids were tinted with a gold or silver paste.

Both men and women used wooden picks to clean their teeth and ears. They also used tweezers and shaving razors, as well as instruments to apply cosmetic substances to their faces.

Both genders also wore earrings. Hair was often adorned with jewels in the parts, and ivory combs were used in the hair. Ankle bracelets often adorn that body part.

A wealthy man prepared for the day by performing several morning grooming rituals, including cleaning his teeth with a special root, then chewing a plant substance to sweeten his breath. He then applied perfumed ointments and used eyeshadow and lip rouge and bathed. On alternating days, he used oil on his body, had a massage, then exercised and had his bath. After the bath came a second application of perfumed ointments and facial makeup. Men of fashion painted designs on their arms and placed a red mark on their foreheads. About twice a week, men shaved their faces. They shaved their other body hair once each five to ten days.

The beauty spot (tilaka) is one of the most recognized cosmetic applications traditional in India. Women applied a red or yellow stain, from the resin of the lac-insect, for this purpose. Women also used this dye to tint the hands and feet. Perfumers sold these dyes in their shops, along with scented oils, incense sticks, eye salves, and other cosmetic items. *See also* EARS; FRAGRANCE; HAIR, STYLING OF; HENNA.

Further reading: Jeannine Auboyer, *Daily Life in Ancient India* (1965); Sengupta Padmini, *Everyday Life in Ancient India* (1955); Ruth Winter, *The Smell Book: Scents, Sex, and Society* (1976).

International Flavors and Fragrances (IFF)

International Flavors and Fragrances (IFF) was founded in the United States in the 1930s as "Van Amerigen-Haebler" and is headquartered in New York City. It has become the world's largest creator and wholesale manufacturer of flavorings and fragrances. After the company joined with the Dutch fragrance firm Polak & Schwarz in 1958, the name became International Flavors and Fragrances (IFF). Its main competitors are Givaudan-Roure and Drugoco.

IFF operates sales offices in 38 different countries and runs numerous factories and laboratories for its extensive work in research and development. Its major manufacturing plants are in Europe, Asia, and South America. By the 1980s, IFF had catalogued more than 30,000 different fragrance and flavor molecules.

The company develops and sells fragrances, which account for about 60 percent of its sales, to firms that produce perfumes, cosmetics, hair care products, and other personal care products. Although IFF protects the privacy of its clients, the company is known to have created a number of prominent perfumes, including Revlon's "Intimate" (1955), Gres' "Cabochard" (1958), Lagerfeld's "Chloe" (1975), Yves St. Laurent's "Paris" (1983), Coty's "Exclamation" (1988), and Calvin Klein's "Eternity" (1989).

One of the foremost perfumers working at IFF during recent decades is the Russian-born American Sophia Grojsman. Known for her keen abilities as a "nose," Grojsman rose to the rank of senior perfumer in the U.S. branch of IFF. Among the scents Grojsman has created are Calvin Klein's "Eternity" and "Escape," Estee Lauder's "Spellbound," Yves St. Laurent's "Paris" and Lancome's "Tresor." *See also* FRAGRANCE; "NOSES."

Further reading: Elisabeth Barille, *The Book of Perfume* (1995); Roy Genders, *Perfume Through the Ages* (1972).

J

Jackson, Victoria (b. 1948)

Makeup artist and beauty expert Victoria Jackson developed a popular line of cosmetics for women and wrote a book about makeup, *Redefining Beauty*. Jackson was one of the first people to launch a cosmetics line through extensive television "infomercials."

As a Hollywood makeup artist for 13 years, Jackson specialized in creating "unmade up" looks for major Hollywood celebrities for magazine covers and ads. In the process, she developed some cosmetic formulas she used in her work. Her goal, says Jackson, was not to drastically change a woman's appearance or make her look a great deal younger but rather "to enhance her natural beauty, to make her look like herself, only better." (Jackson, 1993)

Jackson founded her own cosmetics company in 1987. To market the line, she appeared on an infomercial with actresses Ali MacGraw, Meredith Baxter, Lisa Hartmann, and other women who praised her products. The original makeup sets consisted of foundation, blush, lipsticks, powder, eyeshadow, eyeliner, mascara, eyebrow pencil, and applicators. Cosmetic kits came in three basic color "families"—pink, peach, and red—designed to work well together and to go on with a minimum of time and effort. In 1998, the company stated that more than 700,000 women in America were using Victoria Jackson products, which had expanded to include fragrances.

In her book *Redefining Beauty*, Jackson declared that women are beautiful without makeup and that using cosmetics should be a choice that enhances one's life, not a burden or a necessity. She wrote, "There's no reason to strive to alter your image to match someone else's. I urge you not to try to adapt to someone else's perception of beauty. Instead, I encourage you to strive to raise your self-esteem, to discover your individual beauty, to enhance it, and, above all, to cherish it." (Jackson, 1993) *See also* ADVERTISING (U.S.); AGING AND APPEARANCE; BEAUTY INDUSTRY (U.S.); BEAUTY STANDARDS.

Further reading: "About Victoria Jackson," http://www.vmakeup.com/3about.html; Victoria Jackson, *Redefining Beauty* (1993).

Japan

Special bathing and grooming practices and the use of color cosmetics in Japan began many centuries ago. Traditionally, Japanese men and women placed great emphasis on bathing both for physical cleanliness and spiritual reasons. Massage, including facial massage, is an important Japanese beauty ritual that dates back hundreds of years, as does the philosophy that inner and outer beauty are strongly connected.

Body decoration dates back a very long time as well, when people painted their faces red and ornamented their bodies with tattoos. These tattoos also signified social rank and ethnicity. The Japanese used perfumes and had developed methods of distillation by C.E. 500. Special schools taught the art of perfumery, called kodo. People hung lacquer cases containing perfume on their kimonos.The Japanese attended carefully to the hair, eyebrows, teeth, and complexion. Priests and nuns shaved their heads as another sign that they were entering a spiritual existence apart from the world. During the Asuka age (C.E. 550–710), Prince Shotoku adopted a hairstyle from the Chinese court that featured a topknot.

In the tenth century, women and men used cosmetics, including face powder, rouge, and perfumes. Women also gilded their lower lips. Some hairstyles were so elaborate that a servant might devote as many as six hours to her mistress's coiffure.

Hair was traditionally regarded as an important beauty asset for women, and old tales celebrate women's shining dark hair. To keep their hair glossy, women applied oil with a cloth. During the Heian period (C.E. 794–1185), women's hair might reach the ground or be even longer. Washing this long hair was a time-consuming procedure for women of the higher classes. During this period, women wore their hair parted in the middle and falling long and straight. Ornaments were worn on the head.

Hairstyles often indicated a person's marital status and social class. For example, the lower classes (hinin) and outcasts (eta) had short haircuts instead of the long hair of the upper classes.

For women, a well-rounded figure was considered desirable, and descriptions of attractive females include phrases like "well-rounded and plump" while unattractive women are described as "pitifully thin" or "bony." (Morris, 1964)

When young Japanese men came of age, they received an adult name and their foreheads were shaved, leaving a ponytail in the back. The samurai, or warrior class, wore one of the most distinctive hairstyles for men. These men shaved the tops of their heads, then gathered hair from the sides and back together into a queue. They applied oil to the queue before doubling it forward over the crown, then tying it at the point where it was doubled over. The ends of the bunched hair were kept neatly trimmed. A neat hairstyle and clean shave were considered imperative, and it was humiliating if an opponent cut off the queue during a sword fight.

Distinctive fashions in eyebrows marked different historical periods in Japan. During the Heian era, women and men at court plucked their eyebrows and drew in new brows high on their forehead. Women who plucked their brows during the early part of the Edo era (1601–1867) indicated to others that they were married and had at least one child. The Meiji era (1868) brought more changes. Japan modernized its government and developed more contacts with the outside world. Women rarely shaved off their eyebrows.

Barbershops thrived during the Edo period. Priests, soldiers, merchants, and other men frequented these shops, which were off-limits to women. Patrons could socialize and discuss politics and current events as they had their hair styled and sometimes washed. Shaving services were also available.

Women's styles also became quite elaborate during the Edo period. Courtesans adopted a coiffure that included a forelock, sidelocks, back hair, and a chignon. Hair was adorned with combs, jeweled ornaments, and picks. Different coiffures included the Shimada, Hyogo, and Katsuyama, which was reserved for married women. Some forms of these traditional hairstyles are worn today. A festival called Shimada-mage is still held in Japan on the third Sunday in September. Female beauticians wearing the traditional hairstyle parade in the downtown district of Shimada and the Uda-ji Temple.

The custom of o-haguro involved blackening of the teeth. Bare, white teeth were regarded as unattractive. During the Heian era, men and women blackened their teeth with a dye made by soaking iron ore and powdered gallnut in tea or vinegar. During the Edo period, women blackened their teeth when they became engaged or married. Among women of the lower classes, the teeth were blackened either at the time of marriage or when the woman became pregnant. Aristocratic men in Kyoto also blackened their teeth.

White face powder, made from crushed rice, made its way to Japan from China. During the Heian era, the Japanese viewed white skin a sign of aristocratic birth. A white face was considered most desirable and symbolized beauty, youth, and high social status. Married women added some color to their cheeks and painted their lips. Reddened cheeks were achieved by using rouge, which was also used to redden the lips after the Edo era. This rouge was made from safflowers and was quite costly, so a deeply rouged face was a sign of wealth.

Women's hairstyles changed at the beginning of the 1600s from long and straight to elaborate upsweeps, a shift sparked by courtesans and stylish merchant-class women. The basic style involved dividing hair into six sections—front, sides, back, center and chignon. The center section was then tied with a string. From that point, styles varied but all sections of hair eventually met at that center. Styles were numerous, and each had a name, depending on the way hair was arranged, the size of the different elements, and the types of ornaments that were used. Combs, pads, and frames were also used to create special designs. Different styles and ornaments were assigned to women of different ages and social classes, such as samurai daughters, young wives of merchants, courtesans, brides, and pickpockets. Women used hot wax or a thick greasy substance to help the hairdo remain in place.

During the 1600s and 1700s, women often kept the same style for ten days without washing it. They slept on special pillows that kept their heads propped up away from the mattresses and enabled the hairstyle to remain in place. A traditional punishment for women who committed crimes was to have their hair shaved off.

Certain women called geisha ("beautiful person" or "one who lives by art") represent a specialized feminine look in Japan. These women are traditional entertainers and are called *maiko* (in training) and, later, *geisha*

and *geiko*. The earliest geisha were professional actors, dancers, musicians and storytellers who were men, but women dominated the profession by the eighteenth century. They are trained to speak, move, sing, write, dance, and serve food and drinks in ways that are considered graceful and aesthetically appealing, and they learn special rules of etiquette. They also play a three-stringed instrument called the *samisen* and recite poetry, creating an atmosphere of luxury and relaxation.

These women carefully apply traditional cosmetics and their makeup and ornaments correspond with different seasons and months of the year. For instance, they adorned their hair with cherry blossoms in April and with chrysanthemums in November. Geishas traditionally took mineral baths. Different hairstyles had social significance, as did the use of certain fragrances and colors. Some of the traditional rituals are still practiced by Japanese geishas.

Modern Japanese women believe that diet is vital to a beautiful appearance, and may eat certain foods, including kelp and seafood, for healthy hair. Hairstyles have been influenced by western trends and especially by the styles worn by celebrities and film stars. For example, during the 1950s, numerous women wanted a short, "pixie" style cut with bangs like the one actress Audrey Hepburn wore in *Roman Holiday*. In the next decade, they took to wearing ponytails, which the French actress Brigitte Bardot wore, among others. In recent decades, hairstyles have ranged from long and more traditional-looking effects to curls and feather cuts and the "buzz cut" and other trendy styles that come from the west. Young people are more likely than their elders to experiment with unusual hair colors or streaked heads.

Elegant and elaborate traditional Japanese hairstyles can still be seen during festivals and on special occasions, such as New Year's. Classical styles for women are called *nihongami,* which means "Japanese coiffeur," and some hairstylists specialize in arranging them. They include stylists for kabuki theatrical companies and hairdressers for Japan's traditional Bunraku puppet theater. Some

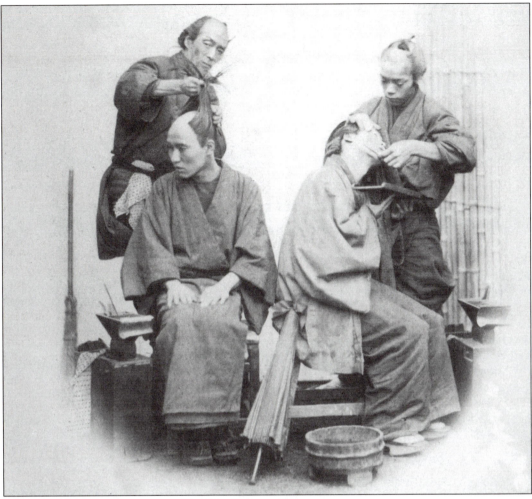

Japanese barbers, ca. 1870–1880. © *Alinari/Art Resource, NY.*

hair salons offer classical styles, too, and Japanese women often choose to wear a nihongami wig on their wedding day. Hideo Tanikawa, who styles hair for the Zenshinza, a theatrical company, has amassed a collection of historical prints and accessories in order to reproduce old hairstyles accurately. Tanikawa has praised the esthetics of the Edo period and says of these classical hairstyles: "Nihongami looks most beautiful when viewed from the back. . . . Nihongami and kimono made a perfect combination." (Takashima, 1999) *See also* AGING AND APPEARANCE; BATHS; COSMETICS; SHISEIDO CORPORATION.

Further reading: Ivan Morris, *The World of the Shining Prince: Court Life in Ancient Japan* (1964); Miki Takashima, "Black and Beautiful," *The Daily Yomiuri,* 18 November 1999, 7.

Johnson, Beverly (b. 1955)

Beverly Johnson broke ground as one of the first prominent black fashion models and cover girls in America. She has appeared in major mass-circulation women's magazines, as well as top beauty magazines, including *Cosmopolitan* and *Glamour.* In 1974, Johnson became the first African American to be featured on the cover of *Vogue.*

Besides appearing in runway shows for designers in the United States and Europe, Johnson was photographed for magazine features on cosmetics and fashion.

Johnson, the mother of a daughter, continued to model during her 30s and into her 40s and also endorsed a line of wigs and hair extensions. In addition, she has appeared on television as a dramatic actress. She actively supports charitable causes and was one of the first celebrities to help raise money for AIDS and visit schools to discuss AIDS prevention. In a 1990 interview, Johnson said, "I broke the boundaries—now I encourage younger minority models to stick with the business." ("Cosmo Cover Girls Then and Now" 1990) *See also* AFRICAN AMERICANS; MAGAZINES; MODELING AND MODELS.

Further reading: "Cosmo Cover Girls Then and Now: Beverly Johnson," *Cosmopolitan,* May 1990, p. 346.

Johnson Products

Johnson Products is a multinational company that is known for its innovative hair care products designed specifically for men and women of color. In 1954, entrepreneur George E. Johnson started the company with $250 he had borrowed from a finance company. He and his wife, Joan Henderson Johnson, began manufacturing "Ultra Wave," a product that straightened men's hair, and within three years, they were also producing their Ultra Sheen line of products for professional beauty operators to use for women clients.

The company began selling in the retail market in 1960. When Johnson Products went public in 1971, its Ultra Sheen cream hair relaxer was among its most popular products. That same year, the company became the first African American advertiser to sponsor its own television show, *Soul Train.*

By the 1990s, the company offered more than 200 products, including Soft Touch, Classy Curl, Sta-Sof-Fro, GT for Men, and Ultra Sheen's Bantu. Johnson Products Research Center was one of the largest development laboratories in the world specializing in hair care products for African Americans. In addition to its hair care products, the company developed several successful lines of cosmetics, including products from Flori Roberts, Posner, and Iman. In July 1998, Johnson Products was acquired by Carson Products, another leader in the ethnic cosmetic industry. *See also* AFRICAN AMERICANS; HAIR, STYLING OF; IMAN.

Further Reading: Johnson Products Company, "How It All Began," "Johnson Products Company, 1996-1998," http://www.sheen.com/history.htm; Rayford W. Logan and Michael R. Winston, *Dictionary of American Negro Biography* (1982).

K

Kan, Yue-Sai (b. 1949)

In 1992, Yue-Sai Kan founded Yue-Sai Kan Cosmetics, a successful business that has become one of the most popular upscale cosmetics lines marketed in Asia. The products are sold in more than 600 stores in China. The company has developed makeup, skin care and sun protection products, and fragrances that are geared to the specific skin types and features of Chinese women.

Kan was born in Guilin, China, then moved to New York City in the 1970s and became a U.S. citizen. After operating a successful import-export business with China, she hosted a television show in English and Chinese, then in 1978 became the host of *Looking East*, a weekly series about Chinese culture. The program ran for 12 years and brought Kan an offer from the Public Broadcasting System to broadcast a live program from China on the thirty-fifth anniversary of the formation of the People's Republic. This was followed by an offer from the Chinese government to produce and host a program called *One World* on China's national television network. Hundreds of millions of people saw the program. (Branna, 1997)

Kan has often expressed her opinion that Chinese women should not use western-style cosmetics. She says that certain shades of red and tan are unflattering to a Chinese woman's complexion and that Chinese women should not let themselves be persuaded to adopt western hairstyles, such as curls, that are less becoming than their own natural hair. She said, "Chinese women are fashion victims. They're curling their hair like crazy and they shouldn't. They have beautiful straight hair!" (Branna, 1997)

In 1996, the company had retail sales totaling $30 million, and employed more than 1,000 people as well as 800 beauty consultants who work with clients. Kan negotiated a joint venture agreement with Coty that involved building a $20 million plant in Shanghai. The American company agreed to provide funding and other resources that enabled her to expand the company. Kan added children's sun care products to the business and made plans for a line of men's products. *People* magazine called Yue-Sai Kan "the most famous woman in China," and Chinese women consumers voted her brands the best on the market. *See also* ASIAN MARKETS (MODERN); COTY COMPANY.

Further reading: Tom Branna, "East Is East," *Happi,* July 1997.

Kennedy, Jacqueline (Onassis) (1929–1994)

As First Lady of the United States (1961–1963) and later, as a prominent private citizen, Jacqueline Kennedy Onassis strongly influenced trends in beauty and fashion. Known for her classic looks and individual style, she increased the prestige of American designers and popularized an "American look" that was described as youthful and casually elegant. Her bouffant hairstyle and refined, understated look in makeup and dress were widely copied by other women. Fashion dolls were created to look like the "chic" Mrs. Kennedy.

According to some observers, Mrs. Kennedy's individuality and wide-eyed dark good looks also altered the prevailing beauty standards that were typified by such actresses as Brigitte Bardot and Marilyn Monroe: "The middle-class dream of the blond sex kitten was replaced by the cultured, feminine brunette. . . . The 'brainy brunette' replaced the 'dumb blonde.' " (Tapert and Edkins, 1997) Mrs. Kennedy was openly intelligent and articulate; she discussed her love of literature, the arts, and history. Between 1961 and 1966, Jacqueline Kennedy topped the Gallup poll list of the most admired women in America.

After leaving the White House when her husband, President John F. Kennedy, was assassinated in November 1963, Mrs. Kennedy, who later wed Aristotle Onassis, continued to fascinate the public and attract attention. The tabloids and mainstream magazines chronicled her hairstyles and clothing, and she appeared on numerous magazine covers. She popularized large sunglasses and a more casual daytime look that included a trenchcoat and slacks. *See also* HAIR, STYLING OF.

Further reading: Annette Tapert and Diana Edkins, *The Power of Style* (1997); Mary Van Renssaeler Thayer, *Jacqueline Bouvier Kennedy* (1962).

L

Langtry, Lillie (1853–1929)

Born Emilie Charlotte Le Breton, the London socialite and actress Lillie Langtry was perhaps the most famous beauty in Edwardian England (1901–1910) and one of the first "international beauties." Langtry was also one of the first celebrities to promote a beauty product.

"Lillie" Le Breton was the only daughter among the seven children born to the dean of Jersey and his wife. In 1884, she married a 27-year-old widower, Irishman Edward Langtry, and within a few years, the couple settled in London. They became part of a select social circle called the "Marlborough House Set" that included the Prince of Wales, Albert Edward, who was later King Edward VII.

At a public reception Langtry attended in London, her looks and mannerisms created a stir. People praised her classic profile, creamy skin, deep violet-blue eyes, and auburn hair, as well as her sensuous figure, set off by a simple dress. The Langtrys were not as wealthy as most of the people in their social circle, and Lillie had a limited clothing budget, so she often wore the same black dress, and it became an admired trademark. She wore her hair in a simple knot or, sometimes, hanging loose.

Frank Miles, John Millais, James Whistler, and other artists asked Lillie Langtry to pose for them. She became part of a group

Lillie Langtry, holding a cigarette lighter shaped like a lizard and smoking a cigarette. *Library of Congress.*

of Englishwomen known as "professional beauties," whose likenesses appeared in photographs that were mass-produced on picture-postcards sold in London shops for a few pennies. Millais chose Langtry as the model for Effie Dean in an illustration he made for *The Heart of Midlothian*, a novel by Sir Walter Scott. An engraving made from this painting sold many copies.

In 1877, Prince Albert Edward chose Lillie as his newest mistress, and she remained his favorite for several years. Although both were married, such relationships were accepted among members of their set as long as people were somewhat discreet. Prince Albert Edward had several mistresses.

In 1881, Langtry became the first English society woman to become a stage actress when she appeared as Kate Hardcastle in the play *She Stoops to Conquer* by the eighteenth-century dramatist Oliver Goldsmith. As she continued to perform and study acting, Langtry toured England, then France and the United States, where she also became famous. Her roles included Cleopatra and Marie Antoinette, and she appeared in several Shakespearean plays.

Americans flocked to see the famous "Jersey Lily," and reporters covered her activities and photographed her as she moved through society. Women copied her clothing and bought "Jersey Lily" hats. Langtry toured the country in a large, custom-made, 10-room railroad car called Lalee, which held a grand piano, kitchen, pantry, two guestrooms, and luxurious furnishings. The car and a New York mansion were gifts from Langtry's wealthy American lover Freddie Gebhard.

Langtry was one of the first celebrities to give a product testimonial when she was hired to promote Pear's Soap. The A. & F. Pears Company, which had been founded in 1800, sold their soap in different sized balls and tablets. Langtry agreed to promote the soap for £132, a sum she came up with because it happened to match her weight. Under a headline that read: "Good Complexion & Nice Hands" were the words, "Testimonial from Mrs. Langtry: I have much pleasure in stating that I have used your Soap for some time and prefer it to any other." The ad covered a whole magazine page. Using the name "Mr. Jersey," Langtry also collected thousands of

pounds from her stable of racehorses. (Brough, 1975) Through the years, she continued to set trends in fashion and beauty. Her hairstyles, hats, and jewelry were widely copied. When Mrs. Langtry began wearing colored nail cream, many other women followed suit.

Long estranged from his wife, who supported him financially, Edward Langtry died in 1897. Lillie Langtry remarried that same year. Her new husband was Hugo de Bathe, 19 years her junior. She continued to perform and operated her own theater in London during the early 1900s. She died at age 75 at her home in Monte Carlo. She was survived by a daughter Jeanne-Marie (Mrs. Ian Malcomb), whose father was a former lover, Prince Louis of Battenberg. *See also* ADVERTISING (U.S.).

Further reading: James Brough, *The Prince and the Lily* (1975); Anita Leslie, *The Marlborough House Set* (1972).

Laser Cosmetic Procedures

During the late 1900s, laser cosmetic procedures were increasingly popular ways to repair sun-damaged skin, reduce wrinkles, and remove unwanted hair. Laser peels were used to eliminate spider veins, varicose veins, and brown aging (liver) spots. They were used on the face and other parts of the body.

Laser—which stands for Light Amplification by the Stimulated Emission of Radiation—works by producing an intense beam of bright light that moves in one direction. By the 1990s, physicians could use lasers with great precision, which made treatments safer and their results more predictable. Laser beams work on skin by peeling off the topmost layer of skin and causing the collagen to thicken and change texture. Different kinds of lasers are used for different cosmetic procedures. Carbon dioxide lasers were used for a process called laser resurfacing, in which the surgeon vaporized one layer of skin tissue at a time with a low risk of scarring or complications.

Laser procedures are regulated by the U.S. Food and Drug Administration. Although physicians have greatly improved both the technology and the techniques, the procedures may still cause side effects, including discoloration, redness, and occasional scarring.

Lasers for hair removal were first approved in the late 1990s. They were compared to the dermatological lasers used for treating skin lesions and removing unwanted tattoos. The devices worked by applying a topical solution capable of absorbing the laser's wavelength on the treatment area. The solution penetrated hair follicles, so that the laser wavelength could then destroy the follicles. *See also* BODY HAIR, MEN'S AND WOMEN'S; PLASTIC SURGERY.

Further reading: American Society For Dermatologic Surgery (ASDS), "Laser Resurfacing," April 1999; Marian Segal, "Hair Today, Gone Tomorrow," *FDA Consumer,* September 1996.

Latin America, Ancient

Ancient peoples of present-day Latin America had distinctive ways of grooming their hair and bodies and applying different cosmetic substances. In pre-Incan times, around 500 BC, people belonging to the Moujik group, left mummies that show styled hairdos and makeup. Women of this era wore their hair in bobs and plucked their eyebrows. They polished both their toenails and fingernails and used red cheek and lip color. Archeologists working in Latin America have also discovered ancient graves with cosmetic containers holding face powder, powder puffs made of feathers, tubes of lip coloring, dark pigments to color eyebrows, and tools to trim nails and pluck hairs.

The Incas, who lived in present-day Peru, altered the shapes of children's skulls when they were very young and their skull bones were still soft enough to be molded into a different shape. The babies were strapped to boards that pressed their heads into the desired shape. Conical shapes and a skull with more than one peak can be seen in Incan skeletal remains.

The Incas' hairstyles indicated their rank. Inca chiefs had the shortest hair, and they wound their headbands around their heads five times. Noblemen had slightly longer hair,

while commoners had the longest. Noblemen wound their headbands around their heads fewer than five times, while commoners wound their headbands the fewest number of times.

The Aztecs of what is now Mexico applied cosmetic substances and styled their hair in ways that used local materials and also revealed the person's social status. Boys who had not yet killed an enemy wore their hair loose and long. Men who had earned the status of warriors wore a topknot. Spiritual leaders wore face paint in special designs, while warriors used vivid face paint in patterns designed to intimidate the enemy. Aztec noblewomen sometimes applied yellow face paint and tinted their lips and teeth red for special occasions.

Some hairstyles were designed to be practical in this hot climate. Married women gathered their hair in bunches or wore braids with colorful fabric woven in, then wound around their heads. Some Mexican women still wear this style. Unmarried women wore their hair loose. To combat the heat and dry air, Aztec women applied a substance called *axim* for their complexions and used jojoba oil on their hair. Avocado was used to moisturize both the skin and hair. Juice from the yucca plant helped to cleanse the hair.

The Mayans, who also lived in what is now Mexico, had specific beauty rituals designed to achieve a look that included an elongated head, long straight nose, and slanted forehead. Like the Incas, they strapped babies to boards that pressed down on their foreheads. The Mayans also thought crossed eyes were attractive, and they hung an object above the center of a baby's forehead to train the eyes to look inward. The Mayan men seemed to have shaved their heads but wore elaborate and high headdresses.

The Aztecs, Incas, and Mayans all used various scented materials. Plants and flowers were used to create fragrances for ointments, incense, and massage oils. They included balsam, cedar, vanilla, and sassafras. *See also* BATHS; BODY DECORATION; BODY ORNAMENTATION; HAIR, STYLING OF; TATTOOS.

Further reading: Warwick Bray, *Everyday Life of the Aztecs* (1968); Michael D. Coe, *The Maya (4th* ed. rev.) (1987); Brian M. Fagan, *The Aztecs* (1984); Michael A. Malpass, *Daily Life in the Inca Empire* (1996); Lawana Hooper Trout, *The Maya* (1991); Alonso de Zorita, trans. Benjamin Keen, *Life and Labor in Ancient Mexico* (1963).

Latinos. *See* Hispanic Americans

Lauder, Estée (b. 1909)

Estée Lauder founded a world-famous high-end cosmetics and fragrance company. By the 1990s, the company controlled 45 percent of the cosmetics market in U.S. department stores.

She was born Josephine Esther Mentzer in Corona, New York (Queens), of Hungarian immigrant parents. From an early age, she was interested in beauty and hair styling. Her uncle John Schotz, a chemist who had moved to America, made skin preparations. Lauder later wrote that she watched her uncle make a special velvety-textured face cream and listened as he discussed proper skin care and the use of different products to cleanse, freshen, and nourish the skin. She helped her uncle sell his products and learned facial treatment techniques. During those years, people often complimented Estée on her beautiful, smooth skin.

In 1930, at age 22, she married Joseph Lauder (1902–1983), and the couple moved to Manhattan, where Leonard, their first child, was born in 1933. Their first business ventures together, including a cafeteria, did not succeed. The couple was divorced in 1939. For several years, Estée Lauder sold her uncle's skin products in various resort areas and hotels and gave demonstrations of facial care. In 1942, the Lauders remarried; their second son, Ronald, was born in 1944. Joseph Lauder became a partner in the company and later directed factory production.

The Estée Lauder company was formed in 1947, and the Lauders worked diligently to market skin care products. In 1948, they obtained their first department store counter-space in Saks Fifth Avenue. Lauder promoted her products by giving free samples and gifts along with purchases (a practice the company retains today). She launched her famous fragrance "Youth-Dew" in 1953. The bath oil version of this fragrance was especially popular and Youth-Dew accounted for 80 percent of the company's business during the mid-1950s. "Youth Dew" has remained popular and earns millions of dollars each year worldwide. In 1957, Lauder launched Re-Nutriv cream, priced at $115 a pound, advertised as their "creme of creams," a product with "rare ingredients" and "youth-giving agents."

In 1960, Lauder's company posted $1 million in sales for the first time. (Lauder, 1994) The 1960s brought new kinds of skin care products to the marketplace and high-priced imports from Europe. In 1965, Lauder introduced a line of men's products called Aramis. Two years later, the company created the Clinique line of products, which emphasized therapeutic care of the skin in three steps: cleansing, clarifying, and moisturizing. The products, geared for younger women, were moderately priced.

Estée Lauder products were sold in department stores around the world as the company expanded to more than 75 in Europe, South America, the Middle East, and Asia. The company's lines included Estée Lauder, Clinique, Aramis, and Prescriptives. Three lines—Aramis, Clinique, and Lauder for Men—offered men's cosmetics. By 1999, the company also included Bobbi Brown Essentials and jane, a line of cosmetics aimed at teenagers. The company bought Aveda, which was distributed in thousands of beauty salons, and Origins, which offered botanical products.

Aramis, a division of the Estée Lauder Companies, is a leading maker of men's grooming products and fragrances. Following its introduction in 1965, Aramis products for men expanded during the late 1960s at a time when many companies were targeting men as cosmetics' consumers. New products included fragrances, shaving products, aftershave lotions, moisturizer, eye pads, hand cream, beard softeners, shampoo, hair lotion, deodorant, skin bronzer, and a coverup for blemishes. A new fragrance,

"Aramis 900," was launched. In the 1990s, as men showed more interest in skin care, Aramis developed new products for men, including its "Lab Series" line with a lightweight gel formula that was designed to protect the skin and fight the affects of aging. Aramis also developed the Tommy Hilfiger franchise, which included men's fragrances, including a Tommy Hilfiger Athletics fragrance line of cologne, body lotion, shampoo, mineral soak, and cooling gel.

Although expanding the men's product line, Lauder continued to introduce new products for women. The company launched several highly successful fragrances after "Youth Dew." They included "Alliage" (1972), "Private Collection" (1973), "White Linen" (1978), "Beautiful" (1986), and "Spellbound" (1991). Men's fragrances included "Aramis," "Aramis 900," "JHL" and "Lauder for Men."

Lauder's company is known for advertisements that feature refined-looking models in elegant, classic surroundings. In 1962, the company decided to select one model to advertise their products exclusively. The first two "Estée Lauder" women were Phyllis Connors and Karen Harris. Beginning in 1971, model Karen Graham was the Lauder model for 15 years, appearing in print ads and on television. Shaun Casey, Willow Bay, and Paulina were followed by model-actress Elizabeth Hurley, who represented the company in the late 1990s.

By 1999, Estée Lauder Companies was a $3.6 billion cosmetics empire (La Ferla, 1999), and the Lauder family owned 70 percent of the stock. Lauder products were sold in 118 countries. Lauder's son Leonard, who officially joined the company in 1958, became chairman and chief executive in 1982; son Ronald served as chairman of Clinique Laboratories and Estée Lauder International. In her autobiography, Estée Lauder also praised the contributions of her daughters-in-law, Evelyn and Jo Carole. Evelyn Lauder was the first public relations director of the company, as well as new products and packaging director; Jo Anne worked with her husband, Ronald, to develop the Clinique division. In the next generation, Ronald's daughter Aerin became director of creative product development for the Lauder brand in the United States and Canada and worked in advertising and marketing; her sister Jane served as marketing manager for Clinique. Leonard and Jo Carole's son William was president of Clinique. *See also* FRAGRANCE; FRAGRANCE FOUNDATION.

Further reading: Lee Israel, *Estée Lauder, Beyond the Magic* (1985); Ruth La Ferla, "The Young Woman Most Invited," *The New York Times*, 28 March 1999, 9-1, 7; Estée Lauder, *Estée: A Success Story* (1994); Gil Y. Roth, "Aramis Takes U-Turn in Men's Market," *Happi*, February 1998, http://www.happi.com.special/feb982.html; Sandra Salmans, "Estée Lauder: The Scents of Success," *The New York Times*, 18 April 1982.

Laws and Regulations (U.S.)

The United States is one of many nations that has passed laws and generated regulations for the cosmetics industry. Governmental agencies, primarily the Food and Drug Administration (FDA), enforce regulations about the safety and purity of cosmetics and toiletries. These regulations often define "cosmetics" and set forth conditions under which they may be produced and traded. They list any banned ingredients and give labeling requirements. Laws may also enumerate safety issues, inspection procedures, and the penalties for infractions. The FDA also sponsors studies to evaluate the safety of products and ingredients.

National and local laws also govern the operation and licensing of the people and businesses that provide beauty services, including beauty salons, hair salons, skin care clinics, barbershops, electrolysis operators, tattoo parlors, and other related services. To safeguard consumers and operators, many states developed an accreditation process for beauty schools. Schools were examined by the national accrediting organization and had to demonstrate that they had adequate facilities and staff, financial resources, and proper equipment and that they used accepted textbooks and conducted appropriate testing.

History of Regulation

Beginning in 1938, with the Pure Food and Drug Act of 1938, the United States Congress passed various laws to increase the safety and purity of cosmetics, prevent misrepresentation, and inform consumers about what they are buying and using. Supporters of these laws contend that cosmetics must be safe for the user and not harm other creatures or the environment. They also believe that cosmetics companies should not be allowed to make false or misleading claims.

The 1938 legislation grew out of earlier laws. During the 1920s, some reformers in America tried to expand the Pure Foods and Drugs Act of 1906, which regulated the drug industry, to include cosmetics. Reformers objected to the unsubstantiated claims cosmetics producers made, and they expressed concerns about the safety of these products. The effort failed, but a licensing act for cosmeticians was passed in New York State and some other states. The act required would-be beauticians to pass an examination that included questions about basic anatomy, common cosmetology equipment and practices, and the effects of various products and chemicals on the body.

Meanwhile, the American Medical Association had set up a Board of Standards for cosmetics advertising. The board said that cosmetics manufacturers could not, in their advertisements, claim that a product would not provoke an allergic reaction. The AMA Board also advocated that companies stop making products they called skin fresheners and tissue creams, because they could not prove that these products could repair or rejuvenate body tissues. In addition, they complained about hair product ads that claimed to restore lost hair. Furthermore, the board said that a list of all ingredients should appear on the package or be available to any customer who requested it. Any manufacturer who did not comply with these guidelines was not permitted to advertise in the AMA magazine *Hygeia*.

The AMA's efforts resulted in the 1938 passage of the Wheeler-Lea Amendment to the Food and Drug Act, which gave the Food and Drug Administration authority over cosmetics. The federal Food and Drug Administration (FDA), an agency of the United States Department of Health and Human Services, administers the Food, Drug, and Cosmetic Act of 1938, the Fair Packaging and Labeling Act, and related laws, which are sometimes called Pure Food and Drug Acts.

Cosmetics Defined

The Food, Drug, and Cosmetic Act of 1938 defines cosmetics as "articles intended to be rubbed, poured, sprinkled, or sprayed on, introduced into, or otherwise applied to the human body or any part thereof for cleansing, beautifying, promoting attractiveness, or altering the appearance." Soaps are not included in this definition, but many other products are—baby powder, bubble bath, deodorants, shaving cream, toothpaste, mouthwash, hair spray, hair tonics, suntan lotions and hair coloring products.

Under new regulations, cosmetics manufacturers could not use misleading names for their products (i.e. "skin food"), nor could they claim that their products lifted muscles or changed facial contours. Manufacturers were no longer allowed to claim they could "cure" skin conditions if they could not prove the claim was true. A key component of the 1938 law is the requirement that manufacturers provide labels listing the nature of the contents of the product when a consumer cannot see the product or easily judge its contents. The law also requires manufacturers to package products in a clear and nondeceptive manner and to produce cosmetics under sanitary conditions.

The laws made it illegal to transport adulterated or misbranded products across state lines and gave the FDA authority to seize defective products and prosecute companies that violate the laws. The FDA's Office of Cosmetics and Colors, later changed to the Office of Cosmetics Technology, was charged with cosmetic regulation.

The cosmetics industry was also regulated by the Federal Trade Commission (FTC), which enacted new regulations regarding the salespeople who gave cosmetics demonstrations as representatives of particular products. The laws required these people to clearly identify themselves with the company they represented. During the late 1930s, the FTC began new investigations into cosmetics advertising. It found that some manufacturers did not comply with the new regulations. As a result, in 1937, the FTC brought legal actions against several leading cosmetics firms, including Yardley, Bristol-Myers, and Helena Rubinstein.

Congress passed more laws requiring that cosmetologists and beauty salons be licensed during and after the 1930s.

Cosmetics Regulation

The FDA has classified cosmetics into various categories. Among them are skin care products (e.g. lotions, creams, powders, sprays); fragrances; eye makeup; manicure products; makeup other than eye (e.g. lipstick, foundation, and blush); and hair coloring preparations.

The Congress subsequently passed more laws to expand on the 1938 act. In 1960, the FDA banned the use of color additives that were shown to cause cancer in laboratory animals. The Color Additive Amendments to the Food, Drug and Cosmetics Act of 1938 (Public Law 86-618) went into effect on July 12, 1960. The amendments required the establishment of regulations that listed the color additives that are safe for use in food, drugs, or cosmetics. The Delaney anticancer clause portion of the amendments banned the marketing of any color additive that the FDA had found to cause cancer in animals or humans in any amount. Color additives that came from plant, animal, or minerals (other than coal and petroleum) were exempt from FDA certification.

Under the act, the FDA must declare an additive safe for use before a cosmetics company can legally market a product that includes that additive. The FDA retains the right to approve or disapprove of color additives that are used in cosmetics. The agency also requires that foreign and domestic manufacturers of certain colors submit samples from every batch of color they produce so that the FDA scientists can test them for safety.

Labels show certification of colors using the designations FD&C, D&C, or external D&C. In 1993, John E. Bailey, Ph.D., acting director of the FDA's Office of Cosmetics and Colors, said, "I think we can say with assurance that today's colors are safe if used properly and that consumers need not be worried." (Henkel, 1993)

The FDA has also banned or restricted specific ingredients from cosmetics. These ingredients are: bithionol, hexachlorophene, mercury compounds (unless they are used as preservatives in eye makeup), vinyl chloride and zirconium salts in aerosol products, halogenated salicylanilides, chloroform, and chlorofluorocarbon propellants.

Another major act followed the 1960 act governing color additives. In 1966, the Fair Packaging and Labeling Act added new labeling requirements that gave consumers more information. Consumers can now read lists of ingredients used in making cosmetics and toiletries on the product label. Merchandisers are required to post lists of ingredients if they are not part of the product label.

To ensure compliance, the FDA may visit factories where cosmetics are prepared to assess cleanliness and manufacturing methods of facilities. The agency cannot, however, regulate cosmetics, except for specific additives, until they are released into the marketplace. It cannot review or approve products until they are sold to the public. Those products that have not been declared safe by the FDA must contain a label that reads: "Warning: The safety of this product has not been determined."

Between 1972 and 1973, the FDA responded to consumer concerns about cosmetics safety by implementing three programs that were proposed by the Cosmetic, Toiletry, and Fragrance Association (CTFA). They provide for the voluntary registration of cosmetic manufacturers, the voluntary filing of cosmetic product ingredient and raw material composition statements, and the voluntary filing of cosmetic product experiences, known as "injury reports."

The FDA programs for regulating and policing the cosmetics industry are funded by a relatively small portion of the overall operating budget. For example, in 1977, funding was $2.8 million, slightly more than 1 percent of the $250 million budget for the entire agency for that year. That same year, the FDA's Division of Cosmetics Technology, charged with regulating the industry, had only 15 employees. As of 1997, the cosmetics division had a budget of about $5.5 million (less than 1 percent of the total FDA budget) and 30 employees. (Yoffe, 1997) Congress appropriated an additional $2.5 million for the fiscal year 1999, and the FDA said that about $1.5 million of that would be used for enforcement programs in the cosmetics division. (U.S. Food and Drug Administration, "Stakeholders' Meeting," 1999)

The FDA publishes various materials, including a magazine called *FDA Consumer*, to inform and educate the public about cosmetics and personal products. These publications discuss safety issues, laws, and the characteristics of different products. They also alert consumers to misleading advertising claims.

Federal law has also made it illegal to manufacture or store cosmetics in unsanitary conditions, to use coloring agents that are not approved by the FDA, or to use any ingredient that is putrid, filthy, or decomposed. However, many consumer advocates continue to push for stricter regulations. Recently, consumers have sought regulations to clarify the labeling of "natural" products versus those that contain some natural and some synthetic ingredients, as well as more ways to protect themselves from allergic reactions.

See also COLOR ADDITIVES; COSMETIC, TOILETRY AND FRAGRANCE ASSOCIATION (CTFA); SAFETY.

Further reading: GMP Institute, "Key National and International Standards, Laws, Regulations and Guidelines," GMP Institute http://www.gmp1st.com/comlaws.htm; John Henkel, "From Shampoo to Cereal: Seeing the Safety of Color Additives," *FDA Consumer*, December 1993; U.S. Food and Drug Administration, Center for Food Safety and Applied Nutrition Report, "Stakeholders' Meeting," 22 January 1999; U.S. Food and Drug Administration, "Color Additives," Center for Food Safety and Applied Nutrition, Office of Cosmetics Fact Sheet, 7 February 1995; U.S. Food and Drug Administration, Food, Drug, and Cosmetic Act of 1936; U.S. Government Printing Office, Code of Federal Regulations, Title 21; Emily Yoffe, "Chemical Good Looks," *U.S. News and World Report*, 11 November 1997.

Legs

Legs have been alternately exposed or covered, emphasized or ignored, considered as physical assets or liabilities. Cleansing and moisturizing products, including lotions and creams, are used on legs, as they are on other parts of the body. Exercises and cosmetic procedures are used to slenderize and tone the legs to achieve the look that is most admired or in style at a given time.

Men's and women's legs have been and still are generally governed by different standards of attractiveness. In ancient Greece, Rome, and some other countries, men's clothing revealed the legs. A strong, muscular appearance was considered attractive, and Greek men did special exercises to build the muscles of their legs both for the sake of appearance and to improve athletic performance. In later centuries, men living in Europe wore clothing that revealed the contours of the legs, which were encased in tights.

Today, men in western countries and most other countries generally favor long trousers for everyday and business wear, although men in Bermuda may wear knee-length shorts with business jackets and ties.

Until recent decades in western societies, women's legs have been covered for purposes of modesty. Women in Asian countries also wore long skirts. A glimpse of a woman's ankle was considered erotic during times when skirts reached the floor. When ankles were on view, beauty standards favored a dainty-looking, slender ankle.

Until the early decades of the twentieth century, in western countries, children knew they were approaching adulthood when they were allowed to put aside short dresses or trousers and wear leg-covering versions. As young women, females wore long, full skirts, while young men replaced short pants with long ones.

During the twentieth century, women's clothing became more revealing and fashions in skirts have often been at the knee or higher on the thigh. Skirts rose during the 1920s when women known as "flappers" rebelled against many conventions and asserted female independence. Skirts stayed relatively short and leg-revealing through World War II (in part due to fabric shortages). In the 1950s, fashion showed less leg, in part because wartime fabric shortages had ended and long, full skirts were again possible. The rebellious sixties brought the miniskirt, which, in its extreme version, revealed most of the leg. Today, almost anything goes. For business or formal occasions in western countries, however, women almost always wear some type of hosiery.

Swimsuits also became far more revealing as the century went on. At the turn of the century, "bathing costumes" covered much of the leg and women also wore stockings in the water. By the 1940s, a one-piece swimsuit revealed the leg from the top of the thigh downward. A number of popular film stars posed in swimsuits for what were called "pin-up" shots, which were often cherished by soldiers serving overseas during World War II. During this era, actress Betty Grable was among the celebrities who were praised for their beautiful legs, and she was a popular "pin-up." It was rumored that Grable's legs were insured for one million dollars.

Today, beauty standards in the United States and many other countries often focus attention on the structure and appearance of the legs. The ideal, as personified by many high-fashion models, is for long, well-toned, slender but shapely legs in proportion to the rest of the figure.

Leg Fashions

People modify their legs in two basic ways: by adorning them and by attempting to reshape them. In places where legs have been on view, they have been decorated or ornamented in various ways. In hot climates, both men and women may wear little clothing, which means the legs are continually revealed. Some ancient cultures and tribes living in

Betty Grable and her famous legs. *Globe Photos, Inc.*

contemporary Africa, South America, and islands in the Caribbean and Pacific have painted designs and applied tattoos to their legs and ankles. These forms of body art are used both for decorative and ceremonial purposes. They may also signify a passage from childhood to adulthood or from single to married status.

In recent years, small tattoos on the thigh and ankle have become more popular in western cultures, too. Women in the entertainment industry are among the celebrities who have permanent or temporary tattoos on the thigh, ankle, or other parts of their legs. Ankle bracelets are the primary jewelry worn on the leg; these ornaments vary in thickness and style.

Reshaping the leg to meet an ideal is done various ways In some cultures, the shape of the legs is mechanically altered to achieve a particular look. The Wauwai of French Guyana use a method called "body swelling" to create swelled calves. The legs of young girls are bound below the knee so the calves take on a round shape, considered desirable. The Dinka of the southern Sudan in Africa use tight gold and silver band as bracelets around their arms and legs to create swelled limbs. Asian Bre women also wear coiled bands below the knee to create a swelled calf.

In western countries, exercise is the most common technique for reshaping legs. During the 1920s and 1930s, exercise to tone the legs and other parts of the body became much more common. Multiple fitness books and exercise routines center on the legs and particularly on ways to trim and tone the thighs. One of the best-selling exercise devices of the twentieth century was the Thigh Master, promoted by actress Suzanne Somers. While sitting, a person can place this device between their inner thighs and squeeze on it repeatedly to firm this area of the body. Somers also appeared in exercise videos and promoted other products associated with Thigh Master. Other exercise routines, including step aerobics and use of the Stairmaster machine, concentrated mainly on the legs.

Legs may also be reshaped or otherwise improved through cosmetic surgery and dermatological procedures. Liposuction can remove fat deposits around the ankle and on the thighs. Some women consider spider veins (telangiectasias—tiny veins that are visible through the outer skin layers) to be a "beauty problem" that should be alleviated. These veins appear as small purple, red, or blue lines or webbed patterns and may be either relatively small or cover larger areas. Varicose veins are larger and tend to be raised areas of skin that are blue-colored. Both spider veins and varicose veins may be covered with concealing makeup. A medical treatment called sclerotherapy is used to minimize or eliminate spider veins and superficial varicose veins. Surgeons inject saline solution into the vessel with a very fine needle, causing the vessel to disappear or fade.

In addition to using leg makeup to hide discolorations, scars, or varicose veins, women also routinely used it during World War II when there was a shortage of silk for stockings. Today, tanning lotions give the appearance of a suntan on the legs. Stockings can also change the appearance of legs and are made in a variety of materials, textures, colors and designs.

Legs Today

In most modern nations, men typically cover their legs in public with full-length pants for daytime professional wear, while women may opt to wear either skirts or pants. In warm weather, both men and women may wear shorts, mainly for casual wear, which are acceptable female attire in Europe and North America, although not in all other places. Women in traditional Middle Eastern or Islamic countries, such as Saudi Arabia, wear black cloaks that cover their bodies in public, along with a traditional veil. Most Malaysian women wear long saris, as do some women in India. *See also* BEAUTY STANDARDS; BODY DECORATION; CELLULITE; DERMATOLOGISTS; FEET; PLASTIC SURGERY; WEIGHT.

Further reading: Howard C. Baron, *Varicose Veins: A Guide to Prevention and Treatment* (1997); Richard Cota, *Great Shapes, Great Legs* (1995); Angela Fisher, *Africa Adorned* (1984); Pat Henry, *Hollywood Legs* (1998); Kate Mulvey and Melissa Richards, *Decades of Beauty: The Changing Image of Women, 1890-1990s* (1998); Julian Robinson, *The Quest for Human Beauty* (1998); Rosemarie Swinfield, *Stage Makeup, Step by Step* (1995).

Liposuction *See* PLASTIC SURGERY.

Lips

Lips, historically, have been the focus of special care and ornamentation. Skin care products and cosmetics have been used to soften, soothe, and color the skin of the lips. Some cultures have chosen to ornament the lips with various objects that may also change their shape. Ornamentation of the lips may serve various purposes, such as signifying a life passage or showing that a culture places great importance on speaking.

Lip moisturizing agents of ancient times, made from oils and other ingredients from plants and animals, gave way to commercially prepared salves and creams designed to smooth the lips and prevent dryness. The oldest known lip preparation, a type of salve, dates back to Mesopotamia around 3,500 B.C.E.

The Egyptians, Greeks, and Romans developed products that tinted and protected the lips by mixing pigments with oils and waxes. By the end of the twentieth century, commercial lipsticks in hundreds of shades and formulations were available to beautify the lips. Women used special brushes and pencils to outline the lips and applied glosses over lipsticks for extra sheen and color. These products were available in different fragrances, flavors, and colors.

During the late twentieth century, some people elected to have cosmetic surgery to add fullness to their lips, fuller lips being regarded as a desirable feature during the 1980s and 1990s. In the movie *First Wives Club*, actress Goldie Hawn satirized the idea of exaggerated lip implants while playing an over-40 actress who has frequent cosmetic surgery.

People in various cultures have also inserted ornamental objects into the lips as a decoration or to change their shape. Lip ornaments range from very simple objects to ornate, finely crafted ones. The use of lip rings, plates, or plugs date back hundreds or thousands of years. The Aztecs created elaborate lip plugs made of gold and precious stones, in the form of serpents and other creatures significant in that culture. Only noble Aztecs were allowed to wear these plugs or other special pieces of jewelry, such as gold ear and nose plugs.

During the 1500s, Spanish conquerors in South America noted that native peoples wore lip plugs made of gold, rock, stone, or crystal. The Botocudo people of South America

were known for their very large lip plates and plugs, which they placed into holes pierced in both the upper and lower lips. The Ge'-speaking peoples of central Brazil also pierced their lips. In Africa, some tribes began wearing lip ornaments as a form of self-protection to deter slave traders. For example, women of the Kichepo in southeastern Sudan began wearing lip plates in the nineteenth century to make themselves look so unusual that slave traders would not be interested in abducting them.

The Tchikrin of the Amazon pierce the lips of infant males, then gradually enlarge the hole as a boy grows. By adulthood, males wear lip disks that measure about four inches in diameter. Similarly, males of the Suya, another Amazonian group, have their lips pierced when they reach the age when they are regarded as men. Their lip ornaments, called labrets, are usually painted red with engraved undersides and remain in place throughout their lives. Labrets are also a tribal ornament among the Tapuya, a tribe in eastern Brazil that dates back to ancient times. They wear their labrets in the lower lip.

Some lip ornaments signify tribal identity, the transition from childhood to adulthood, or some other form of social status. They may also be used to ward off evil spirits. Lip discs worn by the Kayapo of the Amazonian rain forest signified the cultural significance of speaking in this culture. North American native peoples also wore lip ornaments. The Haida Indians of British Columbia were known for their carefully crafted wooden lip rings, decorated with abalone shell inlays.

An Amazonian tribe called the Txukahamei Indians use discs made from balsa to distend their lips. Among the Nilotic herdsmen tribes of East Africa, lip plugs for women are a long-standing tradition. The Nilotic peoples of Kenya, Uganda, and the Sudan also wear small lip studs and pins made from stone, ivory, or rock crystal, which are placed in the upper lip, lower lip, or both.

Lip piercing and lip plates are traditional for Mursi women in Ethiopia's Lower Omo River Valley. They typically have their lower lip pierced when they reach puberty, at which time a lip plate is inserted in the hole.

Lipstick

The use of special substances to add color to the lips dates back thousands of years. The first known lipstick was found in the ruins of ancient Sumeria (c. 3000 B.C.E.). Egyptian women of ancient times colored their lips. Many early lip colors were stains made from berries or plant substances or unguents with pigment added.

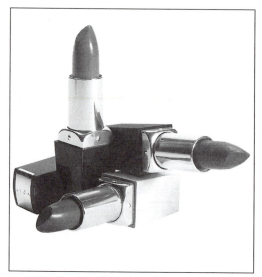

Lipsticks. *Courtesy of Avon Products, Inc.*

Until the advent of commercial cosmetics, women continued to make their own lip tints, trading recipes with one another. Later, these and other cosmetic recipes were published in women's magazines.

The first commercial lipsticks began to appear in the late 1800s. Throughout the early twentieth century, lipsticks came in a limited number of shades, usually only light, medium, and dark, geared for three basic hair and skin tones. During the early 1930s, Elizabeth Arden was one of the first cosmetics executives to introduce the idea of variety. Arden suggested that lipstick colors should be geared toward the colors of women's clothing. To promote her seven-shade lipstick kits, Arden toured the United States with a group of seven ballet dancers who appeared dressed in different color costumes to go along with each of the lipsticks. The success of Arden's lipsticks inspired other manufacturers to develop lipsticks in a variety of shades. Max Factor, a Holly-wood makeup artist, and his son, Max Factor, Jr., who took over the Max Factor Company in 1938, introduced popular lipsticks during and after the 1930s. They claimed their "Tru-Color" lipstick (1940) was more durable than other brands on the market.

Variations on plain lipsticks have included frosted lipsticks, which were made with fish scales, lip glosses that came clear or tinted, and various "lasting" lipsticks that leave a stain on the lips that persists for hours after the lipstick has been applied. Hazel Bishop developed the first so-called "indelible" lipstick in 1950. Well-known lines of long-lasting lipsticks and glosses include Cover-Girl "Marathon" and Revlon "Colorstay."

Most manufactured lipsticks are made of essentially the same ingredients: castor oil and beeswax, color pigment, fragrance, and flavoring. In recent decades, extra ingredients have been added to increase the moisturizing and conditioning qualities of lipsticks. Aloe, vitamin E, castor oil, and sunscreens are among these ingredients. The Food and Drug Administration (FDA) has stated that ingredients for lipsticks must be proven safe, since these cosmetics are worn on the mouth. *See also* ARABIA; ARDEN, ELIZABETH; BISHOP, HAZEL; EGYPT, ANCIENT; FACE; IMPLANTS (COSMETIC); LAUDER, ESTÉE; REVLON COMPANY.

Further reading: Richard Corson, *Fashions in Makeup: From Ancient to Modern Times* (1972); Angela Jackson, *Africa Adorned* (1984); Loren McIntyre, "Amazon: The River Sea," *National Geographic*, October 1972, 456–495; Meg Cohen Ragas, *Read My Lips: A Cultural History of Lipstick* (1998); John Scofield, "Christopher Columbus and the New World He Found," *National Geographic*, November 1975, 584–625; Anthony Seeger, "The Meaning of Body Ornaments: A Suya Example," *Ethnology*, July 1975; Jacques Soustelle, *Daily Life of the Aztecs on the Eve of the Spanish Conquest* (1970); Terence S. Turner, "Tchikrin: A Central Brazilian Tribe and Its Symbolic Language of Bodily Adornment," *Natural History*, October 1969.

"Looks"

Certain looks for men and women have meaning that is symbolic and typical of their times. Most people could recognize these "looks," and many tried to conform to the image in terms of hairstyles, clothing, and other aspects of appearance. In that sense, the looks could be codified and described.

During the 1800s, some men affected the look of the "dandy." Men who inspired this look include the English aristocrats Beau Brummell, who sported this type of appearance during the late eighteenth and early nineteenth centuries, Barbey d'Aureyville, and the French author Charles Baudelaire. These men rejected the standardization that was becoming typical of men's clothing and accessories. They spent hours on their appearance and paid careful attention to each aspect of dress, choosing gloves, ties, canes, scarves, and hats for each outfit. They were also scrupulous about cleanliness and grooming. The look came to be associated with homosexuality, since some prominent "dandies" were either avowed homosexuals or celibate.

For women, the "Gibson Girl" look prevailed at the turn of the nineteenth century. A tall, healthy-looking young woman with a trim waistline, the Gibson Girl was the beauty ideal in America for several decades, and her image became familiar around the world. She was the creation of illustrator Charles Dana Gibson (1867–1944), whose pen-and-ink drawings appeared in the popular *Collier's* magazine and other important magazines, including *Scribner's*, *Harper's*, and *Century*. By 1894, four years after Gibson began illustrating for *Life* magazine, the image was well known throughout America.

The women in Gibson's pictures reflected the lives of middle-class and prosperous American families. They could be seen in leisure settings, such as outdoor picnics or playing croquet. Women who wanted reforms in women's clothing applauded the girls' casual blouses and skirts. Charlotte Perkins Gilman said of the Gibson Girl that she was "braver, stronger, more healthful and skillful and able and free, more human in all ways" than previous beauty ideals. (Banner, 1983, 156) She also appeared modest and ladylike, in keeping with social mores of that era, as well as sporty and energetic. Gibson's sister Josephine later said that her brother's intention was "to portray a totally American type . . . symbolic of a wholesome, healthy, utterly American girl." (Banner, 1983, 165)

In the United States, socialite Irene Langhorne, whom Charles Gibson had married in 1895, was considered to be the epitome of the Gibson Girl. An American-born actress, Camille Clifford, became the British version after she moved to England. In 1999, the U.S. Post Office issued a "Gibson Girl" postage stamp as part of its "Celebrate the Century, 1900s" series.

The "vamp" look for women was associated with film stars of the 1910s and 1920s, notably Theda Bara, Louise Brooks, and Pola Negri. Trademarks of this look were large, made-up eyes and full, vividly colored lips, along with behavior that implied worldly sophistication. The word "vamp" comes from "vampire" and was meant to signify the great powers of attraction female vamps could exercise over men. Theda Bara, who portrayed Cleopatra in a 1917 film of that name, played the lead role in *The Vamp*.

As the 1920s arrived, the "flapper" look replaced the more conservative looking "Gibson Girl," although the vamp look lingered. "Flappers" was the name given to women who adopted certain styles of appear-

The Flapper look: Miss Hardie, championship Charleston dancer, *American Stock/Archive Photos.*

ance and behavior during the Jazz Age of the 1920s. This period, following World War I, was a time when many women in western societies opted to spurn traditional roles and break away from respectable fashions. American women "got the vote," and more young women could be found in the workplace. In Paris, the famous designer Paul Poiret developed a style of loose-fitting dresses that exposed the arms and legs.

The flappers flouted many longstanding ideas about how women should look. To some traditionalists, they were "painted women" who were much too liberated in all areas of their lives. Many people regarded their appearance as an outward rejection of women's traditional roles.

The women, most of whom were young, went against the tradition of long hair for women by "bobbing" their hair—cutting it short. F. Scott Fitzgerald wrote about this subject in his 1920s short story, "Bernice Bobs Her Hair," in which a girl has her hair bobbed on a dare (I will if you will). When the other girl fails to follow suit, Bernice exacts revenge by sneaking in and cutting her rival's beautiful, long hair as she sleeps.

Flappers also wore visible makeup, including round rouged areas on their cheeks. Sometimes, they "touched up" their lipstick and powder in public, something no respectable woman would do, if she wore makeup at all. Their skirts were much shorter than those worn by previous generations, and they wore rolled stockings on their exposed legs. In addition, their dresses were cut so they did not emphasize the breast, giving a straight up-and-down silhouette to the body, and some women wore binding undergarments to flatten their chests. Some also smoked in public, which was considered daring.

Among the celebrities who represented the flapper look and exuberant behavior of the era were actresses Louise Brooks and Clara Bow (known as the "It Girl.") Brooks was thought to be the inspiration for a long-running cartoon called "Dixie Dugan," created by John H. Striebel.

In the 1930s a more feminine style replaced the boyish looks of the 1920s fash-

ions. Synthetic fabrics such as nylon were developed. In the 1940s synthetic fabrics were even more important as the goverment took over stocks of natural fabrics for the war effort. Rayon became very popular, and American designers designed shorter, more form-fitting clothing in order to comply with government restrictions on fabric used by the fashion industry. Clothes, especially for women, became much more functional.

In the 1950s, nonconformist men and women assumed the Bohemian look. This look was also referred to as the Beatnik," and its proponents the Beat Generation. Both genders wore black clothing, often turtleneck sweaters, and women wore black capri pants (which made a come back in the late 1990s). Men wore short narrow beards called goatees and hair slightly longer than the norm. For women, short cropped hairstyles or long simple styles, including ponytails, were part of the look.

During that same era, teenagers took to the "greaser" look," a rebellious look of the 1950s that emerged with the "Teddy-boys" of England. Males wore leather jackets and blue jeans with white T-shirts or drainpipe trousers, bright-hued socks and long fitted jackets. They slicked back their hairdos with pomades that gave a wet or "greasy" look. The Teddy boy hairstyle was long and swept back, while other men preferred a short back and swept-back sides and sideburns. James Dean, in the movie *Rebel Without a Cause,* typified this look. At the same time, American "Bobbysoxer girls" looked clean cut, with ponytails or short bouffant haircuts, white bobby sox and loafers, and full skirts.

The "Mod look" of the mid-1960s developed in London and became popular in other countries. Short "mini" skirts, platform shoes, long straight hair or a short geometric cut, neon colors, and strong eye makeup with pale lips were features of this look. The British teenage model "Twiggy" was one of its main representatives. Men wore jumpsuits and "Nehru" jackets (which were collarless and named after the Indian prime minister), and they wore their hair longer, in the style of pop musicians like the Beatles and Rolling Stones.

The "Hippie" look that began in the United States in the late sixties spread to other countries. Often associated with the movement against the war in Vietnam, hippies championed a "counterculture" that rejected the capitalist values of their parents. Males wore long hair, sometimes with beards; a long, center-parted style was popular with women adherents and could be seen on numerous television and film actresses, including "Mod Squad" star Peggy Lipton and former model and film star Ali MacGraw. Jeans were a standard part of this look. Women also wore long skirts, often in batik or tie-dyed fabrics, with sandals. Men wore ethnic shirts, such as those worn in India, sometimes in bright colors. Both genders wore bell-bottom trousers.

The 1970s brought the "natural look," although students and other young people continued to wear the casual attire of the 1960s. A renewed interest in the environment and a healthy planet, as well as the quality of food, the purity of water, and a healthy, fit body, inspired this preference. Along with natural foods and mineral waters, people began looking for what they called "natural" cosmetics. Exercise became more fashionable as clothing styles revealed more and more of the body, and women rarely wore the tight, constrictive girdles and similar undergarments, of the past. String bikinis, topless swimsuits, and other form-fitting, revealing clothing prompted women to seek a slim, toned body.

An oft-mentioned American "beauty type" has been referred to as the California look, seen on numerous models, actors, and on popular television shows, such as *Baywatch*. Author Nora Scott Kinzer describes it this way:

> The California man or woman is tanned of limb, straight of teeth, short of nose, blond of hair, and without a spare ounce of fat. The man has rippling muscles and the woman has soft-rounded contours with big round breasts Health and fitness are other aspects of this look. A number of television and film personalities and models are identified as representing the "California" type, which became recognized around the world as a result of the mass media. (Kinzer, 1977)

Two famous models from California, Christie Brinkley and Cheryl Tiegs, are considered examples of this look. Both later had successful careers in the fitness industry.

A look known as "punk" (also called the urban guerilla look) originated in England during the late 1970s and has regained popularity in the 1990s to the present. The music called "punk," exemplified by the Sex Pistols, spawned a look that was described as anti-beauty and rebellious. Hairstyles included the Mohawk cut, often tinted or sprayed brilliant and unusual colorings, including turquoise, fluorescent purple, vivid reds and pinks, and sometimes multicolored combinations. Designers Vivienne Westwood and Malcolm Maclaren designed the clothes and "tribal" looks. Punks were early practitioners of body piercing, Day-Glo colors, safety pins and razors on clothing, odd, heavy eye makeup, and black nail polish and lipstick, as well as accessories such as handcuffs. Some of the celebrities who wore features of the punk look were singer Cyndi Lauper, fashion designer Todd Oldham, members of the rock bands Aerosmith and Green Day, and basketball star Dennis Rodman. Boy George, lead singer of the British group Culture Club, individualized the punk look and wore various colored cosmetics and colorful clothes. Elements that began as punk are now more mainstream; as men and women wear "spiky" haircuts and young women routinely wear black nail polish.

This look also developed into what were called "grunge" and "waif" looks, in which people wore torn, disheveled looking clothing and garments held together with safety pins. The waif look evolved into a controversial look called "heroin chic" that was seen on top models in fashion centers such as New York, Paris, and London during the early to mid-1990s. The models were extremely thin and had what some critics called a "strung-out" appearance. Author Joan Jacobs Brumberg said, "Heroin chic suggested a kind of thinness, frailness, emaciatness . . . sickliness as desirable." (Brumberg, 1999) Negative reactions to this look prompted some designers to stop featuring this look in ads and runway shows.

The late 1990s illustrated the circular nature of "looks." Teenage girls wore long hair, parted in the center, and favored bell bottom jeans. The only statement they were making, however, was simple fashion. *See also* AFRICAN AMERICANS; BEAUTY INDUSTRY (U.S.); BEAUTY STANDARDS; COSMETICS; NATURAL PRODUCTS.

Further reading: Lois W. Banner, *American Beauty* (1983); Marilyn Bender, *The Beautiful People* (1965); Joan Jacobs Brumberg, quoted in *Body [I]com: Body as Commodity—mediacraze* (1999) http://www.nm-server.jrn.columbia.edu/ projects/ bodyimage/commodity/media; Kate DeCastelbajac, *The Face of the Century: 100 Years of Makeup and Style* (1995); Paula S. Fass, *The Beautiful and the Damned: American Youth in the 1920s* (1977); Nora Scott Kinzer, *Put Down and Ripped Off: American Women and the Beauty Culture* (1977); Kate Mulvey and Melissa Richards, *Decades of Beauty* (1998); Elizabeth Stevenson, *Babbits & Bohemians: The American '20s* (1967).

L'Oreal

A publicly owned firm based in France, L'Oreal has become the largest beauty products company in the world at present. It offers men and women a wide array of makeup, fragrances, and skin and hair care products under various labels.

The company began as a producer of hair coloring products in the early 1900s. It was founded by a Parisian chemistry student, Eugene Schiller, in 1907 when he created permanent dyes for gray hair. L'Oreal expanded into the cosmetics business, producing lipsticks, foundation, face powder, cheek color, and eye makeup. It added other fragrance and cosmetics lines, including Guy Laroche, Giorgio Armani, Ralph Lauren, Helena Rubinstein, Cacharel, Maybelline, Redken 5th Avenue NYC, and Lancome, another high-end maker of cosmetics. Lancome, founded in Paris by Armand Pettijean in 1935, was known for its successful skin care products and fragrances, including "Magie" (1950) and "Tresor" (1952; reissued in 1991). The company's mass-market labels were L'Oreal and Maybelline.

As of 1984, the company ranked third in the world in sales, after Avon and Revlon, although between 1979 and 1984, the growth rate of L'Oreal surpassed the growth rate of both those companies. L'Oreal continued its expansion as part of the federation that owned Cosmair, which marketed hair mousse products in the United States, by purchasing Warner Cosmetics, which included fragrances from Gloria Vanderbilt and Ralph Lauren. The company also owns Redken and Soft Sheen Products, which are sold in beauty salons. Its Synthelabo subsidiary developed pharmaceutical products. One of its most successful advertising campaigns, "[I use L'Oreal and] I'm worth it" has been used to promote both cosmetics and hair products. *See also* COSMETICS; FRAGRANCE; HAIR COLOR.

Further reading: L'Oreal, Facts and Figures, Finance, History, and Industry http://www.loreal.com/us.

M

Magazines

Magazines have a tremendous impact on the advertising and sale of beauty products. Articles and advertisements in magazines influence beauty standards and trends in fashion, makeup, and personal care. Each month, millions of people around the world read feature articles that promote certain products and grooming practices.

The first woman's magazine to circulate widely in the United States was *Godey's Lady's Book* (1830–1898). During the mid-1800s, this was the most important American women's fashion and beauty publication of its day. By subscribing to the magazine, women living in remote and rural areas could glimpse the latest dress designs, silhouettes, and hairdos, which often originated in Paris before moving to North America and other places.

The illustrations featured natural looking, ladylike women with pale, oval-shaped faces and delicate expressions. Their upswept hairstyles and chignons reflected the styles worn by middle-class Victorian women in western Europe and the United States. In keeping with the values of the day, fictional stories that appeared in the magazine emphasized moral virtues and the spiritual qualities of female heroines. Ebenezer Butterick, who invented the tissue paper dress pattern, began publishing *Ladies Quarterly Review of Broadway Fashions* in 1863, and in 1867, *Harper's Bazar* made its debut as a fashion

magazine (the name changed to its current spelling, *Harper's Bazaar* in 1929). Other women's magazines of the late nineteenth century included *Ladies Home Journal* (1883) and *Good Housekeeping* (1885). Both included articles on hygiene and grooming, and their coverage through the 1950s focused on making a happy, healthy home.

The rise of the teen culture in the 1950s brought with it the first fashion and grooming magazines targeted to teenage girls. *Seventeen* began publishing in 1944, followed by *Teen* in 1957 and *Ingenue*. They advised young women on skin care, fashion, and the management of their romantic lives.

In the mid-1960s, two long-standing magazines revamped their formats, and in doing so, shifted the direction of women's magazines. *Vogue* magazine began publishing in 1892, declaring itself to be dedicated to the "ceremonial side of life." Its intended audience was the elite of New York City, but the magazine's influence has spread far beyond that. *Vogue* has become one of the most influential fashion and beauty magazines for women. As editor-in-chief during the 1960s, Diana Vreeland, herself a member of a socially prominent family, popularized fashion and beauty trends and is credited with inventing the "celebrity model."

In 1965, *Cosmopolitan*, first published in 1886 as a literary magazine, broke new ground as a beauty and fashion magazine for women. The change in content was the work of editor-in-chief Helen Gurley Brown, who wrote the best-selling book *Sex and the Single Girl*. Before she married the well-known film producer David Brown at age 37, Helen Gurley had been a single career woman in Los Angeles.

Brown proceeded to change the focus of the magazine to young career women and male-female relationships. She regarded her magazine as a self-help tool and "inspirational magazine" to help women make the most of their lives. Articles focused on fashion, beauty, and relationships, giving information and advice about clothes, makeup, grooming, diet, exercise, and dating, as well as cooking, decorating, careers, and other subjects. The magazine pioneered the new era of sexual permissiveness. Under Brown's leadership, its circulation increased from 740,000 to 1 million with its first new issue. It became one of the most successful American magazines in history.

One of the magazine's trademarks was a glamorous cover of a model or celebrity wearing a low-cut outfit and full makeup. For years, these covers were photographed by top photographer Francesco Scavullo, who was known for his high-fashion and society photography. In 1972, *Cosmopolitan* published the first nude male centerfold (film star Burt Reynolds, discreetly posed).

By the 1990s, the magazine had a circulation of more than 3 million, with 23 foreign editions (including France, Italy, Spain, Japan, Taiwan, and other countries). Ads continued to refer to that "Cosmopolitan girl"—an attractive, talented, young career woman who wanted success both in love and in her job.

Playboy

Hugh Hefner (b. 1926) founded *Playboy* and *Oui* magazines, publications that prominently feature nude and semi-nude women who fit certain popular western physical standards of beauty. Playboy "centerfolds" are usually young women in their 20s with full breasts, small waists, and slim hips. Many models are posed to appear simultaneously innocent and sexually provocative.

Hefner, with a degree in psychology and experience at writing ad copy and working in circulation at *Esquire*, decided in 1952 to start his own magazine, one that would "thumb its nose at all the phony puritan values of the world in which I had grown up," as he put it. (Blackwell, 1973, 229) The first issue of Playboy went on sale in October 1953. It was geared to appeal to young urban men but became popular throughout the country.

Hefner and his magazine have sometimes been criticized by people who believe that *Playboy* and the idea of the "*Playboy* lifestyle" treat women as sex objects whose main value lies in their physical traits, particularly large breasts, and an idealized, "air-brushed" appearance.

Changes in Magazines

Social change and a growing interest in health and fitness generated new magazines and changed the tone of old ones. More feminist and sports/fitness-oriented magazines appeared. *Ms.* magazine, first published in 1972, was the unofficial journal of the nascent women's movement, and in its early years, deliberately shunned the fashion and grooming articles that had long characterized women's magazines. The 1980s brought more health and fitness magazines for both women and men, along with publications that emphasized modern roles for women, as both mothers and people who work outside the home. *Working Woman* is one example. *Sassy* and *Jane* joined the ranks of teen magazines, and in 1999, a version of *Cosmopolitan* was launched for teenagers.

More magazines for men featuring many articles on appearance emerged during the late twentieth century, including *Gentleman's Quarterly (GQ)*, *Men's Fitness*, *Ebony*, and *Essence*. One of the best-known magazines in this group, *Men's Fitness*, is published in the United States. The magazine focuses on fitness, health, and appearance, and includes regular features on clothing, fitness gear, relationships and sexuality, sports, travel, and nutrition.

Esquire Magazine continues to be one of the most influential men's magazines that features articles on men's grooming and fashions. Based in New York City, this magazine was founded in 1933 in Chicago by Arnold Gingrich, a well-known editor. *Esquire* was originally a men's apparel magazine for the trade but established itself as a forum for modern literary writers. During the 1940s, it began publishing pin-up art of women, including the popular Varga and Petty Girls. The magazine continued to publish up-and-coming male authors and became known for cutting-edge, irreverent humor. It has received numerous journalism awards.

Today, *Esquire* is published in 10 international editions, and it continues to target professional men. Monthly issues show readers new fashions and grooming trends and contain articles on current events, the arts, and the media. An attractive female celebrity is usually profiled each month and often featured in erotic poses on the cover photo and interior of the magazine. In recent months, actresses Charlize Theron and Catherine Zeta-Jones were interviewed and photographed for *Esquire*.

In recent decades, new magazines have emerged to offer more diverse images for women. Some magazines focus on women who belong to certain ethnic groups or nationalities. *Ebony* and *Essence*, for African American readers, include features on appearance as well as current events and various other topics. Hispanic women can turn to *Latina* and *Latina Style*, and women of Asian descent have the online magazine *Jade*. *Radiance*, a magazine geared for larger women, debuted in 1984. A glossy fashion magazine for women size 12 and above, called *Mode*, was well received when it appeared in 1997. *See also* ADVERTISING (U.S.); BEAUTY STANDARDS; BODY IMAGE; COSMETICS; MODELING AND MODELS.

Further reading: Robert Atwan, et al., *Edsels, Luckies, and Frigidaires: Advertising the American Way* (1979); Earl Blackwell, ed. *Celebrity Register* (1973); Helen Gurley Brown, "Step Into My Parlor," *Cosmopolitan*, 25th Anniversary Issue, May 1990, 22.; Max Von Boehn, *Modes and Manners of the Nineteenth Century* (1909); *Jade*, http://www.jademagazine.com.

Makeup Artists

Makeup artists work with photographers' models for magazines, runway shows, and television. They also make up film stars and other celebrities or clients before special events. Their work includes applying regular makeup to enhance appearance and as well as creating specialized looks to transform characters for acting roles.

The profession began with artists who applied makeup to performers in the theater, opera, and ballet. It steadily grew with the film industry during the early 1900s, when Max Factor was one of the best-known makeup artists. Richard Corson (1917–1999) was an eminent theatrical makeup artist in New York City. Educated at DePauw University and Louisiana State University, Corson became an adjunct professor at Southern Methodist University and also taught at the University of Minnesota and Hollywood Academy. He trained numerous future makeup artists who worked in television, the film industry, and at the Metropolitan Opera. His first book, *Stage Makeup* was published in 1942; later books included *Fashions in Hair: The First 5,000 Years* (1965), *Fashions in Makeup: From Ancient to Modern Times*, and *Fashions in Eyeglasses: From the 14th Century to the Present*.

In recent decades, some makeup artists have become celebrities in their own right. They can be seen in magazine articles and books, as well as on television programs where they sometimes perform beauty "makeovers."

Among the most famous American makeup artists of the late twentieth century were George Masters, Way Bandy, and Kevyn Aucoin. During the 1970s, professional makeup artist Way Bandy was regarded as an innovator and one of the best in the business. He developed his technique of "face design" that involved analyzing a person's facial bones and structure and later wrote an influential book describing his approach to beauty and makeup.

Born and raised in the southern United States, Bandy graduated from college and taught American and English literature before moving to New York City in 1967 to pursue an art career, focusing on portraits. During this time, he began working in the field of cosmetics. Bandy soon found himself in demand as customers praised his ability to create natural but glamorous effects with cosmetics. In 1969, he became salon and makeup director for Lanvin-Charles of the Ritz. After leaving the salon in 1971, Bandy worked as a freelance face designer, creating looks for fashion models and magazine covers, including *Vogue, Harper's Bazaar,* and *Cosmopolitan.* In addition, he was often sought for cosmetic advertisements, television commercials, and film and theater. Celebrities and people in the media hired Bandy to create flattering looks for them on special occasions. Bandy died in 1986.

Aucoin, who says he was inspired by Bandy's work, grew up in southern Louisiana during the 1960s. He later said, "While the other boys in my school dreamed of traveling to the moon or winning the Super Bowl, I dreamt of glossy red lips and sparkling skin. By the age of eleven I knew I wanted to be a makeup artist." (Aucoin, 1997).

Some makeup artists have gone on to create their own cosmetic lines. Francois Nars (b. 1959), who began his successful career at 20, had worked with French designer Yves St Laurent, celebrities, and top magazine models in Paris and New York when he brought out a line of 10 lipsticks in 1994. The next year, he launched a full line of cosmetics and made plans to open stores in Paris, London, and Tokyo.

Victoria Jackson developed another successful line of makeup and skin care products bearing her name. Makeup artist Paula Begoun, known as a cosmetics consumer reporter and author, developed her line of cosmetics during the late 1990s. Begoun's line emphasized quality and simple ingredients at a reasonable price.

In 1996, makeup artist Michael Key created a newsletter for people in the business called "Craft News" that developed into *Makeup Artist Magazine.* The magazine publishes articles on the art of makeup, developments in the industry, and famous people. It has an international readership. Key was also instrumental in building the industry's trade union and developing the annual International Make-Up Artist Trade Show, which gets larger each year. Both the magazine and trade shows appeal to nonprofessionals with an interest in films and the craft of makeup. *See also* BEGOUN, PAULA; COSMETICS; EYES; FACE; JACKSON, VICTORIA; LIPS; MASTERS, GEORGE; MAX FACTOR AND COMPANY.

Further reading: Kevin Aucoin, *Making Faces* (1997); Way Bandy, *Designing Your Face* (1978); Richard Corson, *Fashions in Makeup: From Ancient to Modern Times* (1972); Victoria Jackson, *Redefining Beauty* (1993).

Malone, Annie Turnbo (1869–1957)

Born in Metropolis, Illinois, Annie Turnbo Malone grew up as an impoverished orphan and became a successful hair care products entrepreneur who contributed large sums of money to charitable causes. During her childhood, she developed an interest in herbs that she later used in her work. In the 1890s, she started working on hair and scalp preparations for herself and other African American women. Hair was a major focus of women's attention during those years, and black women were eager for products that could reduce hair breakage, hair loss, and scalp ailments.

Malone's first commercial hair treatment was a conditioner that contained egg and sage. She and her sister moved to Lovejoy, a river town in Illinois, and began making "Wonderful Hair Grower," which they sold door-to-door in this African American community. Later, Malone said that she had to convince customers the product was effective by demonstrating it and by discussing cleanliness and hygiene with her customers. As orders for the product increased, the Turnbo sisters hired three assistants to help them make it.

The business continued to grow, and they relocated to St. Louis, Missouri, which offered them larger consumer markets and numerous stores selling drugs and toiletries. From St. Louis, Turnbo expanded into southern states, then across the country. In 1906, she registered a trademark name of "Poro." Poro agents continued to sell products door-to-door. One of the Poro agents in St. Louis, Sarah Breedlove (later Madam C.J. Walker), would later found her own hugely successful hair products business.

In 1914, Turnbo married Aaron Malone. By this time, there was a proven demand for Malone's products, and white-owned businesses agreed to stock them. Malone advertised in newspapers and various periodicals that were popular in the black community. In 1922, she added some skin care products and face powder to her hair care line. As she continued to promote her business, Malone provided jobs for African Americans and contributed time and money to churches and other community organizations. She was active in social welfare, recreational, and educational programs. Malone founded Poro College, which opened in 1918, and contained her offices and factory, along with educational and cultural facilities.

During the 1920s, it was reported that Malone was worth $14 million. This would mean she was the nation's first black female millionaire. She continued to give large sums of money to charitable causes, including $25,000 to Howard University. Malone supported individual students as well. She founded the St. Louis Colored Orphan's Home and served as its president. The institution is now known as the Annie Malone Children and Family Service Center.

In 1927, Malone and her husband divorced, and they embarked on a heated court battle over Poro. Although Malone finally regained control over the company she had founded, its economic condition had deteriorated, a process that deepened during the Great Depression. By the early 1930s, other companies were outselling Poro. Her fortune had dwindled to about $100,000 when she died in 1957. *See also* WALKER, MADAME C.J.

Further reading: M.A. Majors, *Noted Negro Women* (1971); Kathy Peiss, *Hope in a Jar* (1998); Jessie Carney Smith, ed., "Annie Turnbo Malone" in *Notable Black American Women* (1992).

Malone, Jo (b. 1964)

Perfume creator and entrepreneur Jo Malone became famous during the 1990s for her unusual fragrance line made with natural in-

gredients. Born in England, Malone grew up in Bexley, outside London, where her father was an artist and her mother made and sold her own skin care products. Malone helped her to prepare the products, chopping and straining plant products and herbs. At 16, she quit school and got a job in a flower shop. She married Gary Willcox, and she began giving facials to women in their homes.

Malone began experimenting with scents in the kitchen of her Chelsea home during the mid-1980s and made bath oils scented with ginger and nutmeg for some of her clients. The oil was so popular that customers asked to buy dozens more bottles, and Malone and her husband decided to start a fragrance business. Malone developed new fragrances, including "Amber & Lavender," "French Lime Blossom," "Lime, Basil, & Mandarin," (her best-seller) sandalwood soap, and lotion made with grapefruit. As orders increased, and French perfume companies were not interested in mass-producing her scents, Malone and Willcox contracted with factories to take over this job in 1994.

Malone's fragrances, which she said were inspired by personal experiences, contained unusual combinations and were described as sensuous and distinctive. By the late 1990s, her company owned a store in London and Malone fragrances were sold in Paris and New York, as well as by mail. In 1997, the business grossed $2 million. In addition to perfumes, lotions, bath products, and candles, Malone worked on fragrances for other items, including scents for the air at parties, called Scent-an-Event.

In 2000, Malone opened a large new store on London's fashionable Sloane Street, where customers may test products. The company will shortly begin Internet sales as well. See also FRAGRANCE; PERFUME; SKIN CARE.

Further reading: Samantha Miller, et al., "Nose Can Do," *People* 10 August 1998, 75–76; "Jo Malone" http://www.jomalone.com.

Marie Antoinette (1755–1793)

Born in Vienna, Marie Antoinette was the youngest daughter of Francis I and Maria Theresa, emperor and empress of the Holy

Roman Empire (C.E. 962–1806). The young princess grew up in luxurious, palatial surroundings and was often praised for her beauty. In later years, as queen of France at the time of the revolution (1789), she was widely condemned as vain, self-centered, and extravagant.

In 1770, Marie was married to the king of France, Louis XVI. At age 18, she declared that her ambition was to become the most fashionable woman in the kingdom. According to the beauty standards of her era, the queen had several assets: a clear complexion, slender figure, smooth shoulders, and bright blue eyes. Her liabilities were the red tints in her frizzy-textured hair, a slightly protruding lower lip, and her rather high brow.

During the 1770s and 1780s, the queen spent about $700,000 a year on clothing. She spent so much time planning and being fitted for her gowns and accessories that her designer moved to an apartment near the palace. The queen's mother, Empress Maria Teresa, wrote her letter, warning, "This was not the portrait of a Queen of France, but of an actress . . . you know that I think fashion should be followed moderately but never to any extreme. A young and pretty queen, attractive in herself, has no need for these follies." (Cronin, 1974)

Although her gowns were expensive, the queen had championed a new style for simpler dresses, often in a single color. She was expected to change her clothing at least three times a day and to wear fashions that showcased the talents of French dressmakers.

Antoinette followed the custom, originating in England, of piling her hair high on her head, adding artificial hair, and securing the elaborate coiffure with pins and gauze. Plumes were also a key part of these high hairstyles, which often contained numerous objects. The queen's hairdresser Leonard, who called himself a physiognomist rather than a hairdresser, worked with her to create hairstyles that were high but not so high as some women of fashion were wearing. One member of her court had a small model of her son's nursery woven into her hairstyle. It included a nanny, servant, and parrot pecking at a cherry. (Cronin, 1974)

The queen's beauty routines aroused as much interest as her clothing and jewels. She was known to use buttermilk on her face and bosom. The acid in the buttermilk acts as an astringent, removing some oil.

During the economic and political crises that led to the French Revolution, the queen took some steps toward a less lavish way of life. She dismissed some people serving the royal household, which brought strong criticism from the nobility, many of whom held these honorary positions. The king demanded that he review all writs permitting the expenditure of public funds. He also decreed that his brothers and their wives share his kitchens and dining rooms instead of operating separate ones (a change that would save a significant amount of money). Both the king and queen favored certain reforms, but they faced tremendous opposition from the nobility.

The king and his family probably would have fled had the revolutionary forces not imprisoned them outside Paris. Marie Antoinette was accused of passing military secrets to Prussia and Austria, who declared war on France in 1792. King Louis XVI was executed on the guillotine on January 21, 1793. Marie Antoinette was executed on October 16 that same year. *See also* COSMETICS.

Further reading: Katharine Anthony, *Marie Antoinette* (1933); Vincent Cronin, *Louis & Antoinette* (1974); Evelyne Lever, *Marie Antoinette* (1991).

Mary Kay Cosmetics *See* ASH, MARY KAY.

Masters, George (1936–1998)

George Masters was one of the most prominent American hairstylists and makeup artists of the twentieth century. His clients included actresses such as Marilyn Monroe, Jennifer Jones, and Ann-Margret, as well as socialites and other prominent women.

Masters grew up in suburban Detroit and dropped out of high school in Highland Park to study hairdressing. After graduating from a local beauty school, he worked in a Detroit shop where customers quickly began to request his services. He was then hired by an exclusive salon in Grosse Pointe, a high-income community near Detroit, and then received an offer to join the Elizabeth Arden salon on New York.

In 1959, he moved to Beverly Hills to take a job at the Saks Fifth Avenue salon. He soon established a new, casual style in his profession by working in blue jeans and a sweatshirt or open-neck shirt rather than more formal clothing. Clients compared his looks to those of the actor James Dean. After leaving his regular job at Saks, Masters spent evenings styling the hair of wealthy clients in their homes. He was in such demand that he could select his clients. One favorite client was screen legend Marilyn Monroe. Masters changed Monroe's hair color to a paler, whiter tone and designed a new hairdo with soft curls for the actress. In 1966, he designed a new hairstyle and makeup for Lynda Byrd Johnson, the daughter of President Lyndon Johnson, before she appeared at the Academy Awards ceremony that year with her date, the actor George Hamilton.

Masters opened his own Beverly Hills salon in 1966, but the business did not succeed. He then left the hair-styling business to become a traveling makeup artist, working in various expensive salons. He was known for his amazing makeovers of women of all ages. As a consultant, he commanded a $350 fee for his services.

He gained additional acclaim for his work on movie and television sets where he worked with many actresses. For the 1982 movie *Tootsie,* Masters transformed actor Dustin Hoffman into a woman through the artful application of makeup. *See also* MAKEUP ARTISTS.

Further reading: George Masters, *The Masters Way to Beauty* (1978); George Masters, obituary, *The New York Times,* 7 March 1998.

Max Factor & Company

Max Factor & Company, formed by Russian-born American Max Factor, began as a makeup company for the film industry and became an international cosmetics and perfume company. Max Factor is often called the "Father of Modern Makeup."

Factor, who was born "Frank" or "Francis" Faktor in Lodz, Russia, in 1877, became an apprentice to a wigmaker at age 14 and studied theatrical makeup. By age 20, Factor owned his own shop. When he traveled to the United States in 1904 with his family to visit the World's Fair in St. Louis, Factor decided to remain and he opened a cosmetics store in that city.

From there Max Factor moved to California to work as a makeup artist in the film industry. In Hollywood, he revolutionized film makeup by developing panchromatic makeup. Introduced in 1910, Factor's foundations came in a range of skin-toned semi-liquid greasepaint that appeared more natural under the special lighting and other conditions involved in making motion pictures. For this achievement, Max Factor won the Oscar in 1928 from the Academy of Motion Picture Arts and Sciences.

Containers of Factor's makeup rapidly "disappeared" from movie sets because actresses were taking it home to use for professional appearances and social occasions. Other women wanted to use these same products that helped the stars look so glamorous. In 1927, Factor began selling the makeup to the public and he started the Max Factor company, which advertised its products as "makeup of the stars." His children worked with him in the business. Max Factor is often credited with popularizing the term "makeup" and helping cosmetics to become more socially acceptable.

The company grew quickly and, by 1930, it was distributing Max Factor lipstick, foundation, powder, and other cosmetics in 81 countries. When it became possible to film in color, many actors and actresses did not want to appear in these movies because skin tended to reflect the other items in a scene, making the skin look unattractive. Max Factor's "Pancake Makeup" (introduced in 1937) solved this problem. Factor became one of the wealthiest men in Hollywood. He continued working as a top makeup artist. He also tried to quantify beauty by developing a rating system for various physical traits in order to predict whether an actress had the looks to become a star. In 1932, he introduced his Beauty Calibrator, a strange-looking metal headpiece, which measured a person's facial features.

When Max Factor died, his son Max Factor, Jr. took over as head of the company, which continued to introduce innovative products, such as Tru-Color Lipstick (1940) and a refillable mascara wand (1958), as well as numerous fragrances and other color cosmetics. The company was known for the creative work done in its laboratories. One innovation was a Kissing Machine (1939) to determine the durability of its lipsticks. The company produced makeup that flattered actors who appeared in black-and-white television productions and, beginning in the mid-1950s, in color, and it continued to create hairpieces and wigs for theatrical use until 1973. The company remained in the family until it was sold to Procter and Gamble in 1973 for nearly a half billion dollars. Max Factor Jr. died at age 91 in 1990.

Max Factor and Company has produced many popular fragrances. Two of the company's best selling lines during the 1980s were "Le Jardin d'Amour" (1986) and "Le Jardin de Max Factor" (1982). Actress Jane Seymour appeared in ads for these fragrances, which were described as romantic florals. During the 1980s, actress Jaclyn Smith was a popular spokesperson and model for the company. Smith appeared in ads for Max Factor cosmetics and for her signature perfume "California."

In 1969, Max Factor, Sr. and Max Factor, Jr. were honored with a star on Hollywood's "Walk of Fame" in Los Angeles. The Max Factor Beauty Museum is located on Hollywood Boulevard. *See also* COSMETICS; MAKEUP ARTISTS.

Further reading: Fred E. Basten with Robert Salvatore and Paul A. Kaufman, *Max Factor's Hollywood* (1995); Richard Corson, *Fashions in Makeup: From Ancient to Modern Times* (1972); Kate Mulvey and Melissa Richards, *Decades of Beauty: The Changing Image of Women, 1890s-1990s* (1998).

Médicis, Catherine de (1519–1589)

As the wife of a French king, Henry II, Catherine de Médicis influenced fashion and beauty styles and is often regarded as the founder of the French perfume industry. She was one of the best-educated women of her day and one of the most powerful.

The daughter of the Italian duke Lorenzo de' Médicis and his noble French wife, Catherine, became the sole heir to their fortune when both died shortly after she was born. In 1533, at the age of 14, she married Henry, younger son of King Francis I of France. After his brother died, Henry ascended the throne as King Henry II. When Catherine arrived for her wedding, she created a stir with her high-heeled shoes, designed by a Florentine shoemaker to give her a more imposing stature. Observers noted that Catherine was petite and slender with a thin face and blonde hair. She was not regarded as "pretty" according to the standards of the day but gained a reputation for glamour.

With her, the 14-year-old bride brought her personal perfumer, Renato Bianco, and he set up a perfume-making business in Paris where he became famous. (René the Florentine, as he was known, sold not only perfume but poisons he concocted for people who wanted to kill their enemies or inconvenient spouses or lovers.) At Catherine's insistence, laboratories were set up in Grasse, in the south of France, to study different ways of making perfume so that France could compete successfully with the perfume centers in Arabia and Spain. The queen also brought her love of cosmetics, shared by other Italian women, to France. Following her lead, French women began using more lip and cheek color and worked harder to lighten their skin.

Although many French had disdainfully called Catherine "the Italian woman," she had a close relationship with her father-in-law, Francis I, who supported her efforts to develop the perfume industry. Her husband's devotion to his mistress Diane de Poitiers also brought her great pain.

Catherine de Médicis continued to control the French perfume industry after her husband died and two of her sons ruled from 1560–74 and 1574–89, respectively. During those years, she won over many of her former critics and gained the people's respect from her skillful handling of government matters and worked for the good of France. *See also* GRASSE; PERFUME.

Further reading: Frederic J. Baumgartner, *Henry II* (1988); Jean Heritier, *Catherine de Medicis* (1963).

Men's Personal Care Products

Like women, men have worn cosmetics and used personal care or grooming products since time immemorial. Ancient Egyptian men colored their nails, using colors that signified their social status. Pharoahs and high-ranking aristocrats were allowed to wear red, for example. Men also used skin creams, fragrances, lip color, rouge, and elaborate eye makeup. Egyptian preparations were expertly made and durable. When the tomb of the boy pharaoh, Tutankhamen, was opened more than three thousand years after his death, the lip salves, rouge, and skin creams that were buried with him for the afterlife were still in a usable condition.

In the Roman Empire, centurions used a variety of cosmetics on their hair, faces, and hands. These included hair bleach and facial paint. Military leaders also used nail varnish, with lip colors to match. Servants or slaves tended the nails of the nobility, and noblemen had personal barbers.

Ancient Greek men were concerned with appearance, paying special attention to their physiques, and they exercised to build muscles. They also had manicures and pedicures and went to the barber for hair styling.

In North, Central, and South America, Africa, Australia, and various islands in the Pacific, body paint was often worn. Body paint was used both for spiritual reasons and to improve the appearance. Native American men painted designs on their faces to signify status, tribal roles, or for ceremonial purposes. Men in Africa also used cosmetics to adorn their faces and bodies and spent time styling their hair. Male members of the Wodaabe tribe of West Africa are known for their strong interest in appearance. The Wodaabe believe that charm is vital to winning a mate and men follow the traditional custom of spending hours on their appearance, focusing on facial paint, jewelry, and special hair styles.

Some men chose to use more elaborate cosmetics than was customary in their milieu. Around 650 BC, the Assyrian Ashurbanipal, an eccentric ruler, dressed in women's attire and wore cosmetics and large quantities of perfume. In Ireland, monks sometimes dyed or painted their eyelids black with a plant dye, probably from berries.

Both men and women used fewer cosmetics during the Middle Ages, when the clergy dominated daily life and admonished people not to use such materials.

During the early 1500s in England, both men and women were using more grooming preparations. Both genders used face powders, color cosmetics, skin moisturizers, and fragrances. Herbs and flowers were used in several skin care products.

In France, Henry III, who ruled from 1574–1598, was criticized for using cosmetics as well as perfumes. His behavior, which the clergy and French statesmen considered too feminine, made the king an object of ridicule among many of his subjects.

In European courts dating from the 1500s through the 1700s, it was common to see men wearing face paint, face patches, elaborate wigs, and hair powder. By the 1800s, however, attitudes had changed, and Englishmen who adorned themselves in this manner were ridiculed and called "dandies."

More men's grooming products were introduced during the late 1800s and 1900s. They included brilliantines and pomades (both solid and liquid), lotions, emulsions, gels, and aerosols. Brilliantines and pomades lubricated the hair and held it in place, as well as giving it an artificial shine. Lighter grooming lotions were usually made with alcohol. Early lotions contained castor oil and alcohol, which evaporated on the hair, leaving a slight oily film behind. Synthetic oils gradually replaced other oils because they had a longer shelf life and did not darken with time.

During World War II, new cream hair-dressings were created because alcohol was rationed and unavailable for cosmetic use. Mineral oil was a common ingredient in the oil-in-water and water-in-oil emulsions that men used to groom their hair, which was usually worn in a short, neat style.

The use of men's cosmetics increased greatly during the 1940s. During World War II, American companies urged family and friends to send toiletries to men who were in the service. Included in these kits were scented colognes and after-shave lotions. Sales of these items rose steadily during and after the war.

The 1960s brought transparent hair gels with a lighter consistency for men. They were promoted for their greaseless and long-lasting qualities. During the 1970s, more men began using hairspray and other products that had once been associated with women's hair care. Men's hairsprays had "masculine" containers and scents and did not stiffen the hair. In western societies, more men used mousses, hair gels, and other products, all sold in drugstores and variety stores.

Today, men in industrialized countries use a variety of personal care, or grooming, products. These include shaving and various hair care products. Surveys conducted during the 1990s showed that men in European countries used more fragrance, deodorants, and shaving creams per capita than men in the United States. American men, however, used more hair care products than men in the five largest countries in the European Union (EU). European men were also more likely to buy shower gels, but consumption of this product was steadily rising in the United States.

Today, men around the world use a variety of personal care products: fragrance, shaving, and hair care items. Skin care products have become increasingly popular, as are hair care and hairstyling products.

Men who appear on television, including news reporters, politicians, or film actors routinely use makeup. Rock musicians and actors at times use dramatic makeup when performing live, but the average man in de-veloped nations is seldom seen in color cosmetics. Obvious makeup is regarded as a feminine look. Boy George, a British pop music composer and singer, became famous during the 1980s for both his music and striking appearance. He is known for his use of cosmetics and unusual clothing and sometimes affects a look traditionally considered "female." His changing looks rely on colorful eye makeup, foundation, lipstick, and other cosmetics.

Attitudes may be changing. Modern cosmetics for men include tinted foundation, concealers for blemishes or discolored areas, colorless powder, lip balm with little or no color, and clear mascara. Men in Japan are among those who began using more cosmetics during the 1980s and '90s, including eyeliner, face powder, and lip balm.

Makeup artist Michele Probst developed a line of cosmetics for men called Menaji that included skin-care products (for example, eye gel, after-shave lotion, facial masque, and exfoliating toner), lip balm with sunscreen, and a concealer to hide blemishes, under-eye circles, and shaving nicks. The products were promoted as natural and perfume-free, as well as easy-to-use, and were initially sold in beauty salons and dermatology offices. Probst, who favors a natural look, has applied makeup on male celebrities for music videos, album covers, and television commercials.

The late twentieth century saw a growing trend for men to spend more time on physical fitness to build a trim, muscular body and to pay more attention to their looks. The "buff" look of male models also includes little if any visible body hair, so more men are seeking waxing and other hair removal processes. Men are also undergoing cosmetic surgery in growing numbers. More men are also purchasing hair-dyes or having the procedure done in a salon. They are countering thinning hair with hair transplants or other cosmetic procedures for hair loss; drugs are also available to treat male pattern baldness. *See also* ADVERTISING (U.S.); AVON PRODUCTS INC.; COSMETICS; FACIAL HAIR, MEN'S; HAIR COLOR; HAIR LOSS; HAIR TRANSPLANTS; WEIGHT.

Further reading:Further reading: Lucas L. Johnson, II, "Makeup Artist Creates Line of Cosmetics for Men," *The Oak Ridger (TN)*, 9 June 1998; Judith Rodin, *Body Traps* (1992); Nicole Sault, ed., *Many Mirrors: Body Image and Social Relations* (1994); Toni Stabile, *Everything You Want to Know About Cosmetics, Or What Your Friendly Clerk Didn't Tell You* (1984); "You're So Vain," *Newsweek*, 14 April 1986.

Michaeljohn

Michaeljohn, based in London, is a well-known hair salon and hair care products business. It was founded in 1967 by stylists Michael Rasser and John Isaacs, who built up a clientele that included singers Mick Jagger and Madonna and supermodel/actress Iman. Michaeljohn stylists have worked on the models who appeared at showings for Calvin Klein, Chanel, and other top fashion designers.

The company developed professional products for their salons. During the late 1990s, the company decided to offer consumers a line of semiprofessional products for lower prices than their top-of-the-line versions. The new products were developed by a firm called Couture Brands and were tested by stylists in the Michaeljohn salons. They included natural ingredients that were especially popular with consumers during the 1990s, including peppermint, tea tree oil, rosemary, lavender, and sage. The company stated that the fragrances of their new products were a major selling point.

Further reading: "Another British Invasion?" *Happi*, August 1997.

Miss America Pageant

In the United States, the Miss America Beauty Pageant, held every year in Atlantic City, New Jersey, is perhaps the best-known beauty contest in the country.

The pageant began in 1921 and was first called the Natural Beauty Tournament. The contest, which takes place in September, was created by the Atlantic City Business Men's League as a way to prolong the tourist season. The first contestants, who were referred to as "beauty maids," came from communities around Atlantic City, including New York, Philadelphia, and Pittsburgh. They were sponsored by newspapers or came on their own.

Miss America, 1999, Heather French, being crowned by 1998 winner Nicole Johnson. *Courtesy of the Miss America Organization.*

A press release from the Atlantic City *Press* announced that thousands of beautiful girls "including stage stars and movie queens' would "march in full review before judges in the Atlantic City Fall Pageant." A few hundred contestants actually took part. The contest was divided into two parts, with one for professional beauties, such as actresses and well-known athletes, while the young women who had been sponsored by newspapers were called "civic beauties."

The first woman to win the competition was 16-year-old Margaret Gorman of Washington, D.C. Gorman was sponsored by the *Washington Herald* and won the title Miss Washington over 1,500 contestants. The blue-eyed blonde stood 5 feet, 1 inch tall and weighed 108 pounds. As of 1999, she was the youngest woman ever to hold the title and the smallest until 100-pound Suzette Charles became Miss America in August 1984. Her prize was a Golden Mermaid trophy reportedly worth about $5,000.

Through the years, the contest became more elaborate and more judged events were added, including bathing suit competition (changed to "swimsuit" competition in 1946), evening gown competition (1922), and talent competition (1938). Starting in 1948, contestants were chosen in each state and the District of Columbia so that, by 1956, a total of 51 contestants competed each year.

During the 1970s, the contest became the target of critics who protested that such contests demean women and treat them as objects, worthwhile only for their appearance. Demonstrators at the 1968 pageant picketed outside, chanting, and crowning a sheep as the "winner." They threw various objects into a trashcan, including wigs, false eyelashes, bras, girdles, and hair curlers. A group of women drafted a manifesto decrying the fact that men were judged by their actions and achievements, while women were judged on the basis of their looks.

Since the 1970s, the pageant has emphasized the talent and personality components of the contest and prides itself on awarding scholarships worth more than $4 million each year to top contestants in various local, state, and national pageants so they can continue their education. Many pageant winners have gone on to careers in the entertainment industry, but many have also become lawyers, doctors, journalists, politicians, authors, or other professionals. During her year as Miss America, the winner makes numerous public appearances, give speeches, takes part in community service activities, and may champion particular causes.

These changes notwithstanding, beauty remains a key component of the contest, and the contestants are experts at techniques to enhance their appearances. Author Nancie S. Martin reported some beauty tricks commonly used by Miss America contestants. One is to apply petroleum jelly on their lips

for shine and on the teeth to help the lips slide along them when the contestants have to smile for long periods of time. Contestants may wear false eyelashes and pad their rear ends if they wish, and are encouraged to wear sheer hosiery for the swimsuit events. Contestants may also add hairpieces to their own styles and are permitted to dye their natural hair color, something that was banned during the early years of the pageant. *See also* CONTESTS; FEMINISM.

Further reading: Frank Deford, *There She Is* (1971); Nancie S. Martin, *Miss America: Through the Looking Glass* (1985).

Modeling and Models

Male and female models are an important part of the modern fashion and beauty industries. They are featured in runway fashion shows and in advertisements for cosmetics, personal care products, and numerous other consumer goods. They both reflect and influence the standards by which a society judges appearance.

Models have been around for centuries. Artist's models posed for paintings for hundreds of years before they were used to model clothing. Artists paid models to pose with or without their clothing.

During the 1850s, French couturier Charles Worth employed women called "mannequins" as live models to showcase his designs while walking down a runway. Other Paris couturiers followed suit and this practice made its way to other fashion centers in Italy and the United States. During the 1920s and 1930s, designers sometimes asked socialites to model their clothing.

Professional modeling developed around the year 1920 and developed into a large international business. The first large American modeling agencies were founded by Harry Conover and John Robert Powers, an actor. "Powers models" became the top professional models of the 1920s and were respected for their well-groomed, elegant appearance. Until then, designers, artists, and photographers hired their models informally or found them working as chorus girls, for example.

Model, photographed circa 1900. *Library of Congress.*

Powers designed a course to train models and worked to give the profession respectability and prestige. Powers models became known for their good looks, professional preparation, and refined manners. They learned how to apply cosmetics and dress in a way that was regarded as both ladylike and fashionable at the same time. Some of the young women who sought to become Powers models came from upper-class New York families.

Powers expanded his modeling and charm school organization after the 1950s to include the John Robert Powers Modeling and Acting School. Among the celebrities who have attended the school are singers Diana Ross and actor Montgomery Clift. The organization participates in international modeling and talent competitions.

The first female models to receive a great deal of attention modeled in the 1940s and 1950s. One of them was Bettina, a French-born fashion model who influenced fashion and beauty trends during those two decades. Couturier Jacques Fath discovered the young model and launched her career. Bettina was known for her tall, slim figure, youthful movements, short bobbed hair, shapely eyebrows, and bright red lipstick. Women imitated her hairstyle and the way she applied makeup and groomed her eyebrows, and she appeared in magazines read by women in different countries. In the United States, red-haired Suzy Parker and her sister Dorian Leigh were top models for fashions and cosmetics, as were Jean Patchett and Lisa Fonssagrives, who was married to fashion photographer Irving Penn.

During those years, models worked in three different areas: in fashion houses, as runway models for the spring and fall collections, or appearing in print work (photographs). Print work was regarded as the most prestigious, and modeling lingerie was regarded as the least.

During the late 1960s, these areas became blurred as models worked in more than one area. In spring 1970, Valentino, a top couturier, hired the best photographic models to model his new collections. Two of his favorite models were a Spanish beauty named Nati Abascal and Suzy Dyson. It was not until the 1980s that modeling lingerie for high-end companies such as Victoria's Secret also gained status.

The Ford Modeling Agency was founded in 1946 by Eileen and Jerry Ford. The couple began their business by handling bookings for two models from their New York City home. Models who signed with the agency were impressed by the personal attention they received as they adjusted to the business and moved to New York to work. Ford became a prestige name in the modeling business. The Fords also worked to boost pay rates for their models. Hourly rates increased so that by the 1990s, top models earned thousands of dollars a day.

Some of the most famous models of the late 1900s—Jean Shrimpton, Carmen Dell'Orefice, Jerry Hall, Rachel Hunter, Vendela, Rene Simonsen, Christie Brinkley, Christy Turlington, and Patricia Velasquez—began their careers as Ford models. Among the Ford models who have gone on to acting careers are Lauren Hutton, Kim Basinger, Shari Belafonte, Rene Russo, Ali MacGraw,

Candice Bergen, and Sharon Stone. Katie Ford, daughter of the founders, took charge of the business during the 1990s.

Some new modeling agencies became very successful. Wilhelmina, based in New York City, was founded by the former supermodel of the 1960s and 1970s who gave the agency its same name. Elite Model Management, which opened in 1971, has become a leading agency in the international modeling field. As of 1999, Elite had agencies in 30 different cities and billed $100 million (U.S.) each year; it represented more than 600 models on six continents. Elite models include Cindy Crawford, Paulina Porizkova, Linda Evangelista, Naomi Campbell, Stephanie Seymour, and Karen Mulder. It has offices in Paris, Vienna, Hamburg, Milan, Madrid, Lisbon, Toronto, London, Amsterdam, Copenhagen, Tokyo, Hong Kong, Rio de Janeiro, Miami, and Atlanta, among other places. In 1996, Elite launched a major Asian office in Singapore. Among the top regional models Elite manages in that region are Celia The, Charmaine Harn, Junita Simon, Sonia Couling, and Hadya Hutagalung.

African American Models

African American models first appeared on the national scene during the late 1950s and early 1960s. Among them was Donyale Luna, who was particularly popular in France. Dorothea Towles was one of the first women of color to earn a living as a fashion model when she worked in Paris during the 1950s. In the United States, Helen Williams became the first well-known African American model and was featured in glamorous magazine ads. As more black models became visible, cosmetic companies devoted more research to developing products for African-American women. Brandford Models, an African American agency, opened in 1946 at a time when the modeling business segregated races. Mainstream agencies did not hire black models until the 1960s, when they were occasionally offered work in magazines.

Beverly Johnson broke more barriers as a famous African American model of the 1960s.

She was the first to appear on the cover of *Vogue* magazine. Iman, an African model who joined the profession in 1977, also became an actress, activist, and creator of a line of cosmetics for black women. London-born Naomi Campbell (b. 1970), who began modeling during the 1980s, is considered to be the first black "supermodel." Campbell was the first black model to appear on the cover of the French *Vogue*. During the 1990s, she was regarded as possibly the best runway model at couture shows. She also appeared in feature films and joined supermodels Elle MacPherson and Claudia Schiffer to open a chain of restaurants called "Fashion Café."

Naomi Sims was the first African-American model to appear on the covers of *Ladies' Home Journal* (1968) and *Life* (1969). During the 1970s, prominent black models included Beverly Johnson, Barbara Smith, Billie Blair. Later came Mounia, Naomi Campbell, Wanakee, Roshumba, Iman. Veronica Webb and Tyra Banks were among the supermodels of the 1990s appearing in numerous designer fashion shows, ads for cosmetics and clothing, and Banks was one of the Victoria's Secret models.

Naomi Sims later developed a line of wigs and cosmetics. Bethann Hardison headed an international modeling agency bearing her name and was also an advocate for black representation in the fashion industry. Iman's cosmetics line was one of the most successful launches in history when it came out in the 1990s.

Supermodels

The late twentieth century ushered in the age of the "supermodels"—highly paid models who were in demand by designers and cosmetics companies and became international celebrities in their own right. The first supermodels were Americans Cheryl Tiegs and Christie Brinkley. Later supermodels included Czech Paulina Porizkova; Americans Lauren Hutton, Brooke Shields, Cindy Crawford and Christy Turlington; German Claudia Schiffer; African Iman; Dane/Peruvian Helena Christensen; Italian Carla Bruni;

Supermodels Claudia Schiffer, Elle MacPherson, Naomi Campbell, and Christy Turlington (1995). © *Mitchell Gerber/CORBIS.*

Swede Eva Herzigova, and Australian Elle MacPherson. Brooke Shields, Cindy Crawford, and Elle MacPherson went on to careers in acting, and Cheryl Tiegs and Christie Brinkley both went on to achieve success in the fitness industry.

Models' appearances have influenced the styles women adopt. In the 1960s, for example, the British model Twiggy ushered in an era in which extreme slenderness was the ideal.

Echoing that in the 1990s, several top models influenced a style that became known as the "waif look." These very slender models included American Amber Valletta (b. 1973) and British Kate Moss (b. 1970). Both women, who started modeling as teenagers, appeared at couture shows and were photographed for top fashion magazines, as well as representing various products. Moss was chosen as the Face of Calvin Klein, and Valletta was featured in ads for Calvin Klein's fragrance "Escape." Critics of the "waif" look said it encouraged some teenage girls to develop eating disorders in the pursuit of extreme thinness.

Male Models

Until recent decades, most male models were not as well known to the general public or as highly paid as female models. That changed during the last decades of the twentieth century. Male supermodels are now a significant part of the fashion, modeling, advertising, and entertainment world. Male models are also signing exclusive contracts to represent a designer or line of products.

Prominent male models come from around the world. Swede Marcus Schenkenberg has been called the first male supermodel. Schenkenberg began modeling in 1989 when he was discovered rollerblading on Venice Beach in southern California. He became known for his muscular build. His modeling credits include jean ads for Calvin Klein and numerous magazine covers. He has modeled in runway shows for Klein, Ungaro, Gianni Versace, and Donna Karan. Other male models who were featured in Klein's famous underwear ads include Mark Wahlberg and Italian Antonio Sabato Jr. Both men also became actors. Swede Alex Lundquist was featured in ad campaigns for Guess? clothing. Michael Bergin, a native of Connecticut, later became a Calvin Klein model and has appeared in runway shows for Valentino, Donna Karan, and Hugo Boss. Tyson Beckford, whose heritage is Jamaican and Chinese-American, has represented Ralph Lauren fragrances and Lauren's body line, "Sport." Beckford was named VH-1's Male Model of the year (1995) and one of People magazine's 50 Most Beautiful People.

Other top male models of recent years include Scott Barnhill, Tyson Beckford, Jason Fedele, Enrique Palacios, Mark Vanderloo, Charley Speed, Rod Brewster, Johnny Zander, and Jason Lewis, who has been featured in campaigns for Hugo Boss, Tommy Hilfiger, and Byblos, among others. Male models appear in publications such as *Vogue Homme, Vanity Fair, Gentlemen's Quarterly, The New York Times Magazine, Arena, US,* and *People.* Some of the agencies that represent top male models include Boss, Wilhelmina, John Robert Powers International, and Click.

Increasing Diversity

As women and the fashion industry both realized that the size, shape, and needs of the female population were diverse, models that did not fit the traditional tall, slim, young formula were also featured in fashion and beauty ads and on fashion runways. More Asian and Hispanic models also received attention. At the same time, as the Baby Boom women began to reach middle age, the fashion and cosmetics industries began to use more older models. Actress Isabella Rosselini and other over-40 women broke down more barriers during and after the 1980s when they were featured in ads for prestige cosmetic lines (Lancome, in Rosselini's case).

Plus-size models—those who model size 14 and up—were seen in cosmetic and clothing ads and in fashion shows for larger women. Many women, including more than 50 percent of all American women wear plus-sizes, so manufacturers recognized the commercial benefits of designing and producing attractive clothing for this market. Emme (Melinda) Aronson (b. 1964), known professionally as Emme, became a prominent American plus-size model during the 1990s. Aronson, who stood 5 feet 11 inches and weighed 190 pounds, was represented by the prestigious Ford modeling agency. Aronson discussed fashion on television talk shows and became a Revlon spokesperson and encouraged women to accept themselves: "True beauty absolutely comes in every size, shape, age and color." (Johnson, 1999) *See also* AGING AND APPEARANCE; BRINKLEY, CHRISTIE; CRAWFORD, CINDY; IMAN; JOHNSON, BEVERLY; TIEGS, CHERYL; TWIGGY

Further reading: Emme Aronson, *True Beauty* (1998); Eileen Ford, *Secrets of the Model's World* (1970); Michael Gross, *Model* (1995); Lois Joy Johnson, "Emme's Guide to Confident Style," *Ladies' Home Journal,* March 1999, 126–131; Kathy Peiss, *Hope in a Jar* (1998); John Robert Powers, *The Powers Model Book of Beauty, Charm and Personality* (1956); "Who's Who: Christy Turlington," *Vogue* biography, April 1999.

Further reading: (male models): "Boss Models Men," http://www.bossmodels.com/men.html; Michael Gross, Model (1995); "The Insider's Guide to Supermodels and Modeling," http://supermodelguide.com/supermodels; "Ultimate TV News—Having That Keen Fashion Sense — the 1998 VH-1 Fashion Awards," http://www.ultimatetv.vom/news/f/a/98/10/26vh1.html; VH-1 Fashion Awards 1996, 1997, 1998 http://www.madonnafanclub.com/vh1fash.htm; "Yahoo! Model of the Month: Rod Brewster," http://features.yahoo.com/model.

Monroe, Marilyn (1926–1962)

American actress Marilyn Monroe, nicknamed the "Blonde Bombshell" and described as a "sex goddess" was one of the most celebrated beauties and glamorous women of her day and a cultural icon of the twentieth century. Her trademarks were platinum hair, red lips, and a distinctive facial mole, along with a voluptuous figure and sexy walk. She influenced beauty standards and trends during her lifetime, and her influence continued after her death.

Born Norma Jeane Mortenson in California, she spent much of her childhood in foster homes while her single mother was institutionalized for mental illness. For a while, she lived with a caring woman named Grace McKee, who often told Norma Jeane that she would be a beautiful movie star someday. Her screen idol during those years was actress Jean Harlow, a blond whose film roles highlighted her sexuality.

Norma Jeane was briefly married at age 16 to 21-year-old James Doughterty. Doughterty entered the armed services during World War II. While Norma Jeane was working in a parachute factory in 1944 to help the war effort, an army photographer took her picture as part of its program to promote the contributions of women and show that women working in "men's jobs" could look feminine. She quickly became a popular subject, and her picture appeared on 33 national magazine covers during the next two years.

Her image led to her career in acting. Renamed "Marilyn Monroe," she signed a contract with Twentieth Century-Fox in 1946 and had small parts in several movies. She won good reviews for her first significant role, in *The Asphalt Jungle* (1950). Beginning in the early 1950s, Monroe starred in several hit movies, including *Gentlemen Prefer*

Blondes, Some Like It Hot, How to Marry a Millionaire, and *The Seven-Year Itch*. She appeared in both dramas and comedies. Monroe appeared in various dramatic and comedy roles. Her demeanor was often fragile and child-like in contrast to her imposing, womanly appearance. Journalist Paul Rudnick summed up her screen persona this way: "She's the bad girl and good girl combined; she's sharp and sexy yet incapable of meanness, a dewy Venus rising from the motel sheets . . . ." (Rudnick, 1999)

In 1954, having divorced her first husband, she married 39-year-old baseball legend Joe DiMaggio, who asked Monroe to retire from filmmaking. She refused. That same year, she joined a USO tour of Korea and entertained U.S. troops there. Afterwards, she and DiMaggio separated; they later divorced. A third marriage, to playwright Arthur Miller, also ended in divorce.

Monroe died at age 36, of a prescription drug overdose that was labeled a suicide, although some biographers believe it was accidental. During her career, she made 29 films. Her "look" is recognizable nearly everywhere in the world, and has been widely copied. During one period of her successful career, singer-actress Madonna wore a platinum blonde hairstyle and clothing and accessories that are identified with Marilyn Monroe.

See also ADVERTISING (U.S.); BEAUTY STANDARDS; HAIR COLOR.

Further reading: Sara Halprin, *"Look at My Ugly Face!"* (1995); Barbara Learning, *Marilyn Monroe* (1998); Paul Rudnick, "The Blond: Marilyn Monroe," *Time* 100: Heroes and Icons, 12 October 1999; Adam Woog, *Marilyn Monroe* (1997).

Museé International de la Parfumerie

The Museé International de la Parfumerie contains exhibits that show the 3,000-year history of perfume making and information about the process of creating perfume. It is located in Grasse, in the south of France, which has been the center of the world perfume industry since the 1600s. The museum has a conservatory with examples of plants that are often used to produce commercial fragrances. Artifacts from ancient Greece, Rome, and Egypt help visitors and students learn about the long history of perfumes and the kinds of containers that were used by various cultures. Other exhibits include flacons and toilet cases that belonged to French royalty, including Marie Antoinette. *See also* FRAGRANCE; GRASSE; PERFUME.

Mustache *See* FACIAL HAIR, MEN'S.

N

Nails *See* FEET; HANDS.

Natural Ingredients

Natural ingredients are substances that come from nature and are used as ingredients in various cosmetics and toiletries. Some of the most common natural ingredients in cosmetics and personal care items include aloe vera, algae extracts, fruit and vegetable oils and extracts, soy, herbal extracts, and Vitamins A, C, and E. Perfume manufacturers have also used products derived from animals, such as musk, from the musk ox, and ambergris from the sperm whale. (Ambergris is now banned from international trade, because it resulted in the over-destruction of sperm whales.)

Two examples of popular plant ingredients are aloe and jojoba. Aloe is used as a juice derived from the aloe leaf plant and is used as a medicinal plant as well. Four of the more than 300 species of Aloe vera have medicinal value. The juice is mostly water and about 0.5 percent amino acids and carbohydrates.

The promotion of cosmetics containing aloe often stress its value as a natural product that has been used on the skin and as a healthful drink for thousands of years. As of 1999, there were no controlled laboratory studies that proved aloe had special qualities for cosmetic use. However, "extensive research since the 1930s in the U.S. and Russia has shown that the clear gel has a dramatic ability to heal wounds, ulcers and burns, putting a protective coat on the affected area and speeding up the rate of healing." (Chevallier, 1996) It has been used to treat acne, chronic itching, and certain other skin conditions. (*Nature's Impact*, February/March 1999) Today, aloe is also being added to the strip of disposable razor blades men and women use for shaving.

Jojoba oil comes from a shrub in the box family (*buxaceae*), sometimes called the Pignut or Goatnut tree. The oil, which is clear and nearly odorless, is contained in the plant's capsules. It is used in hair products and other cosmetics, including fragrances. The shrub is native to northern Mexico and the southwestern United States. After jojoba oil became more popular during the 1980s, it was also grown commercially in California. In addition to its commercial uses, jojoba is used alone as a hair tonic. People who choose to create their own fragrances at home sometimes use jojoba as a base oil, because it does not compete with the other essences. *See also* BODY SHOP, THE; NATURAL PRODUCTS.

Further reading: Andrew Chevallier, *The Encyclopedia of Medicinal Plants* (1996); Albert Y. Leung and Steven Foster, eds., *Encyclopedia of Common Natural Ingredients* (1996); *Nature's Impact*, February/March 1999.

Natural Products

Natural grooming and beauty products, made from substances extracted directly from plants and animal products rather than synthetic chemicals, became increasingly popular after the 1960s.

Natural products were the first and only cosmetic and grooming products for thousands of years. Even when synthetic alternatives became available, some companies continued to use natural ingredients during the 1900s.

One of the first large companies to provide organic cosmetics with natural ingredients was Aubrey Organics, founded by Aubrey Hampton and based in Tampa, Florida. Hampton had previously operated a business that made chemicals for the printing and wig-cleaning industries. During the 1960s, Hampton developed Relax-R-Bath, an herbal bath product that aimed to relieve muscle pain. He explored and pioneered the idea of natural grooming products and began writing on the subject. Hampton listed all the ingredients in his products on the label before the U.S. Food and Drug Administration (FDA) required it. His books, including *What's In Your Cosmetics: A Complete Consumer's Guide to Natural and Synthetic Ingredients,* inform consumers about the different chemical ingredients found in most cosmetics and their potential effects.

Interest in natural ingredients increased during the 1970s when the consumer movement and the environmental movement gathered momentum. Both expanded after an international Earth Day was celebrated in 1970. Consumers expressed concern about allergies and sensitive skin, as well as a desire for pure, simple preparations.

During the 1970s, more natural and organic products became available and were sold in drugstores and department stores as well as health food stores (although only in 1999 did the FDA announce that it would come up with a formal definition of "organic"). Jojoba oil, yucca, and other plant ingredients appeared in more hair care products. A clay-based product called Indian Earth was marketed for use on several parts of the body—as a rouge, nail color, and facial highlighter. The use of these products was part of a larger trend toward cultural diversity and awareness. Interest in herbs also increased, and many consumers demanded products that had not been tested on animals.

In addition to cosmetics, more companies began making personal care and oral care products using plant ingredients and fewer synthetic chemicals. For example, Tom's of Maine was founded as a company that produces natural products and does not use animal testing for its soaps, toothpastes, and other grooming products. Tom's produces various oral care products, including toothpastes made without fluoride, dyes, sugar, artificial sweeteners, and certain other ingredients found in other commercial toothpastes.

More people have also been experimenting with homemade beauty and grooming products. For example, women mix brewer's yeast with water for facial masks and use mayonnaise, eggs, olive oils, and avocado to condition their hair. As they did in the nineteenth century, before the advent of commercial cosmetics, books and articles include recipes and ideas about making personal care products, including soap and fragrances. People can also find recipes for homemade personal care products and cosmetics on the Internet.

Consumers' desire for natural products has continued through the 1990s. During the late twentieth century, manufacturers offered more and more "natural" cosmetics and grooming products. New companies were formed to manufacture and market these products, and existing personal care companies emphasized the natural ingredients or naturally derived ingredients that they already used in their products. These products are often given names that emphasize their connection to "nature" or "natural." Examples of such ingredients are fruit and vegetable extracts, including lemon oil, chamomile, green tea, peppermint, cucumber, rosemary, aloe vera, and eucalyptus.

Proponents of natural preparations say that organic cosmetics and those made primarily with fruits, herbs, vegetables, and the like are better and safer. Experts, including scientists at the FDA, who disagree with these claims, say there is no scientific evidence to prove that the products are safer or that they perform more effectively than cosmetics made with synthetic ingredients. The FDA has said, "There is no basis in fact or scientific legitimacy to the notion that products containing natural ingredients are good for the skin." (Lewis, 1998) In her book *The Beauty Bible,* and her monthly newsletters, makeup artist and consumer advocate Paula Begoun has said that the so-called "natural" products are not inherently better. Other experts point out that plants are made up of chemicals, too, and may provoke allergic reactions that synthetics do not. Begoun says,

> "Even if an 'all-natural' product did exist, you wouldn't want to use it on your skin anyway. Think about a bunch of plants, fruits, or vegetables sitting in your bathroom. What would happen in a very brief period of time if they didn't contain preservatives? They would become moldy and disgusting in just a few days. Skin-care products contain very 'unnatural' –sounding preservatives, and that's great. According to many cosmetic chemists, a reliable preservative system helps to avoid the risk of microbial contamination, which could cause problems for the eyes, lips, and skin." (Begoun, 1997)

Some authors have said that synthetics may perform better, last longer, resist contamination, and offer more shades and colors.

In addition to standard cosmetics, such as lipsticks, powder, cheek colors, and foundations, companies also offer new brands of hair color made from plant extracts and without ammonia, peroxide, or coal tar dyes. Clairol and other companies that make hair color have brought out new products that contain jojoba oil and other ingredients from plants. Henna, a natural hair coloring agent that has been in use for millennia, also remains popular.

Other products made with "natural" ingredients include bath gels, bath salts, soaps, body lotions, fragrances, and skin care product.

Most of the large drugstores in the United States and Europe sell "natural products," and some large multipurpose stores, such as Wal-Mart, also carry them. More natural products chain stores have also been springing up and expanding during the 1980s and 1990s. One of the best known is The Body Shop, based in the United Kingdom. In 1998, the company sold 604.4 million (British pounds) worth of products. The Limited, a clothing retailer, opened Bath and Body Works. Sales increased from $1.9 million in 1990 to $475 million in 1999, an 11 percent increase over the previous year. Older natural products companies are based in Germany and Switzerland, among other countries.

As more mainstream companies have introduced their own brands of "natural cosmetics" (often at lower prices than those of their competitors), critics say that these products are not 100 percent natural because they contain artificial colors and fragrances, preservatives, and other synthetic ingredients. As of 1999, the U.S. Food and Drug Administration (FDA) was considering how to handle this matter, which may lead to changes in labeling laws. Current laws do not prevent companies from calling their products "natural," even if they contain some synthetic ingredients.

Statistics gathered in the 1990s showed that the majority of consumers choosing natural products were women between the ages of 16 and 45 in high-income brackets. In 1998, sales of natural personal care products in the United States totaled $1.62 billion and accounted for about 6 percent of the total cosmetics and toiletries trade. Sales of skin care products—sunscreens, suntan lotions, anti-aging creams, lotions, toners, astringents, and cleansers—were the fastest growing segment. Sales of men's natural shaving products increased by 24 percent between 1995 and 1999. Oral care product sales rose by 6 percent, and sales of natural soap and bath products increased by 13 percent. Industry analysts predicted that sales of natural products would continue to rise, at a rate of about 10 percent annually. Sales of natural products in other countries in Europe and Asia also grew. (Dunn, 1997; Galinsky, 1999) *See also* BODY SHOP, THE; HENNA; HAIR COLOR; LAWS AND REGULATIONS

(U.S.); MALONE, JO; NATURAL INGREDIENTS; SAFETY.

Further reading: Bath and Body Shop, http://www.bathandbodyshop.com; The Body Shop, http://www.bodyshop.com; Paula Begoun, *Don't Go to the Cosmetics Counter Without Me* (1997); Carolyn A. Dunn, "Natural Appeal," *Happi,* June 1997; Bob Galinsky, "Skin and Hair Products Go Natural," http://www.M@rket Asi@ agribusiness information; Carol Lewis, "Clearing Up Cosmetic Confusion," *FDA Consumer,* May-June 1998.

Nazi Germany

During the Nazi era in Germany (1933–1945), under dictator Adolf Hitler, matters of appearance took on a profound political and social significance. The Nazis launched an intense campaign promote a particular set of physical features, which the Nazis called "Aryan," as the ideal. The beauty ideal promoted by the Nazis emphasized traits associated with people of Nordic, or northern European, ancestry: blond hair, blue or gray eyes, delicate features, and fair skin, as well as a tall, athletic physique. People from ethnic or racial groups who did not have these characteristics were stigmatized and called "inferior" and "unattractive."' This was an early phase in a process of ostracizing particular groups of people, primarily Jews, then depriving them of civil rights and eventually imprisoning and killing them.

Laws regarding the use of cosmetics went into effect, and propaganda was also used to discourage cosmetic use. Women members of the Nazi party and Hitler Youth were banned from using cosmetics of any kind. However, women married to top Nazi officials could be seen patronizing expensive salons, such as one in Berlin owned by the Elizabeth Arden Company, a large beauty products firm based in New York City. (After visiting Germany during the mid-1930s, Arden decided not to mention the Berlin salon in any of her ads because of the negative association with fascism and her personal distaste for Hitler's government.)

Further reading: J. C. Fest, *The Face of the Third Reich* (1970); Raoul Hilberg, *The Destruction of the European Jews* (1985); G. I. Mosse, *Nazi Culture: Intellectual, Cultural, and Social Life in the Third Reich* (1981); William Shirer, *The Rise and Fall of the Third Reich* (1959).

Neck

Changing the shape of the neck for esthetic purposes and adorning this body part with paint and jewelry dates back to ancient times. Cultures also have different ideas about what makes for an "ideal" neck.

The Padaung women of Myanmar (formerly Burma) considered a long neck a strong beauty asset. These women traditionally used coiled rings made of brass to lengthen their necks to about 15 inches (38 centimeters). This process entailed pulling three or four of the thoracic vertebrae (spinal discs) up into their necks. The Karenni people of Myanmar still practice this stretching of the neck in modern times, using long coiled gold necklaces. The practice is now banned by law in many regions.

In modern times, westernized ideals of beauty have included a long neck in propor-

A woman of the Pordaung tribe in Myanmar (circa 1964) wearing brass rings in order to lengthen her neck. © *Archive Photos.*

tion to the figure as a whole. Women cited as examples of "swan-necked" beauties are socialite Gloria Guinness, actress Audrey Hepburn, and model/actress Iman. Jewelry—chokers, pendants, beads, and other neckwear—has been a popular form of adornment for the neck since ancient times. Body paint and tattooed designs are also applied to this part of the body.

The neck has also been the focus of special products and surgical techniques to reduce the signs of aging. Creams and lotions are applied to moisturize and improve the appearance of the skin. Plastic surgery is used to tighten loose, wrinkled skin on the neck. *See also*: FACE; PLASTIC SURGERY.

Further reading: Joseph Agris, *Cosmetic Surgery* (1996).

Nefertari (Thirteenth Century B.C.E.)

Egyptian queen Nefertari, the favorite consort of King Rameses II, who reigned from 1279–1213 B.C.E., has become a symbol of timeless beauty for many people. The name "Nefertari" is said to mean "the most beautiful of them."

The image of this Egyptian beauty can be seen on ancient temple reliefs and sculptures that reveal an elongated head, slender neck and narrow torso. Historians believe that her head was flattened during childhood, according to the custom at that time, and that her ribcage was probably bound to prevent the bones from growing wide, since a narrow silhouette was highly valued. The queen plucked her eyebrows and adorned her nipples with gold paint. Women did not cover their breasts at certain times, so these areas were decorated.

The tomb of Nefertari is the most beautiful and ornate of all those located in the Valley of the Queens, which the ancients called the "Place of Beauty." *See also* EGYPT, ANCIENT.

Further reading: John MacDonald, *House of Eternity: The Tomb of Nefertari* (1996).

Nefertiti (Fourteenth Century B.C.E.)

The legendary Egyptian beauty, Nefertiti, was married to the Pharoah Akhenaten. Nefertiti was probably the daughter of a general in Akhenaten's army. Her given name, Nefertiti ("the beautiful one has come") was changed to Neferfefruaten ("beautiful is the beauty of aten") after she married the king. Aten was an Egyptian god. One of her husband's most important actions was to move Egypt from polytheism to monotheism, the worship of one god, Aten. So great was her beauty that numerous paintings were made of her. Her husband wrote poems that detailed his admiration of her looks and intellect. In one poem, the king praises her as the "mistress of happiness." Her husband's apparent devotion to her notwithstanding, she vanished mysteriously from court before her death, and it is believed the king sent her away because he became displeased with her for some reason.

Nefertiti was particularly admired for her long neck and shapely head. Historians believe that her head may have been bound when she was a child. At that time, the Egyptians valued a long, oval-shaped head and used boards and cloths to bind the heads of young children when the bones were still soft enough to mold. Busts of the queen show that she used eye makeup and colored her lips, in keeping with the custom of the day. A famous bust of the queen is one of the most admired works of ancient art. It was used as a model to train sculptors. *See also* EGYPT, ANCIENT.

Further reading: Mary Chubb, *Nefertiti* (1954); Evelyn Wells, *Nefertiti* (1964).

New Age Cosmetics

The 1980s saw the rise of an ill-defined social trend known as the "New Age" that includes a wide range of fads, rituals, and beliefs with a general unifying belief in creating spiritual unity and social harmony. The New Age practices prompted the created of New Age cosmetics and personal products that purported to enhance spiritual awareness. Companies that produce these products include Philosophy and 5S, a branch of the giant Japanese cosmetics company Shiseido. They produce soap and other bath products, as well as skin creams, moisturizers, makeup, and nail products. The products come in special colors and scents that are supposed to induce particular emotional and mental effects, for example, increased energy or feelings of tranquility. Based in Arizona, Philosophy offers customers a kit of seven bottles of colored bubble bath called the Rainbow Connection. The brochure instructs people to choose the color of their bath bubbles according to "the area of your emotional life that needs attention." (Green, 1999)

Aromatherapy is part of the New Age approach to beauty. Certain scents are said to produce responses in the body that result in emotional and physical states that enhance attractiveness. *See also* NATURAL PRODUCTS

Further reading: Penelope Green, "Spiritual Cosmetics. No Kidding." *The New York Times* 10 January 1999, pp. 9-1, 5.

Nose

Different shapes and sizes of noses have been considered more or less desirable, and these standards vary with cultures and eras. The nose has also been ornamented with paint and jewelry. People have used mechanical or surgical methods to change its natural shape. In western countries, rhinoplasties ("nose jobs") rank among the most popular types of cosmetic surgery and are performed on both men and women and on increasing numbers of teenagers.

Shape

Several cultures have tried to create a certain shape of nose with mechanical devices. The ancient Mayas admired a long, straight profile, and they attempted to press a growing child's nose into this shape. Parents pressed boards against the front and back of the head to create an elongated profile and flattened front. Grown Mayans could attach a cosmetic nose bridge to fill in any crevices that remained on their noses and foreheads. In some places where large noses are admired, such as New Guinea, parents may try to influence the shape of their children's noses at an early age. A baby's nose is often pressed and pinched to make it wider and longer. Austra-lian aborigines pierced the septum and placed a long stick or bone through it in order to flatten the nose, which they regarded as more attractive.

Ornaments

Nose piercing involves perforating the nasal septum, ala (wing) or other part of the nose, usually the nostril, to insert one or more ornaments. Nose ornamentation has been practiced for centuries in certain countries. People in pre-Columbian America, Polynesia, New Guinea, and India, as well as Native Americans, have worn such ornaments. The size of the hole varies from very small to several millimeters in diameter.

Ornaments are often made from precious metals and jewels, or from animal bones, tusks, feathers, or wood. Among the ancient Aztecs, only the ruler and nobles were permitted to wear gold or silver nose plugs made

A man of the Asmat Region of Indonesia (circa 1976), who has inserted large bones in his pierced septa. © *Jack Fields/CORBIS.*

with precious stones. The Aztecs, along with the Mayans and Incas, often wore gold and jade ornaments.

The practice continues in non-western cultures. The Cuna Indians of Panama paint a black line down the center of the nose and wear a gold ring in the pierced septum. Gold rings and sometimes pendants are placed through pierced septa by people in Nepal, Tibet, and India.

Wearing large ornaments made of animal bones or tusks through a pierced septum is most often seen among warrior cultures, perhaps because it gives a fierce look to the face. Men of the Tuburi tribes, the Solomon Islands, and New Guinea insert the tusks of wild pigs in their nose holes. The Asmat tribe of Irian Jaya inserts large bones in their pierced septa. These may be the bones of animals or human enemies they have slain.

In some cultures, nose piercing is part of the coming-of-age rituals. The Bundi of Papua New Guinea usually pierce the noses of young men between the ages of 9 and 22.

Nose rings can still be seen in parts of West Africa as well. Small gold nose rings are worn by the Fulanis of Mali. These people are known for their fine filigree jewelry.

In western countries, nose piercing and other body piercings became increasingly popular. The trend began during the 1970s, fueled by well-known pop music and film stars who exhibited their own piercings. Young people make up the majority of westerners who choose to have nose piercings, but some adults also wear these ornaments. The piercings are done in the septum, nostril, and on the bridge of the nose. Rings or studs are the most common ornaments worn in nose piercings. Health experts have warned about possible hazards, including infection.

Plastic Surgery

Rhinoplasty, colloquially referred to as a "nose job," refers to a surgery performed to alter the shape and/or size of the nose. A person who dislikes the appearance of his or her nose or who has suffered an injury that changed its shape may choose to have this surgery. Rhinoplasty may also improve the functioning of the nose if the internal nasal structures are not properly aligned (a deviated septum) in a way that causes difficulty in breathing. Reconstructive nose surgery is performed on people of all ages, but cosmetic rhinoplasty is usually not done until a person reaches the teen years, when the nose is completing its growth.

Attempts to reshape the nose date back at least several centuries, when surgeons tried to restore noses destroyed by syphilis. Surgical procedures to reshape the nose for cosmetic purposes were first developed during late decades of the nineteenth century. In the 1920s, some doctors offered wax implants to change the shape of the nose. Subsequent decades brought more sophisticated and safe methods of changing the shape of the nose.

The most common reason for wanting a new nose is to conform with the prevailing standards of beauty. In the 1880s, a surgeon named John Orlando Roe put forth the belief that the shape of the nose was an indicator of various mental characteristics. The different shaped noses of different races indicated their inferiority. Roe changed the shape of the nose surgically, which he believed would have the psychological effect of allowing a person to become integrated into the mainstream. His patients primarily were the Irish (pug nose), African Americans, and Asians.

Since then, most people have sought cosmetic rhinoplasty for simple cosmetic reasons. They want their nose, and hence the rest of the face, to look "better." *See also* BEAUTY STANDARDS; BODY ORNAMENTATION; PLASTIC SURGERY

Further reading: Joseph Agris, *Cosmetic Surgery* (1996); Sander L. Gilman, *Making the Body Beautiful* (1999); John Scofield, "Christopher Columbus and the New World He Found," *National Geographic*, November 1975, 584–623.

Nose Job *See* NOSE; PLASTIC SURGERY.

"Noses"

In the perfume industry, people called "noses" are highly valued for their unusual abilities to distinguish among hundreds of different scents. At any given time, only about two dozen people are considered to be the top "noses" in the world.

Experts believe that this talent for understanding and discriminating among different fragrances is inborn and that these people then spend years perfecting their gift. They can detect subtle differences among scents that seem identical to the average person. They are able to detect individual ingredients in mixtures that contain a hundred or more different ingredients. "Noses" can also estimate the amounts of the different ingredients in a fragrance blend and can predict the results of adding or subtracting various ingredients.

Many of these perfume experts prepare for their careers by studying chemistry. They may go on to specialize in a certain area, such as household products, industrial scents, or top-quality perfumes. These perfume-makers also have their own techniques for developing a new scent, which may take several years. Perfume creator Sophia Grojsman has compared the process to music, which requires a blending of different instruments and notes into a harmonious work. She says, "You could have layers of notes coming through the fragrance, but yet you still feel it's pleasing. If the fragrance is not layered properly, you'll have parts and pieces sticking out, it will make you uncomfortable, something will disturb you about it." (Ackerman, 1991) *See also* NTERNATIONAL FLAVORS AND FRAGRANCES (IFF); PERFUME.

Further reading: Diane Ackerman, *A Natural History of the Senses* (1991); William F. Kaufman, *Perfume* (1974).

O–P

Orthodontics *See* TEETH.

Otoplasty *See* EARS.

Paint, Body *See* BODY DECORATION.

Perfume

The art of making fragrances dates back thousands of years. Egyptian perfume recipes from as long ago as 1600 B.C.E. have been found, and Egyptian perfume artifacts go back to 3000 BC. The word perfume comes from French words meaning "through smoke" because early perfumes were incenses used in religious ceremonies. In ancient times, the use of scents was linked to magic and religion. The Greek words for "scent" and "offering" were the same. The Greeks used perfumes as an offering to the gods, for medicinal purposes, and for hygiene and personal appeal. Different scented oils, herbs, and essences were sometimes applied to different parts of the bodies. The Greek historian and geographer Herodotus (485–425 B.C.E.) described the use of fragrances from Arabia in 450 BC and the trade in spices between Greece and Arabia.

A natural philosopher named The-ophrastus (370–288/5 B.C.E.) wrote about the popularity of floral scents and scents based on a single herb, as well as compound scents with special names: Mendesian, Kypros, Oenanthe, and Susinon, among others. His book *An Enquiry into Plants*, written about 295 BCE, and the treatise *Concerning Odours* (the earliest known written work on the subject of perfumery) provide modern historians with information about perfume in ancient Greece. In Greece, most perfume makers were women. During that era, the Greeks also used spices in perfume-making and dried fragrant plants to make powders they could sprinkle on clothing.

In Arabia, the perfume trade flourished. Arab Kindi wrote *Kitah Kimiya' al'-Itr wa' 'l-Tas 'idat* (The Book of Perfume Chemistry and Distillation). Arabia became the center of the perfume industry and specialized in attar of roses, which was made by distilling the essential oils of the rose.

In addition to attar of roses, other early scents included lavender water. Some historians believe that lavender water was first made during the twelfth century by a German Benedictine nun and mystic, Hildegard of Bingen. She distilled several flowers in the process of making this perfume.

In C.E. 1190, King Philippe Auguste of France became the first European ruler to declare perfumers a professional group, with their own charter. New French laws required perfumers to complete four-year apprentice-ships and three years as journeymen before they could qualify as master perfumers. They were also required to be certified by a jury of professional perfumers.

The first perfume atomizers may have come from Persia. During the twelfth century, Europeans who went to the Middle East as part of the Crusades discovered that the Persians used attractive bottles that enabled them to spray fragrances on themselves and into their surroundings. At the same time, the Crusaders brought back various perfumes and fragrances that became popular in Europe.

Improved methods of distilling scents and blending ingredients led to more progress in perfumery during the Renaissance. European explorers found new routes to the Orient and discovered islands previously unknown. They brought back spices and other ingredients that could be used for scents. Spanish explorers brought plants from the Americas, and Spanish perfumers, who had studied the methods of Arabs living in Spain, used them for scenting gloves and creating new perfumes.

First Perfume

A major development took place in Hungary in the thirteenth century. A Hungarian man created the first known perfume based on alcohol for Queen Elizabeth, who was then in her 70s. This popular scent, called "Hungary Water," also contained the herb rosemary. A Milanese perfumer, Jean Paul Feminis, later used this formula to create an improved version using oils of bergamot, lemon, and orange, local to his region. His nephew, Jean Antoine Farina, continued to develop the formula. Farina moved to Cologne, now in Germany, and sold his scent there, naming it "eau de cologne," or cologne-wasser. This fresh-smelling, fruity scent continued to be produced in modern times both by men and women. Crabtree & Evelyn, a British cosmetics company, sells a modern version made with some of the original ingredients.

Italy became another important center for perfume-making. During the early 1500s, Dominican monks in Florence set up a perfume laboratory where they created a lily-based toilet water that was exported throughout Europe. The monks also designed special fragrances to order for wealthy people. After Catherine de Médici, member of a noble family in Florence, married French King Henry II in 1533, she brought her love of perfume to France, along with her favorite perfumer.

Perfume use at court declined during the early 1600s but was revived with the ascension of the perfume-loving King Louis XIII (1610) came to the throne. His son, Louis XIV (1638–1715) promoted perfume even more than his father had, and the French perfume industry reached new heights. Members of the court scented their clothing, wigs, and leather goods, as well as their surroundings. The king suggested that a different scent be used every day. Favorite essences included hyacinth and orange-flower water, obtained from the hundreds of orange trees the king had planted around his palaces.

His grandson, Louis XV (reigned 1715–1774), also declared that a different scent be used each day, a custom that gave his court the nickname La Cour Parfumeé. Two of the king's mistresses, Madame du Barry and Madame de Pompadour, used scents liberally and demanded expensive gifts of perfumes in jeweled cases. Madame de Pompadour spent an estimated 580,000 francs each year on perfumes. Her favorites were called Eau de Portugal and Huile de Venus. The king's glover-perfumer J.H. Fargeon went bankrupt in 1788, when unpaid bills from the king totaled more than 20,000 British pounds at that time.

In 1709, Nicolas Lemery, a French chemist, suggested that three different groups of scents be designated: one for royals, one for the middle class, and one for the poor.

Perfume use declined in England after Charles I was ousted (1649) but made a comeback during the reign of his son Charles II (reigned 1660–1685). Charles Lilly was the most prominent perfumer of that era, and he wrote a book about the art of making perfume.

Throughout the 1700s, Englishwomen used perfumes when laundering their clothing and to scent their underwear. Anne Marie, the Countess of Neroli, Spain, used the oil from orange blossoms to scent her body, gloves, and bath water. The oil extracted from Seville (or bitter) orange blossoms was named after her. (Oil is also extracted from the blossoms of the sweet orange, the mandarin, and lemon blossoms.)

Developments in the Perfume Industry

Paul Feminis's nephew, Jean Farina, altered the first cologne formula (L'eau Admirable) and renamed it eau de cologne. In 1862, Roger & Gallet of Paris bought and modified the formula , renaming it "Jean Marie Farina." New formulas for eau de cologne were produced through the years, including Guerlain's Eau de Cologne Imperial, made expressly for the Empress Eugenie in 1850. The closest to the original in modern times is 4711 from the Mullhens company in Germany. Modern cologne contains about 70 percent alcohol/water and is from 3 to 5 percent perfume oil.

Floris, a London-based company, is the oldest perfume house in the world. The company started out as a barbershop when it was founded in 1730 by Spaniard Juan Floris. Floris began making fragrances shortly after the barbershop opened, starting with "Lavender," which remained in production through the twentieth century. The company produced fragrances for both men and women. During the eighteenth century, Floris added new fragrances based on floral scents, including "Rose Geranium," "Jasmine," and "Lily of the Valley." During the 1800s, Floris introduced "Malmaison," "Sandalwood," and "Special No. 127." Beginning in 1820, Floris supplied fragrances to the royal family. The company is still family-owned. Between 1901 and 1990, "Edwardian Bouquet," "Florissa," and "Zinnia" joined the roster of Floris fragrances.

An Italian alchemist named Giuseppe Balsamo toured Europe with his wife, selling various perfumes and other scented products that they claimed would make women beautiful.

During the 1800s, perfumes became more subtle, in keeping with the more natural looks in hairstyles and cosmetics. Many people made perfume at home using recipes that were handed down and printed in books. Herb gardens and special flowerbeds provided materials for toilet water, sachets, potpourri, and pomanders. During the Victorian era, it was considered unacceptable to put fragrances directly on the skin. Instead, people scented their gloves, handkerchiefs, and other items of clothing. They also preferred the more diluted version of perfume called toilet water, which contained more alcohol than perfume, and they used simple scents, such as rose, orange blossom, lavender, or strawberry. Musk, which had been very popular for many centuries, fell into disfavor. It was considered too sexual.

Penhaligon's, established in England 1870, served such famous people such as Churchills and the Rothschilds, and had warrants to supply Prince of Wales, Duke of Edinburgh. They produced toiletry articles and colognes and toilet waters for men and women, including Lords (1911) and Bluebell (1978). This company became part of the Laura Ashley group in 1987.

Synthetics and Perfumes

The development of synthetic chemicals for perfumes allowed the perfume-making industry to expand. Synthetic sources of perfumes were first used during the 1700s. Paul Poiret, a Frenchman, was first fashion designer to create a fragrance bearing the designer's name. His line was influenced by Asian styles, and he used exotic essences in his perfume.

Aldehyde refers to a group of chemicals derived from alcohol and some natural plant materials. Together, they make up chemical groups called benzenoid compounds, which were discovered at the end of the 1800s and used to make synthetic materials for perfumes. Very small quantities of aldehyde are added to perfume recipes to give them strength and endurance. Ernest Beaux was the first to use aldehyde in perfumes. He created Chanel No. 5, one of the most famous perfumes in history, for the French designer Coco Chanel.

Frenchman Theophile Thore wrote a book called *Arts de Parfums* in 1836. He claimed that scents inspired the imagination and could be as expressive as colors.

The process of making modern perfumes usually begins with the production of oil that contains the essence of the flowers or other material with the desired fragrance. Pounds of flowers may need needed to produce tiny amounts of oil. Alcohol is added to the mixture to dilute the scent. To produce cologne or toilet water, more alcohol is added than is true for perfume, which is the most concentrated form of fragrance. People known in the perfume business as "noses" sniff and judge various scents as they are being developed. Classifications are floral, green, citrus, oriental, chypre, aldehyde, leather and animal.

Contemporary perfumers include IFF, Quest International (based in Kent, England, with centers in Paris, Brazil, the Netherlands, Japan, and the United States), Roure, Givaudan and Firmenich (Swiss). Roure, which was founded in Grasse in 1821 by Claude Roure, is the oldest of the large perfume manufacturers. The main business complex, located near Paris, includes laboratories, a plant for producing synthetic raw materials, and headquarters. Other factories are located in Grasse and the United States, and the company has affiliates in more than 10 other countries. Roure also operates a perfumery school and research center. The company has produced numerous popular and important fragrances, including Balmain's "Vent Vert" (1945) and "Jolie Madame" (1953), Givenchy's "Ysatis" (1984), and Yves St. Laurent's "Opium" (1977). In 1963, Hoffman LaRoche acquired both Roure and Givaudan. Top-selling fragrances have included Chanel's "Chanel No. 5," Coty's "L'Aimant" (1927) and Nina Ricci's "L'Air du Temps" (1948).

In the modern perfume industry, fragrances are often classified according to their dominant notes, which number about 15. They include floral, spicy, Oriental, floral/fruity, floral/aldahydic, the green, and woody.

Each scent is said to have top notes, middle notes, and base notes. The top notes are those that are noticed first; middle notes are more evident after the perfume has dried on the skin, and the base notes remain at the end. Commercial perfumes usually contain three basic ingredients: a solvent; odorous substances that can number in the hundreds; and a fixative.

By the early 1970s, the cost of producing a new fragrance was about one million dollars. In the process of creating their recipes, modern perfumers had more than 5000 raw materials at their disposal. Companies also spent millions of dollars each year advertising their fragrance lines. Large American perfume manufacturers include Avon, Revlon, Jovan (est. 1969), Estée Lauder, and Charles of the Ritz. In 1989, Cacherel's floral scent, "Anais, Anais" was the best-selling perfume in Great Britain.

Ingredients for perfumes come from all over the world. They include essential oils from leaves, flowers, fruits, woods, roots, and stems. From South America come rosewood and petit-grain; United States produces peppermint; lavender from Spain; sandalwood, lemon grass, and patchouli from India; cloves; roses from France, Bulgaria, and North Africa; the ilang-ilang from Malaya. Common animal products used in perfumes have been ambergris (formed in sperm whale intestines, but which is now banned in international trade); musk formed in small gland in sex organs of male musk deer or muskrat; civet by civet cat; castor, a glandular secretion from beaver. These are mainly used as fixatives. Most modern musk is synthetic rather than taken from the musk deer of the northern Himalayas. Individual perfumes are extremely difficult to duplicate. As the cosmetics company entrepreneur Hazel Bishop said, "They could copy my new lipsticks and cosmetics, but they could not duplicate my fragrances." (Winter, 1976)

Perfume in the United States

The American perfume industry began during the late nineteenth century. One of the first perfume-makers in the United States was

Richard Hudnut, a chemist and druggist who launched "Violet Sec" in 1896. Hudnut, who later added hair products to his business, continued to create new fragrances until 1946.

Synthetic fragrances first appeared in commercial products during the mid-1800s as the demand for perfume increased and perfume makers sought ways to cut costs. Chemists worked to isolate important elements of the essential oils that were used in perfumes and then to reproduce them on a mass scale. Chemists also found ways to extract substances from cheaper sources and alter them to emulate the effect of extracts from more expensive and rarer sources.

Rediscovering what the Persians had already found, the industry developed perfume atomizers, bottles made with a pressure device and operated by squeezing a rubber bulb. These appeared around 1910 and were made by an American company, DeVilbiss.

During the 1920s, beauty entrepreneur Elizabeth Arden urged women to match their perfume to the type of clothing they were wearing. According to Arden, certain perfumes were appropriate for morning, afternoon, or eveningwear.

Fashion designers have created their own signature fragrances and fragrance lines. In recent decades, Liz Claiborne, Tommy Hilfiger, Oscar de la Renta, and others have come out with fragrances. Top American fashion designer Calvin Klein influenced women's clothing styles around the world and launched some successful fragrance lines, including "Eternity" and "Obsession."

Among the less costly lines, Houbigant and Fabergé, which are available in drugstores, have produced popular perfumes. Fabergé has introduced several classic fragrances for both women and men. They include women's scents "Woodhue," "Ambush," and "Tigress." For men, "Canoe" was one of the company's best-sellers.

Among the celebrities who have lent their names to a fragrance are Elizabeth Taylor ("Passion" and "White Diamonds"), Cher ("Uninhibited"), Jaclyn Smith ("California"), Candace Bergen ("Cie"), and Jane Seymour ("Le Jardin de Max Factor").

Some scents have been especially created for particular people. For example, the French couturier Hubert de Givenchy, who designed many clothes for the actress Audrey Hepburn, created a perfume called "L'Interdit" for her in 1957. Cosmetics company executive Estée Lauder began marketing her own personal scent, "Private Collection," in 1973.

During the 1960s, musk and patchouli oils from the Middle East were increasingly popular. This trend coincided with an interest in Eastern philosophy and natural ingredients. These long-lasting fragrances were also mixed with other essences to make personalized scents.

New scents are introduced every year. Most of them fade away, but a few remain popular through the years. Another perfume that quickly became successful was "Giorgio Beverly Hills," launched in 1981. "Giorgio," a floral scent, is regarded as the first "linear" perfume, one that is designed to create a strong first impression.

During the 1990s, companies often marketed new perfumes with an advertising method called the "pull" technique. They heavily promoted a new fragrance before it became available so as to build up a demand from potential consumers. Major perfumes of the 1990s included Calvin Klein's "Escape," Estée Lauder "Spellbound," and Gianni Versace's "V'E VERSACE," which was available in a Baccarat crystal bottle that cost $3,500.

Statistics taken to determine the most popular or best-selling fragrances show that certain fragrances endure, although new brands also rise to the top. In 1999, Global Cosmetics Industry magazine published a list of the top-selling prestige fragrances in U.S. department stores for the year 1998. The women's perfumes were

1. Aromatics Elixir
2. Beautiful
3. Chanel No. 5
4. Eternity
5. Happy
6. Pleasures

7. Tommy Girl
8. Tresor
9. White Diamonds
10. White Linen

For men, the top sellers were

1. Acqua Di Gio Pour Homme
2. Aramis
3. Cool Water
4. Drakkar Noir
5. Eternity for Men
6. Hugo
7. Obsession for Men
8. Pleasures for Men
9. Polo Sport
10. Tommy

Another poll, taken in 1997, showed that African American women preferred (Branna, 1997)

1. White Diamonds
2. Red
3. Giorgio
4. Red Door
5. White Linen
6. Eternity
7. Liz Claiborne
8. Avon
9. Escape
10. CK One

People in different countries vary in perfume use. Researchers found that people in Great Britain preferred lighter scents rather than heavy ones. They bought more talc, powder, and scented bath products then perfume. Women in France bought less talcum powder than British women and used perfume but avoided strong ones. German women regarded expensive perfumes as status symbols. Women in America were more likely to use vary their perfumes according to their mood or the time of day.

Recent advances in technology have changed the way perfume is made. Perfumers can now use infrared and ultraviolet spectroscopy, gas-liquid and thin-layer spectroscopy to detect the various components in a scent. Smells can be analyzed at a molecular level, and computers can be used to store information for later use, so that cer-

tain natural odors can be recreated synthetically.

Nevertheless, synthetics notwithstanding, the future of the perfume industry is at least in part tied to changes in the environment. The climate and quality of the air and soil influence the natural materials that are used to create fragrances. In addition, as more land is used for housing and industrial development, less land is available for planning large quantities of flowers and scented plants. The quality of the flowers and plants also differs from year. *See also* ARABIA; FRAGRANCE; FRAGRANCE FOUNDATION; GRASSE; INTERNATIONAL FLAVORS AND FRAGRANCES (IFF); DE MÉDICIS, CATHERINE; MUSEÉ INTERNATIONALE DE LA PARFUMERIE.

Further reading: Elisabeth Barille, *The Book of Perfume* (1995); Tom Branna, "Fragrance and African-American Women," *Happi*, July 1997; Roy Genders, *Perfume Through the Ages* (1972); Ian Jenkins, *Greek and Roman Life* (1986); A. Hyatt Verrill, *Perfume and Spices* (1940); Ruth Winter, *The Smell Book: Scents, Sex, and Society* (1976).

Permanent Makeup

Permanent makeup, which is also called dermapigmentation or micropigmentation, involves placing pigment, colors, and/or dyes into the skin for a cosmetic effect. It can replace regular cosmetics, including lipstick, eyebrow pencil, and eyeliner and has become more popular during the late twentieth century. Using a process like tattooing, colored pigments are injected on the face to color or fill in the eyebrows, apply eyeliner, or to tint the lips and cheeks various shades of pink, peach, or red. Permanent makeup can also enlarge the lipline and disguise aging lines around the mouth.

Permanent eyelining originated in Asia and became available in the United States during the early 1980s. Lining the top and bottom eyelids on both eyes can take from 20 minutes to 1 hour. It can be applied in a line or in the form of shading blended into the row of eyelashes.

The idea of permanent makeup appeals to people who like to accentuate certain features with makeup but want to save time and effort. Besides convenience, permanent makeup is a completely waterproof makeup that need not be removed at night and will not smear or smudge. It can also create the appearance of eyelashes and eyebrows that have been lost due to illness or chemotherapy, camouflage irregular skin pigment from birthmarks or other conditions, and make irregular features look more symmetrical.

Corrective camouflage is the term for permanent makeup that focuses on restoring a more normal appearance to scars, burned tissue, or skin disorders. Permanent makeup may also appeal to people who wear contact lenses or who are allergic to conventional makeup.

The pigments used in permanent makeup come from plants and are applied with needles that implant the color beneath the skin. Local anesthetic may be given to reduce discomfort. The procedures are usually done in beauty salons.

Potential complications of these procedures are similar to those associated with other types of tattoos. They include allergic reactions to the dye, which may lead to persistent itching and the formation of welts or blisters on the site. Nonsterile needles can cause infections. Blindness is a possible risk when protective eyelid covers are not used during eyelining procedures. Other complications include swelling, scab formation, and irritation. Consumer advocates warn that these procedures can lead to problems, including permanent damage, if a serious allergic reaction occurs around the eyes. Surgery to remove pigment that has caused such a reaction can lead to scarring.

In addition, some beauty experts warn that permanent makeup can become a problem if the color and manner of application becomes outmoded. They point out that aging can cause changes in the contours of the face and features that can make permanent makeup on the eyebrows or lips, for example, look odd or off-balance.

Further reading: Paula Begoun, *Don't Go to the Cosmetics Counter Without Me* (1997); Margie Patlak, "Permanent Eyeliner," *FDA Consumer*, April 1993.

Permanent Wave

The permanent wave, a chemical process used to create lasting curls or waves in the hair, was introduced during the 1900s. The chemical solution used in the permanent wave actually changed the structure of the hair shaft, bending the hair into the new shape. Permanents produced lasting hairdos so women could recreate favorite styles with fewer visits to a hair-stylist and less time and effort at home. Before that time, women had to heat curling irons in a stove add curls and waves. A permanent could set short curly styles, as well as longer, waved styles that would last until the hair grew out and withstand shampooing and wet or windy weather.

London hairdresser Charles Nestle invented a permanent-wave machine in 1906. Electricity enabled Nestle to develop his process, which required about 10 hours from start to finish. Early permanents involved a series of steps. The hair was treated with a chemical that broke down certain chemical bonds, then curlers were used to create curls in the desired shape. An oxidizing agent was applied to reform the hair bonds into their new positions.

During the 1930s, beauty salons or parlors had to use heat to augment the chemicals in these early permanents. A type of permanent called the croquinole involved hooking salon customers up to a bulky machine with heated wires and clamps. Permanent wave machines of this era featured sets of clamps that covered the customer's hair curlers and applied the desired levels of heat. A timer and thermostat were part of this apparatus. During this era, short waved styles, such as those worn by screen actresses Jean Harlow and Claudette Colbert, were popular in western cultures.

During the 1940s, hair salons continued to offer permanent wave treatments, and companies began producing kits so people could give themselves or their children home permanents. These kits were relatively inexpensive and became very popular during the 1940s and 1950s, when structured wavy and curled hairstyles were popular.

Early products produced tight curls and had a strong chemical smell. Improvements through the years resulted in products with lighter, more pleasing scents, and processes that could produce looser curls and waves. The modern cold-wave permanents are available in different strengths to suit different hair types and to create various styles, ranging from loose to tight. Different types of permanents are also sold for people with gray hair and for children. *See also* HAIR, STYLING OF.

Further reading: Richard Corson, *Fashions in Hair: The First 5000 Years* (1965).

Peruke/Periwig *See* WIGS AND HAIR-PIECES.

Piercing, Body *See* BODY ORNAMENTATION.

Plastic Surgery

Procedures performed to alter parts of the body to improve their appearance fall under the general term "plastic surgery." Surgeons general divide plastic surgery into two types. Reconstructive surgery includes operations done to repair or restructure a body part deformed from a birth defect, illness, or trauma. Cosmetic surgery (also called esthetic surgery) is the term that describes medical procedures performed when no objective or medical defect exists, but the person wants a part of the body to look better.

Physicians who perform these procedures are generally specialists in dermatology or plastic and reconstructive surgery. With advanced training, they may be certified by the American Board of Plastic Surgery (ABPS) or dermatology. Physicians from other specialties, however, also do cosmetic surgery without board certification.

Since its inception thousands of years ago, societal attitudes about surgery to change physical appearance has changed various times and has always been accompanied by a certain moral element. Reconstructive surgery, to correct a deformity that is not a person's fault, has generally been viewed as acceptable. In contrast, surgery that is done for the sake of "vanity" has been criticized for that reason.

In the 1970s, with the rise of feminism, some women began to see cosmetic surgery (and other ways of changing their appearance through cosmetics) as part of a centuries-old system that kept women in the role of "sex objects"; that is, how they looked was paramount; their other characteristics, such as intelligence or talent, were subordinate or trivial. Women who came of age during this time may continue to use fewer cosmetics and be less concerned about appearance, although the advance of the physical effects of aging on their appearances may cause some to rethink their positions.

History

The practice of cosmetic surgery dates back to ancient times. Historians believe that surgeons performed nose reconstruction in India around 2000 B.C.E. Convicted criminals had their noses cut off as punishment for certain offenses, and surgeons learned to rebuild them, using skin from the forehead. Certain nasal deformities that interfered with respiratory function were also corrected surgically.

At the end of the sixteenth century, syphilis epidemics brought a surge in cosmetic surgery. Among other effects, syphilis erodes the noses of its victims. In the mid-1700s, a Scottish surgeon, John Taylor, removed burn scars from the face of a woman, apparently with very successful results. Taylor went on to do what was apparently the first purely cosmetic surgery when he corrected a drooping eyelid, now among the most common of cosmetic operations. The societal standards of the day, however, did not support such efforts, and his colleagues were highly critical of Taylor and any other "beauty doctor." Health was beauty; humans need not intervene.

A fresh recurrence of syphilis in the late eighteenth century spurred another surge in cosmetic surgery. Surgeons at New York Hospital were working on methods to correct deformities during the 1820s, and they did an increasing number of operations to change the shape of the nose in the late 1800s.They did not always do so purely to improve appearance, however.

It was war, however, not vanity, that led to many of the contemporary techniques in plastic surgery. Soldiers received disfiguring wounds during World War I (as they had during previous wars), and the medical profession developed new techniques to restore their normal appearance as much as possible. That physicians were able to do much more plastic surgery (without which the person would still survive but be deformed) was linked to the availability of anesthesia and antiseptic techniques that prevented postsurgical infections. As the field expanded, new techniques developed to restore the appearance of people who were injured, burned, or born with disfiguring birth marks or birth defects, such as cleft palates.

In the early years of the twentieth century, vanity became a more acceptable motive for plastic surgery. Surgeons began to perform elective operations on people who wanted to change a physical feature they disliked or to look younger, a practice now termed cosmetic surgery. For example, they sought ways to fill in lines and wrinkles, such as silicone injections (first used in the 1950s), collagen injections, and "threading," a technique in which gelatin suture material (the kind used to close surgical incisions or wounds) is placed inside a wrinkle. This technique is often used in the lip and forehead area.The body produces collagen to fill the empty space that remains after the suture dissolves.

Plastic Surgery Today

Plastic surgery, done for whatever reason, does carry some risk. Complications occur in 10 to 15 percent of the procedures, some specific to the type of surgery, others risks that accompany any surgery. They include nerve damage, abnormal scarring, adverse reactions to anesthesia, hemorrhaging, and deformity or, in extreme cases, death. The complication has not deterred those who seek to improve their appearances. More and more people elect to have cosmetic surgery every year.

Multiple factors probably explain this increase. Medical techniques have improved enough so that the procedures yield results highly satisfactory to many patients. At the same time, the aging "baby boom" population may be particularly eager to retain a youthful appearance. People are living longer than they used to, and they want to look youthful as long as possible. Because health insurance does not cover purely cosmetic procedures, patients pay these bills themselves.

In recent decades, however, many younger people are having cosmetic surgery. Some are in their teens and twenties. Many of these patients are also using credit cards or loans, going into debt to finance the procedures. About two-thirds of the people who had cosmetic surgery in the late 1990s reported family incomes below $50,000.

In recent years, surgeons have continued to develop innovations in cosmetic surgery. They created less invasive procedures and were able to make smaller incisions that could be hidden in the hairline and natural folds of the skin. The result was less scarring and shorter recovery periods. Procedures are often performed in outpatient facilities rather than during hospital stays.

The new technology (much of which is used in other types of surgery as well) includes such things as the endoscope, a lighted tube only one-fourth inch in diameter, with a tiny video camera attached. The surgeon can make a small cut and insert the endoscope, which then transmits a much larger image onto a video monitor. Surgeons also began to use precision lasers to remove wrinkles and lines, which has eliminated some of the use of chemicals.

Plastic surgeons now perform cosmetic surgery on virtually all parts of the body. Among the most popular procedures are the following.

Abdominoplasty. Often called a "tummy tuck," it is designed to tighten loose abdominal skin and repair weak muscles in the abdominal wall, both of which may result from substantial weight loss in general or after pregnancy.

Abdominoplasty became more popular during the late twentieth century in the United States and other countries where people placed a high value on a toned, slender, youthful-looking body. Tabloid newspapers and gossip columns sometimes mentioned the names of celebrities who had undergone a "tummy tuck" or other cosmetic procedures to improve their appearance. The desire to retain a youthful appearance is no longer confined to women. Abdominoplasty was one of the ten cosmetic surgeries most often requested by American men. Surgeons can also excise stretch marks. These operations cost around $5,000 to $10,000 in the United States during the 1990s. Although men are turning in increasing numbers to cosmetic surgery, more women still undergo plastic surgery. This and other procedures designed to improve the appearance have become increasingly popular in countries that place a high value on looks and youthfulness.

Liposuction. During the 1970s, plastic surgeons developed a procedure called liposuction (or tumescent liposuction). In this procedure, a tube called a cannula is attached to a suction machine to draw out the fat. Liposuction is considered a contouring or "resculpting" procedure rather than a way to lose unwanted weight. People may dislike fat deposits that remain in certain localized areas of their body, despite dieting and exercise. Surgeons use the technique cosmetically to remove undesired fat from the hips, buttocks, thighs, stomach, knees, face, and other areas. Liposuction may be done in conjunction with other cosmetic surgery. It also has medical uses, such as removing lipomas (noncancercous fatty tumors). Liposuction is now the most frequently performed cosmetic surgery in the United States among people 35-50.

Although many candidates for the surgery view liposuction as a quick fix for an abdomen or thighs that are larger than they like, the procedure remains somewhat controversial in medical circles. Because studies suggest that the offending fat—often deemed "cellulite" —is virtually identical in composition to the fat that people can lose through diet and exercise, some medical professionals and others question the procedure and suggest that liposuction patients not turn to surgical remedies. Any surgery involves risk, and some professionals argue that no surgery should be performed in the absence of a documented medical need.

Brachioplasty. This is a cosmetic surgical procedure to tighten the loose skin of the upper arm. People who dislike the look of sagging skin in that area, caused by the aging process or weight loss, may elect to have this procedure, which may include liposuction to remove excess fat from the arm and tightening or resurfacing the skin on the hands. Women are more likely to have a brachioplasty than men.

Blepharoplasty. An eye-lift, called a blepharoplasty, is a form of cosmetic surgery designed to erase lines from the eye area and/or to eliminate drooping eyelids. After making incisions along the creases of the eye, the surgeon removes excess skin and fat to open up the area and give a more youthful appear-

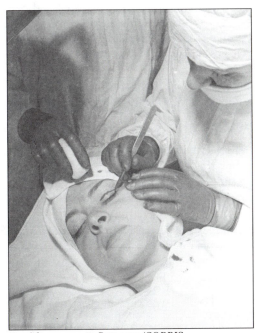

Eye-lift surgery. © *Bettmann/CORBIS.*

ance. A brow-lift may also be done to lift drooping upper eyelids. In this procedure, incisions are made at the hairline, and a portion of the forehead muscle is removed. The surgeon then uses small sutures to close the incisions. Eye surgery is one of the most popular and one of the least complicated types of cosmetic surgery. Eyelid surgery is the most common procedure currently performed for people aged fifty-one and older. It may be performed alone or along with other procedures and does not usually leave obvious scars. Women have made up the majority of people who had eye-lifts, but the number of men seeking the surgery increased after the 1970s.

Soft Tissue Augmentation. These include cosmetic procedures designed to alleviate wrinkles, lines, scarring, and depressed areas of skin. Injections of collagen, body fat, and a substance called Fibrel were being used for this purpose during the 1990s. The main sites for augmentation are on the face and, occasionally, the hands. Procedures on the face are done to get rid of frown lines between the eyes, lines around the mouth, "crow's feet" around the eyes, and scarring that results from acne or injuries.

With the desire to look youthful that currently prevails, surgeons have developed new approaches to counteracting the effects of aging on the area surrounding the eyes. Among other techniques, they surgically smooth out the circular muscle that opens and closes the eye, making the folds of that muscle thinner so that it cannot contract as much. For especially heavy wrinkles, some surgeons remove a part of the muscle itself. The effects of this surgery, which requires deep incisions, last five to ten years.

Controversy surrounds a related procedure called anchor blepharoplasty when it is used to give people with Asian eyes a fold that imparts a Caucasian look. Critics claim that a western ideal of beauty is being foisted upon other cultures and that people should value their own heritage and natural looks.

By 1999, surgeons performed about 700,000 cosmetic operations each year. Ac-

cording to the American Society of Plastic and Reconstructive Surgeons, a 63 percent rise in cosmetic surgery in America occurred between 1981 and 1988. Statistics showed that people were having these operations at younger ages. About one-fourth of the people seeking cosmetic surgery have had one or more procedures before. Most have (43 percent) have more than one procedure done at the same time, and women outnumber men ten to one.

Men and Cosmetic Surgery

Nevertheless, the number of men seeking cosmetic surgery also increased steadily after the 1970s. By 1997, some surgeons reported that about 20 percent of their patients were men. In the past, men had said that their reasons for having such procedures were related more to professional and career concerns than to a desire to look younger; however, by the 1990s, a higher percentage of men said they had chosen to have cosmetic surgery for appearance's sake. Some men still said they wished to maintain a younger appearance for career reasons, given the possibility that some companies are "ageist" and favor younger or younger looking job candidates. In the United States in 1998, more than 99,000 men had liposuction, eyelid surgery, or face-lifts (11 percent of the 89,000 done in the United States in 1997), as well as other cosmetic procedures. In one poll, 53 percent of the men said they approved of cosmetic surgery (compared to 59 percent of women).

Hair transplants were the most commonly performed procedure for men. More than 11,000 men had breast lifts and breast reductions. Men also had cosmetic surgery to firm their chins, alleviate wrinkles, tighten sagging jowls, pin back protruding ears, remove fatty pockets beneath the eyes, and tighten their eyelids. Another popular procedure among men was liposuction to remove fat from around the waistline. Men who had rhinoplasty (nose reshaping) were younger than those who opted for other procedures. A small number of men underwent procedures to augment their cheeks, chins, pectoral muscles, calves, and penises. The American Academy of Cosmetic Surgery (AACS) reported that in 1998 the five most popular cosmetic procedures for men were: abdominal liposuction, nose surgery, hair transplants, eyelid surgery and face-lifts. During the early 1990s, men asked cosmetic surgeons for fuller lips, higher cheekbones, strong chins, and straight noses (in contrast to the narrow concave shape that was more popular in the 1970s).

Surgeons reported that, in general, men had a lower tolerance for pain than their female counterparts and required more medication before and after surgery. Because men's skin is thicker than women's and contains more blood vessels, more bleeding may occur, but for the same reason, men heal more quickly.

Implants

By the 1990s, people could have implants put into their buttocks, cheeks, forehead, nose, jowls, lips, chin, chest, and calves. Facial sculpturing—reshaping the face using implants, liposuction, and other surgery—was increasingly popular. The procedures available for face sculpturing included rhinoplasty ("nose job"), otoplasty (pinning back the ears), genioplasty (chin implants /reshaping), malarplasty (cheek implantation), and removal of facial fat through liposuction.

Plastic surgery on breasts began in the late nineteenth century, with breast reduction or reshaping after a woman had had surgery for cancer or another serious disease. By the 1930s, however, surgeons were performing the surgery for purely cosmetic reasons.

Before World War II, surgeons did little surgery to enlarge breasts, although one Austrian surgeon tried paraffin injection in the 1890s. (Haiken, 1997) They next tried using fatty tissue transplanted from elsewhere on a woman's body, but the body reabsorbs fat. This technique also resulted in lumps, and made it difficult to detect abnormal lumps that might be malignant. The notion of implanting something began in the 1950s and was very controversial. Surgeons first used sponge implants, then began injecting liquid silicone. Liquid silicone "migrates" elsewhere in the body, however, and that practice was became the subject of both controversy and litigation. Breast reconstruction following cancer surgery accounts for about 20 percent of augmentation procedures in recent years.

People who wanted to change the contours of their face sought cheek augmentation, which had originally been used only to correct certain kinds of birth defects. In 1990, surgeons performed more than 2,000 cheek-augmentation surgeries in the United States. They also performed close to 13,300 chin implants on people who wished to increase the prominence of their chins (a receding chin traditionally being associated with a weak character). In some chin implant surgeries, surgeons also repositioned the bones of the chin.

The quest for the perfect body seems unlikely to end. Daily newspapers in major metropolitan areas contain advertisements placed by prominent plastic surgeons. Magazine articles, although they are generally balanced in their coverage and so mention the risks, continue to cover cosmetic surgery. The trend seems likely to continue, given that it is unlikely that humans will ever completely accept the notion that people who are old are not identical to people who are young. Similarly, the quest for the "perfect" body (an ideal that changes) is unlikely to vanish. *See also* BREASTS; CELLULITE; EARS; EYES; FACE; HAIR TRANSPLANTS; IMPLANTS (COSMETIC); LEGS; LIPS; NOSE.

Further reading: Suzanne Alexander, "Egged on By Moms, Many Teen-agers Get Plastic Surgery," *The Wall Street Journal*, 24 September 1990, 1; American Society of Dermatologic Surgeons (ASDS), "Abdominoplasty" (1998), "Tumescent Liposuction" (Form #003, 1994), "Soft Tissue Augmentation" (Form #006, 1996); American Society of Dermatologic Surgeons, Fact Sheets, 1993-1998; Jennifer Drawbridge, "Implants, Dangerous Curves," *Mirabella*, August 1991, 104–108; Sander L. Gilman, *Making the Body Beautiful: A Cultural History of Aesthetic Surgery* (1999); Elizabeth Haiken, *Venus Envy: A History of Cosmetic Surgery* (1997); Claudia Kalb, "Our Quest to Be Perfect," *Newsweek*, 9 August

1999, 52ff; Maggie Paley, "Scalpel Junkies," *Mirabella*, January 1991, 74–76; Janet Carlson Reed and Diane Guernsey, eds., "Comprehensive Guide to Cosmetic Surgery," *Town and Country*, March 1999, 144–162; Judith Rodin, *Body Traps* (1992); University of Iowa, Department of Plastic Surgery, "Plastic Surgery of the Eyes," 1999; Beth Weinhouse, "Cosmetic Surgery for Men," *Town and Country*, March 1999, 158.

Pola

The Pola company, one of the top cosmetics manufacturers in Japan's direct sale industry, was founded in 1929. Pola made women's cosmetics, as well as hair care products and a perfume for men.

The company has been especially active in the area of research and development. More than 300 researchers were working on research about skin and skin care as of 2000. The company also prides itself on its advanced technology and on quality control in order to produce pure, safe products. The company claimed that its laboratory environment was the same as that required in the manufacturing of medical and pharmaceutical products.

By 1999, about 6 million customers used the products, which were sold by 200,000 salespeople in 21 countries. In addition to its cosmetics for women, Pola offered hair care products for men and a men's fragrance called "Testardo." Ads for this fragrance said that the Andract essence used to make it had been scientifically tested and found to produce a state of excitation in women and relaxation in men.

Further reading: "About Pola Japan," http://www.pola.com; Information Sheets from Pola.

Powder Rooms *See* WIGS AND HAIR-PIECES.

Powers, John Robert *See* MODELING AND MODELS.

Presley, Elvis (1935–1977)

Rock-music legend Elvis Presley popularized the duck-tail hairstyle and sideburns that were worn by numerous young men around the world during the 1950s. Presley wore his dark hair in a slight pompadour that swept back behind the ears, then combed back so the sides met at the back of the neck. The hair was slicked down with pomade, and men could be seen slicking back their hair with a comb they sometimes tucked under the sleeve of their T-shirts. A few strands of hair fell onto the singer's forehead.

The singer, who was born in Tupelo, Mississippi, began his career as a child when he performed country gospel music. He recorded his first songs for Sun Records in Memphis in 1954. His backers were excited that a white musician might have the sound and feel of the African Americans who had developed a form of popular music known as "rhythm and blues," the predecessor of "rock and roll."

Colonel Tom Parker began managing Presley's career starting in 1955. Tens of millions of people saw Elvis Presley perform on the popular television shows of the 1950s including *The Ed Sullivan Show* and *The Steve Allen Show*. When he appeared on Milton Berle's *Texaco Star Theater*, he was nicknamed "Elvis the Pelvis" because of the suggestive way he moved his hips onstage. He recorded eight of his lifetime top ten songs during the 1950s.

The popularity of the "Presley" hairstyle created a huge demand for men's hair-care products, including creams, tonics, and brilliantines. These products tended to give hair a wet or greasy appearance, which later gave the hit musical about the 1950s, "Grease," its name. Fans were upset when Presley was inducted into the U.S. Army in 1958, and photographers took pictures of him as he received his short "G I haircut." His situation was satirized in the hit play and movie *Bye, Bye Birdie*.

Presley continued his career after he was discharged in 1959 and appeared in numerous movies. He recorded other songs, eventually charting more songs on Billboard's Hot

Elvis Presley. © *NBC/Globe Photos, Inc.*

ucts, and other items. Sales in the 1999/2000 fiscal year were $9.66 billion.

A soap maker, James Gamble, and a candle maker, William Proctor, formed the company in 1837. Using the expanding railway system and riverboats, their company grew, selling $1 million worth of goods in 1859. During the Civil War, Procter & Gamble was the major source of candles and soaps to the Union forces.

In 1879, an accident at the company's factory led to the production of the famous Ivory brand soap. A worker forgot to add olive oil to a batch of soap and failed to turn off the heating machine. The resulting soap came out colored white and floated because it contained tiny air bubbles. Executives sent samples of this white soap to a chemical laboratory for analysis, and the chemists commented that it was "99 and 44/100 percent pure." The soap was cheaper to produce than higher-quality imports.

An advertising company came up with the name "Ivory" and launched a national campaign describing Ivory as "the soap so pure it floats." Sales of Ivory soap increased, especially after the company advertised the soap on the radio during the 1930s. In 1939, the company spent $9 million on the radio ads that punctuated serial dramas. Soap ads were so common on these shows that they got— and retained—the name "soap operas."

The company, which had set up research laboratories in the 1880s, continued to develop new products, including the well-known Head & Shoulders anti-dandruff shampoo. Procter & Gamble acquired pharmaceutical companies and three cosmetic firms—Max Factor, Noxell, and Ellen Betrix—during the 1980s and 1990s. *See also* ADVERTISING (U.S.); SOAP.

Further reading: Charles Goodrum and Helen Dalrymple, *Advertising in America: The First 200 Years* (1990); Proctor and Gamble, "General Information," "FAQs," http://www.pg.com.

100 than any other artist. During the last years of his life, "The King" often performed in Las Vegas nightclubs wearing vivid and glittering stage costumes. Journalists sometimes criticized the star for his weight gain over the years. As of 1999, Presley's record of 10 consecutive number one hit songs was still unbroken.

Presley died at age 42 of a drug overdose. His memory appears to be eternal, however, as thousands of fans journey to his mansion Graceland each year. He retained the same hair style until his death. *See also* HAIR, STYLING OF.

Further reading: Richard Corson, *Fashions in Hair: The First 5000 Years* (1965); Tony Gentry, *Elvis Presley* (1994); Robert Love, *Elvis Presley* (1986).

Procter & Gamble Company

Based in Cincinnati, Ohio, The Procter & Gamble Company is a large conglomerate that manufactures and sells personal and hair care products, as well as foods, paper prod-

Punk *See* "LOOKS."

R

Renaissance Europe

The historical period known as the Renaissance took place in Europe between the years 1400 and 1600. Along with a general revival of culture and emphasis on art and beauty, the era also brought more stylish clothing and greater use of cosmetics. Women wore upswept hairstyles that suited their fashionable high-collared dresses. By using a wire frame under their hair, they could shape it into a style that resembled a heart.

Red hair became popular during the reign of Elizabeth I (1558–1603), and remained in favor. At the end of the 1500s, the Italian artist Titian painted beautiful women with reddish-gold hair, which has become known as "Titian red." Venetian women used a mixture made from alum, soda, rhubarb, and sulfur to achieve this tint. After applying it, they sat in the sun so that the direct heat would activate the chemicals. Other women (and men, too) who sought lighter hair used dyes made from onion skin.

A new hairstyle for men emerged in sixteenth-century France after King Francis I (reigned 1515–1547) burned the ends of his hair with a torch. Other men copied the king's new, shorter style, along with shorter beards and mustaches. In France, women frizzed the hair around their faces and coiled the back hair in a net above their collars. They applied a mixture made from pulverized flowers to their hair. Hair was also powdered with different substances, depending on the color.

Brunettes used violet powder, blondes chose flour or light powder, and people with gray hair used white. Gummy or paste-like substances helped the powder adhere to the hair.

Subsequently, men's hairstyles became longer and more elaborate. Beards and mustaches, popular during the reign of Henry VIII, remained in vogue for English men. King Louis XIV of France, whose reign lasted from 1643 to 1715, inspired many men to adopt his lush hairstyle with long curls. Usually, they wore wigs to achieve this look.

In the seventeenth century, a time when bathing with water was discouraged, people rinsed their mouths with water that was mixed with wine or vinegar, wiped their ears, and rubbed their heads with a scented towel or sponge before combing. Scented towels were also used to wipe off the armpits, face, and torso.

Wealthier people powdered their hair beginning in the latter part of this era, and the custom spread to include most of Europe and people of all ages by the 1700s. The lack of powder or powdered wigs labeled a person as being of low social status. People powdered their heads at night, then combed it out in the morning, at which time it drew out excess oil.

The heavy clothing of the times, made from embroidered velvets and brocades, exacerbated the build-up of body odors. Perfume was increasingly important during these years and beyond dispelling odors, also indicated a person's social class.

These years marked a time of increased differentiation in the appearance of men and women and their grooming and dressing habits. Increasingly, men in towns rejected bright colors and dressed more somberly, choosing black, gray, and white clothing. This emphasized their roles in government, business, and other serious positions. *See also* MÉDICIS, CATHERINE DE; ELIZABETH I; FRAGRANCE; HAIR COLOR; HAIR, STYLING OF; PERFUME.

Further reading: Francois Boucher, *20,000 Years of Fashion: The History of Costume and Personal Adornment* (1965); E.R. Chamberlin, *Everyday Life in Renaissance Times* (1965); Richard Corson, *Fashions in Makeup* (1972).

Revlon Company

Founded in 1932, Revlon started out with one product, long-lasting nail polish, and became the largest retail cosmetics and fragrance company in the United States. The multinational company, whose vision is to provide "glamour, excitement, and innovation through quality products at affordable prices," had billions of dollars in annual sales by the 1990s.

Charles Haskell Revson (1906–1975) was a primary founder of Revlon, Inc., He was president of Revlon from 1932 to 1962 and chairman from 1962 to 1975. Revson was born in Boston, the son of a cigar-maker. As a young man, he worked as a salesman in a women's clothing store, then left to sell nail polish at a cosmetics firm. In 1932, at the height of the Great Depression, he did not receive an expected promotion and left the company to begin an entrepreneurial venture with his brother Joseph and a chemist named Charles Lachman.

With only $300 among them, they founded Revlon (the "l" came from Lachman's name), focusing on the development of a new and improved form of nail polish. Revlon nail polish was made from pigments instead of dyes, using a unique manufacturing process. Their polish went on more smoothly and covered better than other brands that were available at the time. Revlon polish also came in a variety of colors.

Initially, Revlon sold mostly to beauty salons but expanded its market to drug and department stores. Within six years, Revlon was earning more than a million dollars a year. In 1935, Revson's other brother, Martin, joined the business. The company was the first to offer consumers matching polish and lipsticks, which it began selling in 1940. That year, Revlon sales hit $2.8 million.

During World War II, Revlon factories produced items for the war effort. They included first-aid kits and dye markers for the U.S. Navy. When the war ended, Revlon began making manicure and pedicure tools. Company executives devised clever marketing plans that involved the launching of new lipstick and nail enamel products twice the year, just as fashion designers presented their new design lines each spring and fall. The company also produced creative ads that took advantage of new marketing opportunities in the fast-growing medium of television.

In 1952, the Revlon Company launched a landmark advertising campaign called "Fire and Ice," featuring its new line of lipsticks and nail polish. The ads, which were praised for their stunning visuals and clever text, are considered to be the first in which cosmetics were strongly associated with sexuality. The ads appeared in national magazines, including *Vogue*, the upscale fashion and beauty publication for women, and showed a beautiful dark-haired model dressed in a silver dress and vivid red cape against a glittering background. For this high-priced campaign, Revlon hired Dorian Leigh, a top model in New York during the 1940s and 1950s. The ad copy was designed to encourage women to identify with the glamorous woman and enticing life portrayed in the ad. It asked women questions such as: "Do you close your eyes when you're kissed? Have you ever danced with your shoes off?" Another ad said "Fire and Ice" products were "for you who love to flirt with fire . . . who dare to skate on thin ice." The deep red color of the lipstick and nail enamel was described as "lush and passionate scarlet." Women who worked on the Fire and Ice ad campaign said they were inspired by Italian movies made after World

War II in which women were sensual and feminine but strong.

An astute businessman, Revson realized that he should spend most of his money to promote rather than produce the products. In 1955, he recognized the potential for advertising on television and sponsored a popular quiz show called *The $64,000 Question* (which was later taken off the air when it was found that contestants had been coached). He raised the costs of his products and invested more money in advertising and distribution, giving Revlon product lines alluring and provocative names, such as "Moon Drops," and "Ultima II." Revson was known as a strong executive with excellent marketing insights. Under his direction, the company produced numerous types of makeup items as well as a variety of fragrances. Revlon stock was listed publicly on the New York Stock Exchange in 1956.

The company dramatically increased its name recognition and international sales during the 1960s. Revlon products came to symbolize the "American Look," as ads appeared in magazines and TV ads throughout the world featuring attractive American models.

By 1965, Revson was the only remaining original partner in the firm, which maintained a large market-share in its industry. That year, the company introduced a line of men's products called Braggi. During the 1970s, Revlon products were available in 85 countries, and Revson was spending about $65 million each year on advertising. Revson died in New York City in 1975.

During the 1980s and 1990s, more celebrities, international models, and women of color, representing multicultural views of beauty, were featured in Revlon ads and endorsed Revlon products. A product line called "Revlon Internationals" featured shampoos and conditioners labeled "French," "Far Eastern," "Scandinavian," "Australian," "Latin American," and "Ivory Coast" (African). Reflecting the growing trend toward wider views of beauty, the text for a 1990 ad read, "Because today there is no single standard of beauty . . . "

A series of ads during the late 1980s and early 1990s declared that "the most unforgettable women in the world wear Revlon." This ad campaign featured talk-show host/actress Oprah Winfrey, actress Melanie Griffith, supermodel Cindy Crawford, and others.

The company produced numerous successful fragrance lines. One popular brand called "Charlie," a light scent created by Florasynth perfumers, was billed as the "sexy, young fragrance" and designed to appeal to active modern women, especially career women. Charlie products, which debuted in 1973, had sales topping $1 billion in 1977 and continued to sell well into the 1990s. The fragrance was especially popular in North America and Europe.

Revlon was purchased by a subsidiary of MacAndrews and Forbes Holdings in 1985. In 1987, the group also purchased Almay, another cosmetics company, known for its hypo-allergenic products.

Although Revlon was chiefly known for its cosmetics and fragrances, the company was also a leader seller of skin care and personal care products. Revlon products were sold in 175 countries and territories as of the 1990s, a decade when it reached the position of the number one brand in mass color cosmetics. *See also* ADVERTISING (U.S.); BEAUTY INDUSTRY (U.S.); COSMETICS; HANDS; MAX FACTOR & COMPANY; MODELING AND MODELS.

Further reading: Eileen Ford, *The Ford Models Crash Course in Looking Great* (1985); Andrew Tobias, *Fire and Ice: The Story of Charles Revson* (1976).

Rhinoplasty *See* NOSE; PLASTIC SURGERY.

Roman Empire

The civilization based in ancient Rome, known as the Roman Empire, lasted from around 27 B.C.E. to C.E. 476. Clothing and grooming were important in ancient Rome, and people of means devoted much attention to their appearance. They also took elaborate baths as part of their grooming rituals. Public baths in Rome were large facilities that contained special rooms for exercising, massage, dining, and socializing, as well as bathing. The excrement of crocodiles was used for mud baths.

Beards and long hair were fashionable during the early republic, which began in 500 B.C.E., when Greek styles were still influential. During the late republic and early empire periods (the empire dates from 27 B.C.E.), men shaved off their beards and wore their hair shorter.

Barbers, called *tonsors,* lived in the homes of wealthy people as part of their staff. Less wealthy men visited the local *tonstrina* (barbershop) to have their hair styled and cut. These social shops contained mirrors. A sculptured hairstyle created with the use of curling irons became popular, especially among young men.

Women's hairstyles also changed from the early to the late republic, moving from long hair worn in a bun to short, curled, and pouffed hairstyles. Wealthy women wore a great deal of jewelry, including gold chains, anklets, bracelets, and rings, as well as earrings made from precious metals and gems stones. Women who could not afford real jewels wore fake gems made of colored glass.

Women's makeup included a chalky powder called cerussa, red lip and cheek coloring, and dark eye liner and eyebrow color. Women in the middle and upper classes owned numerous cosmetics and implements, including razors, brushes, wigs, and perfumes. When they went out, many Roman women carried a small grooming kit attached to their belts with a ring. The kit contained nail and hair cleaners, tooth sticks to remove food particles from the teeth, tweezers, a small mirror, and cosmetics.

Young slaves called *cosmetae* were assigned to make beauty preparations for people in wealthy households. Face care included the application of a strong-smelling cream made from sweat extracted fromsheep's wool, which was used at night. Blemishes were treated with barley flour and butter. Different unguents for the skin were made from flowers, eggs, honey, flour, and other ingredients.

Poppaea, wife of the emperor Nero (reigned 54–68 B.C.E.) spent hours on her beauty routines and hair styling. She used the finest perfumes, made from rare floral essences and oil of ambergris, a valuable substance obtained from sperm whales that served as a fixative. Slaves prepared her scented baths and kept her clothing and jewels in scented boxes. Creams were made of milk products and crocodile mucus. It was said that Poppaea's daily bath contained the milk of 500 female asses.

Hair care was elaborate among upperclass Roman women, who set the fashions for women of other classes. Hairstylists called *matrices* applied oils to hair, and used brushing and massage to beautify the hair. Young women often wore simple styles, for example, a knot at the back of the neck fastened with a pin. Another popular style for adolescent girls was to make rod-shaped curls, piled atop the head. Older women were more likely to wear a bun in the back with small curls arranged around the face. Julia, the sister of Augustus (reigned 27 B.C.E.–C.E. 14), popularized tow-

Nero, the fifth emperor (65 C.E.) of Rome. © *Hulton/Archive Photos.*

ers of fancy curls, achieved with hot irons. Later, another member of the royal family, Sabina, chose to wear a simple coiffure parted in the middle and pulled down into waves on either side. Some women wore thin woven nets ornamented with golden flies over their hair, as well as silk ribbons trimmed with jewels and diadems.

Women tinted their gray hairs with dyes made from German herbs, according to the Roman poet Ovid (43 B.C.E.–C.E. 17), who described cosmetic use and hair care in his book *Art of Love*. The hair coloring he mentions may have been some herbs found in the Rhine district, that were called Batavian foam or Wiesbaden soap tablets. This substance could change a woman's hair color from dark to different shades of amber and red. They used another mixture, made of ashes and fat, to cleanse the hair. Ovid also described the use of wigs and false hair. Some people wore wigs after the dyes they used to bleach their hair made it fall out.

During the Roman Empire, particularly during the first and second centuries, fragrances were extremely important, both for household and personal use, even though the sale of perfumes had once been banned by law (in 188 B.C.E.). By the first century B.C.E., both men and women used perfumes, some of which were imported from Egypt, India, and Arabia. Materials for making fragrances came from inside and outside the Roman Empire. Thousands of tons of myrrh and frankincense were brought in from other lands, primarily Arabia. The Romans also extracted oils from flowers, roots, and leaves and used them in their baths, as well as in preparations that were worn on the body. Perfume became so important that at one time, a special women's senate was convened to test different perfumes that were being developed. Pliny (C.E. 23–79), the great Roman historian, describes the use of various fragrant flowers and plants in perfumes and medicinal preparations.

The Romans used scent in different forms, including solid and liquid unguents, scented powders, and scented oils. Single flowers and mixtures of flowers were combined with fats, oils, resins, herbs, spices, and other materials to create these products. Roses were popular ingredients, and Capua, in an eastern region known for its roses, became the perfume center of the empire. In Rome, people visited perfume shops to meet with friends as well as to purchase scented products. Indeed, the Romans used fragrances for so many purposes that people even scented their horses and the water that sprang from their fountains. They sprayed perfumed water on guests during their parties.

Some mirrors, pomade jars, combs, tweezers, hairpins, perfume bottles, and other items from this era have survived and can be seen in museums. *See also* ARABIA; BATHS; COSMETICS; FRAGRANCE; HAIR COLOR; HAIR, STYLING OF; PERFUME; WIGS AND HAIRPIECES.

Further reading: J.P.V.D. Balsdon, *Roman Women: Their History and Habits* (1962); Jane F. Gardner, *Women in Roman Law and Society* (1986); Mary Johnston, *Roman Life* (1957).

Rouge *See* COSMETICS; FACE.

Rubinstein, Helena (1870–1965)

Helena Rubinstein was one of the first and most successful cosmeticians and founders of a large cosmetics business bearing her name. A native of Krakow, Rubinstein was one of eight daughters of a middle-class Polish Jewish family. In 1890, Rubinstein left Poland to visit relatives in Australia, taking along jars of the face cream her mother used. Created by a Polish chemist, the cream contained essence of almonds and various herbs. Friends and acquaintances who admired Helena Rubinstein's complexion asked her if they could buy this skin cream, which helped to reduce the effects of their harsh climate. After her supply ran out, she sent home for more cream, which she sold for $1 a jar.

Rubinstein borrowed money to open her own beauty salon, where she sold face cream and other products made by the Polish chemist. Rubinstein also provided such services as analyzing a woman's skin type and recommending a particular cream. At that time, women used rice powder on their faces, but it tended to clog pores. Rubinstein set out to create more subtle, flesh-tinted powders that would not block pores.

To expand her business and learn more about cosmetology, Rubinstein returned to Western Europe. She studied the makeup techniques of actresses and learned how to use eyeshadow, then taught her clients how to apply it. She also worked with well-known dermatologists. In 1908, she opened a salon in London; four years later, she opened her Paris salon.

Rubinstein moved to New York in 1915 after World War I broke out in Europe. There, she opened a new, larger cosmetics business and salon. She also began a wholesale distribution business, in addition to her research and manufacturing operations and numerous salons. Her cosmetics empire expanded to include salons all over the world. During the 1920s, the Helena Rubinstein Company offered women more than 600 cosmetics, including 115 shades of lipstick and the first-ever line of medicated cosmetics. By 1950, the corporation operated manufacturing plants on five continents.

Rubinstein continued to bring out new products in the early 1960s. She was the first cosmetics manufacturer to create lines for different types of skin—oily, normal, and dry. She also introduced more eye makeup. Rubinstein had been promoting the use of more eye makeup and had applied dramatic eye makeup on actresses for certain movie roles.

When she started her company in 1915, Helena Rubinstein was already widely regarded as one of the world's beauty experts. The Rubinstein Company had a longstanding rivalry with the successful Elizabeth Arden company. The two women did not appear at the same social functions and claimed they had never met throughout their lives.

Rubenstein used some of her profits to help others. She established The Helena Rubinstein Foundation in 1953, and donated millions of dollars to the arts, educational institutions, and charities, especially causes that aided women and children.

The petite, flamboyantly attired Rubinstein became a prominent member of international society. When she died, her personal fortune was more than $100 million, and she owned five lavish residences. After Rubinstein's death, her company was sold to Colgate-Palmolive. Helena Rubinstein cosmetics are now part of the French-based international company L'Oreal. *See also* COLGATE-PALMOLIVE CO.; COSMETICS.

Further reading: Maxene Fabe, *Beauty Millionaire: The Life of Helena Rubinstein* (1972); Helena Rubinstein, *My Life for Beauty* (1965).

Russell, Lillian (1861–1922)

Lillian Russell, an actress known for her performances in light comedies and musicals, was regarded as a model of feminine beauty in turn-of-the-century America where she was called "The American Beauty." She was one of the first celebrities to use her fame to promote beauty products.

Russell, who was born Helen Louise Leonard in Clinton, Iowa, originally planned to become an opera singer. She made her theatrical debut in 1879 as a member of the chorus in Gilbert and Sullivan's *HMS Pinafore*. The next year, her manager, Tony Pas-

Lillian Russell, circa 1893. *Library of Congress.*

tor, convinced her to take the stage name Lillian Russell. She became a frequent member of Pastor's Broadway variety shows. In 1881, she became famous for her role in Edmond Audran's *Grand Mogul*. Audiences also raved about her performance in *Grande Duchesse de Ge* by the French composer Jacques Offenbach.

The actress received even more attention for her appearance than for her performances. People came to see the woman whose skin had been called "luminous" and whose voluptuous curves suited the beauty ideal of that era. Theater critic Lewis Strang said Russell had "the most perfect doll's face on the American stage" and praised her as "a golden-haired goddess with big, rounded cheeks, soft and dimpled like a baby's." (Strang, 1900)

Between 1899 and 1904, Russell, known as "The Toast of the 'Nineties," toured England with a burlesque company. Europeans also flocked to see the woman who had been praised for her beautiful face, hourglass figure, and marvelous complexion. Women on both continents were eager to see Russell's splendid fashion ensembles and jewelry.

Celebrity-watchers followed Russell's private life as well, including her famous affair with "Diamond Jim" Brady, and women were curious about the beauty products she used, such as Caswell-Massey's "Red Jasmine Cologne." Russell capitalized on her reputation as a great beauty to produce and promote face creams and other items she claimed to use herself. She was the most frequently photographed woman in America for 20 years, and the beloved "American Beauty" rose was named for her.

Beginning in 1912, Russell wrote a syndicated newspaper column about love, beauty, and health. She also endorsed beauty products, including a line of skin products made in Germany called Lanoline Toilet Preparations. A photo of her much-admired profile appeared in the ad for "Lanoline," which claimed the products were "used by the nobility throughout Europe." *See also* "LOOKS."

Further reading: Lois W. Banner, *American Beauty* (1983); Lewis C. Strang, *Prima Donnas and Soubrettes of Light Opera and Musical Comedy in America* (1900).

S

Safety

Throughout history, certain beauty preparations have harmed and killed some of the people who used or produced them. One of the best-known examples was a face powder made from white lead, known as ceruse or cerussa, used at least from the time of the Roman Empire (27 B.C.E.–476 C.E.) and at least through the Renaissance (1600s). It is not known how many thousands of women died from prolonged use of this powder, which they applied to lighten their complexions. The factory workers who made the powder, many of them located in the Netherlands, died of lead poisoning even more often than did consumers. Other women were disfigured from using lead powders.

Arsenic, a potentially fatal substance, was another popular but potentially deadly beauty aid. During the seventeenth century, women died because they used a beauty liquid that contained arsenic. This prompted the passage of laws in Italy that required all poisonous substance to be registered with the government. However, some European women still took arsenic. During the early 1800s, they ingested small amounts occasionally to achieve a pale, delicate complexion. The theory behind this practice was traced back to research done by an eighteenth-century Austrian biologist, Johann Blumenbach, who gathered skulls and skeletal remains. Blumenbach developed a theory of racial classification for Europeans, saying that the Circassians, who lived in the Caucasus, were ethnically "pure." The women were reputed to be extremely beautiful, and images of them showed them with pale, almost white, skin.

During the 1830s, these theories were discussed and it was said that Circassian women ate arsenic to achieve their much-envied complexions. Women in other countries continued to eat arsenic, believing it would give them a fairer appearance.

Other substances used cosmetically also caused damage. Safety concerns were raised by various incidents that occurred in the United States early in the twentieth century. During the 1920s, a skin astringent called "Ambrosia" was found to contain carbolic acid. It was removed from the market in New Hampshire, where it was made. In the 1930s, a product made to dye eyelashes caused some women to become blind, disfigured, or even to die.

The U.S. Congress passed the Food, Drug, and Cosmetic Act of 1938 to address these kinds of problems, and appointed the Food and Drug Administration (FDA) as the agency of oversight. The law prohibited what it called the practice of adulteration and banned the use of coal-tar dyes from most cosmetics. It did not require that companies pretest their products, nor did it require labels listing the products ingredients. The soap industry had lobbied long and hard to be excluded from this law, and they were exempted from its provisions. Critics complained that the penalties for breaking the law were too mild—a $1,000 fine for a first offense and $10,000 fine for a second offense. Amendments to the law covered the use of color additives. Labeling laws did not take effect until the 1970s.

As a result of these laws, the FDA can take certain steps to remove unsafe products from the market. The agency can conduct plant inspections and test samples from these factories in its laboratories, as well as samples of cosmetics on the market. Both domestic and foreign products are subject to these regulations. The FDA states that foreign cosmetics "must be safe and made from approved ingredients; and all labeling and packaging must be informative and truthful." (*FDA Consumer*, May 1992) The inspectors look for "signs of filth, spoilage, contamination, or mislabeling."

Around the world, industrialized nations and many developing countries, have passed similar laws to protect consumers from unsafe cosmetics and misrepresentations by manufacturers. Some countries also increase consumer awareness through education programs and conduct impartial research to determine the effectiveness of new products. Laws vary from one country to another. In Spain, the government requires pretesting of cosmetics. France does not permit companies to advertise soaps, hair products, or cosmetics using terms that have a medical definition, such as dandruff or allergies. The Swiss government classifies certain products, such as vaginal deodorants, as drugs subject to drug laws, rather than as cosmetics or personal hygiene products. Swedish laws require labels with specific facts about the product. While laws in the United States require that cosmetics manufacturers be registered, in Japan, they must also obtain official licenses.

New safety issues emerge with new products. During the 1990s, a product called "thigh cream" was sold, with claims that regular use could eliminate an inch or more from the thigh. The products contained aminophylline, a medication that was used to treat asthma. One concern was that asthmat-ics who used it on their thighs would acclimate to it so that it no longer helped their asthma. Also, some of the women who used this product reported side effects, including skin irritation, dizziness, headaches, nausea, diarrhea, and heart palpitations. Some people said they had a metallic taste in their mouths and felt pressure in their chests after using the cream. More serious side effects included coma and circulatory failure. Some companies conducted tests and said they could not detect any aminophylline in the blood of people who used the cream on their skin. However, critics of these tests concluded that side effects could still occur even if tests did not pick up detectable levels of the drug. They claimed that testing of the substance had been too limited before it was marketed. The publicity about these safety concerns resulted in the production of new thigh creams that contained plant extracts or substances other than aminophyllne.

Debates over the safety of hair care and hygiene products and cosmetics continued into the 1990s. In 1994, the FDA received 200 reports of adverse reactions from the use of cosmetics. Sixty-five cases involved skin care products or makeup. Most of the 65 cases were allergic reactions or skin irritations. Other complaints involved the use of soaps, hair products, toothpaste, or mouthwash. The FDA stated that hundreds more people experienced adverse reactions, but they often reported them to the product manufacturer rather than to the FDA. (Stehlin, 1995)

Consumer advocates continue to raise questions about the safety of various products. They claim that the effects of many of the thousands of chemicals used to manufacture cosmetics remain unknown. Safety concerns have also led to the rising popularity of herbs and other natural ingredients (not all of which are safe, either, although many people associate the word "natural" with "safe.") *See also* ALLERGIC REACTIONS; CELLULITE; COLOR ADDITIVES; HAIR COLOR; LAWS AND REGULATIONS (U.S.); ROMAN EMPIRE; SKIN COLORING AGENTS; WEIGHT.

Further reading: "Imports and FDA," *FDA Consumer,* May 1992; Dori Stehlin, "Cosmetic Safety: More Complex Than at First Blush," *FDA Consumer,* May 1995; U.S. Food and Drug Administration, "Cosmetic Handbook," 1992; U.S. Food and Drug Administration, "Inspection of Cosmetics," 6 February 1995; U.S. Food and Drug Administration, Office of Cosmetics Fact Sheet: "Prohibited Ingredients," 2 February 1995; Emily Yoffe, "Chemical Good Looks," *U.S. News and World Report,* 11 November 1997.

Salons, Beauty

The first beauty salons in North America appeared near the end of the nineteenth century. Most of the early salons were operated by women, and some were owned and run by families. One of these early entrepreneurs was Anna B. Adams, a physician who left her profession because of the barriers female physicians faced in their careers during that era. She founded a chain of beauty parlors.

The most successful beauty salon entrepreneur was Martha Matilda Harper (1847–1950), who is also often called the "mother of franchising." Harper was a Canadian-born housewife who worked for 25 years as a servant. During that time, she learned about the use of herbs for hair and skin care. She founded her first beauty salon in Rochester, New York, in 1888 and went on to build a chain of Harper Hair Dressing Salons and beauty schools, which eventually grew to 500 units worldwide at their peak in 1928. Harper, whose trademark was her stunning floor-length auburn hair, called her salons "branches" and they sold Harper products and used the "Harper Method." She recruited working-class women to run the salons, which could be found in New York, San Francisco, Detroit, Edinburgh, and Berlin, Germany, among other places.

Harper criticized potentially dangerous beauty products and processes. Instead, she said that people had natural beauty and her salons focused on skin and scalp treatments that encouraged the hair's natural sheen and enhanced the skin. Harper said, "When a [person] is healthy, [she] is beautiful." She encouraged the staffs at her franchises to emphasize service, treat customers and em-

ployees courteously, set up childcare facilities, and work to improve their communities. Prominent women, including suffragist Susan B. Anthony, actress Helen Hayes, First Ladies, and men, including Presidents Wilson and Coolidge, were among Harper's customers. The Harper Method operated until 1972 when a competitor bought the business.

Beauty salons were also opening in other countries in the early 1900s. In 1905, Hatsuko Endo opened her salon in the Ginza, the main commercial section of Tokyo, Japan. Although the business started as a bridal parlor, Endo began offering makeup and hairstyling services along with planning the wedding kimono, ceremony, and reception. (The company continued to grow and is still in business today and has remained in the family.)

The advent of electricity enabled beauty salons to offer new services, such as the permanent wave. A large permanent wave machine, invented in 1906, became a stock feature in American and European hairdressing salons by the 1930s. Electrical curling implements and hooded hair dryers also appeared by this time.

More western women began patronizing salons and many made weekly appointments to have their hair styled and washed. Salons began to serve other purposes as well; women came to socialize, gossip, and feel pampered while receiving hair and nail care or facial treatments. Salons also sold face creams and other beauty products that were not available elsewhere.

By 1925, the beauty industry in the United States had expanded such that women were spending about $6 million each day buying beauty products and paying for services in hair and beauty salons. The average American woman spent about $150 a year on beauty products and services, while wealthy women might spend a few hundred dollars each week. (Lewis and Woodworth, 1972) Statistics for the year 1927 showed that the American beauty business brought in $2 billion a year. (Lewis and Woodworth, 1972)

A number of Americans deplored these statistics and urged women not to devote time and money to their appearance. Yet changing attitudes about cosmetics and women's jobs and social roles led to steady growth in the beauty parlor industry. During the 1920s, careers in cosmetology opened new opportunities for women in the workplace. Men began to join them, since they could earn more money in this field than in some of their former jobs as salesmen, clerks, or mechanics. A beginning beauty operator could earn between $20 and $30 a week plus about $15 in tips, an income that often doubled by the end of the first year. Some beauty operators earned hundreds of dollars each week, far more than in other jobs then open to women, which paid around $17 a week.

By the mid-twentieth century the beauty parlor was firmly established as a common institution in women's lives, and by the 1960s and 1970s, men were also flocking to beauty parlors to utilize the services of hairdressers and other beauty professionals. *See also* ADAIR, ELEANOR; ARDEN, ELIZABETH; BEAUTY INDUSTRY (U.S.); HAIR, STYLING OF; SASSOON, VIDAL.

Further reading: Alfred Allen Lewis and Constance Woodworth, *Miss Elizabeth Arden* (1972); Jane R. Plitt, *Martha Matilda Harper and the American Dream: How One Woman Changed the Face of Modern Business* (2000). Nancy Shakur, *Elizabeth Arden, Cosmetics Entrepreneur* (1989).

Sassoon, Vidal (b. 1928)

Hair stylist, educator, and creator of hair care products, Vidal Sassoon profoundly influenced twentieth-century hairstyles and the hairstyling industry. His distinctive, simple cuts let hair move in a natural way and reduced the amount of time women had to spend on their hair. It has been said that Sassoon did for hair "what the Beatles did for rock and roll." (Fishman and Powell, 1983)

Sassoon had a difficult early life in London after his father abandoned the family. He and his younger brother Ivor spent six years in a Jewish orphanage until their mother remarried and could support her sons once more. At school, Sassoon was a talented athlete with a strong interest in health and fitness. He left school at age 14 to help support

the family and was accepted as an apprentice to Adolph Cohen at Cohen's Beauty and Barber Shop.

During World War II, Sassoon heard stories about the systematic murder of Jews in Nazi-occupied countries. He joined anti-Fascist groups and went to Israel in 1948 to help Jews in the new Jewish nation fight for independence. When he returned to England, he resumed his career and studied with top stylists Silvio Camillo and Frank Blaschke to perfect his skills. He entered and won several hair-styling competitions.

In 1954, Sassoon opened his first salon, where he created haircuts that were radically different from the stiffly constructed, sprayed styles that were then popular. He claimed that wearing hair rollers to bed was both uncomfortable and unromantic. His freer styles, including the Torro cut, the Bronte, and a style he called Le Swish, worked with the hair's natural movement and texture. Women could enjoy sports and other activities and their hair would still look good afterward.

The 1960s brought revolutionary ideas about beauty and fashion. Revealing new fashions, including mini-skirts, were the rage, and trend-setting British fashion designer Mary Quant became famous around the world. Sassoon's approach suited the bold, youthful fashions. Quant asked him to give her models fresh new hairstyles, and he created the Sassoon Bob, a short style that looked simple but actually required artful cutting. He went on to design a signature asymmetric cut and other important styles. He said his approach was to cut hair "like you cut material. No fuss. No ornamentation. Just a neat, clean swinging line." (Fishman and Powell, 1993)

Sassoon became the most sought-after stylist in London, and his fame spread abroad. French couturiers hired him to style the hair of their runway models. Because Sassoon's styles considered a woman's individual facial shape and bone structure, they flattered women from different cultures and ethnic groups during years when ideas about beauty and fashion were becoming more inclusive. Top fashion magazines featured hairstyles by

Hairdresser Vidal Sassoon styling a "swinging bob," 1963. © *Kent Gavin/Archive Photos.*

Sassoon, and, in 1968, his hairstyles were featured in the first fashion video, *Basic Black*, which showcased clothing by Rudi Gernreich.

In 1968, Sassoon was the first foreigner invited to appear at the prestigious annual French hairstyling event, "Le Style de Paris." The 1968 demonstration drew 600 top stylists from all over Europe. Sassoon demonstrated eight of his famous haircuts.

Sassoon toured other countries, including Japan (1969). One of his most famous jobs during the early 1970s took him to Hollywood, where he cut the long tresses of actress Mia Farrow into the cropped hairdo she wore in the film *Rosemary's Baby.* This became known as the "$5,000 haircut."

By 1974, Sassoon had moved to Los Angeles, where he opened his world headquarters. He eventually opened more than 20 salons in six countries and set up Vidal Sassoon schools and academies to train stylists. Celebrities who patronized his salons included rock star Rod Stewart, singer/actress Liza Minelli, actor Cary Grant, comedian Carol Burnett, and actress Catherine Deneuve. Sassoon salons featured a chic décor and friendly atmosphere, and he said, "In our salons everyone is welcome—social-ites, sociologists, socialists." (Fishman and Powell, 1993)

Sassoon's interest in the health of hair led him to work with chemists on products for men and women, including shampoos, conditioners, and styling products. The Vidal Sassoon hair-care business was sold to Richardson Vicks in 1983; two years later, Procter & Gamble bought Richardson Vicks. Sassoon products continued to sell well; by 1991, they reportedly earned $300 million a year. (Fishman and Powell, 1993) Sassoon also sold his salon and academy businesses.

Sassoon wrote about his career in *Sorry I Kept You Waiting, Madam* (1968) and described his techniques in *Super Cuts* (1972) and *Cutting Hair the Sassoon Way* (1972), both of which were written for hairstylists. In 1975, he and his former wife Beverly, the mother of their four children, collaborated on the book *A Year of Beauty and Health.* A well-received ad campaign starting in 1976 featured the slogan, "If you don't look good, we don't look good." Sassoon made numerous appearances on American television, and, from 1980–81, appeared on a syndicated TV show, *Your New Day.*

Sassoon set up the Vidal Sassoon Foundation for philanthropic purposes, including social programs and institutions, particularly education for disadvantaged youth and minorities, and to the arts. It also supports programs that bring together youth from different racial and religious backgrounds and set up what is now called the Vidal Sassoon Internation Center for the Study of Antisemitism. Sassoon also devotes time and money to HairCares, a fund to help hairstyling professionals with AIDS. He continues to work on new styles that evolve with the times, but are recognizably Sassoon's.

Sassoon has received numerous honors. In 1982, the Fellowship of Hair Artists of Great Britain gave him their Patron of Honour citation "for his outstanding achievements, revolutionary ideas and creative techniques in hairdressing." Six years later, he was inducted into the United States Cosmetology Hall of Fame. In 1991, he was inducted into the British Hairdressing Hall of Fame, and he became the second person ever to receive the North American Hairstyling Award for Lifetime Achievement. Sassoon also received the American Beauty Association Award for Outstanding Achievement in 1993. A 50-year retrospective of his work premiered in London in 1992 and toured the world.

Further reading: Diane Fishman and Marcia Powell, *Vidal Sassoon: Fifty Years Ahead* (1993); Vidal Sassoon, *Sorry I Kept You Waiting, Madam,* (1968).

Scarification *See* SKIN MODIFICATION.

Schiffer, Claudia (b. 1970)

German-born supermodel Claudia Schiffer is one of the most successful women in her profession. The head of the Metropolitan Model Agency discovered her when, as a 17-year-old schoolgirl, she was visiting a discotheque in Dusseldorf. Her first appearance was in *Elle,* a prominent French fashion magazine, and her career advanced quickly. The 5'11" tall, blue-eyed blond was chosen as the new "Face of Chanel" and represented their products, as well as being the featured model in a phenomenally successful ad campaign for Guess? clothing. She has also appeared in ads for Revlon cosmetics as part of a four-year contract for which she received $6 million.

Schiffer went on to appear on more than 500 magazine covers and was the first model on the cover of several publications, including *Vanity Fair* and *People.* In addition, she was frequently invited to model spring and fall couture collections for such luminaries as Gianni Versace and Jil Sander.

Outside of modeling, Schiffer has developed fitness videos and was a partner in the theme restaurant chain, "Fashion Café'" with fellow models Elle McPherson and Naomi Campbell. Schiffer, who speaks several languages, maintains homes in New York City and Monte Carlo. *See also* MODELING AND MODELS.

Further reading: "Claudia Schiffer: Biography," http://www.boxofficemania.com/actresses/c/claudiaschiffer/

Shiseido Corporation

The Shiseido Corporation was founded in Tokyo, Japan, by a formal naval pharmacist, Yushin Fukuhara, in 1872. The company developed into a large, multinational manufacturer of cosmetics and skin care products.

In the early years, Shiseido sold pharmaceuticals and grooming products, including soaps and the first toothpaste produced in Japan. This paste soon outsold tooth powders. Shiseido introduced a skin lotion called "Eudermine" in 1897; it remained in the product line throughout the 1900s.

In 1923, Shiseido developed a network of chain stores throughout Japan to market its products. That same year, a devastating earthquake in Tokyo ruined the Ginza facilities and the pharmaceutical building in Tokyo. New, temporary facilities were built. In 1927, Shiseido was incorporated, and Yushin Fukuhara's son Shinzo became the first president. Under his leadership, the company would grow, develop high-end cosmetics products, and build a following of loyal customers. The company organized its "Camellia Club" in 1937, publishing a monthly beauty magazine for its members, which eventually numbered 10 million Japanese women.

The company expanded its operations overseas beginning in 1957, selling products in Taiwan, Singapore, and Hong Kong, then Hawaii. In the years that followed, new subsidiaries included Shiseido Cosmetics America, Shiseido Cosmetici Italia, and Shiseido New Zealand. During the 1970s, Shiseido sponsored international fashion shows and the first Tokyo International Women's Marathon (1979), which became a regular international event.

As the 1980s began, Shiseido worked with Serge Lutens, who helped to shape the company's international image into one that emphasized high quality, high service, and high image. Shiseido France, Shiseido Deutschland (Germany), and Shiseido Australia were created. The company added an international salon network. Carita salons, a prestigious French-based business, joined the Shiseido Group, followed by Zotos International, a top U.S. supplier of professional hair and salon products (1988). Fragrances also became a key part of the company, as it introduced "l'Eau d'Issey" and "Issey Miyake" in 1992 and "Jean Paul Gaultier" in 1993.

In 1991, Shiseido embarked on a joint venture with the Chinese firm Beijing Liyuan Co., establishing Shiseido Liyuan Cosmetics in that nation. Production in the Beijing factory commenced in 1993. Shiseido established its first European factory in Gien, France, one of seven factories in five countries. The company had gained a 10 percent share of the worldwide cosmetics market by the late 1990s.

The company continued to develop new product lines. In 1997, Shiseido launched its Za ("zee ay") brand of skin care products and makeup for young Pan-Asian women. The products, which included 10 skin care products, lipsticks, and nail polishes, were sold in Japan, Thailand, Hong Kong, Taiwan, Singapore, and Malaysia. Shiseido expected to distribute them in more than 10 countries by the year 2000. The new Za line was heavily advertised on television on music-oriented and entertainment channels.

Shinzo Maeda, the president of Shiseido Cosmetics, said, "The population of Asia is now nearly two-thirds of the world's population, and huge demand is expected from the Asian cosmetics market, which is estimated to grow by $1 billion a year." (Herskovitz and Fannin, 1997) Figures for 1999 showed approximately $5 billion in overall sales, and over $3 billion in cosmetics sales. *See also* ASIAN MARKETS (MODERN)

Further reading:; Jan Herskowitz and Rebecca A. Fannin, "Shiseido Buffs Its Image with first Pan-Asian Line," *Advertising Age International,* September 1997, 12ff; Shiseido Corporation, "About Shiseido," "The Shiseido Story," "Annual Report" http://www.shiseidoco.jp.

Shrimpton, Jean (b. 1940)

Jean Shrimpton was a world-famous model during the 1960s, a time when many people in the fashion and beauty industry called her "the most beautiful girl in the world." Shrimpton was known for her natural, unfussy look, which included wide blue eyes, full lips, and long golden-brown hair. She also personified the popular body shape of that era—thin but rounded rather than angular.

Shrimpton grew up on a farm in England, then enrolled in vocational school where she began studying secretarial skills. One weekend, while attending a local community dance, she was invited to take part in a beauty contest, where she placed third. After her photograph appeared in the newspaper, she was approached by people in the film business and encouraged to become a model. She attended Lucie Clayton's school, a top modeling school in London at that time, and learned how to apply makeup, walk down a runway, and style her hair. After the course ended, she began taking on assignments.

Between 1961 and 1963, Jean Shrimpton became a top model, the first to gain worldwide fame. Top photographers, including Richard Avedon, Peter Knapp, and her boyfriend and manager David Bailey, took her pictures for *Vogue, Glamour,* and other fashion and beauty publications. When she arrived to work in New York in 1965, Shrimpton commanded the highest fees that had been paid to a model up to that time, and she was praised by people in the beauty industry as the woman who personified beauty in the sixties. She endorsed beauty and hair care products for Yardley, a London-based company.

Shrimpton quit modeling after four years to try acting but her first film, *Privilege,* was not a success. She decided to retire from the business during the early 1970s and moved to Penzance, a town on the English Channel, where she opened an antique business. In 1980, she married an antique car collector and hotel owner, Michael Fox. The couple converted an old building above the bay in Penzance into a hotel, which they operated, and lived there with their son. In 1990, Shrimpton published her memoirs.

Further reading: Michael Delmar, "Jean Shrimpton, Star of the '60s," *TopModel,* Sept./Oct. 1996, 82–85; Jean Shrimpton, *Jean Shrimpton, An Autobiography* (1990).

Skin

The skin, the largest organ on the body, is normally at least partly visible to others. Whether on view or covered, however, skin has been a major focus of grooming rituals throughout history. Skin care treatments aim to keep skin soft, smooth, supple, and free of blemishes. Some treatments have been simple, with only one are a few ingredients, while others have been extremely complex and expensive.

Skin Care in History

Care of the complexion and body dates back to ancient times and includes cleansing, deodorizing, moisturizing, and treatments that aim to reduce or eliminate signs of aging, such as lines and wrinkles. In some cases, people are willing to make great sacrifices to care for their skin. Among the Kalahari of Africa, people have used animal fats to moisturize their skin even in times of famine.

Ancient skin preparations were made from materials from plants and animals. People living in ancient Rome used a strong-smelling facial preparation at night made from the sweat extracted from sheep's wool, among other ingredients. The Romans treated blemishes with barley flour and butter. Different unguents for the skin were made from flowers, eggs, honey, flour, and other ingredients. Ancient Egyptians used cucumber juice to soothe the skin and restore facial tone. Egg-white masks also date back to ancient Egypt. Honey has also long been used as a moisturizer. Women in Latin America have used avocado, rich in oils, since pre-Columbian times. Africans often used palm oil on their bodies to alleviate the effects of extreme hot and cold. Brazilians also used this oil. Later, palm oil would be used in commercial soaps.

During Elizabethan times (1558–1603), people applied raw meat to the face to minimize wrinkles. During the 1700s, women of the French court are said to have used aged wine on their faces, a process that is now recognized as helping in exfoliation, since wine contains certain types of acids. The Creoles—settlers of French descent—of the southern United States added berries to their baths and used perfumed milk as a skin lotion.

In Asia, people used both naturally occurring substances and manufactured products on their faces. Japanese women gathered the excreta of nightingales and applied that to their skin as a beauty treatment.. A cream called "Royal Concubine Radiant Beauty Cream," now made in the People's Republic of China, has been popular since the early 1900s. It contains ingredients women in China have used for centuries on their skin, including pulverized white jade, pearl powder, and ginseng.

Cold Cream

Women have long used face creams to create a smooth, clear, and unblemished complexion, which is regarded almost universally as attractive. Topical products used for face care vary from simple oils and plant extracts to creams with multiple ingredients.

Cold creams, the forerunner of modern cleansing and lubricating creams, date back to about 150 AD. The first known cold cream came from Greece, and the formula spread to the Roman Empire. The formula was called "cold cream" because the water evaporated when the cream was applied, leaving the skin feeling cool.

The Greek physician Galen is credited with developing these early cold creams, more for medicinal than cosmetic use. Previously, people had used salves and unguents made from oils and plant materials on their skin. Galen's cream contained water, olive oil, and beeswax, and was scented with rose petals. The oil and wax in the cream loosened dirt, oily secretions, and dry, dead cells on the skin's surface.

Various recipes for cold cream were passed down to new generations and made at home. Creams were made with spermaceti beginning in about 1780, but this product came from whales and led to such large-scale killing in the quest for it that it later contributed to the whales' endangered status.

In the 1800s, manufactured creams became more available to cleanse, soften, and condition the skin. Chief ingredients in the creams were oils and waxes, mixed with water. (A product with similar properties, jojoba oil, gained popularity in the 1970s. This oil comes from nuts of the jojoba shrub. An acre of these plants yields as much oil as 30 whales.) Some cold creams advertised their botanical ingredients. During the Gilded Age (1880–1915) Caswell-Massey's Cucumber Cold Cream was popular; actress Sarah Bernhardt was among those who ordered it often.

Modern cold creams are still used to clean and lubricate the skin. They contain alcohol, glycerin, lanolin, and other ingredients, as well as varying amounts of water, oil, and wax.

Beauty Masks

Facial masks—substances that are applied to the face for a specific length of time, then wiped or rinsed off—to beautify the complexion may be the world's oldest facial treatment. Long before commercial companies offered facial masks, women concocted their own, using natural and, later, household products. They used them to clean the skin, tighten pores, and minimize wrinkles, but they probably accomplished only the first goal, according to some skin experts.

The use of cucumbers to moisturize the skin dates back to ancient Egypt, when Queen Cleopatra is said to have to have applied slices of ripe cucumber to her face. Women continued to use cucumbers as cosmetics, both as a facial mask and to soothe the eyelids. Clay masks also date back to ancient times. Today, homemade masks still often use foodstuffs, such as egg white, oatmeal, cucumbers, tomatoes, lemon juice, honey, milk, avocados, bananas, mayonnaise, baking soda, and oil.

During the late twentieth century, masks containing glycolic acids and alpha-hydroxy acids became popular. The producers of these masks claimed they would help to increase the rate of cell turnover, getting rid of old cells and thus stimulating the production of new skin cells.

Hormones

During the 1950s, hormone face creams came onto the market, most of which contained the female hormone estrogen. Manufacturers recommended that women use these creams for aging skin, saying they would replace hormones that diminished with age. However, no scientific proof exists that hormones in topical face creams change the skin's capacity to retain moisture or lubricate better than other face creams. Nor do any scientific studies show that hormone creams could reverse or correct the degeneration of the elastin and collagen fibers in the skin, also related to aging and sun exposure. The Food and Drug Administration (FDA) limits the amount of hormones that can be used in creams and requires manufacturers to warn consumers not to expose children to these creams. Certain hormone creams have been declared unsafe and taken off the market.

As the 1960s began, European companies, especially those in France, were focusing on skin care and scientific studies about various products to improve skin and reduce signs of aging. These products included hormones, marine algae, and serums. At the same time, the FDA began enforcing stricter laws governing the claims that cosmetics manufacturers could make about their products.

Other Products

Products for the skin are many and numerous and fall into several categories. One of the most basic is cleansers. One type of cleanser is intended to regulate the amount of oil on the skin. Astringents, also known as toners, pore lotions, tonics, and skin fresheners, remove some of the excess oil on the skin.

Before commercial products became available, women used buttermilk or yogurt for this purpose. Later, they found that witch hazel, which comes from a small shrub, made a good astringent because it contains tannic acid. People also used alcohol, and this became the basis of some commercial astringents but can be harsh used alone. To remove dead, dirty skin cells, manufacturers offer products called exfoliants.

Acne treatments remain another large category of skin care products. Acne refers to blackheads, whiteheads, pustules, and other blemishes on the face or other parts of the body. Acne or blemishes result from hormonal activity, buildup of bacteria in the pores of the skin, excess oil, and excessive shedding of dead skin cells. Acne is most common during the teenage years, but may erupt at any time. About 75 percent of teenagers experience blemishes or acne. Nearly 50 percent of adult women and about 20 percent of all adults between the ages of 25 and 44 have experienced problems with skin breakouts at times.

Acne is considered unattractive and may leave scars. Many nonprescription lotions, creams, liquids, and other preparations are available to treat it. Physicians, particularly dermatologists, may prescribe special topical treatments or drugs to clear up the skin. (Litt, 1989)

Moisturizers, also known as emollients, are substances that soften or soothe the skin. Common ingredients include lanolin, a substance that comes from the oil glands of the sheep. Glycerin is a humectant, a substance that attracts moisture from the air. Glycerin is a common ingredient in face creams and other cosmetics because of its moisture-attracting properties and also because it keeps cosmetics from drying out.

People who cannot or do not want to buy manufactured face creams may prefer traditional lubricants, such as cocoa butter, the pure form of an ingredient also found in cosmetics and manufactured creams. Petroleum jelly has also been used since the late 1800s as an all-purpose lubricant for skin on the face, hands, and other parts of the body, as well as to soothe sunburned, chapped, or chafed skin.

Anti-aging products are another category of skin care products. Many claim to give the skin a more youthful appearance. In recent years, many such face creams and lotions have been developed. The claims made about face creams are controversial, especially those that purport to improve or reverse the effects of age on skin. Often, new products are launched with great fanfare, and companies say that they contain "breakthrough" ingredients that can produce amazing results. For example, manufacturers have claimed that their products can penetrate the skin in new and better ways and deliver important materials needed for healthy skin.

Anti-aging products include tretinoin, a substance that stimulates cell turnover and circulation. The two major brands of tretinoin are Retin-A and Renova. Tests using glycolic acid, a natural by-product of sugar cane, were conducted beginning in the 1970s. Makers of this substance claimed it helped to remove dead skin cells from the top layers of skin, thus improving its appearance. The FDA approved tretinoin for treatment of "the appearance of photoaged skin" (i.e., wrinkles). (*Medical Sciences Bulletin*, 1996).

As researchers discovered new ways to treat aging skin, the 1990s brought new treatments. A product called Ethocyn, developed by a California-based company, contains a patented ingredient that acts at the molecular level, blocking receptors for the hormone dihydrotestosterone, which inhibits the elastin-building process in skin cells. Elastin is a skin fiber that tends to lose its resilience through the years, which allows the skin to sag. Elastic tissue increased in test subjects who used this substance on their skin twice a day for at least two months. Some skin experts point out that other factors, including adequate collagen, which adds strength to skin tissue and is stimulated by tretinoin, is also vital for young-looking skin.

One of the most widely touted ingredients for reducing the signs of aging is alpha-hydroxy acids. By the 1990s, alpha hydroxy acids (AHAs)— natural, nontoxic substances found in foods and plants—were being used in skin care products. Dermatologists and beauty experts claimed that these substances can smooth the skin's surface and improve the appearance of aging or sun-damaged skin by helping to slough off dead skin cells from the top layers. Studies showed that this substance increased the speed at which skin cells turned over, so it is a useful exfoliating agent. Numerous cosmetic companies, including Avon, L'Oreal, Revlon, and Estee Lauder, have developed their own products containing these acids, and many generic preparations are also on the market. The products sold over the counter usually contain no more than 10 percent alpha hydroxy acids, but preparations with higher percentages are available from dermatologists and skin care professionals, who use them for mini-face peels.

An increasing number of people are turning to plastic surgery and advanced dermatologic procedures to reduce signs of aging. They include dermabrasion, or facial planing, in which top skin layers (derma) are removed so that new skin grows in their place. After this procedure, skin may look as if the person has suffered a severe sunburn. Recovery may take about 10 days, and complications, such as uneven skin tone, may occur. Various other cosmetic surgeries are performed to remove excess folds of skin or to lift certain areas.

Skin care products are a large part of the total personal care products industry. Many new products are introduced each year. For instance, in 1996, more than 1,700 new products were launched.

During the late 1990s, women in the United States were spending more than $3 billion each year on skin care products. (Dunn, 1997) This was also the decade in which manufacturers began to address cosmetic needs of ethnic groups. They began to produce cleansers, moisturizers, toners, and eye moisturizers geared to African Americans and people of Asian heritage. Some companies were preparing products for people with Hispanic heritage—Mexican, Spanish, Puerto Rican, South American.

The market for skin care products is likely to grow as the age at which their use begins drops. Even babies' skin care products, a market once dominated by Johnson & Johnson, has competitors such as BabySpa, which sells aromatherapy baby bath, BabySoft body lotion, and BabyWash, all considerably pricier than traditional baby products. *See also*

ADAIR, ELEANOR; ADVERTISING (U.S.); AGING AND APPEARANCE; ALLERGIC REACTIONS; ARDEN, ELIZABETH; BEAUTY INDUSTRY (U.S.); COSMETICS; DERMATOLOGISTS; LAUDER, ESTÉE; PLASTIC SURGERY; RUBINSTEIN, HELENA.

Further reading: American Society for Dermatologic Surgery (ASDS), "Dermabrasion Treatment," http://www.asds-net.org/.html; The Body Shop Team, *The Body Shop Book* (1994); Tom Branni, *Happi*, August 1999; Christine Canning, "Filling the Void in Ethnic Skin Care," *Happi*, October 1996; Tony C. Chu and Anne Lorell, *The Good Skin Doctor: A Dermatologist's Guide to Surviving Acne* (1999); Carolyn A. Dunn, "The Skin Care Market," *Happi*, March 1997; Dr. Albert Klingman, "The Rose Sheet, 3 March 1997"; Takie Sugiyama Lebra, *Japanese Women: Constraint and Fulfillment* (1984); Carol Lewis, "Clearing Up Cosmetics Confusion," *FDA Consumer*, May–June 1998; Jonathan Z. Litt, M.D. *Your Skin: From Acne to Zits* (1989); *Medical Sciences Bulletin*, "Tretinoin (Renova) Approved for Treatment of Wrinkles," February 1996, http://pahrminfo.com/pubs/msb/treinoin2.html; Gil Y. Roth, "Ethnic Skin Care Review," *Happi*, October 1997.

Skin Coloring Agents

Various substances and formulations have been used to give the skin a different color, paler or darker. The use of face whiteners made with ceruse, a lead compound, dates back thousands of years, and sickened and killed some users. During the Roman Empire, when a pale complexion was regarded as beautiful, women used ceruse to whiten or lighten their skin. The use of powdered mixtures made with white lead persisted and spread to other places. During the Elizabethan period (1558–1603), ceruse was made from lead and carbon, and both men and women applied it to the face and hair.

A ceruse-making industry developed to satisfy the growing demand. Much of the industry was centered in Holland, and Dutch workmen suffered ill effects from their exposure to lead and its poisonous effects. During the eighteenth century, two well-known victims of ceruse poisoning were the actress Kitty Fisher and a society beauty named Maria Gunning.

Gradually, people became aware of the various problems caused by the use of the substance. Scientists warned that lead could cause corrosion to the surface of objects, and some women realized that prolonged use of what was supposed to improve their skin in fact harmed the texture and caused hair loss. Even when people became more aware of the hazards, some women continued to use the substance. Near the end of the 1700s, they used it less as rice powder, a harmless product, became available.

Pale skin tones have been part of the beauty standard in many places throughout history. Racism, directed against people of color, has affected social attitudes about appearance. In a place where most of the population has dark skin, including India and parts of Africa, some cultures have considered the lighter skin tones more attractive.

Such attitudes led some people to try and lighten their skin to fit the prevailing standard of appearance. They did so not only to make their appearance fit the standards, but also to try to avoid the mistreatment and discrimination that came with being labeled as black or dark-skinned.

During the 1800s and early 1900s, women of color and women with darker skin colors who were oppressed by northern European ideals of beauty tried bleaching their natural dark skin tones. In the United States, women, and a smaller number of men, used household bleaches, among other substances, for this purpose.

As time went on, manufacturers came up with more commercial products for bleaching the skin, especially the face. Products designed to lighten the skin of African Americans were vigorously marketed during the early part of the twentieth century. Many of these creams, treatments, and lotions were made from damaging chemicals, including laundry bleach. Ads for these products openly denigrated dark skin tones, saying light skin was preferable and "better" than dark skin. They often featured light-skinned black women as "better" looking.

The 1920s saw new skin-lightning products come on the market in the United States. Some were injected. Some people died from bleaching their skin, while others were disfigured. People burned their skin or their skin turned strange colors that were neither natural for their race nor like "white" skin. In response, during the twentieth century, some nations, such as Senegal, banned the sale of skin-bleaching preparations. Countries that had been under the domination of white colonialists also began holding national and regional beauty pageants as a way of asserting their new pride in their own standards of beauty.

By the late mid-1900s, particularly with the changing attitudes ushered in by the 1960s, people of color began to appreciate and enhance their own natural attractiveness. Western cultures recognized more men and women of color for their good looks and other qualities.

Modern bleaching creams are sold to lighten freckles, moles, liver spots, and areas of skin that become darkened with age spots or other abnormal pigmentation. Before the 1970s, bleaching creams contained ammoniated mercury, which produced a slight degree of lightening. In 1974, the FDA banned the use of mercury in bleaching creams because mercury compounds are known to cause side effects and allergic reactions. Later bleaching creams contained hydroquinone, which was sometimes effective in lightening small areas of excess pigmentation caused by some form of pathology. Side effects of this substance included a total loss of pigmentation or a deepening of the abnormal coloring.

People may also use products that produce the look of a suntan. A tanned body has been popular in many cultures since the 1920s, when French couturiers showed sun-tanned models wearing resort clothing. A variety of manufactured creams, gels, lotions, and foams can be used on the face and other parts of the body to give a temporary tan without exposure to the sun. *See also* BEAUTY STANDARDS; ELIZABETH I; FACE; SAFETY.

Further reading: Paula Begoun, *The Beauty Bible* (1997); Tony C. Chu and Anne Lorell, *The Good Skin Doctor: A Dermatologist's Guide to Surviving Acne* (1999); Robin Tomach Lakoff and Raquel L. Scherr, *Face Value: The Politics of*

Beauty (1984); Jonathan Z. Litt, M.D., *Your Skin: From Acne to Zits* (1989); Kathy Peiss, *Hope in a Jar* (1998).

Skin Modification

In modern western societies, cosmetics are often temporary, but native peoples tend to modify the appearance of their skin permanantly. Often, they emphasize body parts that have special significance. They introduce designs through tattoos and scarring.

Intentional scarring, or scarification (also called cicatrization from "cicatrice," the French word for scar), offered an alternative to tattooing among dark-skinned people because tattoos and inks showed up poorly on their skin. People living in Africa, New Guinea, Australia, Tazmania, and Melanesia are among those who have marked themselves in this manner and regard the patterns of the scars as attractive. They may be quite intricate and detailed.

Scars are produced through incisions or burning to create decorative patterns. The designs serve aesthetic purposes and may also show a person's social status or ancestry. They may also improve health by introducing bacteria into the skin, which prompts the

Skin modification (intentional scarring) on Karamoja girl from Uganda. © *George Holton, Photo Researchers.*

immune system to develop antibodies that protect against disease.

Scars have also been sometimes regarded as a sign of masculinity. For example, in previous centuries, dueling scars were popular at certain times in history and countries such as Germany, as they showed that a man had successfully fought a duel for "honor."

Members of the Kiv tribe of northeastern Nigeria scarred their faces during youth. Boys who have not yet completed this process are teased and told that their faces look silly or foreign. This custom continued into the twentieth century, but European influence changed certain aspects of the practice. Men began to make flatter scars and tried to flatten their old, lumpier scars, and Kiv women prefered the newer look.

Different methods have been used for scarification. One popular method involves piercing the skin, then rubbing it with ash. This causes inflammation, which results in raised scar tissue after it heals. Sometimes these areas are opened again later, and pebbles or other ornaments are inserted. *See also* PLASTIC SURGERY; TATTOOS.

Further reading: Francois Boucher, *20,000 Years of Fashion: The History of Costume and Personal Adornment* (1965); Basil Davidson, *African Kingdoms* (1966); Julian Robinson, *The Quest for Human Beauty* (1998).

Soap

Soaps are substances that are mixed with water to remove dirt or other unwanted materials from the skin. They have probably been used in some form since the earliest humans lived on earth. People found it necessary or desirable to wash dirt, dust, grease, bodily excretions, and food off their bodies. They discovered that the extracts of plants such as yucca, soapwort, and horsetail secreted substances that cleaned better than water alone.

Ancient peoples, including the Greeks, did not use soap but rubbed themselves with oils, plant juices, and sand to remove dirt and dead cells from the skin's surface. Some ancient tribe must have discovered that combining ashes with water and animal fats produced a substance that had an abrasive and cleansing effect.

Around 2500 B.C.E., the Sumerians found that a mixture of water, alkali, and cassia oil was effective. The Egyptians also discovered the usefulness of mixtures of alkali and animal and vegetable fats, which created suds for cleansing.

The word "soap" comes from a place near ancient Rome called Sapo Hill. People living there sacrificed animals on the hill, and the fats dripped through the wood ashes into the clay soil and moved downhill near the Tiber River. Women found this clay-oil-ash mixture at places where they came to wash clothing in the river. For whatever reason, they tried it as a cleaning agent, and it worked.

By about 100 C.E., people in Gaul (present-day France) were using a rough sort of soap. As Roman conquerors moved throughout Europe, they learned about these techniques and began making their own soaps. In his writings, the Latin scholar Pliny the Elder (C.E. 23–79) described two kinds of soap (soft and hard) used by people in Gaul. Pliny wrote this soap could brighten the hair. Roman soapmakers treated their work as a craft and developed better, more refined soaps, using olive oil and ashes from the barilla tree. During the seventh century, European men founded soap makers' guilds to promote their trade and regulate the training process.

Elsewhere, North Africans were using certain clays as soap, sometimes combining them with perfumed oils. In parts of Africa, people shaped ash, papaya, and fat into grainy balls. Bees' honey was used in soaps in China, Brazil, and other places. Substances obtained from plants were also used as soaps. For people in South America, the fruit of the soapberry tree provides a substance called saponin, which produces a foam. This substance can also be found in the yucca plant, which can be found in the American southwest and Latin America, the soap bark tree that grows in the Andes, and the wild flowering plant called the soapwort that grows in North America.

By AD 800, Spain was known as the European country that produced the best soaps, which were made from the high-quality olive oil produced in the district of Castile. Castile soap was white and finer in texture than other soaps. Possession of this soap became a status symbol among people in other countries.

Soapmakers in other countries continued to try different methods and ingredients. By the tenth century, soaps made in France were considered to be the best quality. During the 1400s, this honor went to Italian soap, then shifted to English products. (However, English soap was costly and was heavily taxed until the soap tax was repealed in 1853.)

Europeans' manufactured soap was first sold in stores in the 1300s, but only wealthier people could afford it. Most people continued to make their own soap.

North American colonists brought this custom with them to new homes. To make soap, colonial families saved fats from bits of lefover candles and cooking grease. Lye came from fireplaces and cooking ashes. The ash was placed in a leach barrel, layered with straw, and water was poured over it. The brown liquid that was created by this process dripped out of a hole in the bottom of the barrel into a container. People tested the lye to see if it was strong enough by trying to float an egg or potato on top; if it floated, the lye was suitable for making soap. The lye and fat were placed in a large kettle and cooked outdoors over an open fire, where they simmered for hours until the mixture became thick. Someone, often a child, was assigned to stir the soap from time to time so it would not boil over.

Soap making was usually done in the spring or fall and produced a substance that was used for all personal, housecleaning, and laundering purposes. The finished product was stored in jars or buckets and might last the rest of the year. It did not have a pleasing fragrance, nor did it foam into lather like the factory-made soaps of today, and it irritated some people's skin.

During the 1700s and 1800s, soap manufacturers used whale oil in some products. Whaling was big business as crews of whaling ships pursued these large marine mammals and sold the oil for use in oil lamps and manufactured goods. Whalebone was used in women's corsets and hoop skirts, among other things. Some of the soaps made during the 1700s was affordable to average people in Europe.

In the early 1790s, a French chemist named Nicholas Leblanc developed a method for making alkali from common salt. This provided an inexpensive way to make soda ash for soaps, making them less expensive. New discoveries in the early 1800s helped soap makers to find better ways to produce soda ash and to combine some basic ingredients of modern soaps: fats, fatty acids, and glycerine.

By the 1840s, soaps for bathing and shaving were being made in American factories. People could buy soap in general stores or from salesmen who went door-to-door. Coal-tar soap was one of the most common types for everyday use, but new kinds were being made for different uses.

The 1900s brought steady progress in the quality and appeal of soap products. Manufacturers added ingredients such as coconut oil, sandalwood, florals, glycerine, and lanolin to improve the scent and texture. Soap making became a fast-growing industry, and many companies competed for customers. To boost sales, companies started using advertisements featuring lovely famous women, such as stage actresses. Americans used more soap than people in any other country.

Luxury products were also available. One leading manufacturer of fine soaps and grooming products, Caswell-Massey, continued to produce high-end specialty soaps and bath products. One Caswell-Massey line, called the Presidential Soap Collection, featured the favorite soaps of three U.S. Presidents: George Washington, who named Number Six Cologne as his favorite; Dwight D. Eisenhower, who preferred Almond Cold Cream; and John F. Kennedy, who chose Jockey Club (woodsy). Their sandalwood-scented Tricorn was used by actor John Barrymore and composer-lyricist Cole Porter.

New kinds of soaps were made during the late twentieth century. The 1970s brought soaps with various deodorant and emollient ingredients, while others were designated for sensitive or acne-prone skin. Companies also developed liquid soaps, shower gels, and body washes, available in different scents and price ranges. Varieties of bodywashes included florals and fruits, such as peach, raspberry, and grapefruit, as well as vanilla and other food-related scents. Body washes, which manufacturers described as "high-margin items," were popular with American consumers, but, as of 1996, soap continued to bring in higher profits. In that year, bar soap was a $1.5 billion business, while body washes brought in $300 million. Retail stores displayed body washes both in the bath and cosmetics departments. (Dunn, 1996) Body washes increased their share of the "personal cleanser marketplace" by 18.6 percent from August 1997 to August 1998. (*Happi*, December 1998) Bar soap sales grew by 2 percent in the same period.

Although large corporations had the biggest share of the soap market, specialty shops attracted customers by providing attractive and unusual products, creatively packaged. Some featured soaps in various bright colors and shaped like animals, fruits, and flowers, designed to appeal to children and young people. These soaps are also popular gifts. *See also* ADVERTISING (U.S.); BATHS; COLGATE-PALMOLIVE CO; LANGTRY, LILLIE.

Further reading: Carolyn A. Dunn, "The Bar and Liquid Soap Market," *Happi*, December 1996; Gregory Frazier and Beverly Frazier, *The Bath Book* (1972); Charles Goodrum and Helen Dalrymple, *Advertising in America: The First 200 Years* (1990); "Soap's Up!" *Happi*, December 1998; U.S. Food and Drug Administration, Center for Food Safety and Applied Nutrition, "Soap," 3 February 1995.

Society of Cosmetic Chemists (SCC)

Founded in 1945, the Society of Cosmetic Chemists (SCC) works to promote high standards of practice in the cosmetic sciences, which involve research and development in the cosmetics and toiletries industries. The

SCC also aims to set high ethical, professional, and educational standards and to increase and disseminate knowledge in the field of cosmetics science.

As of 1999, the SCC had over 3,700 members in the United States and Canada. Members included people engaged in scientific or technical work in the cosmetics and toiletries industries. To qualify for membership, a person must also have earned a bachelor's degree in the chemical, physical, medical, pharmaceutical, biological, or related sciences and technology.

The SCC publishes a journal called the *Journal of Cosmetic Science,* which contains technical papers and information about the SCC's activities. The group sponsors continuing education programs, as well as local and national meetings and scientific seminars.

Further reading: Society of Cosmetic Chemists, http://www.scconline.org.

South and Central America (Ancient)

See LATIN AMERICA, ANCIENT.

Spas, Beauty and Health

Spas are special places where people go for health or beauty treatments.Even in ancient times, people visited springs that they believed contained curative waters; these were the earliest spas. The word "spa," however, is more recent and derives from the Belgian town of Spa, a resort with baths and mineral springs located near Liège. Spa became popular with European royalty during the nineteenth century, but people had been going there since Roman times. Other famous European spas were located in Carlsbad and Baden-Baden in Germany, Aix-les-Bains and Vichy in France, Aquincum and Hunyadi Janos in Hungary, Karlovy Vary in Czech Republic, and Tunbridge Wells in England. In the United States, Saratoga Springs in New York and French Lick Springs in Indiana are among the oldest, best-known spas.

Early health spas in Europe were known for their healing waters. Their modern counterparts, which originated in the 1930s, had resort settings where clients could receive beauty treatments, lose weight, and become healthier and more physically fit.

The first American spa devoted exclusively to beauty treatments was Maine Chance, the brainchild of cosmetics tycoon Elizabeth Arden. Arden turned her Maine estate into a luxurious retreat where women could come to lose weight and obtain beauty treatments for high weekly fees. Maine Chance, as it was called, opened in 1934, with luxurious guestrooms and suites, a swimming pool, steam rooms, exercise rooms, and recreation rooms. Beautifully landscaped, the buildings were decorated in colors of red, white, blue, and pink (Arden's signature hue). Guests were served breakfast in bed at 7:30 on trays bearing fine china and silver, a pink rose, and pale pink linens. Their day included exercise sessions, swimming, steam baths, facials, weighing sessions, massage treatments, and various sports. Light meals were especially planned for the spa by a leading nutritionist, and alcoholic beverages were forbidden.

After World War II, the Arden Maine Chance spa was moved to Phoenix, Arizona. It was known for its luxurious accommodations, excellent service, tasty low-calorie food, and exercise program. Clients could receive treatments for hair, skin, nails, scalp, and body.

By then, the Rancho la Puerta Spa, located in Mexico not far from San Diego, was operating. This spa, which opened in 1940, is known for its mountain scenery and low-fat vegetarian cuisine.

Other spas offered similar services. They were often referred to as "fat farms" because most clients were women who went there to lose weight. Later, spas focused on weight management and long-term changes in eating habits and exercise routines. Modern spas have evolved into a big business.

By the 1980s, hundreds of different types of spas were operating in the United States alone, and people could contact spa-referral agencies or guidebooks to various spas to chose the one that met their needs. In addition to hotel-like resorts, there were spa cruises aboard ships and day spas where people could receive a sampling of spa services for a half or full day. Women still made up the majority of clients, and most female spa-goers were between the ages of 25 and 50.

Men, however, are going to spas in increasing numbers. During the 1990s, the percentage of men using spas steadily grew, and some spas catered to couples as well as individual clients. By 1999, men made up 35 to 45 percent of the customers at some spas, up from 5 percent in the early 1990s. They went for facial treatments, including masks and stress-relief facials, as well as manicures, pedicures, full-body massage treatments, and hand treatments. They also had scalp treatments and anti-aging treatments.

Many new spas focused more on overall fitness and health, as well as ways to revitalize mind and spirit. Some spas emphasize New Age approaches that target inner health and spiritual well-being. They offer programs on yoga and Eastern philosophies, t'ai chi, alternative healing therapies (for example, aromatherapy, reflexology, and biofeedback), believing that inner health is vital to physical beauty. Today, luxury spa businesses can be found in the United States, Mexico, Bermuda, Switzerland, and Yugoslavia, among other places. Different spas may offer regional specialties. For instance some spas in Hawaii give seaweed body wraps as well as lomi lomi massage; Chinese spas may do acupuncture treatments and give herbal supplements; Malaysian spas often feature hydrotherapy. *See also* ARDEN, ELIZABETH; BATHS; FITNESS MOVEMENT.

Further reading: Eli Dror and Joseph Bain, eds., *Spas: The International Spa Guide* (1999); David Howard, "It's a Guy Thing Now at the Spa," *The New York Times (Ct.)* Section 14, pp. 1, 6; Jenifer Miller, *Healing Centers and Retreats* (1998); Pam Martin Sarnoff, *The Ultimate Spa Book* (1989).

Steinem, Gloria (b. 1935)

Gloria Steinem, journalist and founder/editor of *Ms.* magazine was one of the best-known members of the American feminist movement that flourished during the 1970s. During those years, the press called her "the thinking man's Jean Shrimpton" (a reference to the best-known international model of that era). A tall, shapely brunette who modeled on the pages of *Glamour* magazine and dated attractive, successful men, Steinem served to contradict stereotypes about "unattractive" or "male-hating feminists" when she became a leader of the women's liberation movement.

Steinem grew up in an economically depressed neighborhood in Toledo, Ohio, where she lived with her mentally ill mother. Young Gloria had so many household responsibilities that she did not attend school full-time until she was 12. However, her academic abilities earned her a scholarship to prestigious all-women's Smith College, where she graduated with highest honors. Later, Steinem was named a Woodrow Wilson International Scholar. In New York City, Steinem embarked on a career as a journalist. In 1963, she went undercover as a Playboy Bunny so she could write an exposé about her experiences for *Show* magazine. She also helped to start *New York* magazine.

Steinem contributed to women's changing attitudes about the importance of appearance and grooming through the pages of *Ms.*, as well as through her personal speaking and writing. She also heightened women's awareness of how appearance and attire affected their progress in the working world. The generation of women who came of age in the 1970s used fewer cosmetics and placed less emphasis on mainstream fashion than had their older sisters.

Some of her remarks have been quoted often, including one she made about aging and appearance. On her 40th birthday, someone told Steinem she did not look 40 years old, and Steinem replied, "This is what 40 looks like. We've been lying so long, who would know?" (Anderson, 1988) *See also* FEMINISM.

Further reading: Walter Anderson, "Gloria Steinem Talks About Risk," in *The Greatest Risk of All* (1988); Carolyn G. Heilbrun, *The Education of a Woman: The Life of Gloria Steinem* (1996); Gloria Steinem, *Revolution From Within* (1993); Sydney Ladensohn Stern, *Gloria Steinem: Her Passions, Politics, and Mystique* (1997).

Sunglasses *See* EYES.

Suntan

Tanned skin has been in and out of fashion in various places and times in history. In some cultures in hot climates, tanned skin was and is both a normal and valued part of appearance. In contrast, a suntan has usually been regarded as undesirable during eras and in places where tanned skin signified a lower social status. Laborers who performed manual work outdoors were members of lower socioeconomic classes. Pale skin, on the other hand, signified a life of privilege and leisure, always protected from the sun, which gave a person more social status.

People living in ancient Greece, Assyria, Babylonia, and Rome, all located in hot climates, were exposed to the sun, and tanned skin was normal. At certain times, women in these places tried to lighten their skin with lead-based powders. In addition, they used some substances to protect their skin against intense sunlight and its drying effects.

In ancient Egypt, where eye makeup was particularly elaborate, both men and women used kohl to line both the upper and lower lids because it helped to protect the eyes from the glaring sun. Eyeshadow often extended from the eyelids to the temples. These powders were made from malachite, copper oxide, and iron oxide.

As political and economic power moved northward, pale skin tones were considered more desirable. People of the higher classes stayed out of the sun, while peasants and farmers were likely to have tanned skin. This was true in northern Europe and the British Isles. A pale and delicate look was highly valued in medieval and Renaissance Europe.

After centuries during which pale complexions were in vogue, suntans again became more popular during the 1920s. French couturier Coco Chanel was among those who deliberately sunbathed. Another French couturier, Jean Patou, is credited with inventing the first manufactured suntan oil (1927). Patou called the lotion "Chaldee" after a legendary beauty known for her gold-toned skin. "Ambre Soleil" was introduced and became

the most successful suntain oil during this era. More suntan lotions came on the market during the 1930s and 1940s; they were intended to promote, not prevent, tanning.

During the late twentieth century, a suntan was sometimes viewed as a status symbol because it showed that a person could afford to vacation in a sunny place or spend time on the beach or another outdoor leisure activity. At this time, too, physicians and skin-care experts began to warn that spending too much time in the sun was dangerous because of the risk of skin cancer, as well as the aging effects of certain ultraviolet rays. Many people have and continue to ignore the warnings and seek suntans, which they consider attractive. Some celebrities have become known for their tanned looks. For example, American actor George Hamilton has sported a year-round tan that observers credit to the use of a sunlamp.

Eventually, however, warnings about cancer began to have an effect. Sales of sunscreen and sun-blocking products increased dramatically during the last decades of the twentieth century as many people used these products to prevent sun damage. In the year that ended January 1, 2000, sales of sunblocking products rose 8.4 percent for a total of $483 million in sales in the United States. Various products are available in creams, lotions, and sprays, including formulations for babies and children. Some sunscreens are also formulated for "sensitive skin." Recently, more companies have been making sunscreens for younger children in novelty formulations that include colorful foams and "mousses."

Tanning salons are also popular with people who want to have a tan even during the winter months. Consumers pay a fee to lie on "tanning beds" and expose themselves to tanning lights for a specified length of time. The tanning beds help people avoid some, but not all, types of damaging rays.

Companies also sell makup that gives skin an artificial tan. These products, which have been available for several decades, tint the skin on the face and/or body various shades of tan. They come in the form of creams, lotions, and foams. Some women use these products on their legs as warm weather approaches when they want a tanned look without stockings. *See also* SKIN COLORING AGENTS.

Further reading: Paula Begoun, *The Beauty Bible* (1997); Alexandra Greeley, "On the Teen Scene:

Dodging the Rays," *FDA Consumer*, July-August 1993 (FDA Publication 95-1212); Greeley, "No Safe Tan," U.S. Food and Drug Administation, May 1991, http://www.fda.gov; James P. Hickey, "The Sun Care Market," *Happi*, March 2000, http://www.happi.com/current/mar002.htm.

T

Tattoos

Tattoos are permanent markings made with pigment inserted into breaks in the skin. In modern times, tattooing has been done mostly for aesthetic reasons or to honor a particular person ("Mom"); in earlier societies, the purpose may have been to protect the wearer against evil spirits or to produce other magical results. The color and designs of a tattoo likely had social significance and showed a person's rank or affiliation.

It is unclear when and where tattooing began, but historians think that ancient Egyptians developed this practice sometime between 4000 and 2000 BC. Mummies uncovered in what is now Siberia include a woman who lived about 2000 years ago who had intricate blue designs tattooed on her left arm. Inside her tomb were jewelry and other objects that indicated a person of high social status.

In addition to ancient Egyptians, the Nubians, Greeks, Germans, Celts, and people in Gaul and the Roman Empire practiced tattooing. The Romans tattooed criminals and slaves as a way to brand these people. Later, Christian leaders in Europe banned tattooing, but it was still done in the Middle East and certain other regions. In Africa, the custom continued among lighter-skinned people, such as the Berbers, a group in northern Africa who tattoo their hands and feet.

In North America, the Inuit (Eskimos), Arapaho, Creek, and Mohave were among the native groups that tattooed certain designs on their faces and bodies for spiritual purposes. Men and women of the Mandan tribe both wore tattoos, on their faces and breasts. Comanche men and women also practiced tattooing. Native Americans typically applied tattoos to the face, body, or both. The designs were often simple. The Mayans covered their bodies with intricate tattoos, and usually also applied body paint, preferring the color red.

How these early peoples applied tattoos varied. The Native Americans usually did so through scratches cut into the skin. Some peoples in eastern Siberia and most of those living in Arctic regions made tattoos by puncturing the skin with a needle holding a thread coated with a pigment, such as soot, then pulling it in different directions. The Maori of New Zealand, who tattooed their faces, used a bone instrument to carve the design, after which they applied soot under the skin.

The Ainu, aboriginal people of the northernmost Japanese island, Hokkaido and the Russian islands of Kurils and Sakhalin, used thorns to cut their skin for tattooing, using soot for colored designs. Women typically tattooed their arms and faces. Tattoos above the upper lip formed a sort of "mustache" design. After they married, Ainu women were tattooed on their hands, eyebrows, and lips. The design around the lips created a larger mouth that was turned up in a permanent smile. Sociologists have concluded that these tattoos reflected the expectations that a married Ainu woman would work only for her husband, think only of him, and speak only for him.

Tattooing was also a popular form of body art in China and India. Today, women of the Todas, people living in southern India, are tattooed.

For native peoples in New Zealand, the Maori and Tamoko, tattoos have been used to show status. Women tattoo artists in Borneo had special tattoos on their hands and fingers that signaled they were "weavers." The Maori of New Zealand wore unique tattoos on their faces. The Maori were known for their development of color tattoos. Among the Tobriand Islanders of Papua, New Guinea, it is customary to tattoo the genital region and thighs of youths in puberty as a sign of sexual maturity. In Samoa, tattoos are traditionally applied using a mallet to inject tiny slivers of carved boar's tusk into the skin. Black coloring in the designs comes from ink that contains soot. Tattoos are sometimes applied to the back, torso, and upper thighs, a process that can take several sessions that total 18 hours. The tattooing process is quite painful, and the discomfort lasts for weeks afterward.

There was a long tradition of tattooing in Polynesia for both sexes. Women wore fewer tattoos, for example, on the tongue and in the genital region. Some male islanders covered their entire bodies with tattoos, as did residents of the Marquesas Island. Polynesians believed that people who did not have tattoos indicating their rank and family history were not a true human being. In Samoa, tattoos signify leadership positions and other roles in a community.

Tattooing in Developed Countries

After he visited Tahiti in 1769, Captain James Cook brought a tattooed prince home to Great Britain. Members of the aristocracy were so fascinated by the prince's tattoos that some of them also had tattoos put on their bodies. Native people with tattoos were exhibited as curiosities at fairs, circuses, and other gatherings.

Before the 1700s, professional tattoos in Japan showed a person's place in society, whether that be fireman, carpenter, or criminal. Criminals were given tattoos around the eyes and forehead.

Early in the eighteenth century, tattooing (*irezumi*) became an art form in Japan, and people wore tattoos for personal adornment. Tattoo artists used needles attached to a wooden handle. Some tattoos were large and colorful, covering the torso or upper arms or both. The most complex designs could take years to complete. They were commonest among wealthy merchants, although the fad spread to the poorer classes over the course of the century. Popular designs included flowers, animals, dragons, and human figures. In Japan now, artists continue to create elaborate tattoos, some that cover the entire body. However, the upper and middle classes now tend to disapprove of this body decoration.

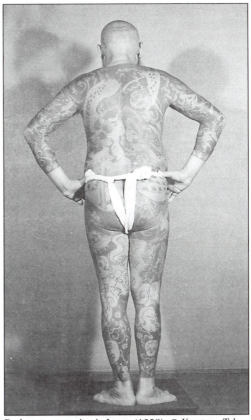

Body art—tatooing in Japan (1958). © *Keystone-Tokyo/ Archive Photos.*

In some countries, tattoos became a fad among daring upper-class people. For instance, at the turn of the nineteenth century, Tsar Nicholas of Russia, King George V of England, and Lady Randolph Churchill (mother of Winston) all had tattoos.

When Samuel O'Reilly invented the tattoo machine in 1891, upper-class people lost interest in tattoos because they had become accessible to the masses. About this same time, tattooing became a circus attraction in the United States. Most of the people who wore tattoos were male, including members of the military. Tattoo parlors sprang up in port cities to accommodate sailors.

During the early twentieth century, in Western societies, tattoos were a sign of antisocial tendencies or rebellion against the status quo. Safety issues arose from time to time. When a boy in New York City died in the 1950s from blood poisoning he contracted from a contaminated tattoo needle, the government began to regulate tattoo artists and tattoo parlors. In New York City, officials banned tattooing and enacted statutes that made it illegal under the city health codes. During the early 1960s, tattooing was banned in other American cities after an outbreak of hepatitis was traced to contaminated needles. Some American cities and towns did not ban tattooing, but required that the person be at least 18 years old. Some religions or cultures, such as Orthodox Jews, forbid tattoos.

Tattooing became more popular during the late twentieth century. Movie and television personalities in the United States and models and other celebrities revealed small tattoos they had on their hips, ankles, buttocks, and other places not necessarily visible when they were fully clothed. The singer Janis Joplin had small heart tattooed above her ankle. By 1990, statistics showed that about 3 percent of women and 5 percent of the men in one survey of 10,000 Americans had tattoos. The numbers continued to rise during that decade. (Larkin, 1993)

In the United States, the Food and Drug Administration (FDA) regulates tattoo needles, and local health departments impose guidelines on the way tattooists may operate. Tattoo artists have organized self-regulating groups that set standards and protect customers. They include the Alliance of Professional Tattooists (APT), a nonprofit organization organized in 1988 by a physician and a tattooist. The APT promotes the use of sterile equipment and sanitary procedures that prevent diseases transmitted through unsafe tattooing procedures. APT runs courses for tattooists and certifies those who complete the course and adhere to APT standards.

Although people who run safe tattoo parlors sterilize their equipment, critics say that tattooing is still risky. The dangers include infection, diseases (including AIDS and hepatitis), allergic reactions, and scarring, because tattooing breaks open the skin and introduces foreign substances and materials.

A person who opts for a tattoo should be convinced that he or she wants it permanently because the process of removing tattoos can be painful, expensive, or both, and scars may remain. At times, people who no longer wanted a particular design had it covered with a different one. Other methods included dermabrasion, skin grafts, plastic surgery, and laser surgery. Lasers can remove the pigments from a tattoo, but the ink from the tattoo remains in the body. During the late 1990s, it cost between $500 and $1,000 to remove one square inch of a tattoo using laser technology. *See also* BODY ART; SKIN MODIFICATION.

Further reading: John Batchelor, *Ainu Life and Lore* (1927); Robert Booth, "The Two Samoas: Still Coming of Age," *National Geographic*, October 1985, 452–473; Marilynn Larkin, "Tattooing in the '90s: Ancient Art Requires Care and Caution," *FDA Consumer*, October 1993; Donald Ritchie, "The Japanese Art of Tattooing," *Natural History*, December 1973; Julian Robinson, *The Quest for Human Beauty* (1998); Anthony Seeger, "The Meaning of Body Ornaments: A Suya Example," *Ethnology*, July 1975.

Taylor, Elizabeth (b. 1932)

Award-winning screen actress Elizabeth Taylor is often called one of the most beautiful women of the twentieth century. She has appeared on hundreds of magazine covers around the world and influenced numerous beauty trends during her film career. Taylor has also endorsed beauty products, including two successful perfumes, Elizabeth Taylor's "Passion" and "White Diamonds."

Born Elizabeth Rosemond Taylor in London to American art dealer parents, she grew up in Los Angeles, California, where she became a popular child actress. Her first starring role, *National Velvet*, earned critical and popular acclaim. From a young age, she was regarded as a stunning beauty. Her distinctive eyes, which have been called violet in color, are said to have a double row of eyelashes. During her teen years, the 5'4" actress developed a full-busted figure and small waist that fit the beauty ideals of 1940s and 1950s. As a young woman, Taylor moved into ingenue, then into adult, roles. She was still a teenager when she was married (for the first of seven times) to hotel business heir, Nicky Hilton. Taylor was the number one female star at the box office from 1958–1968. Throughout the 1950s and 1960s, the press avidly chronicled Taylor's romances and other activities; her image appeared in hundreds of magazine and newspaper stories.

Taylor won her first Academy Award (Oscar) in 1960 for her performance in *Butterfield 8*; a second Oscar came in 1966 for her portrayal of Martha in *Who's Afraid of Virginia Woolf?* For the latter role, Taylor wore a decidedly unglamorous look, featuring disheveled hair and little makeup. Her starring role in the *Cleopatra* (the first time an actress was paid $1 million for a film role) helped to inspire women's use of more dramatic eye makeup during the 1960s.

In recent decades, the media has publicized Taylor's fluctuating weight, serious health problems, and struggles with alcohol and painkiller addictions. Likewise, they noted her devotion to her children and grandchildren and her humanitarian work, especially in the fight against AIDS. In 2000, Queen Elizabeth of England named Taylor a Dame of the British Empire, the highest honor the British government can bestow on an artist.

Further reading: Kitty Kelley, *Elizabeth Taylor* (1982); Sheridan Morley, *Elizabeth Taylor* (1999).

Teeth

The shape, color, size, and alignment of teeth have all been regarded as important aspects of personal appearance. Teeth have been colored with various substances, as well as bleached to achieve a whiter look. They have also been adorned in various ways and filed to particular shapes. Different treatments are available to alter their appearance and alignment of teeth and to repair diseased or missing teeth. In modern times, clean, well-maintained teeth have been associated with youth and health, which are regarded as desirable traits in a mate, as well as a higher economic status.

The care of teeth dates back at least to the ancient Egyptians, when physicians learned how to treat oral problems, including swollen gums and diseased teeth. The Egyptians considered tooth doctors to be a specialty of medicine as early as 3000 B.C.E. They developed methods of filling decayed teeth with enamel and gold and also made false teeth to replace missing ones. The Etruscans replaced missing teeth as early as 700 B.C.E.

Later, dentists in Rome devised methods of drilling into diseased teeth and filling the holes with substances that reduced the pain from aching teeth. The ancient Romans also replaced missing teeth with false ones. During Elizabethan times, high-ranking Englishwomen placed tiny wax balls inside their mouths where back teeth were missing. These balls, called puffers, were used to maintain the normal shape of the cheeks despite the gaps.

In some cultures, the natural color of teeth is considered boring or quite unattractive. Ancient Egyptians tinted their teeth with red ocher, which they considered more appealing. Blackened teeth were popular in some parts of Asia and remained in vogue for several centuries in some places. In Japan, the custom of blackening teeth, called *o-haguro*, took hold during the Heian era (C.E. 794–

1185). Women of noble birth painted their teeth black to show they had come of age; women also painted their teeth black after they married. This custom persisted for hundreds of years. The blackening mixture contained powdered iron filings and water, vinegar, or saki. It helped to protect decayed teeth but was primarily a means to hide a woman's mouth expressions, something that was also achieved by graceful movements of the hand or a fan. The Japanese also thought that white teeth made humans look more like dogs. By the 1500s, Japanese samurai (men of the warrior class) blackened their teeth, but most other Japanese had ceased to follow this custom. At the turn of the twentieth century, the Japanese empress set an example of white teeth for women.

Some South American tribes have retained the old practice of darkening their teeth. They use a substance from the yanamuco tree that also helps to prevent decay, so the custom may have developed for reasons of health rather than aesthetics.

Clean white teeth are also highly regarded by certain cultures. To gain the desired look of whiter teeth, Moroccan women chew a plant bark that darkens their gums. Against darker gums, the teeth appear lighter.

In some cultures, people have changed the actual shape of teeth or removed parts of teeth for ornamental purposes. In the period before the ninth century, Mayans filed their teeth and bored the incisors so that they could attach inlays made of jade, obsidian, and iron pyrite. In Sumatra and some parts of Central Africa, people file their teeth into sharp points. The Kiv people of northeast Nigeria customarily file the teeth of small boys so they are pointy. According to author Olivia Vlahos, girls compliment boys who have gone through this procedure and call them "handsome little sharpteeth," while those with unfiled teeth are called "crabclaws," a derogatory term. (Vlahos, 1979)

The Toradja people of the Celebes (now Sulawesi) changed their teeth in a different way. So they would not appear to be like the fangs of the dog, men's teeth were shortened

A Kelahit woman in Sarawak shows a style of sharpened teeth. © *Hedda Morrison, Globe Photos, Inc.*

and blackened. Women's teeth were shortened to prevent them from having teeth like those of a dangerous legendary villainess. People in Bali also regarded sharp teeth as signs of monsters and filed them flat.

During the nineteenth century, some people had gold caps put on their teeth because they thought it would enhance their smile. Dentures were sometimes made with gold teeth placed among the white ones. During the late twentieth century, some celebrities, including athletes and musicians, had diamond inlays placed in their teeth.

Along with the teeth, the gums may also be the focus of attention. In Senegal, gums were traditionally tattooed, in a painful process, when women came of age. Certain groups of people have chosen to remove certain teeth for reasons of appearance. Among the Nilotic tribes of East Africa, tradition dictated that they remove the two lower incisors during childhood. The custom of removing teeth decreased in modern times.

Orthodontics

The word "orthodontics" comes from Greek words meaning "straight" and "teeth." This specialized branch of dentistry deals with the regulation of the position of the teeth. Orthodontists correct a condition called malocclusion, which entails irregularities in the position of teeth and the relationship between the upper and lower jaws. They use devices and appliances to achieve the goals of orthodontia, which affect the health and appearance of the teeth, jaw, and face.

Historians believe that dentists in ancient times tried to straighten crooked teeth. The grave of a Phoenician woman who lived around 600 B.C. revealed wires twisted around several teeth. However, scientists could not determine if these wires were intended to straighten crooked teeth or to hold her false teeth. Early physicians and medical writers discussed the problem of crooked teeth and ways they could be straightened. Some doctors gave their patients mechanical devices to use for this purpose.

Little progress was made in the field of orthodontics until the early 1700s. In 1728, a Frenchman, Pierre Fauchard, suggested the problems that irregular teeth might cause and proposed ways to fix them. About 100 years later, another Frenchman, Pierre-Joachim Lefoulon, called the process of straightening teeth *"orthodontosie."*

In Great Britain, dentist Joseph Fox removed certain teeth to make room for others. Pulling teeth was painful, because there were no anesthetics. American dentists continued to work in the field of orthodontics during the 1800s. Although they developed methods for straightening teeth, the results were short-lived until the 1920s, with the creation of better methods for stabilizing teeth. At first, the cost prevented all but wealthier families from having their teeth straightened, but health insurance plans began to cover some of the costs, and more people sought orthodontic care.

By 1970, about 10 percent of all American youth were receiving some type of orthodontic therapy. Orthodontists emphasized that the treatment was not just for cosmetic purposes—to improve one's appearance—but that malocclusion could have serious consequences on oral health. By the late 1990s, as more parents sought cosmetic orthodontic treatment for their children, the figure had risen to at least one third.

Cleansing the Teeth

Different methods of cleaning the teeth have often relied on readily available natural materials. Africans used chew sticks from the Peelu (or "toothbrush") tree to clean their teeth, gums, and tongues. Other tribes in Australia and Africa mashed the ends of small twigs and used them to brush their teeth. Some tribes continue this practice today.

In some ancient cultures, people cleaned their teeth with ashes or urine or a mixture of these two substances. In ancient Wales, people rubbed their teeth with green hazel sticks wrapped in woolen cloth. The Welsh believed that very hot foods and drinks and beverages containing acid must harm teeth, so they avoided these things.

Nobility in the Roman Empire (27 B.C.E. to 476 C.E.) had special slaves who were assigned to clean their masters' teeth.

In Elizabethan England, the mid-sixteenth to early seventeenth centuries, people cleaned their teeth by rubbing them with cloths and toothpicks. Royals and nobles used fine cloths, often embroidered or with decorative edging, and toothpicks made of ivory or gold. They also used a mixture of boiled vinegar, spices, and pine tar called Vaughan's Water. The inventor of this mixture, Vaughan, advised people to rinse with it after every meal and to use pieces of linen to rub off food or any coatings that remained on their teeth.

A form of bristle brush for cleaning teeth arrived in Europe around the 1600s. This type of brush, made with animal bristles and a wooden handle, may have been Chinese in origin. Dentists in France, England, and other countries encouraged the regular use of bristle toothbrushes.

That early toothbrush was followed by many others. Their inventors filed thousands of patents for these brushes around the world during the last half of the twentieth century alone. Modern toothbrushes are made with nylon bristles and plastic handles.

The first known electric toothbrushes were sold during the 1880s. Dental floss was introduced in the 1890s and was first made from silk thread; in the 1940s, a wax-coated dental floss became available. A variety of other products have also been developed to clean the teeth, both for reasons of hygiene and appearance. Modern teeth cleaning involves brushing and flossing between the teeth. Some people use various appliances, such as electric toothbrushes, brushes that claim to clean through sonic waves, the Water-Pic, and polishers.

During the twentieth century, bright white teeth became the desired look in most cultures. Tooth powders made of pumice (a volcanic rock) were used to remove stains and tartar; unfortunately, they also stripped teeth of enamel. Other early tooth powders used ground charcoal or chalk, soap, lemon juice, ashes, tobacco mixed with honey, powdered spices. Salt and baking soda were also used, as was hydrogen peroxide as a rinse.

Modern dental paste arrived during the late 1800s. An American company, William Colgate & Company, started selling jars of dental cream in 1877. In 1896, the company introduced toothpaste in tubes, launching a campaign informing consumers about the convenience of squeezing a strip of paste from the tin tube. Regular use of toothpaste and brush became more common after World War II, when soldiers were instructed in health care practices. New products were introduced regularly during the late 1900s.

Modern toothpastes claim to clean teeth, keep gums healthy, and freshen breath. For instance, print ads for Pepsodent toothpaste, which was introduced in the 1920s, claimed that this product removed the film that robbed teeth of their beauty and kept them from being clean. The ad said, "Those pearly smiles.... fight the dingy film on teeth." Buyers were offered a 10-day period to try out this new product for free. These advertisements also used a scientific argument to sell the product; they informed consumers that

the film also "holds food substances which ferment and form acid. It holds the acid in contact with the teeth to cause decay." (Twitchell, 2000)

Whitening products include toothpastes, gels to be worn for long periods, and dentist-prescribed solutions. Special preparations to whiten teeth are available over the counter in drug stores and by mail order. Dentists offer more customized treatments in which they make special trays designed to fit a patient's upper and lower teeth that hold whitening material that must be applied daily for a certain number of days.

By 1997, consumers in the United States were spending $383 million a year on over-the-counter tooth whitening kits. (Hammel, 1998) Critics say that some methods of do-it-yourself teeth whitening may damage the enamel on the teeth. The American Dental Association and U.S. Food and Drug Administration have investigated reports from people who developed holes in the enamel of their teeth. The cost of repairing this damage can amount to thousands of dollars. *See also* BREATH, BAD; TATTOOS.

Further reading: Sara Hamel, "Do-it-Yourself Tooth Whitening is Risky," *U.S. News and World Reports*, April 20, 1998, at http://www.usnews.com/usnews/issue/980420/20whit.htm; Elizabeth Jenkins, *Elizabeth the Great* (1958); Daniel Kandelman, *Keep Your Smile* (1995); Alice McGinty, *Staying Healthy: Dental Care* (1998); Marvin J. Schissel and John E. Dodes, *Healthy Teeth* (1999); James B. Twitchell, *Twenty Ads that Shook the World* (2000); Olivia Vlahos, *Body: The Ultimate Symbol* (1979); Susan Watkins, *The Public and Private Worlds of Elizabeth I* (1999); Alison Weir, *The Life of Elizabeth I* (1998).

Temple, Shirley (b. 1928)

Child actress Shirley Temple was one of the most popular performers of the 1930s and one of the most popular child stars in history. The dimpled youngster with the bright eyes and golden sausage curls endeared herself to audiences around the world with her singing, dancing, and personality. Fans were inspired to adopt the curly hairstyle that was part of the Shirley Temple look.

When Shirley Temple was a toddler in Santa Monica, outside Los Angeles, her mother enrolled her in dancing classes. A studio scout who visited the dance studio chose Shirley, along with several other children, to appear briefly in a series of short films called Baby Burlesks. The hazel-eyed three year old was a natural performer, and studio executives offered her the chance to star in her own films. At age six, she appeared in *Stand Up and Cheer*, which was followed by four more films that same year. She received a special Academy Award for her "outstanding contribution" to the motion picture industry. Soon, she was earning upwards of $1,000 a week, a large sum during the Great Depression. More than 100,000 people from around the world sent Shirley gifts on her eighth birthday.

Ideal Toy Company created "Shirley Temple" dolls, often dressed in outfits young Shirley wore in her films. These dolls, made in vinyl and porcelain, have been popular with both children and collectors from the 1930s to the present. Mothers wound their daughters' hair in curlers to duplicate the popular Shirley Temple look, and many young children took tap-dancing classes.

Shirley Temple's childishly charming appearance vanished as she reached adolescence, and although she made several films when she was in her teens, she retired. After marrying Charles Black in 1950, Shirley Temple Black devoted her time to her family, which grew to include three children. She later appeared on television in the 1950s as the host of a program featuring dramatized fairy tales. In 1969, she embarked on a new career as a diplomat, serving as chief of protocol for the U.S. Department of State and U.S. ambassador to Ghana, then Czechoslovakia, for a total of 27 years in the diplomatic corps. She later wrote two autobiographical books.

In her film roles, Shirley Temple played characters who were charming and well behaved and were dressed and groomed in a manner typical of young children. Unlike many of the child stars who followed her, she appeared unsophisticated and unspoiled, and in the plots of the films, her goodness was rewarded. The image of this talented child star is one of the most recognizable of the twentieth century. *See also* HAIR, STYLING OF.

Further reading: Jeanne Basinger, *Shirley Temple* (1975); Robert Windeler, *Shirley Temple* (1976).

Tiegs, Cheryl (b. 1948)

One of the first and most famous "supermodels," Cheryl Tiegs was a popular cover girl for more than a decade. She has held lucrative contracts to represent Cover Girl cosmetics, various hair care products, and other commercial products.

Tiegs was born in Minnesota and raised in California, where she began modeling as a teenager, then signed with the prestigious Ford Modeling Agency. Tiegs was 30 when her career took off. She was featured on the cover, as well as inside photographs, of the annual *Sports Illustrated* swimsuit issue. *Time* magazine did a cover story on Tiegs, who was appearing in nearly every major magazine around the world.

Expanding into other areas, Tiegs did regular fashion and beauty segments on ABC's weekday show, *Good Morning, America*, and endorsed a line of clothing for the Sears department store, the "Cheryl Tiegs" line, from 1980 to 1990. In later years, Tiegs endorsed a line of eyewear and wigs bearing her name, as well as Light 'n Lively food products. She wrote a beauty and fashion guide called *The Way to Natural Beauty* and appeared on television programs talking about fitness, fashion, beauty, and travel. Her exercise video, "Aerobic Interval Training," was produced by *Sports Illustrated,* and she has publicly promoted yoga as a means of physical fitness and mental well-being. *See also* MODELING AND MODELS.

Further reading: Cheryl Tiegs, *The Way to Natural Beauty* (1980).

Toenails *See* FEET.

Toothpaste *See* TEETH.

Turkish Bath

The Turkish bath, which originated in the Middle East, involves the use of different chambers or rooms where a bather is exposed first to warm air, then hot air or steam, followed by a massage and then a cold-water bath or shower. This style of bathing may have developed as middle easterners blended their own traditions with those of East India and ancient Rome. The baths in ancient Rome, however, were large spaces where people socialized, but rooms in the Turkish bath were small and private, geared for quiet and relaxation, as well as bathing.

After Christian crusaders from Europe returned from Constantinople and other parts of the Middle East during the twelfth century, they introduced this novel form of bathing. European plumbing, however, was inadequate for Turkish-style baths. In later centuries, people in western Europe and the United States popularized the Turkish bath, and they were built in resorts, hotels, and luxury liners, including the ill-fated *Titanic*. The baths were taken occasionally rather than daily. Modern public baths in Turkey remained open and could be used by men and women on different days.

The five-stage bathing process that developed in the Turkish baths—dry heat, moist heat, massage, cold, rest—laid the foundation for modern spa bathing. Variations on this sequence are used in spas around the world. *See also* BATHS.

Further reading: John J. Cosgrove, *Design of the Turkish Bath* (1913); Gregory Frazier and Beverly Frazier, *The Bath Book* (1972); David Urquhart, *The Turkish Bath* (1856).

Twiggy (b. 1949)

Lesley Hornby, nicknamed "Twiggy," was one of the best-known international models of the late 1960s. At 5'7" tall, weighing slightly more than 90 pounds, the very slender Twiggy influenced the trend toward thinness as a female beauty ideal.

Twiggy was a teenager living with her family in the London suburb of Neasdon when she began modeling. Her figure and style suited the short, short skirts, hip-hugger pants, high boots, and vividly colored fashions that had first become popular in her homeland and were called the "Mod look." People said she was as skinny as a twig, with measurements of 31" 23" 31". Twiggy's blond hair was cropped short and tucked behind her ears and smoothed with hair cream. Her large round eyes were made up with thick false lashes and painted lashes under the lower lid and shadow. Young girls around the world copied her appearance.

Twiggy shifted her career in the 1970s, when she recorded her first solo album and was recognized as a singer. She married Leigh Lawson in the late 1980s and starred on Broadway with dancer-choreographer Tommy Tune in a revival of the popular 1920s musical *The Boyfriend*, and starred in the motion picture of the same name. Throughout the 1980s and 1990s, she continued her successful acting and singing career. *See also* MODELING AND MODELS.

Further reading: Marilyn Bender, *The Beautiful People* (1967).

V

Valentino, Rudolph (1895–1926)

Silent screen idol Rudolph Valentino, known as "The Sheik," was a trend-setter and icon of male beauty during the early twentieth century. During the 1920s, he was widely regarded as one of the handsomest men in the world, and he influenced standards of appearance for men during and after his brief life. Admirers praised his expressive dark eyes, smooth olive complexion, full lips, and graceful movements. He was one of the first international celebrities to represent a romantic type sometimes called the "Latin lover."

He was born Rodolfo Alfonzo Rafaelo Pierre Filibert Guglielmi di Valentine D'Antonguolla in Italy. At age 13, he completed a course at a military school but failed the physical exam required for admission to the Naval Academy.

When he was 18, Valentino left for America. He worked at various low-paying jobs in New York City. He finally found work as a dancer in 1914 and worked hard to improve his English skills. After some career setbacks, Valentino was chosen by Bonnie Glass as her new dancing partner, and they worked at Maxim's, a popular club. He then danced with Joan Sawyer and toured in vaudeville, hoping to move to California.

Once in California, he sought work in Hollywood as an actor. Between 1917 and 1926, he appeared in more than a dozen silent films, where he was known for his "exotic sensuality." (Lawton, 1974) Valentino's

critics charged that the actor, known for his smoldering gaze and slick appearance would have "a degenerating influence on American manhood." (Lawton, 1974) He appeared with some of the leading ladies of the day, including Gloria Swanson, Mae Murray, and Vilma Banky. Three of his most famous roles

Rudolph Valentino, circa 1924. © *Hulton/Archive Photos.*

were *Blood and Sand* (1922) and *The Sheik* and *The Four Horsemen of the Apocalypse* (1921). He was briefly married to actress Jean Acker in 1919, then to Russian actress Natacha Rambova in 1923.

Together, in 1923, Valentino and Rambova promoted Mineralava Beauty Clay products during a very successful dancing exhibition tour. Valentino, who greatly influenced men's styles during those years, also received much publicity in 1924 when he returned home from a European trip with a beard. The Barbers of America Association threatened to boycott all of his films unless he shaved, which he did.

Valentino had problems with his makeup colors after the advent of color films. The usual stage makeup gave his skin a pasty look. Hollywood makeup artist Max Factor solved this problem with his innovative line of different colored foundations, which he blended to match a person's skin tones. Factor's product looked much more natural on Valentino's olive complexion.

After filming *Son of the Sheik* in 1926, (which many critics consider his best work) Valentino was stricken with a perforated ulcer and died from a postsurgical infection. Thousands of mourners tried to enter the New York funeral parlor where his body lay. Police estimated that 100,000 people wanted to pay their last respects to the Sheik. Valentino was buried amid great fanfare in a Hollywood cemetery. Several of his fans committed suicide after his death. *See also* FACIAL HAIR, MEN'S.

Further reading: William K. Everson, *Love in the Films* (1979); Richard Lawton, *A World of Movies: 70 Years of Film History* (1974); Robert Overfirst, *Rudolph Valentino: The Man Behind the Myth* (1962).

Vamp. *See* "LOOKS."

W

Walker, Madame C. J. (1867–1919)

An inventor and entrepreneur, Madame C.J. Walker founded a successful cosmetics line and became the first African American woman to run a large and highly profitable business. In addition, she helped to change attitudes about beauty to recognize women of color, not only women with Caucasian features and light skin colors.

Walker was born Sarah Breedlove in Delta, Louisiana, the child of former slaves turned sharecroppers. Her early life was poor and difficult. She was orphaned at age six and moved to Vicksburg to live with her sister when she was 10. Married at 14 to Moses (Jeff) McWilliams, she gave birth to daughter A'Lelia in 1885, then was widowed when she was 20. With no means of support, she moved to St. Louis, Missouri, where she worked as a laundress for about $1.50 a day.

After she lost some of her hair at an early age, she experimented with tried various remedies, trying in vain to restore her hair. She later said that one night in 1905, she dreamed of a recipe for a hair treatment. When she tried this mixture, which may have contained sulphur, her hair began to grow again, and the formula also helped to improve the condition of her friends' hair. She later said, "I made up my mind I would sell it." She sold the product door-to-door in the black neighborhoods of St. Louis.

After moving to Denver, Colorado, in 1905 and marrying newspaperman Charles Walker, she went by the name Madame C.J. Walker and again sold her hair treatment door-to-door. In addition to her salve for restoring hair, she developed other treatments to clean and improve the hair: a coconut oil shampoo, a salve for ringworm and eczema, a salve for receding hairlines, and Glossine,

Madame C.J. Walker, entrepreneur, hair-care industry pioneer and philanthropist, 1911. *Courtesy of New York Public Library.*

a pressing oil to straighten and smooth hair. Walker designed a special pressing comb that could be heated and used to straighten the hair.

As her business grew, Walker hired other women to sell her hair product directly to consumers. These women, called "Walker Agents," were trained to give hair treatments to people in their homes. Ads describing the products appeared in African American newspapers, such as the *The Nation*. By 1908, Walker had enough money to open another office, this time in Pittsburgh, where her daughter A'Lelia had moved in 1903.

In 1910, the Madame C.J. Walker Manufacturing Company opened in Indianapolis to make her hair and beauty products. Of this achievement, Walker said proudly, "I have built my own factory on my own ground." These products included cleansing products, since Walker believed cleanliness, good grooming, and pride were the most important aspects of beauty. Among the products were Hair Grower and Temple Grower, shampoo, Glossine pressing oil, and Tetter Salve, which was used for skin diseases. Walker's company was incorporated in 1911, and she was the sole shareholder. In 1912, she and husband Charles were divorced, possibly because of conflicts over her business.

Walker's factory employed several thousand African American women. These workers received higher wages and enjoyed better working conditions and more respect than they could find elsewhere at a time when most female African Americans in the workforce were relegated to domestic work and low-paying agricultural or service jobs. Walker encouraged black women to recognize and appreciate their beauty and reject the idea that pale skin and features associated with Caucasians were inherently "better" than their own.

In addition, Walker built beauty schools in Indianapolis and other cities. She organized her representatives into a national group and made sure that her sales agents were trained in the use of the products. The company continued to prosper, and in 1917, Walker earned a total of $276,000 from sales, speaking fees, and other business sources. (*Madame C. J. Walker Collection* [1910–1980])

Operating from company headquarters in Denver, Walker traveled throughout the South and East, lecturing on beauty products and giving demonstrations. In addition, she dedicated herself to humanitarian causes in America and abroad, donating money to the black community and giving prizes to employees for their community service work. The National Association for the Advancement of Colored People (NAACP), Tuskegee Institute, and other institutions and individuals were beneficiaries of Walker's generosity.

Although Walker has been referred to as a millionaire, she denied this during her lifetime. When she died in 1919, her assets totalled over $500,000. In 1916, she bought two adjoining homes in Harlem, which she turned into a beauty parlor and school, along with living quarters. She also purchased land in Irvington-on-Hudson, where, working with African American architect Vertner W. Tandy, she built a $350,000 mansion with a swimming pool and formal Italian-style garden. At the age of only 51, Walker died in 1919 from kidney failure associated with high blood pressure. *See also* AFRICAN AMERICANS; BEAUTY INDUSTRY (U.S.); HAIR CARE; HAIR, STYLING OF.

Further reading: A'Lelia Perry Bundles, *Madam C.J. Walker* (1991); Indiana Historical Society Manuscripts & Archives, *Madame C. J. Walker Collection (1910–1980)*; Rayford Logan and Michael R. Winston, eds., *Dictionary of American Negro Biography* (1982); Jennifer S. Uglow, *International Dictionary of Women's Biography* (1985).

Weight

Through the ages, body weight has been a key element in standards of appearance. Notions about "ideal weights" for men and women have changed throughout history and also differ from one culture to another. Changing views about the most desirable shapes, both for men and for women, have reflected regional preferences and social and economic circumstances, including attitudes about food. For example, in places with food shortages, and the poorest people were thin; a plump figure was often considered attractive.

A well-rounded figure has been considered ideal in many cultures and eras. In ancient Asian countries, a plump wife signified a successful husband and hence was desirable. Ancient European works of art, such as the Venus de Medici and Venus de Milo, show full-figured women with broad shoulders, muscles, and busts. During the seventeenth and eighteenth centuries, Flemish, Dutch, German, and French painters portrayed beautiful women with rounded contours. Rubens's female subjects were known for their ample hips, bosoms, and limbs, and the term "Rubenesque" is still used to describe such women.

Among several African peoples, including the Efik, Ganda, and Nyoro, a heavy female shape has been considered beautiful. When girls reached puberty, they were fattened up to make them more desirable wives. The Tuareg people, who traditionally live in the Sahara Desert, also admire very heavy women. Many of these women, who would be considered obese in modern western cultures, are so heavy that they cannot walk. Certain cultures in the Middle East also purposely fattened women, including those in harems.

In western cultures, a woman's weight became more of an issue after the 1850s when women's magazines disseminated images of beauty ideals to the masses, and mass manufacturing brought standardized sizes in clothing and dress patterns. Mirrors also became more common as they were mass-produced and placed in more rooms and buildings.

Women's fixation on slimness intensified in the 1920s, when the discovery of the calorie made eating a more scientific enterprise. In *The Body Project*, Joan Jacobs Brumberg describes the case of Yvonne Blue, who as a teenager in 1926, bemoaned her "fat" body and determined to slim to from 150 to 119 pounds. The reducing plan she followed recommended 1,000 to 1,500 calories per day, but Yvonne was so zealous that she decided to eat only 500 calories. She did lose 25

pounds in three months, but she put herself at a severe health risk.

In the 1940s and 1950s, the quest for slimness abated some, and women aspired to be shapely, although not overly slim. Marilyn Monroe was much admired for her buxom figure. This trend can be seen in the mass media, the modeling industry, and in beauty contests. The women featured in *Playboy* centerfolds grew steadily slimmer between the 1950s when the magazine was founded and the 1970s. Between 1954 and 1978, the average winner of the Miss America pageant grew five pounds thinner and one inch taller. A desire for a slim fit body reflected a growing emphasis on health and exercise that spread during the 1970s.

By the mid-1960s, however, slimness was again the standard. The changing sizes of fashion models also reflected this trend. In 1965, the average female fashion model weighed about 8 percent less than the average American woman. By the 1990s, that figure had increased to 23 percent. (Kilbourne, 1999)

Eating Disorders

The term eating disorder encompasses several problems: anorexia (an avoidance of eating that leads to malnutrition and serious weight loss) and bulimia (the process of overeating, then vomiting what was eaten). These have been increasingly recognized as health problems since the 1970s. A related problem is the use of laxatives and diuretics without medical supervision to cause rapid weight loss. During the 1980s, scientists estimated that up to 10 percent of all American females and 20 percent of all the women on college campuses suffered from one of these disorders. (Kilbourne, 1999) These figures rose during the 1990s. In 1995, researchers at the U.S. Centers for Disease Control and Prevention estimated that at least 11 million American women suffered from eating disorders. The American Anorexia and Bulimia Association estimates that every year, one million women develop an eating disorder, and 150,000 die of anorexia. (Boskind-White, 2000)

The girls at the highest risk are white, in the mid- to-upper income groups. Studies of at-risk populations during the 1980s and 1990s showed that they tend to have a negative body image. The age at which girls were most likely to develop eating disorders was 14–17, but that appears to be dropping. A study published in 1999 found that among 548 girls in grades 5 through 12, only 29 percent actually were overweight, but 66 percent wanted to lose weight. (Boskind-White, 2000).

Concern about the problem of eating disorders increased as well-known people, including Olympic gymnast Cathy Rigby McCoy, top model Carol Alt, and Diana, Princess of Wales, discussed their personal struggles with bulimia and anorexia. Some young women, including singer Karen Carpenter and gymnast Christy Henrich and other athletes and performers, have died from complications caused by their eating disorders. In 1983, Carpenter died of heart failure at age 32 after years of battling anorexia. Complications may include liver and kidney damage, heart damage, loss of bone mass, amenorrhea, infertility, and anemia.

Researchers have concluded that eating disorders result from various factors, including cultural messages about the importance of being thin. The development of these disorders results from the interplay of "personal psychology, physiology, family dynamics, and culture," according to some experts. (Brumberg, 1988) During the 1990s, researchers found that, in addition to teenagers and mature women, girls as young as seven express unhappiness with their weight and diet to become thinner. (Boskind-White, 2000)

Weight Loss

Dieting refers to the process of reducing one's intake of calories or certain foods in order to lose weight. The phrase "going on a diet" was frequently heard in certain cultures, particularly in the United States, during the last half of the twentieth century. In earlier decades,

people dieted when they were overweight, and the definition of "overweight" was heavier than it was after the 1960s.

The first known weight loss book to become a bestseller in the United States may be *Diet and Health With a Key to Calories* by Dr. Lulu Hunt Peters and published in 1918. Numerous other "diet" or weight-loss books and articles would follow, along with products and services that purport to help people lose weight.

Weight-loss support groups and diet centers sell new brands of diet foods, diet supplements, and other diet-related products appear regularly. Weight Watchers and Jenny Craig are among the best-known dieting organizations in the United States. Weight Watchers was founded in 1963 by Jean Neiditch, a woman who had lost weight herself. The organization recruited half a million members and grossed $5.6 million in revenues that year. Low-calorie foods were produced with the Weight Watchers label.

Magazines for both men and women feature articles on how to lose weight. These include articles on low-calorie recipes and menus, low-fat foods, special diet regimes, and exercise programs. Author Judith Rodin noted that a survey of issues of *Ladies' Home Journal* during the 1960s showed, on average, one diet article every six months. By the mid-1970s, that figure had risen dramatically, and by the 1990s, weight control articles appeared in magazines monthly. (Rodin, 1992)

Magazines also discuss people's attitudes about weight and how they affect their self-image. In a survey of readers in 1984 in *Glamour* magazine, 75 percent said they were too heavy, while only 15 percent considered their weight just right. During the 1980s, social scientists found that younger and younger people in the United States were dieting to lose weight. Ninety percent of people who enroll in weight loss programs are women. However, more men have been using these services since the 1970s, when magazines and other media presented images of toned, trim men's bodies. Male actors, models, pop singers, and entertainers, such as the male strip-tease performers at the nightclub "Chippendales," who were popular in the 1990s, have shaped new cultural "ideals" about attractive male bodies.

Polls taken between 1987–89 by Nielsen showed that about 72 percent of the women between ages 24 and 56 polled said they were on a diet at the time. During those years, the Baby Boom generation was beginning to reach middle age, a time when men and women both often gain weight. As more people, particularly women, sought to lose weight, books and magazines began promoting new diets, some of them quite unusual and some in conflict with others. Examples included the grapefruit diet, the hard-boiled egg diet, the pineapple diet, the cottage cheese diet, low carbohydrate diets, low fat diets, high protein diets, and high carbohydrate diets. Certain medical professionals, such as Dr. Richard Atkins, Dr. Herman Tarnower, and Dr. Stillman, became associated with the diets they had created. Other authors published books that claimed certain exercise programs would result in weight loss.

By 1990, Americans, who were among the world's most avid consumers of weight-loss products, were spending $33 billion on diets and diet-related services. One year earlier, that figure had been $29 billion. (American Dietetic Association, 2000)

Celebrity diet books have also been big sellers. Actresses Suzanne Somers and Marilu Henner are among the celebrities who have written books describing their eating and fitness plans. Celebrities have also become spokespeople for the diet industry. Sarah Ferguson, an author, international socialite, and former wife of Andrew, Britain's Duke of York, became a spokesperson for Weight Watchers. Monica Lewinsky, who was at the center of a scandal involving President Bill Clinton, had a brief career in ads for Jenny Craig in 2000.

The weight-loss industry has also taken advantage of people's desire to lose weight painlessly. Numerous products offered consumers ways to lose inches and pounds without the effort of diet and exercise. Among these were "body wraps," topical ointments, injectable hormones, and pills.

Foods that claim to replace high-calorie meals with nutritious low-calorie substitutes have also been popular. Liquid-protein diets are an example. However, some consumers have had problems after trying these diets. In 1977, the FDA temporarily banned liquid protein diets after three deaths were reported and blamed on this diet regime.

"Diet aids" have also been produced and marketed. In 1959, the U.S. Food and Drug Administration (FDA) approved an appetite suppressant called "Phen"—phentermine— as an aid to weight loss. It purported to speed up the metabolism. Some people asked their doctors to prescribe drugs called amphetamines to help curb their appetites. Other "appetite depressants" and pills claim to move food through the digestive system so fast that the calories have no time to be absorbed. The prescription drug Fenfluarmine—Fen—was approved by the FDA in 1973. This substance suppresses the appetite by changing levels of a neurochemical called serotonin. The FDA approved an appetite suppressant called Redux in 1996 for use with obese people. However, the next year, the makers of Redux and fenfluramine took these drugs off the market voluntarily at the request of the FDA after studies showed that they might cause heart valve disorders. Fen/phen, as one diet drug was known, was banned by the FDA in 1997 because of the high incidence of heart problems among people who were taking it. (Kilbourne, 1999)

Untested diet aids have come onto the market, with their creators claiming they should be classified as "foods," not drugs. An example was "starch-blocking pills." They supposedly blocked starch digestion, thus preventing calories from being absorbed into the body. Ads claimed that people could enjoy their favorite starchy foods without fear of gaining weight. Some consumers complained of nausea, diarrhea, and other side effects, and the FDA demanded that the pills be removed from the market until safety tests were performed.

Custom garments called body wraps have been advertised as a way to melt away fat as people go about normal daily activities, exercising, or sleeping. Made of rubber or plastic, they are designed to be worn on the waist, hips, thighs, and other areas. They do result in weight loss, but scientists attribute this to removal of body fluids temporarily, not loss of body mass.

Responding to complaints from consumers, the FDA has investigated some products that make these kinds of claims. The FDA advises manufacturers not to mislead consumers by claiming that products can "melt away fat." The agency further states that a product that could actually perform this function –i.e. "alter the size, shape, or conformity of the body" or affect the functioning of the body—must be classified as a drug and regulated as a drug under federal laws.

Absent any quick fixes for the weight problem, both men and women people have resorted to surgery to get rid of unwanted pounds or to help them reduce their food intake. Liposuction is used to remove fat deposits on the body. Removing fat around the sides of the stomach and abdomen is one of the most commonly performed types of liposuction on men. Some people have also had their stomachs stapled to reduce the capacity to hold food.

Social Attitudes

In an age where slim, fit figures are the beauty standard for both genders, overweight people are often viewed with disdain. Some of these people who resent the way they are treated because of their weight have become more vocal. They have formed support groups to discuss how society's attitudes about weight have affected their lives. Some authors/activists claim that weight prejudice is one of the only remaining types of intolerance that is still accepted in the United States. They have also pointed out that recent scientific studies show genetics play a large role in how much people weigh, so that weight is not simply a matter of willpower.

The National Association to Advance Fat Acceptance (NAAFA) is a human-rights organization that works to improve the quality of life for people who are regarded as overweight. They have published the results of studies showing that people who are labelled as "fat" experience higher rates of verbal and physical abuse, including teasing and ridicule, in their personal lives and employment than do people of normal weight. In studies of social attitudes, people tended to rate obese people as less industrious, intelligent, disciplined, successful, and popular than people of normal weight. A 1994 study on size discrimination also showed the overweight people were less likely to be hired or promoted in many jobs, mostly in the private sector. (NEA, 1994) *See also* BEAUTY, STANDARDS OF; BODY IMAGE; FITNESS MOVEMENT; "LOOKS."

Further reading: American Dietetic Association, "Weight Management," http://www.eatright.org/adap0197.html; Marlene Boskind-White and William C. White Jr., *Bulimia/Anorexia: The Binge/Purge Cycle and Self-Starvation* (2000); Joan Jacobs Brumberg, *The Body Project: An Intimate History of American Girls* (1997); Brumberg, *Fasting Girls: The Emergence of Anorexia Nervosa as a Modern Disease* (1988); Center for the Study of Responsive Law, *Being Beautiful: Deciding for Yourself* (1986); Patricia Fallan, Melanie Katzman, and Susan Wooley, eds., *Feminist Perspectives on Eating Disorders* (1994); W. Charisse Goodman, *The Invisible Woman: Confronting Weight Prejudice in America* (1995); Jean Kilbourne, *Deadly Persuasion* (1999); National Education Association, "Report on Discrimination Due to Physical Size," http://www.lectlaw.com/files/con28.htm; A. Miller, "Diets Incorporated," *Newsweek*, 11 September 1989, 56; Dr. Judith Rodin, *Body Traps* (1992); Joan Ryan, *Little Girls in Pretty Boxes* (1995); Jean Seligman, "The Littlest Dieters," *Newsweek*, 27 July 1987, 48; Karen Springen, "Making Calories Count," *Newsweek*, Spring/Summer 1999, http://www.newsweek.com/nw-srv/printed/special; Sallie Tillsdale, "A Weight that Women Carry: The Compulsion to Diet in a Starved Culture," *Harper's*, March 1993, 49–55; Judith Willis, "About Body Wraps, Pills and Other Magic Wands for Losing Weight," *FDA Consumer*, November 1982.

Wigs and Hairpieces

The use of wigs and hairpieces—full or partial head coverings made from artificial or human hair—dates back to the earliest periods in recorded history. Both men and women have worn wigs for religious or professional reasons, for personal adornment, to replace missing hair, or as a means of disguise. Wigs have also been worn for reasons of health and hygiene during eras when bathing was infrequent, and hair was plagued with lice. People shaved their heads and used wigs instead.

Material for the earliest known wigs came from horses and other animals, cotton wool, plant fibers, grasses, and human hair (obtained from slaves, people who sold their hair, or dead persons). In recent decades new types of synthetic hair have been developed using vinyl and other materials.

Ancient Assyrians, Egyptians, Greeks, Phoenicians, and Romans were among those who used wigs. Egyptians of both genders wore wigs, which helped to shield their heads and faces from the hot sun. Wigs were also placed on the heads of the dead when they were mummified for burial. Some wigs were dyed. Indigo gave both wigs and natural hair a bluish-black cast while henna imparted reddish tones. Wigs made after 1150 were dyed in brighter shades of red, blue, and green. In Greece, actors on stage used wigs along with their masks and other makeup. Patrician women in Rome wore wigs created from golden curls that were shorn from slaves captured by Roman warriors. In contrast, people in China and Japan rarely used wigs except for theatrical purposes.

During the Roman Empire (27 B.C.E. – C.E. 476), women bought wigs made of human hair to cover thin or damaged hair (often the result of harsh dyes and overuse of hot tongs) or balding that resulted from aging. Many wigs were blond, created from the hair of German captives. In his book *The Art of Love*, the Roman poet Ovid wrote:

> There is nothing graceful about becoming bald. Snatched by
>
> age, our hairs fall out like autumn leaves torn by a chill
>
> wind from the trees. . . . She has a mass of hair—all
>
> bought. She puts the money down, and some other woman's
>
> hair is hers. She buys it without a blush. . . (Humphries, trans. 1957)

The use of wigs by French royalty had a far-ranging influence on hairstyles in the western world. For generations, kings of France had experienced early hair loss, dating back to the days of Charles the Bald, the grandson of King Charlemagne, in the eighth century. During his early 20s, King Louis XIII (1601–1643) began wearing a wig, called a *perruque* in French. French noblemen, most of whom were not bald like the king, followed suit, and wigs became more elaborate and costly. By 1665, a wigmaker's guild had been formed.

By the late 1600s, English royalty had also adopted this style, calling their hairpieces perukes or periwigs, a word that was eventually shortened to wigs. King Charles II covered his thin, graying hair with a large wig featuring long black curls. Aristocrats in England copied the look, as did socially conscious middle-class people.

Throughout the 1700s, a wide variety of wigs, more elaborate than before, were made for men and women for different occasions. Englishmen were more likely to wear wigs than were women. People also wore different types of wigs that signified their profession or trade. For example, English soldiers wore a style called a ramillie that featured side curls and a long braid down the back with a large bow at the nape of the neck and a smaller bow tied to the bottom. Judges and noblemen chose long, straight wigs with one tail down the back, known as the square wig.

Wigs also revealed a person's class. Poor people wore bushy wigs with a center-part called a minor bob. Commoners wore Sunday buckles—wigs with long tight curls circling the bottom half.

Powdered wigs were worn throughout Europe during the eighteenth century. The wealthy powdered their wigs with scented powders that came in pastel shades of pink, violet, and blue, while commoners used flour. This was a time-consuming and messy process that often took place in special parts of the home called powder rooms. People put on robes and held a cone-shaped shield over their noses, then covered their wigs with pomade or grease so the powder would adhere. Servants poured powder over their heads to

A William Hogarth engraving (ca. 1767) of a scene from the novel *The Life and Opinions of Tristram Shandy, Gentleman* by Stern. All men are wearing wigs. *Hulton/ Archive Photos.*

feathers, fruits and vegetables, and flowers. Some people created tableaux on their heads, with scenes of sea battles, furniture, and other objects.

By the late 1700s, before the French Revolution (1789), people were making high rolls of hair by combing them over frames and pads attached to the head. In eighteenth-century France, the size of the wig showed one's social status. These tall hairstyles were called Macaronis. Some wigs were so heavy that the wearers developed sores on their temples and even infections that became abscessed.

As Europeans immigrated to North America, they brought their wigs with them. High-ranking English settlers wore wigs and other fashionable clothing, which they usually ordered from England. Affluent southern colonists wore wigs, as did members of other socioeconomic classes, except the poorest rural residents.

Wigmakers opened shop in the colonies to supply people who could not afford expensive imports. Dozens of wigmakers could be found in the Virginia colony, for example. They made wigs and hairpieces from human hair or the hair of horses, goats, and yaks. In addition to creating new wigs, they repaired old ones or refreshed fading powder and perfume. They could restore relaxing curls as well. Most wigmakers were also barbers, and they shaved male customers' heads to measure them for wigs. Wig-buyers could choose from a variety of colors and dozens of different styles as the wigmaker worked with them to design an individual wig to fit.

A good quality wig took several steps to make but would last a long time. Wigs were made from high-quality human hair, sold by hair merchants. Colonial wigmakers then cleaned, combed, and separated this hair into different bundles, according to color. Clay curling pins were used to hold the style in place while it was boiled, dried, and baked. After the clay pins were removed, the hair was inspected again, then trimmed and woven onto a frame made of silk threads. The strips of hair were sewn onto a support made of silk ribbons and net, which had been carefully constructed to fit the customer's head. To complete the wig, the maker finished—

coat the wigs. Late in the 1700s, a new law passed in England requiring people who wore wig powder to pay for an annual license that cost one guinea. The use of flour as wig powder became a serious political issue before the French Revolution, when people were going hungry for the lack of bread. Yet some people hoarded flour to use on their wigs.

Partial wigs are called toupees (also spelled "toupet"). The first toupees were worn in eighteenth-century Europe as an adjunct to wigs. During the early 1700s, fashionable French men and women adopted a hairstyle that included combing a roll of their own hair above the hairline to blend in with their wigs. Artificial rolls of hair were also made for this purpose. Men wore toupees to cover thinning hair.

Wigs became larger and more elaborate, and there were dozens of wigmakers on the staff at the royal court of Versailles. Wigs were adorned with all manners of gems, hairpins,

shaped and trimmed— the wig, using combs, scissors, and a curling iron. Wigs were also dressed, that is, perfumed and powdered or accessorized with various trims, as the customer desired. For example, the bagwig style involved securing the long hairs at the back of the neck inside a small silk bag.

Wigs for men became controversial in the American colonies. In 1675, Puritan religious leaders in the colony of Massachusetts attacked the practice, claiming that men who wore wigs resembled women. They urged their parishioners not to wear them. Other religious Puritans disagreed, and supported the fashion. Students at Harvard College wore wigs, although their president urged them to refrain. After the Revolutionary War, the use of wigs died out as new political ideas influenced styles of clothing and appearance. The idea of a democracy ruled out these symbols of class distinctions in both America and postrevolutionary France.

However, some people have continued to wear wigs for personal, professional, or religious reasons. Actors and actresses and other performers, Orthodox Jewish women, and people who have lost their hair because of illness are among those who use wigs. In Great Britain, people in the judicial court system continue to wear specific kinds of wigs.

People also add hairpieces or extensions to their own hair. During the nineteenth century, these hairpieces were called switches and were made from human hair that other women had sold. The sacrifice of selling of one's hair provided dramatic material for nineteenth-century authors. In the novel *Little Women,* Louisa May Alcott's heroine Jo March sells her beautiful chestnut-colored hair to raise money to help her father, a Civil War chaplain who is ill in a Washington hospital. Members of her family regarded Jo's long, thick chestnut-colored hair as her best feature—"your one beauty." In O. Henry's classic Christmas short story, "The Gift of the Magi," a loving young wife sells her hair to buy her husband an attractive chain for his pocket watch, not knowing that he has sold the watch to buy combs for her beautiful long hair.

After the 1950s, people, both male and female, were more likely to consider using wigs for styling variety or for fun. The wig business grew more than 1,000 percent between 1960 and 1970, and sales reached $1 billion in 1971 (*Saunders,* 15 November 1971), particularly as synthetic materials used for artificial hair became more natural looking and lowered the cost of wigs. People changed hairstyles and haircolors by using wigs. They could also add length and thickness with hairpieces designed for that purpose or with hair extensions.

Wigs remain popular today. They are sold around the world, and millions of men and women wear them. Some people use wigs because of hair loss, while others use them for variety. They are made from synthetic fibers, human hair, and combinations of synthetic materials and human hair. Hair extensions are also popular and have been seen on popular young celebrities, including Academy-Award winning actress Gwyneth Paltrow. The Hair Club for Men is one of the largest sources of ready-made men's hairpieces. It has been grossing over $100 million annually in recent years from its retail Hair Clubs in the USA, Canada, and Australia. ("Men's Hair Replacement Workshop Bald Talk Report") Modern technology has made men's hairpieces less easy to detect than in years past. Stock and custom-made hairpieces are available for both women and men. Most manufactured wigs and hairpieces are made in China. Do-it-yourself kits to make hairpieces are also available. People can buy materials and learn how to create hairpieces for their particular needs with the help of manuals and videos. *See also* EBER, JOSE; EGYPT, ANCIENT; HAIR COLOR; HAIR LOSS; HAIR, STYLING, OF; ELIZABETH I; ROMAN EMPIRE.

Further reading: Janet Arnold, *Perukes and Periwigs* (1970); Mary Botham and L. Sharrad, *Manual of Wigmaking* (1968); Richard Corson, *Fashions in Hair: The First Five Thousand Years* (1965); Rolfe Humphries, *The Art of Love (1957);* Rebecca Hyman, *The Complete Guide to Wigs and Hairpieces* (1968); "Men's Hair Replacement Workshop Bald Talk Report" http://www.mhrw.com/b_conclusion.html; *Dero A. Saunders,* ed., "25 Years Ago," (from *Forbes,* 15 November 1971), http://www.forbes.com/

forbes/102196/; James Stevens-Cox, *Hair and Beauty Secrets of the 17th Century* (1977); Stevens-Cox, *An Illustrated History of Hairdressing and Wigmaking* (1984).

Wodaabe

The Wodaabe, an egalitarian, nomadic group that lives in Niger in northern Africa, are known for the time and attention they give to their appearance. The word for physical beauty in Wodaabe is *boodal;* the word for personal charm and appeal is *togu,* and both are highly valued. Among the Wodaabe, men adorn themselves and display themselves for women, who then choose the partners they find most attractive.

The group's standards for appearance include a preference for long rather than short hair. Women dress their long hair in braids, a process that can take hours to complete. Author Carol Beckwith, who experienced the process firsthand, described how a Wodaabe woman separated her hair into sections and drew them into tight braids on each side of the head, a topknot, and "an elaborately layered arrangement reaching from my crown to my nape." (Beckwith, 1983) Butter was used to groom the partings.

Jewelry is a popular form of adornment. Wodaabe women wear multiple earrings in both ears, which are pierced with a sharp thorn. The earrings are large brass and silver loops. Numerous bangle bracelets, necklaces, and an ornamental band around the forehead are also worn.

Men spend a lot of time grooming their hair and bodies and try to achieve the beauty ideal of their group: tall stature, long noses, high foreheads, white teeth, and a golden skin tone. Some shave their hairlines to create a higher forehead. To lengthen their noses, they press them between their thumb and forefinger. They apply yellow powder to their skin to lighten it and use black kohl on their eyelids, eyebrows, and lips, where it serves to highlight the whiteness of the teeth. A white line is painted vertically from the forehead to the chin to make the nose look longer.

Men spend a substantial amount of time on their looks and dress in elaborate costumes and jewelry to perform traditional courtship dances and to attract women. Because great romantic importance is placed on the eyes, men practice rolling their eyes and roll them vigorously during the dancing. At two special dances called the *yaake* and *geerewol,* a man is chosen as the most charming and the most beautiful, which are high honors among the Wodaabe. For the week-long *geerewol,* where the best-looking men are chosen, men wear red ochre paint on their faces. Young women, who have been selected for their own good looks, judge the event.

Tattooing is a popular form of body art among the Wodaabe. Geometric designs are tattooed on the cheeks, corners of the mouth, and temples. Black is a favored color. *See also* BODY DECORATION.

Further reading: Carol Beckwith, "Niger's Wodaabe: People of the Taboo," *National Geographic,* October 1983, 483–309; Angela Fisher, *Africa Adorned* (1984); Sara Halprin, *"Look at My Ugly Face!"* (1995).

Wong, Anna May (Wong Liu Tsong) (1905–1961)

Born Wong Liu Tsong in the Chinatown section of Los Angeles, Anna May Wong was the first Chinese-American actress to achieve stardom and one of the best-known Asian-American actors of the 1920s through the 1950s. She experienced racism during her childhood and later as an actress. When she and her siblings entered public school, some classmates pulled their hair, which they wore in a long braid down their backs and taunted them with the insulting name "Chink." She later recalled that her father advised, "Accept everything in life as it comes. Hold no malice in your hearts toward anyone." ("The True Story of a Chinese Girl," at http://www.mdle.com/ClassicFilms/FeaturedStar/star49e1.htm) She and her siblings then transferred to a different school closer to their home. When she returned to her original school in the fifth grade, recalls Wong, "we found out that our schoolmates were willing to accept us and let us share in their games at recess time." Wong was an excellent student who enjoyed art, music, and tennis, as well as her other subjects. She eventually learned to speak several languages.

Wong loved to go to "flickers" shown in the nickelodeons during those years. The film industry was growing and she had opportunities to watch movies being filmed on the streets of Los Angeles. Despite her shyness, Wong approached the people who were making the films. At age 14, she was hired for a bit part in a motion picture called *The Red Lantern.* Despite the disapproval of her traditional father, she pursued a film career. She changed her name to "Anna May Wong" and began landing parts in movies with well-known actors. In 1921, she received on-screen billing. She overcame the intense bias against Asians that existed during those years to win film roles. In "Bits of Life," she portrayed the wife of Lon Chaney's character. She had a supporting role in the movie *Shame,* which starred John Gilbert, one of the top actors of that era. In 1922, she starred in *The Toll of the Sea,* which is regarded as the first true Technicolor film ever made in Hollywood. Wong received good reviews for her performance in "Madame Butterfly."

During the next decade, Wong appeared in numerous films, including fantasies, dramas, and comedies. In 1925, she appeared as a dancer; that same year, in *Forty Winks,* she played the role of a vamp. She became an international star and appeared in German films, as well as on the British stage and in musical comedies. Her performance in *Shanghai Express* (1932) received critical acclaim. Her biggest professional disappointment came when an Austrian actress named Luise Rainer was given the lead role of a Chinese woman in *The Good Earth* (1937).

Wong continued to act on stage and screen. During the 1950s, she appeared in various television shows and starred in her own series, a crime drama called *The Gallery of Madame Lui-Tsong* in 1951. She portrayed the beautiful owner of a chain of art galleries who was also an amateur detective. In her lifetime, she appeared in 54 films.

Wong was acclaimed for her appearance, particularly her luminous ivory skin with its delicate rose blush and her tall, slender figure. People admired her trademark hairstyle, which featured thick shining bangs and her long fingernails. When she refused a part in the *film The Bitter Tea of General Yen,* the director had the actress who played the role wear a wig made to look like Wong's hairstyle.

Wong never married and lived alone in a large home in the Hollywood Hills decorated with Oriental furnishings. She was known for her elegant appearance and gracious manners. Wong often wore a form-fitting Chinese-style dress called the *cheong sam* but also enjoyed wearing casual clothing and loved sports. She claimed she maintained her slender figure by playing golf and tennis. Through determination and talent, she overcame racism and inspired many other aspiring Asian actors.

Further Reading: Arleen Keylin and Suri Fleischer, *Hollywood Album* (1977); Ephraim Katz, *The Film Encyclopedia* (1979); "The True Life Story of a Chinese Star, Part I and Part II" (excerpts from the memoirs of Anna May Wong) at http://www.mdle.com/ClassicFilms/FeaturedStar/star49e1.htm.

Wrinkles *See* AGING AND APPEARANCE; IMPLANTS (COSMETIC); SKIN.

Y

Yardley of London

Yardley of London, founded in England in 1770 by the Cleaver family, began as a soap manufacturer and became known around the world for its cosmetics, colognes, soaps, lotions, and talcum powder, many of them featuring lavender and other floral scents.

Early in the 1800s, William Yardley, who owned a firm that made swords, spurs, and buckles, bought the business from his son-in-law, William Cleaver. The Yardley family operated the business, which became a joint stock company in 1890. As the company expanded, it brought out a perfume called "White Rose" in 1910, "Lavender" in 1913, and "Tete a Tete" in 1921. Another popular fragrance, "April Violets," debuted in 1923.

Two of the best-selling fragrances of the late twentieth century were "White Satin" (1985) and "You're the Fire" (1989). Yardley creams, packaged in pots created by Wedgewood and Royal Worcester, were regarded as attractive additions to the dressing table, as were their Baccarat perfume bottles. By the 1920s, Yardley was widely known for its line of products based on lavender and the company produced more lavender products than any other company, using materials from its large lavender farms in East Anglia.

The British American Tobacco Company, then the Beecham Group, later acquired Yardley. Jovan, a company known for its mass market fragrance products, particularly those with a musk scent, became part of the group in 1985. In 1990, an American conglomerate, Wasserstein-Perella, took over. As of 2000, Yardley of London was headquartered in Memphis, Tennessee. Products, including products with the traditional English Lavender and Lily of the Valley fragrances, were sold in drugstores and on the company's Web site.

Further reading: Yardley of London, "About Us" and "Customer Service" http://www.yardley.com.

BIBLIOGRAPHY

Books

Ackerman, Diane. *A Natural History of the Senses.* New York: Vintage Books, 1991.

Adams, Amy. "Ancient Egyptians Make Up Chemistry," *Academic Press, Daily InScight,* 13 February 1999, http://www.apnet.com/inscight/02121999/grapha.htm.

Adamson, Joy. *The Peoples of Kenya.* New York: Harcourt, Brace, Jovanovich, 1967.

Agris, Joseph. *Cosmetic Surgery.* Houston: Eclectic, 1996.

Alexander, Paul J., ed. *The Ancient World: To 300 AD.* New York: Macmillan, 1963.

Allen, Margaret. *Selling Dreams: Inside the Beauty Business.* New York: Simon and Schuster, 1981.

American Association of University Women Educational Foundation. *Shortchanging Girls, Shortchanging America: Executive Summary.* Washington, DC: AAUW, 1991.American Medical Association. *The AMA Book of Skin and Hair Care.* Philadelphia: Lippincott, 1976.

American Society for Aesthetic Plastic Surgery, "Statistics" http://surgery.org/media/statistics.

Andelin, Helen. *Fascinating Womanhood.* New York: Bantam, 1965.

Anderson, Walter. *The Greatest Risk of All.* Boston: Houghton Mifflin, 1988.

Angeloglou, Maggie. *A History of Makeup.* New York: Macmillan, 1970.

Anthony, Katharine. *Marie Antoinette.* New York: Knopf, 1933.

Arnold, Janet. *Perukes and Periwigs.* London: HMSO, 1970.

Aronson, Emme. *True Beauty.* San Francisco: Pedigree, 1998.

Ash, Mary Kay. *Mary Kay.* New York: Perennial Library, 1986.

———. *You Can Have It All.* Rocklin, CA: Prima Publishing, 1995.

Atwan, Robert, Donald McQuade, and John W. Wright. *Edsels, Luckies, & Frigidaires: Advertising the American Way.* New York: Dell, 1971.

Auboyer, Jeannine. *Daily Life in Ancient India, 200 BC to 700 AD.* New York: Macmillan, 1965.

Aucoin, Kevyn. *Making Faces.* New York: HarperCollins, 1997.

Ayer, Margaret Hubbard, and Isabella Taves. *The Three Lives of Harriet Hubbard Ayer.* Philadelphia: Lippincott, 1957.

Baillen, Claude. *Chanel Solitaire.* New York: Quadrangle, 1974.

Baker, Nancy C. *The Beauty Trap, Exploring Women's Greatest Obsession.* London: Piatkus, 1984.

Balsdon, J.P.V.D. *Roman Women: Their History and Habits.* Westport, CT: Greenwood Press, 1962.

Bandy, Way. *Designing Your Face.* New York: Random House, 1978.

Banner, Lois. *American Beauty.* New York: Knopf, 1983.

————. *In Full Flower: Aging Women, Power, and Sexuality*. 1993.

Barille, Elisabeth, and Catherine Laroze. *The Book of Perfume*. Trans. by Tamara Blondel. Paris, New York: Flammarion, 1995.

Baron, Howard C. *Varicose Veins: A Guide to Prevention and Treatment*. New York: Morrow, 1997.

Basinger, Jeanne. *Shirley Temple*. New York: Pyramid, 1975.

Basten, Fred E., with Robert Salvatore and Paul A. Kaufman. *Max Factor's Hollywood*. Los Angeles: General Publishing Group, 1995.

Batchelor, John. *Ainu Life and Lore*. Tokyo: Kyobunkwan, 1927.

Baudelaire, Charles. Eloge du Maquillage. 1860, in *Oeuvres Completes*. Paris: Gallimard, 1975.

Baumgartner, Frederic J. *Henry II: King of France, 1547–1559*. Durham, NC: Duke University Press, 1988.

Bedrick, Roy. *The Sense of Smell*. Garden City, NY: Doubleday, 1960.

Beer, Thomas. *Mauve Decade: American Life at the End of the Nineteenth Century*. New York: Vintage, 1926.

Begoun, Paula. *The Beauty Bible*. Seattle: Beginning Press, 1997.

————. *Don't Go to the Cosmetics Counter Without Me: An Eye-Opening Guide to Brand-Name Cosmetics*. Seattle: Beginning Press, 1997.

————. *Don't Shop for Hair Products Without Me*. Seattle: Beginning Press, 1997.

Bell, Roseann P., et al. *Sturdy Black Bridges: Visions of Black Women in Literature*. Garden City, NY: Doubleday, 1979.

Bender, Marilyn. *The Beautiful People*. New York: Coward-McCann, 1967.

Berdan, Frances F. *The Aztecs*. New York: Chelsea House, 1989.

Bernier, Olivier. *The Eighteenth-Century Woman*. New York: Doubleday, 1981.

Bettelheim, Bruno. *The Uses of Enchantment: The Meaning and Importance of Fairy Tales*. 1997.

Bibby, Geoffrey. *Four Thousand Years Ago: A World Panorama of Life in the Second Milennium B.C.* New York: Knopf, 1963.

BillyBoy. *Barbie: Her Life and Times*. New York: Crown, 1987.

Bish, Barry. *Body Art Chic: The First Step-by-Step Guide to Body Painting, Temporary Tattoos, Piercing, Hair Design, Nail Art*. North Pomfret, VT: Trafalgar Square Publishing, 1999.

Blackwell, Earl, ed. *Celebrity Register*. New York: Simon and Schuster, 1973.

Blumner, H. *The Home Life of the Ancient Greeks*. Trans. by Alice Zimmern. New York: Cooper Square, 1966.

The Body Shop Team. *The Body Shop Book*. New York: Dutton, 1994.

Bogle, Donald. *Dorothy Dandridge, A Biography*. New York: Amistad Books, 1997.

Bordes, Francois. *The Old Stone Age*. New York: MacGraw Hill, 1968.

Boskind-White, Marlene, and William C. White. *Bulemia/Anorexia: The Binge/Purge Cycle and Self-Starvation*. New York: W.W. Norton, 2000.

Botham, Mary, and L. Sharrad. *Manual of Wigmaking*. New York: Funk and Wagnalls, 1968.

Boucher, Francois. *20,000 Years of Fashion: The History of Costume and Personal Adornment*. New York: Harry N. Abrams, Inc., 1965.

Breasted, James Henry. *Ancient Times: A History of the Early World*. Boston: Ginn, 1944.

Brain, Ronald. *The Decorated Body*. New York: Harper & Row, 1979.

Bray, Warwick. *Everyday Life of the Aztecs*. New York: Putnam, 1968.

Brough, James. *The Prince and the Lily*. New York: Coward, McCann and Geoghegan, 1975.

Brownmiller, Susan. *Femininity*. New York: Linden Press/Simon and Schuster, 1984.

Brumberg, Joan Jacobs. *The Body Project: An Intimate History of American Girls*. New York: Vintage, 1997.

————. *Fasting Girls: The Emergence of Anorexia Nervosa as a Modern Disease*. Cambridge, MA: Harvard University Press, 1988.

Bundles, A'Lelia Perry. *Madam C. J. Walker*. New York: Chelsea House, 1991.

Burgher, Mary Williams. Images of Self and Race in Autobiographies of Black Women." In Bell, Roseann, et al. *Sturdy Black Bridges: Visions of Black Women in Literature.* Garden City, NY: Anchor. 1979

Burstein, Patricia. *Farrah.* New York: Fawcett, 1977.

Campbell, Naomi. *Naomi.* New York: Universe Publishing, 1996.

Camden, Carroll. *The Elizabethan Woman: A Panorama of English Womanhood, 1540 to 1640.* London: Cleaver-Hume, 1952.

Carcopino, Jerome. *Daily Life in Ancient Rome: The People and the City at the Height of the Empire.* New Haven, CT: Yale University Press, 1940.

Casson, Lionel. *Daily Life in Ancient Rome.* New York: American Heritage, 1975.

Center for the Study of Responsive Law, *Being Beautiful: Deciding for Yourself.* Washington, DC: Center for the Study of Responsive Law, 1986.

Chapman, David. "The Mr. America Contest: A Brief Background," http://www.musclememory.com/articles/MrAmerica.

Charles-Roux, Edmonde. *Chanel and Her World.* London: Vendome Press, 1979.

Chase, Edna Woolman, and Ilka Chase. *Always in Vogue.* Garden City, NY: Doubleday, 1954.

Chevallier, Andrew. *The Encyclopedia of Medicinal Plants.* New York: DK, 1996.

Chu, Tony C., and Anne Lorell. *The Good Skin Doctor: A Dermatologist's Guide to Surviving Acne.* Thorson's, 1999.

Chubb, Mary. *Nefertiti.* London: Bles, 1954.

Clark, Eric. *The Want Makers: The World of Advertising: How They Make You Buy.* London: Penguin, 1988.

Coe, Michael D. *The Maya.* 4th Ed. New York: Thames and Hudson, 1987.

Cole, Hubert. *Beau Brummell.* New York: Mason/Charter, 1997.

Conrad, Earl. *Everything and Nothing: The Dorothy Dandridge Tragedy.* New York: HarperCollins, 2000.

Contenu, Georges. *Everyday Life in Babylon and Assyria.* London: Edward Arnold, 1954.

Contini, Mila. *Fashion: From Ancient Egypt to the Present Day.* New York: Odyssey, 1965.

Cooper, Wendy. *Hair, Sex, Society, Symbolism.* New York: Stein and Day, 1971.

Cormack, Margaret Lawson. *The Hindu Woman.* New York: Bureau of Publications, Teacher's College, Columbia University, 1953.

Corson, Richard. *Fashions in Hair.* Peter Owen, 1965.

———. *Fashions in Makeup: From Ancient to Modern Times.* New York: Universe Books, 1972.

Cosgrove, John J. *Design of the Turkish Bath.* Pittsburgh, PA: Standard Sanitary Manufacturing Co., 1913.

Cota, Richard. *Great Shapes, Great Legs.* Personal Fitness Publishers, 1995.

Crone, Patricia. *Meccan Trade and the Rise of Islam.* Princeton, NJ: Princeton University Press, 1987.

Cronin, Vincent. *Louis & Antoinette.* New York: Crown, 1974.

Dache, Lilly. *Lilly Dache's Glamour Book.* Philadelphia/New York: Lippincott, 1965.

Davidson, Basil. *African Kingdoms.* New York: Time, 1966.

Davis, William Stearns. *Life On a Mediaeval Barony.* New York/ London: Harper & Brothers, 1932.

DeCastelbajac, Kate. *The Face of the Century: 100 Years of Makeup and Style.* New York: Rizzoli, 1995.

Deford, Frank. *There She Is: The Life and Times of Miss America.* New York: Viking Press, 1971.

Delay, Claude, *Chanel Solitaire.* Trans. by Barbara Bray. Paris: Gallimard, 1973.

Delderfield, R.F. *Napoleon in Love.* New York: Simon and Schuster, 1959.

Densmore, Frances. *Krakow Indians Use Wild Plants for Food, Medicine, and Crafts.* New York: Dover, 1974.

Devereux, Anthony Q. *Juan Ponce de Leon, King Ferdinand, and the Fountain of Youth.* Spartansburg, SC: Reprint Co., 1993.

Dolan, Sean. *Juan Ponce de Leon.* Broomall, PA: Chelsea House, 1995.

Douglas, Susan. *Where the Girls Are: Growing Up Female with the Mass Media.* New York: Times Books, 1994.

Dowling, Colette. *The Cinderella Complex.* New York: Simon and Schuster, 1981.

———. *Perfect Women.* New York: Summit Books, 1988.

Dror, Eli, and Joseph Bain, eds. *Spas: The International Spa Guide.* BDIT, Inc., 1999.

Drucker, Philip. *Indians of the Northwest Coast.* Garden City, NY: Natural History Press, 1963.

Dubois, Cora. The People of Alor. Minneapolis: University of Minnesota Press, 1944.

Dunbar, Andrew. *Body Piercing.* Griffin Paperbacks, 1999.

Eber, Jose. *Shake Your Head, Darling!* New York: Warner, 1983.

———. *The Ultimate Makeover.* New York: Simon and Schuster, 1990.

Ebin, Victoria. *The Body Decorated.* London/New York: Thames and Hudson, 1979.

Editors of *Latina* Magazine and Belén, Aranda-Alvarado. *Latina Beauty.* New York: Hyperion, 2000.

Edwards, Anne. *Ever After: Diana and the Life She Lived.* New York: St. Martin's Press, 2000.

Edwards, Audrey, ed. *Essence: 25 Years Celebrating Black Women.* New York: Harry N. Abrams, 1995.

Elkin, A.P. *The Australian Aborigines.* New York: Doubleday, 1964.

Ellyson, Steve L., and John F. Dovidio. *Power, Dominance, and Nonverbal Behavior.* New York: Springer, Verlag, 1985.

Epstein, S.S., and R.D. Grundy. *Consumer Health and Product Hazards: Cosmetics and Drugs, Pesticides, Food Additives.* Cambridge, MA: Massachusetts Institute of Technology, 1974.

Estrin, Norman F., ed. *The Cosmetic Industry: Scientific and Regulatory Foundations.* New York: Marcel Dekker, 1984.

Etcoff, Nancy. *Survival of the Prettiest: The Science of Beauty.* Garden City, NY: Doubleday, 1999.

Evans, Nekhena. *Hairlocking: Everything You Need to Know: African Dread and Nubian Locks.* 3rd ed. A & B Publishers, 1999.

Everson, William K. *Love in the Film.* Secaucus, NJ: Citadel Press, 1979.

Fabe, Maxine. *Beauty Millionaire: The Life of Helena Rubinstein.* New York: Crowell, 1972.

Fagan, Brian M. *The Aztecs.* New York: Freeman, 1984.

Falkus, Christopher. *The Life and Times of Charles II.* Garden City, NY: Doubleday, 1972.

Fallan, Patricia, Melanie Katzman, and Susan Wooley, eds. *Feminist Perspectives on Eating Disorders.* New York: Guilford Press, 1994.

Faludi, Susan. *Stiffed: The Betrayal of the American Man.* New York: William Morrow, 1999.

Fantham, Elaine, et al. *Women in the Classical World.* New York: Oxford University Press, 1994.

Fass, Paula S. *The Beautiful and the Damned: American Youth in the 1920s.* New York: Oxford University Press, 1977.

Fest, J.C. *The Face of the Third Reich.* New York: Pantheon, 1971.

Fisher, A. A. *Contact Dermatitis.* 2d ed. Philadelphia: Lea and Febiger, 1973.

Fishman, Diane, and Marcia Powell. *Vidal Sassoon: Fifty Years Ahead.* New York: Rizzoli International, 1993.

Ford, Eileen. *The Ford Models Crash Course in Looking Great.* New York: Simon and Schuster, 1985.

———. *Secrets of the Model's World.* New York: Trident, 1970.

Forde, Daryll, ed. *African Worlds.* London: Oxford University Press, 1954.

Foss, Michael. *The Search for Cleopatra.* New York: Arcade Publishing, 1997.

Foster, G. Allen. *Advertising: Ancient Market Place to Television.* New York: Criterion, 1967.

Fox, Stephen. *The Mirror Makers: A History of American Advertising and Its Creators.* New York: Vintage, 1984.

Frame, Grant. *Rulers of Babylonia.* Toronto: University of Toronto Press, 1995.

Fraser, Antonia. *Mary Queen of Scots.* New York: Dell, 1969.

Frazier, Gregory, and Beverly Frazier. *The Bath Book.* San Francisco: Troubadour, 1973.

Freedman, Rita. *Beauty Bound.* Lexington, MA: D.C. Heath and Co., 1986.

Friday, Nancy. *The Power of Beauty.* New York: HarperCollins, 1975.

Gardner, Jane F. *Women in Roman Law and Society.* Indianapolis: Indiana University Press, 1986.

Garrett, Elisabeth Donaghy. *At Home: The American Family 1750-1870.* New York: Harry N. Abrams, 1989.

Genders, Roy. *Perfume Through the Ages.* New York: G. P. Putnam's Sons, 1972.

Gentry, Tony. *Elvis Presley.* New York: Chelsea House, 1994.

Giddings, Paula. *When and Where I Enter: The Impact of Black Women on Race and Sex in America.* New York: William Morrow, 1996.

Gilman, Sander L. *Making the Body Beautiful.* Princeton, NJ: Princeton University Press, 1999.

Goldman, Irving. *Ancient Polynesian Society.* Chicago: University of Chicago Press, 1970.

Goodman, W. Charisse. *The Invisible Woman: Confronting Weight Prejudice in America.* Carlsbad, CA: Gurze Books, 1995.

Goodrum, Charles, and Helen Dalrymple. *Advertising in America: The First 200 Years.* New York: Harry N. Abrams, 1990.

Gornick, Vivian and B. Moran, eds. *Woman in Sexist Society.* New York: Basic Books, 1971.

Graham, James Walter, et al. *The Palaces of Crete.* Princeton, NJ: Princeton University Press, 1977.

Grant, Michael. *The Ancient Mediterranean.* New York: Penguin Books, 1969.

————. *A Social History of Greece and Rome.* New York: Scribners, 1992.

Groom, Nigel. *Frankincense and Myrrh: A Study of the Arabian Incense Trade.* London: Longman, 1981.

Gross, Michael. *Model: The Ugly Business of Beautiful Women.* New York: William Morrow, 1995.

Gunn, Fenja. *The Artificial Face: A History of Cosmetics.* New York: Hippocrene, 1973.

Haiken, Elizabeth. *Venus Envy: A History of Cosmetic Surgery.* Baltimore: Johns Hopkins University Press, 1997.

Halprin, Sara. *Look at My Ugly Face.* New York: Viking, 1995.

Hamill, Dorothy, with Elva Fairmont. *Dorothy Hamill On and Off the Ice.* New York: Knopf, 1983.

Hampton, Aubrey. *Natural Organic Hair and Skin Care.* Tampa, FL: Organica Press, 1987.

Haney, Lynn. *Naked at the Feast.* New York: Dodd, Mead, 1996.

Hanley, Susan B. *Everyday Things in Premodern Japan.* Berkeley: University of California Press, 1987.

Hart, C.W.M., and Arnold R. Pilling. *The Tiwi of North Australia.* New York: Holt, Rinehart, and Winston, 1960.

Heilbrun, Carolyn G. *The Education of a Woman: The Life of Gloria Steinem.* New York: Dial, 1996.

Helmer, Diana. *Belles of the Ballpark.* Brookfield, CT: Millbrook Press, 1993.

Henry, Jules. *Jungle People.* New York: Random House, 1964.

Henry, Pat. *Hollywood Legs.* Harvill Press, 1998.

Heritier, Jean. *Catherine de Medici.* Trans. by Charlotte Haldane. New York: St. Martin's Press, 1963.

Hilberg, Raoul. *The Destruction of the European Jews.* New York: Holmes and Meier, 1985.

Hooks, Bell. *Black Looks: Race and Representation.* Boston: South End Press, 1992.

Hollis, Alfred Claud. *The Masai: Their Language and Folklore.* Oxford: Clarendon Press, 1905.

Honychurch, Penelope N. *Caribbean Wild Plants and Their Uses.* London: McMillan/Caribbean, 1986.

Hyman, Rebecca. *The Complete Guide to Wigs and Hairpieces.* New York: Workman, 1968.

Israel, Lee. *Estee Lauder, Beyond the Magic.* New York: Macmillan, 1985.

Iverson, William. *O The Times! O The Manners!* New York: William Morrow, 1965.

Jackson, Carole. *Color For Men.* New York: Ballantine, 1984.

———. *Color Me Beautiful.* Washington, DC Acropolis Books, 1980.

———. *Color Me Beautiful Makeup Book.* New York: Ballantine, 1988.

Jackson, Victoria. *Redefining Beauty.* New York: Warner, 1993.

James, Peter, and Nick Thorpe. *Ancient Inventions.* New York: Ballantine, 1994.

Jenkins, Elizabeth. *Elizabeth the Great.* New York: Coward-McCann, 1958.

Jenkins, Ian. *Greek and Roman Life.* Cambridge, MA: Harvard University Press, 1986.

Jennings, John L. *Theatrical and Circus Life.* St. Louis: Sun Page, 1882.

Johnson, Wanda, and Barbara Lawson (illus). *The Art of Dreadlocks.* Ub & Us Books and Things, 1991.

Johnston, Mary. *Roman Life.* Glenview, IL: Scott, Foresman, 1957.

Kandelman, Daniel. *Keep Your Smile.* New York: Vantage Press, 1995.

Katz, Ephraim. *The Film Encyclopedia.* 2d ed. New York: HarperCollins, 1998.

Kaufman, William F. *Perfume.* New York: E.P. Dutton, 1974.

Keylin, Arleen, and Suri Fleischer. *Hollywood Album.* New York: Arno Press, 1977.

Kilbourne, Jean. *Deadly Persuasion: Why Women and Girls Must Fight the Addictive Power of Advertising.* New York: Free Press, 1999.

Kinzer, Norma. *Put Down and Ripped Off: The American Woman and the Beauty Cult.* New York: Crowell, 1977.

Kolbenschlag, M. *Kiss Sleeping Beauty Good-Bye.* New York: Doubleday, 1979.

Krakow, Amy. *The Total Tattoo Book.* New York: Warner, 1994.

Lakoff, Robin Tolmach, and Raquel L. Scherr. *Face Value: The Politics of Beauty.* Boston: Routledge & Kegan Paul, 1984.

Langdon, William Chauncy. *Everyday Things in American Life, 1607–1776.* New York: Scribner's, 1937.

Lauder, Estee. *Estee: A Success Story.* New York: Random House, 1994.

Laver, James. *Dandies.* London: Weidenfeld & Nicolson, 1968.

———. *Taste and Fashion: From the French Revolution to Today.* London: G.G. Harrap & Co. Ltd., 1937.

Lawhead, Stephen R. and Steve Lawhead, *Byzantium.* New York: Harper Prism, 1997.

Lawton, Richard. *A World of Movies: 70 Years of Film History.* New York: Dell, 1974.

Leaming, Barbara. *Marilyn Monroe.* New York: Crown, 1998.

Lebra, Takie Sugiyama. *Japanese Women: Constraint and Fulfillment.* Honolulu: University of Hawaii Press, 1984.

Leffell, David J. *Total Skin.* New York: Hyperion, 2000.

Lefkowith, Christie Mayer. *The Art of Perfume.* New York: Thames and Hudson, 1994.

Lefkowitz, Mary R., and Maureen B. Fant. *Women's Life in Greece and Rome.* Baltimore: Johns Hopkins University Press, 1982.

Leigh, Michelle Dominique. *The New Beauty: East-West Teachings in the Beauty of Body and Soul.* Tokyo, New York: Kodansha International, 1995.

Leslie, Anita. *The Marlborough House Set.* Garden City, NY: Doubleday, 1972.

Leung, Albert Y., and Steven Foster. *Encyclopedia of Common Natural Ingredients.* 2d ed. New York: John Wiley & Sons, 1996.

Lever, Evelyne. *Marie Antoinette.* Paris: Fayard, 1991.

———. *Marie Antoinette.* Trans. by Catherine Temerson. New York: Farrar, Straus, Giroux, 2000.

Levi, Howard S. *Chinese Footbinding.* New York: Walton Rawls, 1966.

Levy, Howard S. *Chinese Footbinding.* New York: W. Rawls, 1966.

Lewis, Alfred Allan, and Constance Woodworth. *Miss Elizabeth Arden.* New York: Coward, McCann, & Geoghegan, 1972.

Lindsay, Jack. *The Ancient World: Manners and Morals.* London: Weidenfeld & Nicolson, 1968.

Liversidge, Joan. *Everyday Life in the Roman Empire.* New York: G.P. Putnam's Sons, 1976.

Logan, Rayford, and Michael R. Winston, eds. *Dictionary of American Negro Biography.* New York: Norton, 1982.

Lott, B. *Becoming a Woman.* Springfield, IL: Charles Thomas, 1981.

Lougee, Carolyn C. *Le Paradis des Femmes: Women, Salons, and Social Stratification in Seventeenth-Century France.* Princeton, NJ: Princeton University Press, 1976.

Love, Robert. *Elvis Presley.* New York: Franklin Watts, 1986.

MacDonald, John. *House of Eternity: The Tomb of Nefertari.* Los Angeles: Getty Conservation Trust and J. Paul Getty Museum, 1996.

Mackrell, Alice. *Coco Chanel.* New York: Holmes and Meier, 1992.

Macy, Sue. *A Whole New Ballgame.* New York: Henry Holt, 1993.

Mainiero, Lina, ed. *Guide to American Women Writers.* New York: Ungar, 1979.

Majors, M.A. *Noted Negro Women.* Freeport, NY: Books for Libraries Press, 1971.

Malpass, Michael A. *Daily Life in the Inca Empire.* Westport, CT: Greenwood Press, 1996.

Mandeville, A. Glenn. *Doll Fashion Anthology and Doll Fashion Anthology and Price Guide.* Cumberland, MD: Hobby Horse Press, 1987.

Manos, Paris, and Susan Manos. *The World of Barbie Dolls.* Paducah, KY: Collector Books, 1983.

Marlowe, Francine. *Male Modeling: An Inside Look.* New York: Crown, 1980.

Marron, Aileen. *The Henna Body Art Book.* Boston: Journey Editions, 1998.

Martin, Nancie S. *Miss America: Through the Looking Glass.* New York: Little Simon, 1985.

Mastalia, Francesco, and Alfonso Pagano. *Dreads.* New York: Artisan, 1999.

Masters, George, and Norma Lee Browning. *The Masters Way to Beauty.* New York: E.P. Dutton, 1978.

McGinty, Alice. *Staying Healthy: Dental Care.* New York: Power Kids Press, 1998.

McKeever, Susan. *Ancient Rome.* New York: DK Publishing, 1995.

Melamed, Elissa. *Mirror, Mirror: The Terror of Not Being Young.* New York: Linden Press, 1983.

Milady's Art & Science of Nail Technology. Albany, NY: Milady, 1997.

Miller, Jean-Chris. *The Body Art Book: A Complete, Illustrated Guide to Tattoos, Piercings, and Other Body Modifications.* New York: Berkley, 1997.

Miller, Jenifer. *Healing Centers and Retreats.* Santa Fe, NM: John Muir, 1998.

Miller, Melba. *The Black Is Beautiful Beauty Book.* Englewood Cliffs, NJ: Prentice-Hall, 1974.

Miller, Richard Alan, and Iona Miller. *The Magic and Ritual Use of Perfumes.* Rochester, VT: Destiny, 1990.

Millman, M. *Such a Pretty Face: Being Fat In America.* New York: Berkeley Books, 1980.

Moers, Ellen. *The Dandy: Brummel to Beerbohn.* New York: Viking, 1960.

Molloy, John T. *Dress for Success.* New York: P.H. Wyden, 1975.

———. *New Women's Dress for Success.* New York: Warner Books, 1996.

Moncrieff, R.W. *Odour Preferences.* London: Leonard Hill, 1966.

Moran, Jan. *Fabulous Fragrances.* Beverly Hills: Crescent House, 1994.

Morella, Joe and Edward Z. Epstein. *The "It" Girl: The Incredible Story of Clara Bow.* New York: Delacourte, 1976.

Morris, Edwin T. *Fragrance.* New York: Scribner's, 1984.

Morris, Ivan. *The World of the Shining Prince: Court Life in Ancient Japan.* New York: Knopf, 1964.

Morton, Andrew. *Diana: Her True Story.* Thorndike, ME: Thorndike Press, 1993.

Mosse, G. I. *Nazi Culture: Intellectual, Cultural and Social Life in the Third Reich.* New York: Schocken Books, 1981.

Mulvey, Kate, and Melissa Richards. *Decades of Beauty.* New York: Checkmark Books, 1998.

Musil, Alois. *The Manners and Customs of the Rwala Bedoins.* Vol. 14. New York: American Geographical Society, 1928.

Oberfirst, Robert. *Rudolph Valentino, The Man Behind the Myth.* New York: Citadel, 1962.

Orbach, S. *Fat Is A Feminist Issue.* New York: Berkeley Medallion, 1978.

Orenstein, Peggy. *SchoolGirls.* New York: Doubleday, 1994.

Oswalt, Wendell. *Alaskan Eskimos.* San Francisco: Chandler, 1967.

Ovid. *The Art of Love.* Trans. by Rolfe Humphries. Bloomington: University of Indiana Press, 1957.

Owen, Nicholas. *Diana, The People's Princess.* Pleasantville, NY: Reader's Digest Association, 1997.

Packard, Vance. *The Hidden Persuaders.* New York: D. McKay Co., 1957.

Padmini, Sengupta. *Everyday Life in Ancient India.* Bombay: India Branch, Oxford University Press, 1955.

Peiss, Kathy. Hope in a Jar: *The Making of America's Beauty Culture.* New York: Metropolitan Books, 1998.

Perricone, Nicholas, M.D. *The Wrinkle Cure: Unlock the Power of Cosmeceuticals for Supple, Youthful Skin.* Emmaus, PA: Rodale, 2000.

Perutz, Kathrin. *Beyond the Looking Glass.* New York: William Morrow, 1970.

Phillips, M.C. *Skin Deep: The Truth about Beauty Aids—Safe and Harmful.* New York: Vanguard, 1934.

Plitt, Jane R. *Martha Matilda Harper and the American Dream: How One Woman Changed the Face of Modern Business.* Syracuse, NY: Syracuse University Press, 2000.

Plumb, Richard A., and Milton V. Lee. *Ancient and Honorable Barber Profession.* Indianapolis: Barbers, Beauticians, and Allied Industries International Association, 1974.

Powers, John Robert. *How to Have Model Beauty, Poise, and Personality.* Englewood Cliffs, NJ: Prentice Hall, 1960.

Procter, R. *Racial Hygiene: Medicine Under the Nazis.* Cambridge, MA: Harvard University Press, 1988.

Quennell, Marjorie. *Everyday Things in Ancient Greece.* London: Batsford, 1954.

Ragas, Meg Cohen. *Read My Lips: A Cultural History of Lipstick.* San Francisco: Chronicle, 1998.

Reynolds, Reginald. *Beards.* London/New York: Oxford University Press, 1950.

Rice, Tamara Talbot. *Everyday Life in Byzantium.* New York: Putnam's, 1967.

Robbins, Clarence R. *Chemical and Physical Behavior of Human Hair.* 3d ed. New York: Springer-Verlag, 1994.

Roberts, J.A.G. *A Concise History of China.* Cambridge: Harvard University Press, 1999.

Robinson, Julian. *The Quest for Human Beauty: An Illustrated History.* New York: W.W. Norton, 1998.

Rodin, Judith. *Body Traps: Break the Binds That Keep You From Feeling Good About Your Body.* New York: Morrow, 1992.

Romer, John. *Valley of the Kings.* New York: Henry Holt, 1981.

Rooks, Noliwe. *Hair Raising: Beauty, Culture, and the African American Woman.* New Brunswick, NJ: Rutgers University Press, 1996.

Ronsard, Nicole. *Cellulite: Those Lumps, Bumps, and Bulges You Couldn't Lose Before.* New York: Bantam, 1973.

Rose, Phyllis. *Jazz Cleopatra: Josephine Baker in Her Time.* 1991.

Rosen, T. *Strong and Sexy: The New Body Beautiful.* New York: Delilah, 1983.

Roszak, B., and Roszak, T., eds. *Masculine/Feminine.* New York: Harper & Row, 1969.

Rowan, A.N. *Of Mice, Models, and Men: A Critical Evaluation of Animal Research.* Albany: State University of New York, 1984.

Rubinstein, Helena. *My Life for Beauty*. London: Bodley Head, 1965.

Ryan, Joan. *Little Girls in Pretty Boxes: The Making and Breaking of Elite Gymnasts and Figure Skaters*. New York: Doubleday, 1995.

Sagay, Esi. *African Hairstyles*. Oxford: Heinemann, 1983.

Sanford, L., and M. Donovan. *Women & Self-Esteem*. Garden City, NY: Doubleday, 1984.

Sarnoff, Pam Martin. *The Ultimate Spa Book*. New York: Warner Books, 1989.

Sartre, Jean-Paul. *Baudelaire*. Trans. by Martin Turnell. Norfolk, CT: New Directions, 1950.

Sassoon, Vidal. *Sorry I Kept You Waiting, Madam*. New York: G.P Putnam's Sons, 1968.

Sault, Nicole, ed. *Many Mirrors: Body Image and Social Relations*. New Brunswick, NJ: Rutgers University Press, 1994.

Schissel, Marvin J., and John E. Dodes. *Healthy Teeth*. New York: St. Martin's, 1999.

Schroeder, David. *Engagement in the Mirror: Hairdressers and Their Work*. R & E Research Associates, 1978.

Seid, Roberta Pollack. *Never Too Thin: Why Women Are at War With Their Bodies*. New York: Prentice Hall, 1989.

Sher, Lyn, and Jurate Kazickas. *The American Woman's Gazetteer*. New York: Bantam, 1976.

Shirer, William. *The Rise and Fall of the Third Reich*. New York: Simon and Schuster, 1959.

Shorter, Edward. *A History of Women's Bodies*. New York: Basic Books, 1982.

Shrimpton, Jean. *Jean Shrimpton, An Autobiography*. London: Ebury Press, 1990.

Shuker, Nancy. *Elizabeth Arden, Cosmetics Entrepreneur*. Englewood Cliffs, NJ: Silver Burdett, 1989.

Simon, Diane. *Hair: Public, Personal, and Extremely Political*. New York: St. Martin's, 2000.

Simon, Rosemary. *The Price of Beauty*. London: Longman, 1971.

Smith, Jessie Carney, ed. *Notable Black American Women*. Detroit: Gale Research, 1992.

Solomon, Herbert, and Walter J. Zinn, *The Complete Guide to Eye Care, Eyeglasses, and Contact Lenses*. New York: Frederick Fell, 1977.

Soustelle, Jacques. *Daily Life of the Aztecs on the Eve of the Spanish Conquest*. Stanford, CA: Stanford University Press, 1970.

Spence, Jonathan D. *The Chan's Great Continent: China in Western Minds*. New York: W.W. Norton, 1998.

Stabile, Toni. *Cosmetics: Trick or Treat?* New York: Hawthorn Books, 1966.

———. *Everything You Want to Know About Cosmetics, or What Your Friendly Clerk Didn't Tell You*. New York: Dodd, Mead, 1984.

Stearns, Peter. *Fat History: Bodies and Beauty in the Modern West*. New York: New York University Press, 1997.

Steinbach, Ronald D. *The Fashionable Ear: A History of Ear Piercing Trends for Men and Women*. New York: Vantage Press, 1995.

Steinem, Gloria. *Revolution From Within*. Boston: Little Brown, 1993.

Steinman, David, and Samuel S. Epstein, *The Safe Shopper's Bible*. New York: Macmillan, 1995.

Stern, Sydney Ladensohn. *Gloria Steinem: Her Passions, Politics, and Mystique*. Secaucus, NJ: Carol Publishing Group, 1997.

Stevens-Cox, James. *An Illustrated History of Hairdressing and Wigmaking*. London: Batsford Academic and Educational, 1984.

———. *Hair and Beauty Secrets of Queen Victoria's Reign*. St. Peter Port, Guernsey: Toucan Press, 1977.

———. *Hair and Beauty Secrets of the 17th Century*. St. Peter Port, Guernsey: Toucan Press, 1977.

Stevenson, Elizabeth. *Babbits & Bohemians: The American '20s*. New York: Macmillan, 1967.

Steward, T.D. *The People of America*. New York: Scribner's, 1973.

Stoddart, D. M. *The Scented Ape: The Biology and Culture of Human Odor.* New York: Cambridge University Press, 1990.

Strang, Lewis C. *Prima Donnas and Soubrettes of Light Opera and Musical Comedy in America.* Boston: L.C. Page, 1900.

Stuart, George E., and Gene S. Stuart. *The Mysterious Maya.* Washington, DC: National Geographic Society, 1983.

Sulieman, Susan R., ed. *The Female Body in Western Culture.* Cambridge, MA: Harvard University Press, 1986.

Tapert, Annette, and Diana Edkins. *The Power of Style.* New York: Crown, 1994.

Tedlow, Richard S. *New and Improved: The Story of Mass Marketing in America.* Boston: Harvard University Press, 1990.

Teish, Luish. *Jambalaya.* San Francisco: Harper and Row, 1985.

Thayer, Mary Van Renssaeler. *Jacqueline Bouvier Kennedy.* Garden City, NY: Doubleday, 1962.

Tiegs, Cheryl, with Vicki Lindner. *The Way to Natural Beauty.* New York: Simon and Schuster, 1980.

Tobias, Andrew. *Fire and Ice: The Story of Charles Revson—The Man Who Built the Revlon Empire.* New York: William Morrow, 1976.

Trout, Lawana Hooper. *The Maya.* New York: Chelsea House, 1991.

Trusty, Sherman L. *The Art and Science of Barbering.* Pasadena, CA: 1963.

Turnbull, Colin. *The Forest People.* New York: Simon and Schuster, 1961.

Twitchell, James B. *Twenty Ads that Shook the World.* New York: Crown, 2000.

Uglow, Jennifer S., comp. and ed., *International Dictionary of Women's Biography.* New York: Macmillan, 1985.

University of Michigan Research Center. *Adolescent Girls.* Ann Arbor: University of Michigan Press, 1957.

Urquhart, David. *The Turkish Bath, With A View To Its Introduction Into The British Dominions.* London: D. Bryce, 1856.

Van Deusen, Edmund. *What You Can Do About Baldness.* New York: Stein and Day, 1978.

Verrill, A. Hyatt. *Perfume and Spices.* Boston: L.C. Page & Co., 1940.

Vickers, Michael. *The Roman World.* New York: Peter Bedrick Books, 1989.

Vlahos, Olivia. *Body: The Ultimate Symbol.* New York: Lippincott, 1979.

von Boehn, Max. *Modes and Manners of the Nineteenth Century.* New York: B. Blom, 1909.

Wade, Carlson. *Health Secrets from the Orient.* New York: Signet, 1973.

Wald, C. *Myth America.* New York: Pantheon, 1975.

Ward, John William, ed. *Society, Manners, and Politics in the United States.* 1961.

Walton, John, Jeremiah A. Barondess, and Stephen Lock, eds. *The Oxford Medical Companion.* New York: Oxford, 1994.

Watkins, Julian Lewis. *The 100 Greatest Advertisements, Who Wrote Them and What They Did.* New York: Dover, 1959.

Weaver, Rebecca, and Rodney Dale. *Machines in the Home.* New York: Oxford, 1992.

Wynbrandt, James. *The Excruciating History of Dentistry.* New York: Griffin, 2000.

Weinberg, Norma Pasehoff. *Henna From Head to Toe.* Pownal, VT: Storey Books, 1999.

Weir, Alison. *The Life of Elizabeth I.* New York: Ballantine, 1998.

Wells, Evelyn. *Nefertiti.* Garden City, NY: Doubleday, 1964.

What Is Beauty? New York: Universe Books, 1998.

Wilkinson, Beth. *Coping With the Dangers of Tattooing, Body Piercing and Branding.* New York: Rosen Publishing, 1999.

Wilkinson, Sir John Gardner. *The Manners and Customs of the Ancient Egyptians.* London: J. Murray, 1878.

Windeler, Robert. *Shirley Temple.* London: W.H. Allen, 1976.

Winter, Ruth. *A Consumer's Dictionary of Cosmetic Ingredients.* New York: Crown, 1998.

———. *The Smell Book: Scents, Sex, and Society.* Philadelphia: Lippincott, 1976.

Wolf, Naomi. *The Beauty Myth: How Images of Beauty Are Used Against Women.* New York: William Morrow, 1991.

Woog, Adam. *Marilyn Monroe.* San Diego: Lucent Books, 1997.

Wright, Lawrence. *Clean and Decent: The Fascinating History of the Bathroom and the Water Closet, and Sundry Habits, Fashions and Accessories of the Toilet, Principally in Great Britain, France, and America.* New York: Viking Press, 1960.

Wyse, Lois. *Blond Beautiful Blonde: How to Look, Live, Work and Think Blonde.* New York: M. Evans, 1980.

Yutang, Lin. *My Country and My People.* New York: John Day, 1939.

Zorita, Alonso de. *Life and Labor in Ancient Mexico.* Trans. by Benjamin Keen. New Brunswick, NJ: Rutgers University Press, 1963.

Periodicals and Web Sites

Abercrombie, Thomas J. "Arabia's Frankincense Trail," *National Geographic* (October 1985): 474–513.

———. "Change Comes to a Changeless Land," *National Geographic* (March 1977): 312–343.

"About Bobbi." http://www.bobbibrowncosmetics.com/bobbi/bio, June 2000.

"About Cindy." Cindy.Com, The Official Cindy Crawford Web site, http://www.cindy.com/about/biography, June 2000.

Adams, Amy. "Ancient Egyptians Make Up Chemistry," *Academic Press, Daily InScight,* http://www.apnet.com/inscight/02121999/grapha.htm, 13 February 1999.

Aguila, Justino. "Zoot-Suiting Up," *Seattle Times* June 7, 1998, http://www.seattletimes.nwsource.com/news/lifestyles/html98/zoot_060748.html.

Ahrens, Frank. "Why Is This Rat Smiling?" *The Washington Post,* 17 August 1995.

Alexander, Suzanne. "Egged on By Moms, Many Teen-agers Get Plastic Surgery," *The Wall Street Journal,* 24 September 1990, p.1.

Alireza, Marianne. "Women of Saudi Arabia," *National Geographic* (October 1987).

American Beauty Association. "To Expand, Serve and Protect," 1999.

American Dental Association. "ADA Statement on Intraoral/Perioral Piercing," 1999.

———. "Consumer Frequently Asked Questions: Bad Breath (Halitosis)," http://www.ada.org/consumer, June 2000.

American Dietetic Association. "Weight Management," http://www.eatright.org/adap0197.html, June 2000.

American Society for Aesthetic Plastic Surgery. "Statistics" http://surgery.org/media/statistics, June 2000.

American Society of Dermatologic Surgeons. "Abdominoplasty" (1998), "Dermabrasion Treatment," "Laser Resurfacing" (April 1999), "Soft Tissue Augmentation" (#006, 1995), "Tumescent Liposuction" (#003, 1994), "Statistics, 1993-1998," http://www.asds-net.org/.html, June 2000.

"Another British Invasion?" *Happi,* August 1997.

Associated Press. "Men Slowly Accept New Clothing Choices," 8 February 1996.

Beckwith, Carol. "Niger's Wodaabe: People of the Taboo," *National Geographic* (October 1983): 483–309.

Booth, Robert. "The Two Samoas: Still Coming of Age," *National Geographic* (October 1985): 452–473.

"Boss Models Men." http://www.bossmodels.com/men.html, June 2000.

Bradford, Laura, "On the Teen Scene: Cosmetics and Reality," *FDA Consumer* (May 1994).

Branna, Tom. "East Is East," *Happi* (July 1997).

———. "Fragrance and African-American Women," *Happi* (July 1997).

———. "No Sweat," *Happi* (March 1997).

Brown, Helen Gurley, "Step Into My Parlor," *Cosmopolitan: 25th Anniversary Issue* (May 1990): 22.

Brumberg, Joan Jacobs. Quoted in *Body [I]com: Body as Commodity—mediacraze,* (1999), http://nm-server.jrn.columbia.edu/projects/bodyimage/commodity/media.

Bussmiller, Elisabeth. "Ms. Universe," *Equity* (February 1999): 29–30.

Calistro, Paddy. "Shades of Meaning," *Los Angeles Times,* 26 October 1986.

Canning, Christine. "Animal Testing Alternatives: The Quest Continues," *Happi* (February 1997), http://www.happi.com/special/febmain2.html.

———. "Filling the Void in Ethnic Skin Care," *Happi* (October 1996).

———. "Fine Fragrances," *Happ,* (November 1996): 12–19.

"Cindy Crawford," *Cosmopolitan* (October 1990): 42.

Clarke,De. http://www.igc.apc.org/nemesis/ACLU/Nikki/BeautyClarke2.html, June 2000.

"Classic Beauty," *Beauty Handbook* (June 1992): 29.

"Claudia Schiffer: Biography," http://www.boxofficemania.com/actresses/c/claudia_schiffer/, June 2000.

Code of Federal Regulations, Title 21: U.S. Government

Colgate Palmolive Company. "Our History," "When It Happened," from Colgate Palmolive Company Web site, http://www.colgate.com/html, June 2000.

Cosmetic Executive Women. "About CEW," "Cosmetic Executive Women 1997 Beauty Awards," "Cosmetic Executive Women 1999 Beauty Awards," http://www.cew.org and www.beautyawards.com, June 2000.

"Cosmo Cover Girls Then and Now: Beverly Johnson," *Cosmopolitan* (May 1990): 346.

Darling, Lynn. "Age, Beauty, and Truth," *New York Times*, 23 January 1994, sec. 9, p. 5.

De La Haba, Louis. "Guatemala, Maya and Modern," *National Geographic* (November 1974): 661–689.

Delmar, Michael. "Jean Shrimpton, Star of the '60s," *TopModel* (Sept./Oct. 1996): 82–85.

Denker, Debra. "Pakistan's Kalish: People of Fire and Fervor," *National Geographic* (October 1981): 458–473.

Dero A. Saunders, ed. "25 Years Ago" (from *Forbes*, 15 November 1971), http://www.forbes.com/forbes/102196/, June 2000.

Devillers, Carole. "What Future for the Wayana Indians?" *National Geographic* (January 1983): 66–83.

Dion, K. "Children's Physical Attractiveness and Sex Determinants Adult Punitiveness," *Developmental Psychology* 24 (1974): 285–290.

Drawbridge, Jennifer. "Implants, Dangerous Curves," *Mirabella* (August 1991): 104–108.

Dunn, Carolyn A. "The Anti-perspirant and Deodorant Market," *Happi* (March 1998).

———. "The Bar and Liquid Soap Market," *Happi* (December 1996), http://www.happi.com, June 2000.

———. "The Ethnic Hair Care Market," *Happi* (April 1997), http://www.happi.com, June 2000.

———. "Natural Appeal," *Happi* (June 1997), http://www.happi.com, June 2000.

———. "The Skin Care Market," *Happi* (March 1997), http://www.happi.com, June 2000.

Faludi, Susan. "Male-ady," *People* (25 October 1999): 143–146.

Fillingham, Christine. "Quick-Fix Beauty—Botched!" *Glamour* (January 1999): 62–63.

Firestone, Lois. "Barbie Arrived 40 Years Ago, Never Left," *The Salem (Ohio) News*, 23 March 1999, pp. 1, 4.

Fragrance Foundation. "Historical Highlights of the Fragrance Foundation," "The Award," "History," "Time Line," "The 26th Annual Fragrance Foundation "FiFi" Awards," "The 27th Annual Fragrance Foundation "FiFi" Awards," The Fragrance Foundation http://www.fragrance.org/tff-hist.html, June 2000.

Freed, Janet Carlson. "Signature Scents," *Town and Country Weddings,* http://tncweddings.women.com, June 2000.

Freed, Janet Carlson, and Diane Guernsey, eds. "Town and Country's Comprehensive Guide to Cosmetic Surgery," *Town & Country* (March 1999): 144–162.

Friedman, Steve. "The Importance of Being Farrah," *Mirabella* (March/April 1998): 122ff.

Galinsky, Bob. "Skin and Hair Products Go Natural," *M@rket Asi@ Agribusiness information* (11 November 1999).

Garver, Rob. "Bye-Bye Barbershops," *New Jersey Monthly*, http://www.hairinternational.com/bar_conv.htm, June 2000.

"Generation N," *Newsweek*, July 12, 1999, pp. 53–58.

George Masters. *The New York Times* Obituary, 7 March 1998.

Gerster, Georg. "River of Sorrow, River of Hope," *National Geographic* (August 1975): 152–189.

Gilliard, E. Thomas. "New Guinea's Rare Birds and Stone Age Men," *National Geographic* (April 1953).

GMP Institute, "Key National and International Standards, Laws, Regulations and Guidelines," GMP Institute online: www.gmp1st.com/comlaws.htm, June 2000.

Goleman, Daniel. "Equation for Beauty Emerges in Studies," *The New York Times*, 5 August 1986.

Gordon, Robert J. "Papua New Guinea: Nation in the Making," *National Geographic* (August 1982): 143–171.

Greeley, Alexandra. "No Safe Tan," US Food and Drug Administration (FDA) May 1991, http://www.fda.gov

———. "On the Teen Scene: Dodging the Rays," *FDA Consumer* 95-1212 (July-August 1993).

Gregory, Sophronia Scott, and Lan N. Nguyen. "Powder Broker," *People* (7 July 1997): 91–92.

"Gynecomastia," University of Iowa, Department of Plastic Surgery.

Hair International, "Purpose" and "Objectives," http://www.hairinternational.com/bar_conv.htm, June 2000.

Hall, Alice J. "Dazzling Legacy of an Ancient Quest," *National Geographic* (March 1977): 292–311.

Hamel, Sara. "Do-It-Yourself Tooth Whitening Is Risky," *U.S. News and World Reports*, April 20, 1998, http://www.usnews.com/usnews/issue/980420/20whit.htm.

Hanover, Larry, "Hair Replacement: What Works, What Doesn't," *FDA Consumer* (April 1997).

"Heightism: Short Guys Finish Last," *The Economist* (23 December 1995): 21.Henkel, John. "A Colorful History," *FDA Consumer* (December 1993).

Her Generation, "Mary Kay Ash," http://www.hergeneration.com/Achievers, June 2000.

———. "From Shampoo to Cereal: Seeing the Safety of Color Additives," *FDA Consumer* (December 1993).

Herskowit, Jan, and Rebecca A. Fannin. "Shiseido Buffs Its Image with first Pan-Asian Line," *Advertising Age International* (September 1997): 12ff.

Hession, Colin. "Men's Grooming," *Happi* (July 1997), http://www.happi.com.special/julmain3.htm, June 2000.

Hickey, James P. "A Market Gelling Together," *Happi* (March 1999), http://www.happi.com.special, June 2000.

———. "The Sun Care Market," *Happi* (March 2000), http://www.happi.com/current/mar002.htm, June 2000.

Hilboldt-Stolley, Lise. "Pretty Babies," *Good Housekeeping* (February 1999): 102ff.

Howard, David. "It's a Guy Thing Now at the Spa," *The New York Times* (Ct.), sec. 14, pp. 1, 6.

Hudson, Patrick. "Causes of Male Pattern Baldness," "Hair Transplant," http://www.phudson.com, June 2000.

"Iman" in *Unforgettable Women of the Century*. Time-Life/People Books, 1998.

"Iman: All You Want, All You Need," http://www.sheen.com/iman/iman.htm, June 2000.

Indiana Historical Society Manuscripts & Archives. "Madame C. J. Walker Collection (1910–1980)."

"The Insider's Guide to Supermodels and Modeling," http://supermodelguide.com/supermodels, June 2000.

"It's Not Your Mother's Nail Polish Anymore," *Happi* (May 1997).

Jacobson, Doranne Wilson. "Purdah in India: Life Behind the Veil," *National Geographic* (August 1977): 270–286.

Johnson, Lois Joy. "Emme's Guide to Confident Style," *Ladies' Home Journal* (March 1999): 126–131.

Johnson, Lucas L. II. "Makeup Artist Creates Line of Cosmetics for Men," *The Oak Ridger (TN),* 9 June 1998.

Johnson Products Company. "How It All Began," "Johnson Products Company, 1996–1998," http://www.sheen.com/history.htm, June 2000.

Jones, Jessica. "Young Men Care About Hair Care," *Staten Island Advance,* 8 October 1999.

"Josephine Baker," Special Report: Remarkable American Women, *Life Magazine* (1976): 91.

Kalb, Claudia. "Our Quest to Be Perfect," Newsweek (9 August 1999): 52ff.

Kendall, Timothy. "Kingdom of Kush," *National Geographic* (November 1990): 96–125.

Koenderman, Tony. "The Avon lady comes calling in SA [South America] too," *Advertising/Marketing* http://www.fm.co.za/97/0711/admark/avon.htm, 11 July 1997.

Kuszynski, Alex. "Trading on Hollywood Magic," *The New York Times,* 30 January 1998, pp. C1, C4.

La Ferla, Ruth. "The Young Woman Most Invited," *The New York Times,* 28 March 1999, p. 9-1, 9-7.

Larkin, Marilynn. "Tattooing in the '90s: Ancient Art Requires Care and Caution," *FDA Consumer* (October 1993).

"Lasting Legacy," *People* (11 January 1999): 138.

Leigh, Michelle Dominique. "Ageless Beauty," *Natural Health* (July-August 1996): 80–82, 145.

Lewis, Carol. "Clearing Up Cosmetics Confusion," *FDA Consumer* (May-June 1998).

Liebmann, Lisa. "The History of Rouge: Cheek Chic," *Mirabella* (July 1991): 52–54.

L'Oreal. "Finance," "History," "Industry," http://www.loreal.com/us, June 2000.

Madden, Normandy. "Maybelline Turns to Eurasian Model," *Advertising Age* (21 September 1998): 12ff.

"Many Benefits of Aloe Vera," *Nature's Impact* (February/March 1999).

Mary Kay. "About Us," http://www.marykay.com/marykay/About, June 2000.

McDowell, Bart. "The Aztecs," *National Geographic* (December 1980): 704–751.

McIntyre, Loren. "Amazon: The River Sea," *National Geographic* (October 1972): 456–495.

"Men's Hair Replacement Workshop Bald Talk Report," http://www.mhrw.com/b_conclusion.html, June 2000.

Miller, A. "Diets Incorporated," *Newsweek* (11 September 1989): 56.

Miller, Samantha, et al. "Nose Can Do," *People* (10 August 1998): 75–76.

Montaigne, Fen, "Iran: Testing the Waters of Reform," *National Geographic* (July 1999): 2–33.

"Moody Hues," *People* (7 December 1998): 111.

Morris, Lois B. "Body Appreciation," *Allure* (September 1999): 98.

Morrison, Margaret. "Hypoallergenic Cosmetics," *FDA Consumer* (June 1974).

Museum of Menstruation and Women's Health. "Zonite" http://www.mum.org.

"NAACP Targets Beauty Industry for Failure to Empower Blacks," *New Amsterdam News*, 17 May 1997, p. 3.

National Clearinghouse of Plastic Surgery Statistics. "1998 Plastic Surgery Statistics," and "As 'Boomers' Age, Cosmetic Surgery Increases," http://www.plasticsurgery.org/mediactr/trends92-98.htm, June 2000.

National Education Association. "Report on Discrimination Due to Physical Size," http://www.lectlaw.com/files/con28.htm.

"Norman Orentreich, M.D.," (interview) *Cosmopolitan* (February 1990): 122,124.

Ogunnaike, Lola. "Some Hair Is Happy to be Nappy," *The New York Times*, 27 December 1998, pp. 9-1, 9-3.

Olsen, E. A., et al. "Five Year Follow-Up of Men With Androgenetic Alopecia Treated with Topical Minoxidil," *Journal of the American Academy of Dermatology* (April 1990): 643–646.

O'Neill, Anne-Marie, et al. "Custom-Made Cachet," *People* (22 February 1999): 107–108.

Paley, Maggie. "Scalpel Junkies," *Mirabella* (January 1991): 74–76.

Pan, Esther. "Scary Hair," *Newsweek* (30 November 1998): 72.

Parish, L.C., and J.T. Crissey. "Cosmetics: A Historical Review," *Clinics in Dermatology* 6, no. 3 (1998): 1–3.

Patlak, Margie. "Hair Dye Dilemmas," *FDA Consumer* (April 1993).

———. "Permanent Eyeliner," *FDA Consumer* (April 1993).

Paula's Choice. "Paula Begoun," http://www.cosmeticscop.com, June 2000.

Pine, Devera. "Hair! From Personal Statement to Personal Problem," *FDA Consumer* (December 1991).

Plastic Surgery Information Service. National Clearinghouse of Plastic Surgery Statistics, "1998 Plastic Surgery Procedural Statistics," http://www. plasticsurgery. org/mediactr/trends92-98.htm, June 2000.

Procter and Gamble Corporation. "General Information," "FAQs," http://www. pg.com, June 2000.

Quintero, Nita. "Coming of Age the Apache Way," *National Geographic* (February 1980): 262–290.

Ritchie, Donald. "The Japanese Art of Tattooing," *Natural History* (December 1973).Roth, Gil Y. "Aramis Takes U-Turn in Men's Market," *Happi* (February 1998), http://www.happi.com.special/feb982.html, June 2000.

———. "Ethnic Skin Care Review," *Happi* (October 1997).

Rudnick, Paul. "The Blond: Marilyn Monroe," *Time* 100: "Heroes and Icons" (12 October 1999)

Salmans, Sandra. "Estee Lauder: The Scents of Success," *The* New York Times, 18 April 1982.

Scofield, John. "Christopher Columbus and the New World He Found," *National Geographic* (November 1975): 584–625.

Seeger, Anthony. "The Meaning of Body Ornaments: A Suya Example," *Ethnology* (July 1975).

Segal, Marian. "Hair Today, Gone Tomorrow," *FDA Consumer* (September 1996).

Seligman, Jean. "The Littlest Dieters," *Newsweek* (27 July 1987): 48.

"Seventeen Survey," *Cosmetics Fair* (July 1967): 17–18.

Shiseido Corporation. "About Shiseido;" "The Shiseido Story," http://www. shiseidoco.jple/index.htm, June 2000.

Shultz, Harald. "Brazil's Big-Lipped Indians," *National Geographic* (January 1962).

Sinnott, Abby. "Study Finds No Association Between Hair Dye and Non-Hodgkin's Lymphoma," *Daybreak* (2 December 1998), http://www.ucsf.edu/daybreak.

"Silicone Update: Safer Than You Thought?" *Longevity* (October 1994): 14, 16.

"The Sleeping Giant Awakes," *Soap, Perfumery & Cosmetics* 70, Issue 5 (May 1997): 23ff.

Society of Cosmetic Chemists Web site, http://www.sccconline.org, June 2000.

Sontag, Susan. "The Double Standard of Aging," *Saturday Review,* 23 September 1972, 29–38.

Springen, Karen. "Making Calories Count," *Newsweek* (Spring/Summer 1999), http://www.newsweek.com/nw-srv/printed/special, June 2000.

Stehlin, Doris. "Cosmetic Allergies," *FDA Consumer* (November 1986), http://vm.cfsan.fda.gov/~dms/cos-224.html, June 2000.

———. "Cosmetic Safety: More Complex Than at First Blush," *FDA Consumer* (May 1995).

Stoloft, Charles I. "The Fashionable Tooth," *Natural History* (February 1972).

Stuller, Jeff. "Cleanliness Has Only Recently Become a Virtue," *Smithsonian Magazine* (February 1991): 126–134.

Takashima, Miki. "Black and Beautiful," *The Daily Yomiuri,* 18 November 1999, p. 7.

Teufel, Nikki. *Roseanne* show, interview with Nikki Teufel, Fox Network, 29 March 1999.

Tien, Ellen. "Brow Tools for Him and Her," *The New York Times,* 11 April 1999, p. 3.

Topping, Audrey. "Return to Changing China," *National Geographic* (December 1971): 801–833.

"The True-Life Story of a Chinese Star," Part I and II (excerpts from the memoirs of

Anna May Wong). http://www.mdle.com/ClassicFilms/FeaturedStar.

Tucker, Randy. "P & G Puts $1.72 Billion into Ads," *Cincinnati Enquirer*, 23 March 1999, http://www.Enquirer.com.editions/1999/03/23.

Turner, Terence S. "Tchikrin: A Central Brazilian Tribe and Its Symbolic Language of Bodily Adornment," *Natural History* (October 1969).

UltimateTV.com. "Ultimate TV News—Having That Keen Fashion Sense—the 1998 VH1 Fashion Awards," http://www.ultimatetv.com/news/f/a/98/10/26vh1.html, June 2000.

U.S. Food and Drug Administration. Center for Food Safety and Applied Nutrition, "Color Additives," Office of Cosmetics Fact Sheet, 7 February 1995.

———. Center for Food Safety and Applied Nutrition, Office of Cosmetics Fact Sheet, "Lead Acetate Used in Hair Dye Products, 8 October 1998.

———. Center for Food Safety and Applied Nutrition, Office of Cosmetics Fact Sheet, "Prohibited Ingredients," 2 February 1995.

———. Center for Food Safety and Applied Nutrition, "Soap," 3 February 1995.

———. Center for Food Safety and Applied Nutrition Report, "Stakeholders' Meeting," 22 January 1999.

———. Center for Food Safety and Applied Nutrition, "Thigh Creams," 30 March 2000.

———. "Collagen and Liquid Silicone Injections," August 1991, http://www.fda.gov/opacom/backgrounders/collagen.html.

———. "Cosmetic Handbook," 1992.

———. "FDA Completes Two Clinical Studies on the Safety of Alpha Hydroxy Acid," study summary, 7 March 2000.

———. "Food, Drug, and Cosmetic Act of 1936."

———. "Imports and FDA," *FDA Consumer,* May 1992.

———. "Inspection of Cosmetics," 6 February 1995.

———. Position Paper, October 1992.

University of Iowa, Department of Plastic Surgery. "Plastic Surgery of the Eyes," 1999.

Vespa, M. "A Two-Year-Old in False Eyelashes," *Ms.* September 1976, 61–63.

VH1 Fashion Awards 1996, 1997, 1998, http://www.madonnafanclub.com/vh1fash.htm, June 2000.Weinhouse, Beth. "Cosmetic Surgery for Men," *Town and Country* (March 1999): 158.

Weiss, Michael J. "Father's Day Special: Guys Who Dye," *American Demographics* (June 1999).

Wentzel, Volkmar. "Zulu King Weds a Swazi Princess," *National Geographic* (January 1978): 47–61.

"What Price Beauty?" *Glamour* (April 1991): 297.

White, Paul W. "Our Booming Beauty Business," *Outlook* (22 January 1930): 133–135.

"Who's Who: Christy Turlington," *Vogue* biography, April 1999

"Who's Who: Cindy Crawford," *Vogue* biography http://www.vogue.co.uk/content/ie4/295/357491-0-1-1.html, June 2000.

"A World of Flavors and Scents," *Montsanto Magazine* (First Quarter 1973).

"Yahoo! Model of the Month: Rod Brewster," http://features.yahoo.com/model, June 2000.

Yardley, Jim. "Building Fame for $15 a Head," *The New York Times*, 5 March 1999, p. B1, B13.

Yardley of London. "About Us" and "Customer Service" http://www.yardley.com, June 2000.

Yoffe, Emily. "Chemical Good Looks," *U.S. News and World Report,* 11 November 1997.

"You're So Vain," *Newsweek* (14 April 1986).

INDEX

by Christine Karpeles